William D. McCready

Signs of Sanctity
Miracles in the Thought of Gregory the Great

Distinguished for his skilful administration of the papal office and for his learned theological works (principally the *Moralia on Job*), in no small measure over the centuries Gregory the Great has also owed his fame to his authorship of the *Dialogues*, a collection of miracle stories that purports to record the wonders of modern, sixth-century saints. This study takes as its point of departure a close reading of the *Dialogues*, its primary object being to determine whether Gregory really believed the miracle stories he relates. But a number of other, related issues are also pursued, among them Gregory's conception of the history of miracles in the Christian church, of their purpose in the New Testament and in his own times, and of their connection with Christian sanctity and doctrine. Gregory's attitude to factual veracity, as well as his understanding of the natural realm and the order it possesses, are fundamental to the argument and method of the work.

Without being guilty of the naive credulity of which he has often been accused, Gregory did believe in the miracles of modern saints. Miracles function primarily as *ostensio sanctitatis*, a visible representation of the inner life of sanctity to which we are all called. In developing a fuller description of Gregory's views, this work seeks to analyze the interrelationship of ideas about miracles implicit in the stories of the *Dialogues* and explicit in the more strictly theological works, and to consider both within the context established by late antique/early medieval theological, philosophical, historiographical, and hagiographical traditions.

Signs of Sanctity engages critically a large body of recent scholarship on these questions, drawing on a careful reading of sources that would have been available to Gregory himself, in particular the influential texts of Augustine. The portrait of Gregory that emerges is intended as a contribution to the continuing reappraisal of a major figure in the intellectual history of late antiquity, and a significant influence on the cultural life of the middle ages.

STUDIES AND TEXTS 91

SIGNS OF SANCTITY

MIRACLES IN THE THOUGHT OF GREGORY THE GREAT

WILLIAM D. McCREADY

PONTIFICAL INSTITUTE OF MEDIAEVAL STUDIES

Acknowledgment

This book has been published with the help of a grant
from the Canadian Federation for the Humanities, using
funds provided by the Social Sciences and Humanities
Research Council of Canada.

CANADIAN CATALOGUING IN PUBLICATION DATA

McCready, William D. (William David), 1943-
    Signs of sanctity

(Studies and texts, ISSN 0082-5328 ; 91)
Bibliography: p.
Includes index.
ISBN 0-88844-091-X

1. Gregory I, Pope, ca. 540-604. Views on miracles.
2. Gregory I, Pope, ca. 540-604. Dialogi de vita.
I. Pontifical Institute of Mediaeval Studies. II. Title. III. Series: Studies and
texts (Pontifical Institute of Mediaeval Studies) ; 91.

BR65.G56M32 1989   231.7'3   C88-094863-9

Pontifical Institute of Mediaeval Studies
59 Queen's Park Crescent East
Toronto, Ontario, Canada M5S 2C4

PRINTED BY UNIVERSA, WETTEREN, BELGIUM

Distributed outside North America by
E.J. Brill, Postbus 9000,
2300 PA Leiden, The Netherlands
Brill ISBN 90 04 08869 5

Valeriae carae

Contents

Acknowledgments ix

Abbreviations xi

Introduction 1

1. Miracles Past and Present 7

2. The Purpose of Miracle 33

3. Miracles and Sanctity 65

4. Miracles and Virtue 84

5. Miracles: Fact or Fiction? 111

6. Miracles and Truth 155

7. Miracles and Belief 176

8. Miracles and Nature 206

Epilogue   The Structure of Miracle 241

Appendix A   The Sources of the *Dialogues*:
    An Alphabetical Register 261

Appendix B   The Sources of the *Dialogues*:
    An Analysis by Episode 264

Bibliography 273

Index 303

Acknowledgments

At the risk of offending the many friends and colleagues who offered me the benefit of their advice, criticism and encouragement during the writing of this book, not all of whom can be mentioned here, I would like to take this opportunity to acknowledge a few special debts of gratitude. Chiefly deserving of mention is my research assistant, Diane Glasgow, from whose patient labour and expertise I have profited in countless ways. She has left her imprint on virtually every page of the book. I should also like to express my gratitude to the anonymous readers appointed by the Canadian Federation for the Humanities and the Pontifical Institute of Mediaeval Studies; the book has been improved considerably by their many valuable suggestions.

My greatest debts undoubtedly are owed to Sofia Boesch Gajano, Giorgio Cracco, Claude Dagens, Adalbert de Vogüé and the many other scholars who have worked this field before me. Although I have not always endorsed their conclusions, even a brief perusal of the notes will indicate how much I have benefited from their scholarship in trying to make my own contribution to a continuing discussion. I regret that the proceedings of the 1982 conference on Gregory the Great held at Chantilly arrived too late to be used fully or systematically. However, I have included the titles of some of the more important papers in the bibliography, and have inserted a few references in the notes. I regret as well that the major study by Francis Clark, *The Pseudo-Gregorian Dialogues*, did not appear before this book was virtually complete. Indeed, I did not learn that Clark's work was on the horizon until my own had reached an advanced stage. But perhaps there is little point in lamenting the difficulties to which all scholarship is subject. Since Clark's perspective is very different from my own, an adequate treatment of his thesis would have required more than a few minor additions to my text.

Queen's University
Kingston, Ontario

W.D.M.

Abbreviations

Many of the abbreviations used in the Notes are fully expanded in the Bibliography. The following, however, should be especially noted:

AAST.M	*Atti dell'Accademia delle scienze di Torino.* Classe di scienze morali, storiche e filologiche
ABoll.	*Analecta Bollandiana*
ABPO	*Annales de Bretagne et des Pays de l'Ouest*
ABR	*American Benedictine Review*
ADip.	*Archiv für Diplomatik, Schriftgeschichte, Siegel- u. Wappenkunde*
AHDLMA	*Archives d'histoire doctrinale et littéraire du moyen âge*
AHP	*Archivum Historiae Pontificiae*
AKG	*Archiv für Kulturgeschichte*
Annales E.S.C.	*Annales. Economies, sociétés, civilisations*
BEC	*Bibliothèque de l'Ecole des chartes*
BenM	*Benediktinische Monatschrift*
BISIAM	*Bullettino dell'Istituto storico italiano per il medio evo e Archivio Muratoriano*
BLE	*Bulletin de littérature ecclésiastique*
BTB	*Bulletin de théologie biblique*
ByzF	*Byzantinische Forschungen*
CCist.	*Collectanea Cisterciensia*
CCL	Corpus Christianorum. Series Latina. Turnhout: Brepols, 1953-
CCM	*Cahiers de civilisation médiévale*
CSEL	Corpus scriptorum ecclesiasticorum latinorum. Vienna, 1866-
DAEM	*Deutsches Archiv für Erforschung des Mittelalters*
DCom.	*Doctor communis*
DR	*The Downside Review*
DSp.	*Dictionnaire de spiritualité.* Paris: G. Beauchesne, 1932-
DVJS	*Deutsche Vierteljahrsschrift für Literaturwissenschaft und Geistesgeschichte*

EuA	*Erbe und Auftrag*
GIF	*Giornale italiano di filologia*
GRBS	*Greek, Roman and Byzantine Studies*
HTh.	*History and Theory*
HZ	*Historische Zeitschrift*
JBL	*Journal of Biblical Literature*
JEA	*Journal of Egyptian Archaeology*
JEH	*Journal of Ecclesiastical History*
JMH	*Journal of Medieval History*
JS	*Journal des savants*
JTS	*Journal of Theological Studies*
MA	*Le moyen âge*
MGH	Monumenta Germaniae Historica
SRL	Scriptores rerum Langobardicarum et Italicarum. Hannover: Hahn, 1878
SRM	Scriptores rerum Merovingicarum. Hannover: Hahn, 1885-
MHum.	*Medievalia et Humanistica*
Moricca	Gregory the Great, *Dialogorum libri quatuor de miraculis patrum italicorum,* ed. Umberto Moricca (Fonti per la storia d'Italia pubblicate dall'Istituto storico italiano: scrittori secolo VI). Rome, 1924
PG	Patrologiae cursus completus. Series Graeca, ed. J.P. Migne. Paris, 1857-1866
PL	Patrologiae cursus completus. Series Latina, ed. J.P. Migne. Paris, 1844-1864
QS	*Quaderni Storici*
RAug.	*Recherches augustiniennes*
RBén.	*Revue Bénédictine*
RBenS	*Regulae Benedicti Studia*
REAnc.	*Revue des études anciennes*
REAug.	*Revue des études augustiniennes*
RHE	*Revue d'histoire ecclésiastique*
RHEF	*Revue d'histoire de l'église de France*
RHSp.	*Revue d'histoire de la spiritualité*
RMon.	*Revue monastique*
RQCAKG	*Römische Quartalschrift für christliche Altertumskunde und Kirchengeschichte*
RSCI	*Rivista di storia della chiesa in Italia*
RSLR	*Rivista di storia e letteratura religiosa*
RSR	*Recherches de science religieuse*

RSSR	*Ricerche di storia sociale e religiosa*
RTAM	*Recherches de théologie ancienne et médiévale*
SAns.	*Studia Anselmiana*
SC	Sources chrétiennes. Paris: Cerf, 1942-
SCat.	*La scuola cattolica*
SE	*Sacris erudiri*
SM	*Studi Medievali*
SMon.	*Studia Monastica*
SMSR	*Studi e materiali di storia delle religioni*
SPatr.	*Studia Patristica*
SSR	*Studi Storico Religiosi*
SStor.	*Studi storici*
ThPh.	*Theologie und Philosophie*
TRHS	*Transactions of the Royal Historical Society*
TS	*Theological Studies*
TTZ	*Trierer theologische Zeitschrift*
VetC	*Vetera Christianorum*
VigC	*Vigiliae Christianae*
VMon.	*Vita monastica*
WS	*Wiener Studien*
WW	*Wissenschaft und Weisheit*
ZBAW	*Zitzungsberichte der Berliner Akademie der Wissenschaften.* Philol.-Hist. Klasse
ZBLG	*Zeitschrift für bayerische Landesgeschichte*
ZDGG	*Zeitschrift für deutsche Geistesgeschichte*
Zimmerman	Gregory the Great, *Dialogues*, trans. Odo John Zimmerman (The Fathers of the Church 39). New York, 1959
ZKTh.	*Zeitschrift für katholische Theologie*

Introduction

Although he was born into a Roman patrician family that had already seen two of its members (Pope Felix III 483-492, and Pope Agapitus 535-536) rise to the dignity of the papal office, in the early part of his career it probably seemed that the Gregory who would become Pope Gregory the Great (ca. 540-604) was destined to make his major contribution in civil administration. Of his early life we know relatively little, other than the fact that he received the finest liberal education then available, with particular emphasis on law. He steps into full view for the first time around the year 570, when he was appointed prefect of Rome, the highest civil officer, whose jurisdiction included all the territory within a hundred miles of the city. In this capacity Gregory presided over the Roman senate, and was generally responsible for all matters relating to public works, defence, supplies and finance.

Within a few years, however, Gregory's spiritual calling became apparent. In the year 575 or thereabouts he transformed his ancestral home on the Clivus Scauri of the Coelian Hill into a monastery dedicated to Saint Andrew, making provision for the establishment of six other monasteries on his family property in Sicily. Having given the rest of his patrimony to the poor, there is every indication that Gregory would have been perfectly content to live out the rest of his life as a simple monk at Saint Andrew's. In 579, however, he was ordained a deacon, and was drawn into the papal service with his appointment as *apocrisiarius*, papal representative, at the imperial court in Constantinople. Thereafter he was never able successfully to withdraw from the wider service to the church to which he was being summoned. He had a brief opportunity to taste the joys of the contemplative life once again after his recall to Rome, which occurred sometime around 586, although even then he continued to function as a trusted advisor of Pope Pelagius II. But in September 590, Gregory himself was elected pope, during a turbulent time in the history of the early medieval church. In addition to the ecclesiastical burdens implicit in the office, major social and political responsibilities were thrust upon him as well, particularly the necessity of dealing with the Lombard invaders of Italy.

As Bishop of Rome and vicar of Christ, Gregory the Great left an important and lasting imprint on the church over which he presided. His

contribution to the history of Christian thought was equally significant, however. The author of the *Moralia on Job* and of several other Biblical commentaries, he was the foremost theologian between Augustine and Aquinas; he would do much to shape the basic categories of Christian theology for the entire Middle Ages. But it is his decisive influence on the early medieval hagiographical tradition that is our concern here, for Gregory was also the author of a collection of miracle stories known as the *Dialogues*.[1] Written in 593/594 at the prompting of Gregory's monastic brethren, the *Dialogues* purport to offer a record of the miracles of modern, contemporary saints, the saints of sixth-century Italy. They include miracles as astonishing as any of those attributed to Christ and the apostles. It is not surprising, therefore, that they have been a major source of puzzlement to students of early medieval thought, the present author included, and that they have given rise to an enormous scholarly literature, especially in this century.

Although it is perhaps to oversimplify a complex development, it may be said that learned opinion on the *Dialogues* has generally fallen into one of two categories. Nineteenth- and early twentieth-century scholars tended to take Gregory's stories seriously, and to be astonished by what they perceived as the blind credulity of their author. Although this judgment has not been completely superseded, more recent research has tended to discount Gregory's claims to factual veracity, and to emphasize that, in the final analysis, it is the moral or spiritual significance of his miracle stories that Gregory would have regarded as of prime importance. Taking them literally is to accept chaff for grain, as one recent student of Gregory's thought would have it, for their real value is to be found in their supra-historical sense.[2]

The present book has arisen out of a dissatisfaction with both these alternatives. Whereas the first tends to identify belief in miracles with a credulity that would make most of us blush, the second is often content to assume that, having discovered a deeper meaning to Gregory's stories, their status as factual statements can be safely ignored. With the exception of a major article by Pierre Boglioni, the question of Gregory's own belief in

---

[1] Gregory's authorship of the *Dialogues* has been accepted by the virtually universal consensus of modern scholars. However, cf. Francis Clark, "The Authenticity of the Gregorian *Dialogues*: A Reopening of the Question?" in *Grégoire le Grand*, Chantilly, 15-19 septembre 1982 (Paris, 1986), pp. 429-442. Clark argues that the *Dialogues* date from the latter part of the seventh century, although the "Dialogist" did indeed incorporate some genuine Gregorian material into his work. Although the argument is not persuasive, it is stated more fully in Clark's recently published book: *The Pseudo-Gregorian Dialogues* (Leiden, 1987). Unfortunately, this arrived too late to be taken into account here.

[2] W.F. Bolton, "The Supra-Historical Sense in the Dialogues of Gregory I," *Aevum* 33 (1959): 206-213.

miracles is rarely confronted directly in current scholarship.[3] Did Gregory the
Great really believe in the modern miracles recorded in the *Dialogues*? This
is the major question addressed in the following pages, and given Gregory's
importance for the entire Middle Ages, it deserves an answer. Dealing with
it adequately, however, requires taking positions on a host of other issues as
well, on many of which historians have been equally as divided.

The first chapter of this book explores Gregory's views on the history of
Christian miracles. Several scholars have noted a tension in Gregory's
thought about contemporary miracles: on the one side, patient exposition of
a plethora of modern wonders; on the other, statements that seem to imply
the end of the age of miracles. Here it is argued that Gregory maintained a
consistent position throughout his career. He would acknowledge that
miracles are not as frequent as they were when the church was in its infancy.
But he would also insist that the grace of miracles has not been withdrawn
entirely. God still deigns to perform miracles on whatever occasions, for
whatever purposes and through whatever agents he thinks appropriate.

The purpose of modern miracles is explored more systematically in
chapter two. Because Gregory was greatly impressed by the apologetic
function of New Testament miracles, he was strongly inclined to see analogous contemporary phenomena in much the same way. Miracles are a means
of evangelization, designed to reach those still outside the church and to
draw them to the true faith. Primarily, however, Gregory believed that
miracles were necessary because the work of conversion was far from
complete within the bosom of the church itself. Hence he conceived of
miracles as being addressed for the most part to an audience of Catholic
Christians, but Catholic Christians whose lives demonstrated that they had
not yet passed beyond the stage of external observance to make their faith
a lived reality. Miracles continued to take place, and Gregory thought they
were worthy of being recorded, chiefly because of the multitudes whose
lapses in understanding and in practice indicated that their grasp on the
Christian faith was tenuous at best.

God's agents for the performance of miracles were, of course, the saints.
Hence chapters three and four investigate the connection between miracles
and sanctity. Some of the miracles recorded in the *Dialogues* follow the
traditional hagiographical pattern, in that they serve simply to establish that
the individuals who performed them were in fact saints. However, this was
not Gregory's primary thought on the matter. Gregory is quite insistent that,

---

[3] P. Boglioni, "Miracle et nature chez Grégoire le Grand," in *Cahiers d'études médiévales*
1: *Epopées, légendes et miracles* (Montreal and Paris, 1974), pp. 11-102; cf. his *Pour l'étude
du miracle au moyen âge: Grégoire le Grand et son milieu* (Montreal, 1972).

although miracles are performed by saints, they are not of the essence of
sanctity. Miracles are simply external signs of the grace possessed within.
Rather than limit their importance, however, this assessment actually enhan-
ces it. It invests miracles with a larger spiritual significance on which Gregory
is particularly insistent. Above all, miracles are an *ostensio sanctitatis*. They
provide a visible representation of the inner virtue that characterizes the life
of the saints, and they encourage those who witness them or hear about them
to emulate the same virtuous behaviour. On occasion, miracles are invested
with doctrinal content as well. Instructing us on the life that is to be led, they
also reveal the truth that is to be believed. By the end of the *Dialogues* this
has become Gregory's primary concern: the miracles recorded in book four
serve mainly to reinforce orthodox Christian teaching about the afterlife.

Chapter five focuses more directly on the place of miracles in Gregory's
world view. Recent scholarship has argued that historical veracity was not
one of Gregory's fundamental concerns; he was much more interested in the
pastoral purposes his miracle stories were intended to serve. Hence it has
also been claimed that, his protestations of truthfulness notwithstanding,
many of the episodes in the *Dialogues* can be shown to be clearly dependent
on an earlier literary tradition. Gregory, it is alleged, borrowed liberally from
St Augustine, Sulpicius Severus, John Cassian and the *Vitae patrum*, to name
only a few of his sources. In chapter five it is argued that, if Gregory did
engage in literary invention of this sort, as of yet the case has not been
proved.

Of course, the sheer number of doubtful cases increases the probability of
such pious invention on Gregory's part, as does the fact that there was ample
precedent for such practice. Conceivably, Gregory might have acquitted
himself by appealing to the doctrine of the justifiable lie, which had some
currency throughout the Middle Ages, or to some form of truth intrinsically
more important than mere factual veracity. However, as we shall see in
chapter six, in point of fact Gregory could have done neither. His consistent
position in all his theological works is that lying is always sinful, and can
never be justified; and his systematic appeal to witnesses who could verify his
stories seems calculated to convince the reader that truth is to be found in
the story itself, and not just in the higher significance it bears. Gregory
believes the miracle stories he relates, and he wants us to believe them as
well.

It has sometimes been suggested that, in the world of late antiquity or the
early Middle Ages, an openness to miracles was paralleled by a relatively low
degree of cultural attainment. Chapter seven examines this hypothesis,
arguing that it has no explanatory force in Gregory's case at all. Although
Gregory demonstrated a certain detachment from the literary traditions of the

ancient world, he was far from being the cultural philistine or the simple fideist on matters of faith and doctrine that he has sometimes been accused of being. He was one of the most cultivated men of the sixth century, the beneficiary of the finest education available in his time; he was also predisposed to believe in the miraculous, as an examination of the methodology of the *Dialogues* clearly shows. When witnesses whose honesty and integrity could not be doubted informed him of the miracles of the saints, Gregory was inclined to take their word at face value. He did try to verify their reports whenever the opportunity presented itself, but he was satisfied by much less in the way of confirmation than most modern observers would demand.

A variety of possible factors may explain Gregory's willingness to believe, but it is often argued that it was ultimately contingent on a world-view that made nature dependent at every instant on the direct governance of God. Whereas the modern age regards the natural realm as a closed system possessed of its own intrinsic rhythms and laws, the sixth century, or so it is suggested, had no such conception of a fixed natural order, and consequently was inclined to see the hand of God at work in even the most familiar of natural processes. In chapter eight, and in the epilogue, it is argued that such a view is fundamentally mistaken in Gregory's case. Gregory, like most medieval writers, was inclined to view the world allegorically. Rather than investigate the causes of things, he often showed himself to be more interested in exploring their significance; and the meaning invested in things was to be deciphered by analogical reasoning linking orders of reality—the physical and the moral, for example—that we prefer to keep distinct. However, this does not mean that he could not perceive the world in causal terms as well. If he was more willing than most of us to accept tales of the miraculous doings of the saints, it was not because he was unaware of nature's own intrinsic causal order, but was rather because he was much less confident than we are of his ability to understand it. Gregory had to accept a good deal more mystery in his life than we do, and was consequently readier to acknowledge that many of these mysteries have only God for explanation.

Several other issues are raised in the course of the discussion, but the foregoing will have to suffice as an outline of the main thrust of the argument. Although attention is focused on the *Dialogues* throughout, systematic use is made of Gregory's more strictly theological works as well. The object of this study is not simply the miracles of the *Dialogues*, but Gregory's whole concept of miracle, of which the miracles in the *Dialogues* are an important articulation. An effort has also been made to place Gregory clearly in his proper intellectual context: to read what he had probably read, and to determine the influence it may have had upon him. Hence, whenever

appropriate, Gregory's thought is elucidated by comparing it, for example, to that of Sulpicius Severus, John Cassian, or Gregory of Tours.

Gregory was undoubtedly much more aware of the sources of eastern spirituality than has sometimes been supposed, and one can no longer assume that his intellectual life was formed only by the western, Latin tradition.[4] Even if his knowledge of Greek was limited, by the late sixth century there was an extensive body of literature that would have been available to him in translation. Thus sources from eastern Christendom such as the *Vita Antonii*, the *Historia monachorum* and the *Vitae patrum* have been taken into account as well. However, a large part of this study has been devoted to exploring Gregory's indebtedness to Augustine: Augustine's influence, which is universally acknowledged, was undoubtedly very great.[5] The comparison of the two writers will serve to show that, in all the main features of Gregory's thought, the debt to the Bishop of Hippo was significant; but it will also demonstrate that Gregory remained a distinctive thinker whose unique contribution would have a profound influence in following centuries.

[4] The point has recently been emphasized in a number of studies by J.M. Petersen. Her views are set out in detail in *The Dialogues of Gregory the Great in their Late Antique Cultural Background* (Toronto, 1984).

[5] See, for example, L. Weber, *Hauptfragen der Moraltheologie Gregors des Grossen* (Freiburg in der Schweiz, 1947), esp. pp. 40-42; R. Gillet, Introduction to *Grégoire le Grand, Morales sur Job, Livres 1 et 2* (Paris, 1952), esp. pp. 86-89; M. Frickel, *Deus totus ubique simul. Untersuchungen zur allgemeinen Gottgegenwart im Rahmen der Gotteslehre Gregors des Grossen* (Freiburg, 1956), esp. pp. 133-134; and more recently, V. Recchia, "La memoria di Agostino nella esegesi biblica di Gregorio Magno," *Augustinianum* 25 (1985): 405-434.

1

Miracles Past and Present

Gregory's *Dialogues*, written in 593/594, were composed for the express purpose of recording miracles performed by the saints in Italy in his own time. At the very outset, his interlocutor expresses doubts as to whether any such miracles have occurred: "This land of ours," Peter says, "has undoubtedly produced its virtuous men, but to my knowledge no signs or miracles have been performed by any of them; or, if they have been, they were till now kept in such secrecy that we cannot even tell if they occurred." However, Gregory immediately corrects his disciple. In fact, he says, there have been so many such miracles that "the day would not be long enough for me to tell you about those saints whose holiness has been well established, and whose lives are known to me either from my own observations or from the reports of good, reliable witnesses." The rest of the book follows directly from this initial exchange, in response to Peter's request that Gregory tell him more. "Interrupting the study and explanation of the Scriptures for such a purpose," says Peter, "should not cause grave concern, for the amount of edification to be gained from a description of miracles is just as great."[1]

If we were to judge by the *Dialogues* alone, Gregory's opinion on contemporary miracles would be beyond dispute. Not only are modern miracles possible, but they occur in significant numbers. Yet scholars have noted a tension in Gregory's thought that becomes particularly apparent when the *Dialogues* are compared with his other works, principally the *Homilies on the Gospels* and the *Moralia*, where he seems to advance the view

---

[1] *Dial.* 1 Prol. 7-9, Zimmerman 5-6, sc 260:14-16. On the identity of Peter, whom Gregory describes as "dilectissimus filius meus Petrus diaconus ..., mihi a primaevo iuventutis flore in amicitiis familiariter obstrictus atque ad sacri verbi indagationem socius" (*Dial.* 1 Prol. 2, sc 260:10), see A. de Vogüé, *Grégoire le Grand, Dialogues* 1: *Introduction, bibliographie et cartes* (Paris, 1978), p. 44. He is probably to be identified with the former *rector* of the papal patrimony and Gregory's own vicar in Sicily, who is known to have been in Rome in 593-596.

that the age of miracles has come to an end. Miracles were necessary only in the early years of the church, he seems to say, to allow the new faith to become established; in the present world they have lost their *raison d'être*. Scholarly reaction to this puzzle has been varied. Boesch Gajano, for example, argues that there is no solution at all, because of what she regards as "l'assenza di una coerente teoria e storia del miracolo" in the thought of Gregory the Great. Somewhat more plausibly, Cracco argues that Gregory evidently changed his mind, and in the *Dialogues* was prepared to accept the existence of modern miracles, which he had rejected earlier.[2] This study will argue that, in his handling of this issue as of others, Gregory was consistent, and that nowhere did he mean to suggest that the age of miracles was over. Miracles were an essential part of Gregory's spiritual universe; he regarded them as an enduring fact of Christian experience, from the time of the apostolic church to the present day.[3]

On this subject, like many others, Gregory would have been significantly influenced by Augustine. Hence it seems prudent to preface a detailed analysis of Gregory's views with an excursus on the position of the Bishop of Hippo. Augustine's views, on a cursory view at least, seem to have changed dramatically. In texts such as *De utilitate credendi* and *De vera religione*, which date from early in his career, he maintains that the miracles described in the New Testament were appropriate only to the church in its infancy, when they were required to draw the minds of the erring to the Saviour. Before anyone could be fit to reason about divine truths, it was essential to stimulate belief in the Gospel. But once the church was firmly established, miracles were no longer necessary. Indeed, their continuation could have undermined their original purpose by deflecting our attention from spiritual matters to things visible. In all likelihood they simply would have failed to move us at all; we would have come to take them for granted, just as we do the many wonders of nature which, because of their very familiarity, we

---

[2] S. Boesch Gajano, "La proposta agiografica dei 'Dialogi' di Gregorio Magno," *SM* 3rd. ser. 21 (1980): 623-664 at 647; G. Cracco, "Uomini di Dio e uomini di chiesa nell'alto medioevo (per una reinterpretazione dei 'Dialogi' di Gregorio Magno)," *RSSR* n.s. 12 (1977): 163-202 at 173-176. See also de Vogüé, *Introduction*, pp. 90-91; cf. C. Dagens, *Saint Grégoire le Grand. Culture et expérience chrétiennes* (Paris, 1977), pp. 225-229.

[3] For a similar assessment, see P. Boglioni, "Miracle et nature chez Grégoire le Grand," in *Cahiers d'études médiévales* 1: *Epopées, légendes et miracles* (Montreal and Paris, 1974), pp. 11-102, esp. p. 86. On the general tenor of Gregory's thought, see, for example, L. Weber, *Hauptfragen der Moraltheologie Gregors des Grossen* (Freiburg in der Schweiz, 1947), pp. 68-69, who argues that there was no significant development in Gregory's theological teaching.

scarcely give a moment's thought.[4] Hence, says Augustine, the physical miracles that Christ once performed no longer occur. They have been replaced by spiritual miracles more appropriate to the circumstances of the contemporary church, and of much greater intrinsic value:

> The blind body does not now open its eyes by means of a miracle of God, but the blind heart opens its eyes at the word of the Lord. Now the mortal corpse does not arise, but the soul which lay lifeless (*quae mortalis iacebat*) in a living corpse rises again. The deaf ears of the body are not now opened; but how many have the ears of their heart closed, ears which nonetheless are opened at the penetrating word of God, so that they who were unbelievers believe, and they who lived evilly live well, and they who were disobedient obey![5]

By the time of Augustine's writing these ideas had been firmly established in theological tradition. Although, for the most part, orthodox Christian authors had had no difficulty accepting the reality of the miracles reported in Scripture, as early as the second and third centuries many seem to have been troubled by the thought that such miracles could continue to take place in the church of their own time. Origen, for example, admitted the possibility, but chose to emphasize the spiritualization of the wonders that had been performed in the age of the apostles. It is a very much greater thing, he says, for a soul to be redeemed from sin than for a blind man to be cured of his physical infirmity. Later thinkers went further, suggesting that the age of miracles in the traditional sense of the term was over, for the gift of miracles was appropriate only to a nascent Christianity.[6] At first glance at least, the young Augustine seems to have shared their conviction. However, Augustine's position towards the end of his career was significantly different. If his earlier writings seem to suggest that the age of miracles has come to an end, his later works expressly state that this is not the case.

Many of the later sermons, which date from 425/426 or later, contain explicit references to the miracles then being witnessed at the shrines of the

---

[4] Cf. *De vera religione* 25.47 (ca. 387-391), CCL 32:216-217; *De utilitate credendi* 16.34 (ca. 391-392), CSEL 25.1:43-44.

[5] *Sermo* 88.3.3 (ca. 400), PL 38:540, ed. P.-P. Verbraken, "Le sermon LXXXVIII de saint Augustin sur la guérison des deux aveugles de Jéricho," *RBén.* 94 (1984): 71-101 at 76. Cf. *Sermo* 98.1.1-2.2, PL 38:591; *De baptismo* 3.16.21, CSEL 51:212-213.

[6] Origen, *Contra Celsum* 2.48, SC 132:390-394. Cf. J. Speigl, "Die Rolle der Wunder im vorkonstantinischen Christentum," *ZKTh.* 92 (1970): 287-312, esp. 307-310. See also H. Delehaye, "Saint Martin et Sulpice Sévère," *ABoll.* 38 (1920): 5-136, esp. 73-79; and more recently M. Van Uytfanghe, "La controverse biblique et patristique autour du miracle, et ses répercussions sur l'hagiographie dans l'Antiquité tardive et le haut Moyen Age latin," in *Hagiographie, cultures et sociétés, IVe-XIIe siècles* (Paris, 1981), pp. 205-231, esp. pp. 210-211.

martyrs, particularly the shrines of St Stephen. Similar claims can be found in the famous twenty-second book of *The City of God*, where Augustine says quite clearly that even at the present time God is actively at work performing miracles by means of his chosen agents, especially St Stephen. At the various *memoriae* of the saints, in Hippo and elsewhere, there have been miracles that rival those recorded in the New Testament.[7] Unfortunately, says Augustine, these miracles are not as widely acknowledged as they should be. Often they are unknown even to the inhabitants of the particular city in which they occur, especially if it is a city of any great size; and so when news of them is carried elsewhere, it frequently lacks sufficient confirmation to ensure ready acceptance. Hence, he continues, he decided to have accounts dictated or written by those who had benefited from such miracles, and to have them read to the people. In the two brief years that had passed since the establishment of the shrine of St Stephen at Hippo, he claims, he had managed to accumulate seventy such *libelli*, and even these did not cover all the miracles that had taken place.[8] Regrettably, the practice of reading them in public was not an immediate and unqualified success.[9] But this was not for lack of effort on Augustine's part. Indeed, that effort extends to *The City of*

---

[7] See, for example, *Sermones* 286.5.5, PL 38:1299; 316.1.1, PL 38:1432; 317.1.1, PL 38:1435; 319.6.6, PL 38:1441-1442. See especially *Sermones* 320-324, PL 38:1442-1447, where, in addition to mentioning the many miracles performed at Ancona, Augustine gives detailed accounts of the miraculous power that St Stephen demonstrated both at Hippo and at Uzalis. See also *De civitate Dei* 22.8, CCL 48:825: "Fiunt ergo etiam nunc multa miracula eodem Deo faciente per quos vult et quem ad modum vult, qui et illa quae legimus fecit."

On the *memoriae* of the saints and the various forms they took, as well as the various meanings the term could assume in different contexts, see V. Saxer, *Morts, martyrs, reliques en Afrique chrétienne aux premiers siècles* (Paris, 1980), pp. 125-133; and Y. Duval, *Loca sanctorum Africae. Le culte des martyrs en Afrique du IVe au VIIe siècle* (Rome, 1982), pp. 753-756.

[8] *De civitate Dei* 22.8, CCL 48:816, 823-825. For an example of one of these *libelli*, see *Sermo* 322, PL 38:1443-1445; cf. H. Delehaye, "Les premiers 'libelli miraculorum'," *ABoll.* 29 (1910): 427-434; "Les recueils antiques de Miracles des Saints," *ABoll.* 43 (1925): 5-85, 305-325, esp. 78-79. For more recent comment on the *libelli miraculorum* of Hippo, Calama and Uzalis, and the leading role which Augustine assumed in their production, see Saxer, *Morts, martyrs, reliques*, pp. 269-270. See also Saxer's "Zweck und Ursprung der hagiographischen Literatur in Nordafrika," *TTZ* 93 (1984): 65-74. Focusing on the period from 180 to 260, Saxer argues that the earliest examples of hagiographical literature produced in North Africa were conceived for essentially liturgical purposes.

[9] Cf. *De civitate Dei* 22.8, CCL 48:825: "Nam et ubi diligentia est, quae nunc apud nos esse coepit, ut libelli eorum, qui beneficia percipiunt, recitentur in populo, semel hoc audiunt qui adsunt pluresque non adsunt, ut nec illi, qui adfuerunt, post aliquot dies quod audierunt mente retineant et vis quisque reperiatur illorum, qui ei, quem non adfuisse cognoverit, indicet quod audivit."

God itself, where, although it is not part of his primary purpose, Augustine records many of these modern miracles, lest they fall into oblivion. Time will not allow him to relate all the miracle stories that he knows, but he prays for the indulgence of Christian friends who might be grieved to discover that he has omitted a very great deal.[10]

The contrast between the early and mature Augustine is so striking that some scholars have posited a radical change of mind towards the end of his career.[11] If this is the way the contrast should be characterized, conceivably Augustine's volte-face was facilitated by a corresponding change of temperament. The young Augustine was initially attracted to the Manichaeans because they offered a strictly rational explanation of the universe; their ultimate failure to fulfill this promise was a major disappointment. However, the mature Augustine had been taught by the many paradoxes of human existence to temper his demands for strictly rational explanations, and presumably therefore was more prepared to acknowledge the possibility of divine intervention in the ordered structure of the cosmos. Even more significant, it is usually argued, was a pronounced change in the practice of Christian piety itself. Up to the end of the fourth century, miracles were, at the very least, uncommon occurrences in the western Church. Apart from a few rare exceptions, wonders performed at the tombs of the saints or through the influence of their relics were virtually unheard of. But the situation changed suddenly and dramatically with the discovery of the relics of St Stephen at Caphar Gamle in 415, and their rapid diffusion, first in Italy, and then in Africa itself. If Augustine changed his mind about the possibility of modern miracles, it was primarily because the experience of Christians was proving that he had been wrong. Men whose personal sanctity and veracity he could not doubt—men like Paulinus of Nola and Evodius of Uzalis, his former disciple—were telling him of the wondrous way in which God was still at work in the world. In 424/425 the relics of St Stephen were finally enshrined in Augustine's own church at Hippo. From then on Augustine was able to confirm everything he had been told by witnessing the miraculous virtue of St Stephen himself.[12]

---

[10] *Ibid.*, p. 823. For an analysis of the miracle stories contained in the twenty-second book of *The City of God*, see Delehaye, "Les recueils antiques," pp. 74-80; and Saxer, *Morts, martyrs, reliques*, pp. 262-269.

[11] Cf. D.P. de Vooght, "Les miracles dans la vie de saint Augustin," *RTAM* 11 (1939): 5-16; and P. Courcelle, *Recherches sur les Confessions de Saint Augustin* (Paris, 1950), pp. 139-153.

[12] On Augustine's change of temperament, see Courcelle, *Recherches sur les Confessions*, pp. 144-145. Although they take various positions on Augustine's attitude toward contemporary miracles, cf. G. Bardy, "Les miracles contemporains dans l'apologétique de saint

There are, however, major difficulties in positing a radical and sudden change of mind, not least of them Augustine's own denial. In his *Retractions*, which were completed in 427, long after the miraculous virtues of the holy martyrs had been made manifest to him, he acknowledges no error in his earlier writings, only the need for clarification. He explains that in *De utilitate credendi* he did not mean to say that miracles no longer occur at all, but simply that modern miracles are neither as great nor as frequent as the miracles reported in the New Testament. His comments on *De vera religione* make the same point. In the apostolic church new Christians received such an infusion of the Holy Spirit that they were able to speak with tongues, and the sick could be cured of their ailments when the shadows of the passing apostles fell upon them. Miracles of this kind no longer happen. But, Augustine maintains, he never meant to imply that miracles do not now happen at all, for he knew perfectly well that they did. It was only shortly before writing *De vera religione*, he says, that he had heard of the miraculous healing of the blind man that took place in Milan, at the time of the invention and translation of the remains of the sainted martyrs, Protasius and Gervasius.[13]

Since *De utilitate credendi* itself seems to contain a reference to modern miracles, it could be argued that Augustine's clear statements in the *Retractions* should be enough to settle the matter.[14] But the text of *De utilitate credendi* is not entirely unequivocal at this juncture. In itself it is not sufficient

---

Augustin," in *La Cité de Dieu, livres XIX-XXII*, Oeuvres de Saint Augustin 37 (Paris, 1960), pp. 825-831 at p. 829; P. Brown, *Augustine of Hippo* (London, 1967), pp. 416-417; and most recently, Saxer, *Morts, martyrs, reliques*, p. 295. On the change in Christian piety, cf. Courcelle, *Recherches sur les Confessions*, pp. 145-148; Bardy, "Les miracles contemporains," pp. 829-830; and Saxer, *Morts, martyrs, reliques*, esp. p. 292. For a discussion of the spread of the cult of St Stephen in north Africa in the early decades of the fifth century, see Duval, *Loca sanctorum Africae*, pp. 624-632, 758.

[13] On *De utilitate credendi*, see *Retract.* 1.14.5, CCL 57:44: "Hoc autem dixi, quia non tanta nec omnia modo, non quia nulla fiunt etiam modo." On *De vera religione*, see *Retract.* 1.13.7, CCL 57:39.

[14] See *De utilitate credendi* 17.35, CSEL 25.1:45, where, after mentioning the self-denial, endurance and charity that have characterized the lives of the saints over the centuries, Augustine remarks: "hoc factum est divina providentia per prophetarum vaticinia, per humanitatem doctrinamque Christi, per apostolorum itinera, per martyrum contumelias, cruces, sanguinem, mortes, per sanctorum praedicabilem vitam *atque in his universis digna rebus tantis atque virtutibus pro temporum oportunitate miracula.* cum igitur tantum auxilium dei, tantum profectum fructumque videamus, dubitabimus nos eius ecclesiae condere gremio, quae usque ad confessionem generis humani ab apostolica sede per successiones episcoporum frustra haereticis circumlatrantibus et partim plebis ipsius iudicio, partim conciliorum gravitate, *partim etiam miraculorum maiestate* damnatis columen auctoritatis obtinuit?" The emphasis has been added.

to dispel the suspicion that in his much later "clarification" Augustine has not been absolutely straightforward. There, of course, he appeals to one of the miracles that took place in Milan in 386. But these miracles are not mentioned in any of the earlier writings in which contemporary miracles seem to be denied. Their first mention occurs in the *Confessions*, written in 397/398, where they are reported as both genuine and authenticated, and are described in considerable detail. But what of the earlier period? Did Augustine accept these as genuine miracles at the time they occurred? Possibly not. Although he was present in Milan at the time and was a witness to the stir they created among the people, it seems clear that he did not actually witness any miracles himself.[15] Moreover, Augustine was not yet a Christian, and what was reported to him by others was insufficient to induce him to make the final act of commitment. That would transpire only several months later, and the miracles at Milan would have nothing to do with it. Conceivably the true import of what had happened at Milan became clear to him only at some later date, when his own Christian faith was firmly established, and when he had been compelled to acknowledge, at least to himself, that his former assessment of the possibility of miracles had been mistaken.[16]

At least one thing *is* clear in all of this, however. By the time he wrote the *Confessions*, if not earlier, Augustine was convinced of the possibility and, indeed, the reality of modern miracles. This lends weight to Saxer's more precise statement of the thesis we have been considering about Augustine's change of mind. In Saxer's view, Augustine did not believe in contemporary miracles in the years 390-400. Around 400 there is evidence that his views

---

[15] *Conf.* 9.7.15-16, CCL 27:141-142. In *Sermo* 286.5.4, PL 38:1299, Augustine might be taken as implying that he actually witnessed the healing of the blind man: "Ibi eram, Mediolani eram, facta miracula novi, attestante Deo pretiosis mortibus sanctorum suorum: ut per illa miracula jam non solum in conspectu Domini, sed etiam in conspectu hominum esset mors illa pretiosa. Caecus notissimus universae civitati illuminatus est, cucurrit, adduci se fecit, sine duce reversus est." However, for an extensive discussion of the issue, see Courcelle, *Recherches sur les Confessions*, pp. 148-151.

[16] In the *Confessions* Augustine does not place these miracles where one would expect to find them had he been following a strictly chronological order. Although they occurred a few months before his conversion, Augustine discusses them only later in his narrative, in the context of his baptism. This curious fact prompts Bardy, "Les miracles contemporains," p. 827, to ask: "Serait-ce par hasard qu'il n'en a pas été très frappé lui-même lorsqu'ils se sont produits? On serait tenté de le croire."

For a recent discussion of Augustine's treatment of these miracles in various contexts and for various audiences, see V. Zangara, "L'*inventio* dei corpi dei martiri Gervasio e Protasio. Testimonianze di Agostino su un fenomeno di religiosità popolare," *Augustinianum* 21 (1981): 119-133.

on the matter began to change, but for the most part this was limited to an intellectual acknowledgment of the possibility of modern miracles and their occasional occurrence. Since the agents of the change in Augustine's attitude were miracles that happened elsewhere and were witnessed by others, miracles were not yet part of his own experience. It was only the efflorescence of miracles that followed the invention and dispersal of the relics of St Stephen in the period after 415, and the need to come to terms with the pastoral problems to which they gave rise, that transformed Augustine into an apologist for the very wonders whose existence he had previously denied.[17]

If Saxer's thesis has a major weakness, it lies in the firm denial that the young Augustine believed in the possibility of modern miracles. One of the miracles described in the twenty-second book of *The City of God* concerns the extraordinary healing of Innocentius, onetime counsellor of the vice-prefecture, who was suffering from a fistula that his physicians had despaired of healing without dangerous surgery. The miracle took place at the time of Augustine's return to Africa in 388, precisely when he was not supposed to believe in modern miracles, and yet Augustine tells us that he was an eyewitness.[18] Unless Augustine wishes deliberately to deceive us about his willingness to accept miraculous events at that stage in his life, his explicit statement on the matter is absolutely conclusive. It may seem surprising that more than thirty-five years passed before Augustine saw fit to mention this extraordinary event, but not on the assumption that he regarded such miracles as genuinely rare occurrences, the expectation of which was not to be encouraged. The same assumption makes sense of his early pronouncements on the matter of miracles in general, the point of which is not that miracles have ceased completely, but rather that they are no longer of central importance for the propagation of the Gospel. They are neither so great nor so frequent as they once were, and so the vast majority of us cannot expect to witness them. This seems to have been Augustine's position from the

---

[17] Cf. Saxer, *Morts, martyrs, reliques*, esp. pp. 240ff. Cf. pp. 295-296: "Le théologien, familier des spéculations les plus hautes, a été conduit par son ministère à se pencher sur les besoins des humbles. Tout en continuant pour lui et pour une élite la poursuite de la perfection, il a achevé et complété son expérience pastorale par la découverte de la religion populaire. Ce n'est sans doute pas le moindre de ses mérites. Il pourrait être médité par les pasteurs de notre temps."

[18] *De civitate Dei* 22.8, CCL 48:816: "Apud Carthaginem autem quis novit praeter admodum paucissimos salutem, quae facta est Innocentio, ex advocato vicariae praefecturae, ubi nos interfuimus et oculis aspeximus nostris?" On the date of this and the other miracles reported in the twenty-second book of *De civitate Dei*, see Saxer, *Morts, martyrs, reliques*, p. 266.

period immediately following his conversion right up to 413 or 414,[19] and perhaps even later. Although there are a few isolated shrines renowned for miracles, Augustine would say, we have not seen them here in Africa, nor do we have reason to expect them.[20] We are not like the Jews who witnessed Christ's miracles at first-hand, but more like the Samaritans, who did not have the benefit of supernatural authentication of the Christian message: "We have heard the Gospel; we have assented to the Gospel; through the Gospel we have believed in Christ. We have seen no signs; we demand none."[21]

Towards the end of his career, primarily because of the sudden increase of miracles that followed the spread of the relics of St Stephen, there was a decided shift of emphasis in Augustine's thought, for miracles were obviously not quite as rare as he had believed. Indeed, to speak of a shift of emphasis is perhaps not to do full justice to the situation. More than the tone changed, for the principal reason he had advanced ca. 390 for the relative rarity of modern miracles could now no longer be maintained.[22] But however we choose to characterize the shift in attitude, it should not be described as a change from unbelief to belief. Although he had not expected to encounter them in such large numbers, Augustine had believed in modern miracles from the earliest stages of his Christian life.[23]

[19] See *Enar. in Psalmos* 110.4, CCL 40:1623, which can be dated at Easter 414: "*Memoriam fecit mirabilium suorum*: hunc humilans, et hunc exaltans. *Memoriam fecit mirabilium suorum*: reservans opportune inusitata prodigia, quae infirmitas hominis novitati intenta meminerit, cum sint eius miracula quotidiana maiora. Tot per universam terram arbores creat, et nemo miratur: arefecit vero unam, et stupefacta sunt corda mortalium; sed *memoriam fecit mirabilium suorum*. Hoc enim miraculum maxime adtentis cordibus inhaerebit, quod assiduitas non vilefecerit." The central thrust of the argument here parallels closely *De utilitate credendi* 16.34, CSEL 25.1:43-44.

[20] See *Epist.* 78.3, CSEL 34.2:335-336, probably written from Carthage in 404. After referring to the miracles reported at the tomb of Felix of Nola and at the shrine of the saints in Milan, he says: "numquid non et Africa sanctorum martyrum corporibus plena est? et tamen nusquam hic scimus talia fieri. sicut enim, quod apostolus dicit, non omnes sancti dona habent curationum nec omnes habent diiudicationem spirituum, ita nec in omnibus memoriis sanctorum ista fieri voluit ille, qui dividit propria unicuique, prout vult."

[21] *In Iohannis Evangelium* 16.3, CCL 36:167. This can be dated July 413.

[22] In *De vera religione* Augustine proclaims: "Cum enim ecclesia catholica per totum orbem diffusa atque fundata sit, nec miracula illa in nostra tempora durare permissa sunt, ne anima semper visibilia quaereret et eorum consuetudine frigesceret genus humanum, quorum novitate flagravit" (*De vera religione* 25.47, CCL 32:216-217). This was written in the period 387-391. Towards the end of his career, however, we find him saying something quite different: "Non cessat Deus attestari: et novit quomodo ipsa miracula sua debeat commendare. Novit agere, ut magnificentur: novit agere, ne vilescant" (*Sermo* 286.5.5, PL 38:1299).

[23] Bardy, "Les miracles contemporains," p. 828, speaks of a bias against miracles on the part of the early Augustine: "N'y a-t-il pas ... chez lui une sorte de parti-pris contre les

Much the same can be said of Gregory the Great's attitude towards contemporary miracles. Like Augustine, he was never seriously tempted to believe that the age of miracles had come to an end. To be sure, the two church fathers were not without their differences. Augustine focused his attention on the miracles taking place at the *memoriae* of the martyrs; Gregory's main concern was to describe the miracles performed by modern, living saints. Perhaps even more important, Gregory adopted a more consistent position throughout his career, and did not have to adjust his views as Augustine did. In Gregory's judgment, modern miracles are relatively rare occurrences compared to the miracles of apostolic times. However, in its most essential features—the conviction that there is continuity between apostolic and modern times, and that even now God continues to act in a wondrous manner—the position of Gregory the Great was identical to that of his great mentor.

* *
*

Two passages most frequently cited in discussions of Gregory's thought on this issue occur in his *Homilies on the Gospels*. These were delivered in 591-592, just a few years before the *Dialogues* were written, but published in the same year they appeared. The fourth homily is based on Christ's commission to the apostles in Matthew 10, where they are instructed to go out and preach the coming of the Kingdom of Heaven, a doctrine, says Gregory, that is relatively easy for modern believers to accept. Even if the Gospel had said nothing about the approaching end, the condition to which the modern world has been reduced would teach the same lesson. Worn down by the many blows it has endured, it has fallen from its former glory, and thus announces the coming of another kingdom.

Gregory commented often on the devastation of the world around him. It led him early in his pontificate to liken himself to the captain of a vessel threatened with shipwreck: "I am tossed by so many waves of this world," he says in a letter of April 591 to Leander of Seville, "that by no means am I able to direct to port the ancient and rotting ship which, through God's hidden dispensation, I undertook to guide."[24] If in this letter Gregory was

---

miracles contemporains, parti-pris qui cesse à un moment donné sous l'influence de circonstances nouvelles?" Brown, *Augustine of Hippo*, p. 415, offers a more precise assessment when he maintains that "within the immensely complex structure of Augustine's thought, the centre of gravity had shifted."

[24] *Ep.* 1.41, CCL 140:47-49 at 47: "Tantis quippe in hoc loco huius mundi fluctibus quatior, ut vetustam ac putrescentem navim, quam regendam occulta Dei dispensatione suscepi, ad portum dirigere nullatenus possim."

more concerned about his own personal loss of the contemplative life than he was about the destruction of the civilized world, there is no mistaking the anguish in a letter of June 595 to the Emperor Maurice: "Behold, everything in the regions of Europe has been handed over to the jurisdiction of barbarians, cities destroyed, encampments overturned, provinces depopulated. No cultivator of the soil inhabits the earth; worshippers of idols have dominion, and vent their rage daily in the slaughter of the faithful."[25] In circumstances like these, he says elsewhere, the Gospel of the coming kingdom can readily be believed. It is relatively easy for those of us who have witnessed destruction on a universal scale to take it to heart, and to put out of our minds any preoccupation with the delights of the world.[26]

However, things were very different when the church was in its infancy, Gregory argues, and as a result miracles were necessary, for the fortunate circumstances of the earth at that time were not such as to encourage belief in another world:

> With the earth flourishing, the human race on the increase, the physical body enjoying the benefits of long life, material wealth abounding, who, when he heard of it, would believe that there is another life? Who would prefer invisible things to the visible? But when the sick returned to health, when the dead were raised to life, when the bodies of the leprous were cleansed, when the possessed were snatched from the rule of unclean spirits—so many visible miracles having been performed—who then would not believe what he heard concerning things invisible?

For Gregory, the circumstances of the early church were such that miracles were necessary in accomplishing the work of conversion. Miracles were required to bring people to the faith. But now that the church has been firmly established, he says, the need for miracles has waned: "since the number of the faithful has now increased, there are many within Holy Church who lead a life of virtue without possessing the signs of virtue, because in vain is a miracle displayed on the outside if the inner purpose which it serves is

---

[25] *Ep.* 5.37, CCL 140:308-311 at 309.

[26] *Hom. in Evan.* 1.4.2-3, PL 76:1090. At least, it *should* be relatively easy. Cf. *Hom. in Evan.* 2.28.3, PL 76:1212-1213: "Ecce jam mundus in seipso aruit, et adhuc in cordibus nostris floret. Ubique mors, ubique luctus, ubique desolatio, undique percutimur, undique amaritudinibus replemur; et tamen caeca mente carnalis concupiscentiae ipsas ejus amaritudines amamus, fugientem sequimur, labenti inhaeremus. Et quia labentem retinere non possumus, cum ipso labimur, quem cadentem tenemus. Aliquando nos mundus delectatione sibi tenuit; nunc tantis plagis plenus est, ut ipse nos jam mundus mittat ad Deum." Cf. also *Dial.* 3.38.3-4, SC 260:430.

lacking."[27] In all this Gregory has sometimes been taken to mean that the age of miracles is over, but he does not say so in as many words. Indeed, read carefully, he seems to deny it. The need for miracles in the modern world is not as great as it once was. But if there are *many* saints who do not perform miracles, by implication it would seem that there are some, a few at least, who do—precisely what we would expect Gregory to say in a series of homilies published in the very year the *Dialogues* were written.

The second passage to which reference is often made is perhaps more troublesome. It occurs in the twenty-ninth homily, where Gregory preaches on Christ's words of Mark 16:15-18. In this passage Christ commissions the apostles to "go into all the world and preach the Gospel to the whole creation," promising that "these signs will accompany those who believe: in my name they will cast out demons; they will speak in new tongues; they will pick up serpents, and if they drink any deadly thing, it will not hurt them; they will lay their hands on the sick, and they will recover." Gregory maintains that such miracles were necessary in the early years of Christianity, because the church at that time was like a freshly planted vineyard that needed to be watered until the plants took root. Now, however, that the vineyard of the faith has been firmly established and is able to flourish on its own, the miracles promised by Christ and accomplished by the apostles are regularly performed in a spiritual fashion. We may not be able to speak in tongues, but we can banish worldly discourse and sing the praises of the Creator. Healing the physically sick may be beyond our power, but our good example can assist the spiritually ill by strengthening their efforts to lead the Christian life. Indeed, these spiritual miracles are even greater than physical miracles. Physical miracles may revive bodies, but spiritual miracles revive souls; physical miracles sometimes demonstrate sanctity, but spiritual miracles actually create saints.

As we have already seen, there were several sources from which such thoughts could have been drawn, perhaps most notably the early Augustine.[28] Like Augustine, Gregory may be taken to imply that the age of miracles is over, and that the crude wonders necessary to the apostolic age have now been replaced by spiritual deeds of far greater significance. A more careful consideration of the context of the passage, however, leads to rather different conclusions. The homily is addressed to simple believers whose faith might

---

[27] *Hom. in Evan.* 1.4.3, PL 76:1090, 1091: "nunc quoque cum fidelium numerositas excrevit, intra sanctam Ecclesiam multi sunt qui vitam virtutum tenent, sed signa virtutum non habent, quia frustra miraculum foris ostenditur, si deest quod intus operetur."

[28] Cf. *Sermo* 88.2.2-3.3, PL 38:539-540, Verbraken 75-76; *Sermo* 98.1.1-2.2, PL 38:591; *De baptismo* 3.16.21, CSEL 51:212-213.

be jeopardized because they are incapable of the miracles that Christ seemed
to say would be performed by all the faithful. Hence at the very outset he asks:
"Surely, my brethren, you don't have trouble believing because those signs
are beyond your power?" (*Nunquidnam, fratres mei, quia ista signa non
facitis, minime creditis?*) Gregory tells them not to despair, for by the grace
of God there are greater miracles within their power, miracles that may not
win renown among men but that nonetheless have their assured reward in
heaven:

> If you wish, dearest brethren, you can perform these [spiritual] signs with
> God's help (*auctore Deo*). ... Do not, therefore, dearest brethren, be enamoured
> of signs that can be held in common with the reprobate, but love these miracles
> of charity and piety of which we have just spoken. The more hidden they are,
> the more are they secure; and the less their glory is among men, the greater is
> their reward before God.[29]

The point of the passage is not that the physical miracles mentioned in the
Gospel are never performed any more, but rather that the ordinary Christian
believer should not be troubled if they are beyond his power. In the apostolic
church the grace of miracles was widely distributed; today, however, miracles
are relatively rare occurrences. In these same homilies Gregory states quite
clearly that miracles do still occur—at the tombs of the martyrs, for example,
a claim he corroborates with a story of a religious woman who, as a reward
for her charity, was privileged to be visited by Saints Processus and
Martinianus, and to receive assurance of their assistance at the Day of
Judgment. This is not an isolated example. In this same series of homilies
Gregory tells the story of the monk, Martyrius, who met Christ in the form
of a leper to whom he extended his compassion, as well as several other
miracle stories, many of which he later incorporated almost word for word
in the *Dialogues*.[30] It is doubtful that he would have wished to tell the popular

---

[29] *Hom. in Evan.* 2.29.4, PL 76:1215, 1216.

[30] *Ibid.* 2.32.6, PL 76:1237: "Ad exstincta namque eorum corpora viventes aegri veniunt
et sanantur, perjuri veniunt et a daemonio vexantur, daemoniaci veniunt et liberantur." For
the story of the religious woman, see *ibid.* 2.32.7, PL 76:1237-1238. For the story of
Martyrius, see *ibid.* 2.39.10, PL 76:1300-1301.

The story of Romula, which is found in *Hom. in Evan.* 2.40.11, PL 76:1310-1312, is
repeated in almost precisely the same words in *Dial.* 4.16, SC 265:62-68. The episode about
the wondrous death of Tharsilla in the story of Gregory's three aunts found in *Hom. in Evan.*
2.38.15, PL 76:1290-1292, is repeated, again in almost the same words, in *Dial.* 4.17, SC
265:68-70. In *Hom. in Evan.* 2.38.16, PL 76:1292-1293, Gregory speaks of an unfortunate
monk from his own monastery who, on his death bed, was snatched from the jaws of the
dragon by the prayers of the brethren. This, too, is repeated in virtually the same words in *Dial.*
4.40.1-5, SC 265:138-142, where the monk is given the name of Theodorus. For a complete

audience privileged to receive these edifying tales that the age of miracles had come to an end.

Perhaps the most important passage for a consideration of the issue, and Gregory's clearest statement on the problem, occurs in the *Moralia on Job*, a work begun in Constantinople, but not completed until after his return to Rome. The *Moralia* were edited and put together in 595, a year or two after the *Dialogues* had been written. In the twenty-seventh book Gregory maintains that miracles were necessary in the apostolic age, when the church was suffering the trials of persecution. But after the pagan persecutors had been won over to the Christian faith, the church required not so much miracles as works of Christian virtue. Once again, however, it is quite clear that Gregory does not mean that miracles have disappeared entirely, but only that they have become less frequent. He states unambiguously that they are still performed by many people today when the need arises.[31]

He does admit in the same passage that, according to both the words and the example of Saint Paul, miracles in the early church were performed for the benefit of non-Christians. They were granted to the apostles as an aid in the process of conversion, and once that work was completed, they were not as necessary as they had been before. As Saint Paul points out (1 Cor. 14:22): "'Tongues are a sign not for believers but for unbelievers.' Therefore, when all are believers, what cause demands that signs should be shown?" Again, however, Gregory clearly does not wish to imply that there are no modern miracles at all, only that there are not as many.[32] Hence in the same twenty-seventh book of the *Moralia* he can rejoice over the fact that, through the miracles of modern apostles, the hearts of the distant *Angli* have been won over to the Christian faith:

> The Lord Almighty, ... through the illustrious miracles of preachers, has led even the ends of the earth to the faith. For behold, he has penetrated already the hearts of nearly all peoples. Behold, he has joined in one faith the boundaries of East and West. Behold, the tongue of Britain, which had known

---

list of the miracle stories in the *Homilies on the Gospels*, see de Vogüé, *Introduction*, p. 29 with n. 15. There are thirteen such stories (fourteen in total, since he repeats one of them), of which nine are repeated almost literally in the *Dialogues*, although two of the nine are truncated.

[31] *Mor.* 27.18.36, CCL 143B:1358: "Tunc quippe sancta Ecclesia miraculorum adiutoriis indiguit, cum eam tribulatio persecutionis pressit. Nam postquam superbiam infidelitatis edomuit, non iam virtutum signa, sed sola merita operum requirit, *quamvis et illa per multos cum opportunitas exigit ostendat.*" The emphasis has been added.

[32] Slightly further on he asks: "Quid est igitur mirum si, propagata fide, *crebro* miracula non fiunt, quando haec ipsi quoque apostoli in quibusdam iam fidelibus non fecerunt" (*Mor.* 27.18.37, CCL 143B:1359)? The emphasis has been added.

nothing other than to gnash its teeth in barbarous fashion, for some time now has begun to echo the Hebrew Alleluia in divine praises.[33]

For the sake of completeness, we should probably consider one additional passage. It occurs in his *Homilies on Ezechiel*, where he is commenting on *Cant.* 4:4: "Your neck is like the tower of David, which has been built with its own fortifications. A thousand shields hang from it, all the armour of brave men." The neck, he says, is a symbol for Sacred Scripture, and the fortifications and the shields symbolize respectively the miracles and the deeds of virtue performed by the Biblical saints. Both the fortifications and the shields are instruments for our defence. We can be encouraged in our own efforts by the good example of the Biblical saints, and we can be assured of the truth of what they said by the fact that God chose to confirm their preaching in such a wondrous manner. However, to explore the allegory a little further, shields can be taken up and wielded by us directly, whereas fortifications cannot. Although we are capable, *praecedente nos gratia*, of assuming our own defence in the Christian life by fortifying ourselves with the virtues of patience and compassion, the performance of miracles is beyond our reach: "we do not command any authority over them, for we do not have the power to do such things."[34]

It seems clear, however, that Gregory cannot here be speaking for his entire generation. In the same *Homilies on Ezechiel* he states that the saints frequently perform miracles as striking as any reported in Scripture: "Now, generally, we see holy men do wonderful things, perform many miracles, cleanse lepers, cast out demons, dispel bodily sicknesses by touch, predict things to come by the spirit of prophecy."[35] *We* may not be able to perform miracles, but *the saints* can. In the *Homilies on Ezechiel* as elsewhere Gregory maintains a consistent position on the issue of modern miracles. In the entire corpus of his work there is no evidence that he changed his mind on the matter, that he altered his basic position to suit his audience, or that he was in any way confused. Modern miracle stories are most prominent in the *Dialogues*, of course, but they are systematically reported and referred to elsewhere as well, whenever the occasion makes it appropriate, and their reality is never challenged. Above all, they are reported in the very treatises in which other scholars have found indications of a contrary belief.

Further evidence is available in the many references to contemporary miracles in Gregory's correspondence. A few examples from the early,

---

[33] *Mor.* 27.11.21, CCL 143B:1346.
[34] *Hom. in Ezech.* 2.3.23, CCL 142:254-255.
[35] *Ibid.* 2.5.22, CCL 142:291.

middle and later periods of his pontificate should suffice. In a letter of August 593 to the Emperor Maurice, Gregory protests against a new imperial policy designed to prevent soldiers from becoming monks unless they had already completed their terms of service or had been rejected for bodily infirmity. If, says Gregory, the motives of these men are being impugned, he can testify to the miracles performed by such converts. In a letter of July 598 to Eulogius, Bishop of Alexandria, Gregory reports that Augustine and his companions in the English mission are resplendent with such great miracles that they seem to imitate the powers of the apostles.[36] In a letter to Augustine himself, in June 601, Gregory comments on the great miracles that God has deigned to perform in the nation of the *Angli*. In the days of the apostolic church God chose to convert the world through unlettered men, and he does the same even now through Augustine and his associates. Augustine is informed that there is cause for rejoicing, because the souls of the *Angli* are being drawn by outward miracles to inward grace. Finally, in a letter of February 601 to Rusticiana, Gregory describes a number of miracles that had taken place in his own monastery of St Andrew, miracles of which he had been informed by the abbot and the prior. Rusticiana, a patroness of this same monastery, would appreciate knowing that such great miracles are performed there that one would think that the monastery were presided over by Saint Andrew himself.[37]

Especially striking to anyone who takes time to read through the register of his correspondence is Gregory's belief in the miraculous properties of relics, a belief evident at every stage of his career in the papal office. His clearest statement occurs in a letter of June 594 to the Empress Constantina, who had asked that Gregory send her the head of Saint Paul, or some other part of his body, for the church that was being built in the saint's honour. Gregory regrets that he cannot perform the favour. The bodies of Saint Peter and Saint Paul are responsible for so many miracles and terrors in their churches that they cannot be approached without great fear. He goes on to say that, when his predecessor attempted renovations near the remains of Saint Peter and Saint Lawrence, his temerity was rewarded with frightening signs. When Gregory himself desired to make improvements near the sepulchre of Saint Paul, similar warnings were received. The prior (*praepo-*

---

[36] *Ep.* 3.61, CCL 140:209-211 at 210; *Ep.* 8.29, CCL 140A:550-553 at 551. The miracles of the English mission are also mentioned in a letter of June 601 to Brunichild, Queen of the Franks: see *Ep.* 11.48, CCL 140A:946-947.

[37] *Ep.* 11.36, CCL 140A:925-929 at 925-926; *Ep.* 11.26, CCL 140A:898-901 at 899: "tanta miracula, tanta cura, tanta custodia monachorum in eodem monasterio eiusdem apostoli est, acsi specialiter abbas monasterii ipse sit."

situs loci ipsius) accidentally unearthed some bones, and even though they were not connected with the sepulchre of the saint, terrible signs appeared when he presumed to lift them up and move them to another place, and he suddenly died. Hence, Gregory tells Constantina, in the western church it is considered sacrilegious to want to touch the bodies of the saints. If anyone presumes to do so, it is certain that such rashness will be punished.

Although the Greeks may claim to handle the bodies of the saints, Gregory continues, their claim is scarcely credible. At the time of the martyrdom of the blessed apostles, some believers from the East attempted to recover the remains. However, they were frightened off by violent thunder and lightning, and were unable to take their treasure any further than the second milestone from the city.[38] In all likelihood, therefore, the Greeks have been no more successful than Latin Christians in approaching the remains of the saints. Indeed, says Gregory, some of their claims are certainly fraudulent. Two years ago some Greeks were discovered to have dug up bones that were lying in an open field; they later confessed that they had intended to take them home and pass them off as relics. Be this as it may, however, Constantina is informed that relics are not treated in such a disrespectful manner in the western church. Knowing what we do of the virtues of these relics, says Gregory, who would be so temerarious as even to look at the bodies of the saints, let alone handle them? When a relic is desired, therefore, it is the custom of the Roman church to put a piece of cloth (*brandeum*) into a small box and place it near the bodies of the saints. When this cloth is deposited in the church being dedicated, its effects are such as to rival those of the holy bodies themselves. At the time of Pope Leo certain Greeks who were inclined to be sceptical were given a vivid demonstration of the efficacy of such relics. Leo cut one with some scissors, and blood flowed from the incision.[39]

---

[38] On the background for this story, see S. Mazzarino, "L'"èra Costantiniana' et la 'prospettiva storica' di Gregorio Magno," in *Passaggio dal mondo antico al medio evo* (Rome, 1980), pp. 9-28 at pp. 9-10.

[39] *Ep.* 4.30, CCL 140:248-250. On the background to Gregory's letter, see N. Herrmann-Mascard, *Les reliques des saints. Formation coutumière d'un droit* (Paris, 1975), pp. 26-70; and J.M. McCulloh, "The Cult of Relics in the Letters and 'Dialogues' of Pope Gregory the Great: A Lexicographical Study," *Traditio* 32 (1976): 145-184. In McCulloh's judgment, the letter is "a thoughtful description of traditional—and contemporary—Roman practice" (p. 181). It may contain some rhetorical exaggeration: "Only with difficulty can one accept at face value Gregory's doubts, expressed in this letter, as to whether the Greeks actually move the bodies of the saints. He had spent sufficient time in Constantinople to know that the Eastern church did practice translation and division, and it seems unlikely that he intended to label as false all of the relics moved by the Greeks" (p. 180n). To this one should add that, despite Gregory's statements about the inviolability of the tombs, in some circumstances at least the

Although Constantina's request for corporeal relics is ultimately denied, Gregory promises to send her some filings from Saint Paul's chains if they can be obtained. Many people come to Rome, he says, in the hope of receiving fragments from the chains, and a priest of the Roman church has been assigned the task of producing them. Sometimes his efforts yield quick results; at others even strenuous labour is in vain. But Gregory promises to send filings if he can, and he assures Constantina of their miraculous properties. These filings, usually described as filings from the chains of Saint Peter rather than Saint Paul, were sent to many of Gregory's correspondents, often enclosed in keys representative of the keys to Saint Peter's sepulchre, but occasionally contained in a cross.[40] Sometimes the meaning of these

---

Roman church as well allowed cult-related translations. Indeed, Gregory himself gave permission for the reburial of St Donatus. However, there cannot be much doubt about the basic accuracy of Gregory's description of Roman practice, particularly with regard to the distribution of corporeal relics. Papal policy as Gregory represents it would continue in effect for some time. Cf. J.M. McCulloh, "From Antiquity to the Middle Ages: Continuity and Change in Papal Relic Policy from the 6th to the 8th Century," in *Pietas. Festschrift für Bernhard Kötting* (Münster-en-Westfalen, 1980), pp. 313-324. Although there was considerable dissatisfaction with the papal position on this matter, even in the West, "no major change in papal policy occurred before the middle of the eighth century, when Paul I (757-767) began to distribute corporeal relics among the Franks" (p. 321). Until that time the distribution of relics was normally limited to contact relics of the kind described for Constantina.

Such *brandea* are mentioned in two places by Gregory of Tours as well: *Liber in gloria martyrum*, chap. 27, MGH, SRM 1.2, p. 54, where Gregory describes the customs that applied at the tomb of St Peter in Rome; and *De virtutibus S. Martini* 1.11, MGH, SRM 1.2, p. 145, where Gregory tells us of a miracle that occurred at the shrine of St Martin at Tours. In the first of these texts Gregory's comments also illustrate the manner in which the supernatural transfer of virtue from the body of the saint could be publicly confirmed. The method he describes involves the use of scales rather than scissors; but in principle it is much the same as the method that Gregory the Great ascribes to Pope Leo, and to any onlookers it certainly would have been equally as striking. On the practices of the sixth-century Frankish church with respect to such relics, see M. Vieillard-Troiekouroff, *Les monuments religieux de la Gaule d'après les oeuvres de Grégoire de Tours* (Paris, 1976), pp. 377-378; and M. Weidemann, *Kulturgeschichte der Merowingerzeit nach den Werken Gregors von Tours* (Bonn, 1982), 2:161-169.

[40] Eulogius, Patriarch of Alexandria, was sent a small cross containing filings from the chains of both Saint Peter and Saint Paul (*Ep.* 13.43, CCL 140A:1047-1049 at 1049). Dynamius, a patrician of Gaul, was sent a small cross containing benefits from the chains of Saint Peter and from the gridiron of Saint Lawrence (*Ep.* 3.33, CCL 140:179). Adaloald, the son of Theodelina, Queen of the Lombards, received a cross containing fragments from the true cross (*Ep.* 14.12, CCL 140A:1082-1083 at 1083). In addition to a key with filings from Saint Peter's chains, Reccared, King of the Visigoths, received a cross containing wood from the Lord's cross as well as hairs of John the Baptist (*Ep.* 9.229, CCL 140A:805-811 at 810). However, keys seem to have been the norm.

Gregory of Tours mentions similar keys to St Peter's sepulchre, although their miraculous

presents is not explained, or only vaguely, and it is difficult to determine precisely what sort of blessing Gregory thought the recipients of the gifts could expect. At other times Gregory mentions only spiritual benefits, the hope that the chains that bound the neck of Saint Peter for martyrdom might loosen that of the recipient from all sins.[41] In several cases, however, it is miraculous benefits he has in mind. To Anastasius, Patriarch of Antioch, he sends keys which, he says, are wont to shine with many miracles when placed on the bodies of sick persons. To Eulogius, Patriarch of Alexandria, who had been suffering from failing eyesight, he sends a *benedictio* to be applied to his eyes. Many miracles, he says, have been effected through this same blessing.[42]

Gregory customarily describes these gifts as *benedictiones*; they are therefore to be distinguished from *reliquiae* or *sanctuaria*, relics in the strict sense of the term. *Reliquiae* were physical remains of the saints used for the dedication of churches and altars. *Brandea*, mentioned above, were their precise equivalent: they had absorbed the virtues that were proper to the bodies of the saints from having been placed in direct contact with them. *Benedictiones* functioned more like charms or talismans, for they were sent to individuals to protect them from a variety of evils.[43] But it is significant that they too had come in contact with the bodies of the saints, and so in a number of letters, written throughout his career, Gregory attributes miraculous powers to them. The letter to Anastasius was written in February 591, shortly after Gregory's assumption of the papal throne; the letter to Constantina in mid-career, in June 594; the letter to Eulogius in July 603, shortly before his death. Together they provide strong evidence that Gregory

---

properties seem to have been due to their simply having been brought in contact with the tomb. See *Liber in gloria martyrum*, chap. 27, MGH, SRM 1.2, p. 54.

[41] No comment on the accompanying presents is offered in the letters to Hospito, Duke of the Barbaricini (*Ep.* 4.27, CCL 140:246), and to Theodelinda, Queen of the Lombards (*Ep.* 14.12, CCL 140A:1082-1083 at 1083). There is only a vague comment on the present sent to Childebert II, King of the Franks: "Claves praeterea sancti Petri, in quibus de vinculis catenarum eius inclausum est, excellentiae vestrae direximus, quae collo vestro suspensae de malis vos omnibus tueantur" (*Ep.* 6.6, CCL 140:373-374 at 374). Cf. the letters to Columbus, Bishop of Numidia (*Ep.* 3.47, CCL 140:191-192 at 192), and to Asclipiodotus, patrician of Gaul (*Ep.* 11.43, CCL 140A:940-941 at 941). Spiritual benefits are mentioned in the letters to Leontius, the ex-consul (*Ep.* 8.33, CCL 140A:557-559 at 559), to the patrician Dynamius (*Ep.* 3.33, CCL 140:179), to Theodore, physician at Constantinople (*Ep.* 7.25, CCL 140:480-481 at 481), to Reccared (*Ep.* 9.229, CCL 140A:805-811 at 810), and to Savinella, Columba and Galla (*Ep.* 12.2, CCL 140A:969-970 at 970).

[42] To Anastasius: *Ep.* 1.25, CCL 140:33-34 at 34; cf. the letters to Andrew, *vir illustris* of Constantinople (*Ep.* 1.29, CCL 140:36-37 at 37), and to John, ex-consul, patrician and *quaestor* (*Ep.* 1.30, CCL 140:37). To Eulogius: *Ep.* 13.43, CCL 140A:1047-1049 at 1049.

[43] McCulloh, "The Cult of Relics," pp. 177-178.

was a believer in contemporary miracles throughout his career in the papal office.

It should be emphasized, however, that Gregory also thought that miracles were relatively less frequent than in the days of the apostolic church. The one significant exception was the occurrence of miraculous visions, which Gregory believed were actually on the increase in his time. In the fourth book of the *Dialogues* Peter asks why so many previously hidden truths about the life of the soul should have been clarified in recent years. Gregory replies that the reason is the approaching end of the world: as eternity looms nearer, it manifests itself by increasingly clearer signs.[44] Some scholars have sought to minimize the eschatological dimension of Gregory's thought by pointing to its traditional and literary quality, or by suggesting that it was intended primarily to serve a pastoral purpose.[45] However, these suggestions fail to do justice to the sincerity of Gregory's conviction, which seems to have been shared by at least one other contemporary observer of the signs of the time.[46]

Gregory did indeed use the notion of the coming end of the world to reinforce his call for repentance and conversion.[47] But nothing could have been more natural, and rather than cast doubt on his sincerity, it seems to presuppose it. Gregory admits that no one knows the day or the hour, of course; and he seems to feel that they are probably not imminent, for he tells us that the coming generation will have to suffer evils even greater than those suffered by his own. But he speaks of the signs that can be seen even in his own time too often for there to be much doubt that, to his mind, the consummation of the age would soon transpire. Despite the very different perspective of his great mentor, Augustine, there is every indication that

---

[44] *Dial.* 4.43.1-2, SC 265:154.

[45] For example, H. de Lubac, *Exégèse médiévale*, part 2, vol. 1 (Paris, 1961), p. 527ff, argues that medieval pronouncements about the approaching end of the world were commonplace. He also comments on their ambivalence. The end of the world is coming, it is frequently said, but not immediately. In de Lubac's judgment: "De tels textes expriment plus la tension de la conscience chrétienne, sachant la précarité de l'existence terrestre et l'incessante urgence de la fin dernière, qu'une prévision particulière et ferme" (p. 531). Contrast S. Boesch Gajano, "'Narratio' e 'expositio' nei Dialoghi di Gregorio Magno," *BISIAM* 88 (1979): 1-33, esp. 26-28, who acknowledges Gregory's "angoscia per gli orrori, le stragi, i dolori del presente, ma non attesa imminente di fine palingenetica: la drammaticità dei tempi è utilizzata dal pastore d'anime per rafforzare la quotidiana fede dei credenti" (p. 27).

[46] See G. de Nie, "Roses in January: A Neglected Dimension in Gregory of Tours' *Historiae*," *JMH* 5 (1979): 259-289.

[47] See in particular P. Catry, "Amour du monde et amour de Dieu chez saint Grégoire le Grand," *SMon.* 15 (1973): 253-275, esp. 260-262. On the issue of whether or not Gregory really believed in the approaching end of the world Catry is non-committal, contenting himself with the observation (p. 261n) that perhaps his thought underwent some evolution.

Gregory was convinced that the second coming of Christ would take place in the relatively near future, and that this conviction assumed central importance, not only in his theology, but in virtually every aspect of his life and thought.[48]

Augustine claims that the teaching of the New Testament is clear: the time of the Lord's second coming simply cannot be known, and so it would be folly to speculate about it. If God has wrapped these matters in secrecy, it is for our own good, so that our hearts might ever be ready for what surely must come, although we know not when.[49] Scripture also teaches, of course, that this is indeed "the last hour," and that the Day of the Lord, or of the Kingdom of Heaven, is "at hand." Hence Augustine frequently maintains that the world is approaching its end; that more time has already elapsed than remains in the future; that we are now living in the sixth and final age, which parallels the sixth and final day of creation.[50] But none of this means that the second coming should be expected soon, for of that we have no assurance whatever. This is indeed the last hour; yet we cannot know what the length of the hour will be, and it has already proven to be quite long.[51] If anything,

---

[48] See the studies of R. Manselli: "L'escatologia di S. Gregorio Magno," *Ricerche di storia religiosa* 1 (1954): 72-83; *Gregorio Magno* (Torino, 1967), pp. 100-114; "Gregorio Magno nelle sue opere," in *Passaggio dal mondo antico al medio evo* (Rome, 1980), pp. 559-568. In the last of these Manselli discusses Gregory as a transitional figure between the world of late antiquity and the Middle Ages. It is in this context that he mentions Gregory's expectation of the end of the world and of the second coming of Christ: "Siamo qui ad uno dei punti più delicati in tutto il mondo spirituale di Gregorio Magno, e allo spartiacque più preciso fra mondo antico e mondo medioevale" (p. 564). See also R. Wasselynck, "L'orientation eschatologique de la vie chrétienne d'après saint Grégoire le Grand," in *Assemblées du Seigneur 2: Temps de l'Advent* (Bruges, 1962), pp. 66-80; M.McC. Gatch, "The Fourth Dialogue of Gregory the Great: Some Problems of Interpretation," *SPatr.* 10 (1967): 77-83, esp. 78-79; C. Dagens, "La fin des temps et l'église selon saint Grégoire le Grand," *RSR* 58 (1970): 273-288; *Saint Grégoire le Grand*, pp. 345-400; Boglioni, "Miracle et nature," pp. 62-66; R.E. McNally, "Gregory the Great (590-604) and his Declining World," *AHP* 16 (1978): 7-26; and G. Cremascoli, '*Novissima hominis*' nei '*Dialogi*' di Gregorio Magno (Bologna, 1979), pp. 35-36. V. Recchia, *Gregorio Magno e la società agricola* (Rome, 1978), pp. 120-123, discusses the centrality of the eschatological perspective for Gregory's approach to papal administration, although the examples he provides illustrate concern with regard to the Last Judgment more than Gregory's conviction about the imminent end of the world.

[49] Cf. *De civitate Dei* 18.53, CCL 48:652; *Epist.* 197.1, CSEL 57:231-232; *Enar. in Psalmos* 6.1, CCL 38:27; 9.35, CCL 38:73; 36.1.1, CCL 38:336-338. Cf. Matt. 24:36; Mark 13:32-33; Acts 1:7; 1 Thess. 5:2.

[50] *Epist.* 137.4.16, CSEL 44:120; *Enar. in Psalmos* 30.2.1.8, CCL 38:196; 36.3.4, CCL 38:370; 92.1, CCL 39:1290-1291 (cf. *De civitate Dei* 22.30, CCL 48:865-866). Cf. Matthew 3:2; 4:17; Romans 13:11-12; 1 John 2:18.

[51] *Epist.* 199.6.17, CSEL 57:257-258. Referring to the words of the Evangelist in 1 John 2:18, he says: "neque enim dixit 'novissimum tempus est' aut 'novissimus annus' aut 'mensis'

Augustine is inclined to push the date into the indefinite future. Before the return of the Lord the Gospel must be preached to all nations. But this, says Augustine, has not yet been done, nor can we be confident that it will be done soon. Indeed, even when it is accomplished, Christ's second coming need not follow immediately.[52] Hence at several places in his work Augustine suggests that the end of the world is not to be expected in his own times, that his is not the last generation.[53] In the final analysis, however, Augustine asks us not to indulge our fancy but to acknowledge our ignorance, and attend to our own immediate end rather than the end of this world: "Let no one, therefore, search out the last day, when it is to be; but let us all keep watch by living well, lest the last day of any one of us find us unprepared." We must not believe that Christ will come sooner or that he will come later, but rather long for his coming, whenever it may be, with watchful care and faithful love.[54]

Gregory's emphasis is profoundly different. Whereas Augustine discourages any state of expectancy, Gregory continually strives to decipher the signs of the times, many of them learned from Augustine himself. In a letter of April 593 to the church of Milan, Gregory sees in the ravages of war indications of the coming Judgment. He urges his correspondents to consider the transitoriness of all things, and to cleanse their souls from the stain of every transgression by means of the tears of repentance:

> Behold, all the things of this world, which we heard in Sacred Scripture were to perish, we now see destroyed. Cities have been overturned, encampments uprooted, churches demolished. No tiller of the soil dwells in our land. Among the very few of us who have been left behind for a short time, the human sword rages incessantly with the devastation of a celestial blow. We now see, therefore, the evils of the world which formerly we heard were to come. The very afflictions of the earth have now become as it were the pages of books written for our benefit (*quasi paginae nobis codicum factae sunt ipsae iam plagae terrarum*). In the face of the destruction of all things, therefore, we ought to consider what we have loved to have been nothing. Hence, look toward the approaching day of the eternal Judge with a careful mind, and anticipate the terror of that day by repenting. Wash away the stains of all your sins with tears. Check the wrath that looms eternal with a temporal lament. For when our

---

aut 'dies', sed: Novissima hora est. et ecce ista hora quam longa est!" Cf. *Ibid.* 199.8.22, CSEL 57:262; 199.10.35, CSEL 57:274-275.

[52] *Ibid.* 197.4, CSEL 57:234; cf. 199.12.46, CSEL 57:284-285.

[53] *Ibid.* 199.3.8, CSEL 57:250-251; *Enar. in Psalmos* 36.1.10, CCL 38:344-345; 36.3.14, CCL 38:377; 37.28, CCL 38:401.

[54] *Sermo* 97.1.1, PL 38:589; *Epist.* 199.13.52-53, CSEL 57:290.

righteous Creator comes to judgment, the more he perceives that we have punished our own faults ourselves, the greater will be the grace with which he comforts us.[55]

Similar thoughts about the imminent end of the world and the coming Judgment are found in a letter to the Emperor Maurice of August 593. In a letter of June 601 to Ethelbert, King of the *Angli*, Gregory enumerates the signs of the coming end, informing the king that they are granted us so that we might be solicitous of our souls and prepare ourselves to meet Christ in judgment.[56]

This theme recurs several times in the *Dialogues*, and in book four Gregory calls upon it to explain the apparent increase in visions of the hereafter. He compares this world to a dark night, and the life to come to the light of day, and continues:

> In the transitional hour before sunrise, when the night comes to an end and the new day is about to begin, darkness is somehow blended with light until the remaining shadows of the night are perfectly absorbed in the brightness of the coming day. In this way the end of the world merges with the beginnings of eternal life. Earth's remaining shadows begin to fade as the beams of spiritual light filter through them. We can, therefore, discern many truths about the future life, but we still see them imperfectly, because the light in which we see is still dim and pale, like the light of the sun in the early hours of the day just before dawn.[57]

---

[55] *Ep.* 3.29, CCL 140:174-175 at 175.

[56] To Maurice: *Ep.* 3.61, CCL 140:209-211 at 210. In this letter Gregory protests against Maurice's new policy that would effectively prevent soldiers from becoming monks. The policy, he says, is particularly unfortunate now that the Last Judgment is approaching: "Ecce enim mora non erit, et ardente caelo, ardente terra, coruscantibus elementis, cum angelis et archangelis, cum thronis et dominationibus, cum principatibus et potestatibus tremendus iudex apparebit."

To Ethelbert: *Ep.* 11.37, CCL 140A:929-932 at 931. It is clear, however, that Gregory does not expect the end to come in his own time: "Praeterea scire vestram gloriam volumus quia, sicut in scriptura sacra ex verbis Domini omnipotentis agnoscimus, praesentis mundi iam terminus iuxta est et sanctorum regnum venturum est, quod nullo umquam poterit fine terminari. Appropinquante autem eodem mundi termino multa imminent quae antea non fuerunt, videlicet immutationes aeris terroresque de caelo et contra ordinationem temporum tempestates, bella, fames, pestilentiae, terrae motus per loca. Quae tamen non omnia nostris diebus ventura sunt, sed post nostros dies omnia subsequentur. Vos itaque si qua ex his evenire in terra vestra cognoscitis, nullomodo vestrum animum perturbetis, quia idcirco haec signa de fine saeculi praemittuntur, ut de animabus nostris debeamus esse solliciti, de mortis hora suspecti et venturo iudici in bonis actibus inveniamur esse praeparati."

[57] *Dial.* 4.43.2, Zimmerman 251, SC 265:154. For additional examples of the eschatological theme, see *Dial.* 3.37.21-22, SC 260:426; and 4.36.12, SC 265:122. Especially significant

The current increase in supernatural visions, however, remains an exception to the general pattern, and so elsewhere in the *Dialogues* Gregory agrees with Peter about the relative scarcity of miracles in his own day.[58] Moreover, in the *Moralia* he links their decline to another sign of the imminent end of the present order, the coming of the Antichrist. It is another favourite Gregorian theme.[59]

---

is *Dial.* 3.38.3-4, SC 260:430. After describing a vision of the end of the world which was experienced by Redemptus, Bishop of Ferentis, Gregory observes: "Mox effera Langobardorum gens, de vagina suae habitationis educta, in nostra cervice grassata est, atque hominum genus, quod in hac terra prae multitudine nimia quasi spissae segitis more surrexerat, succisum aruit. Nam depopulatae urbes, eversa castra, concrematae ecclesiae, destructa sunt monasteria virorum atque feminarum. Desolata ab hominibus praedia atque ab omni cultore destituta in solitudine vacat terra. Nullus hanc possessor inhabitat. Occupaverunt bestiae loca, quae prius multitudo hominum tenebat. Et quid in aliis mundi partibus agatur ignoro, nam hac in terra, in qua vivimus, finem suum mundus non iam nuntiat, sed ostendit. Tanto ergo nos necesse est instantius aeterna quaerere, quanto a nobis cognoscimus velociter temporalia fugisse. Despiciendus a nobis hic mundus fuerat, etiam si blandiretur, si rebus prosperis demulceret animum. At postquam tot flagellis premitur, tanta adversitate fatigatur, tot nobis cotidie dolores ingeminat, quid nobis aliud quam ne diligatur clamat." Cf. Boesch Gajano, "'Narratio' e 'expositio'," pp. 26-27, who notes "la drammatica descrizione delle rovine provocate dai Longobardi," but goes on to argue that "un improvviso ridimensionamento geografico limita la sua portata escatologica ('quid in aliis mundi partibus agatur, ignoro; nam hac in terra, in qua nos vivimus, finem suum mundus non iam adnuntiat, sed ostendit') e il vigore dell'imminenza, dell'urgenza si stempera nell'ammonimento finale a 'aeterna quaerere'."

[58] *Dial.* 1.12.4, SC 260:116; cf. *Dial.* 3.37.21-22, SC 260:426. See M. Van Uytfanghe, "La controverse biblique," p. 219. As Van Uytfanghe points out, the idea of the relative rarity of contemporary miracles is reinforced throughout the *Dialogues* wherever Peter expresses his astonishment at the fact that the miracles of which he is being informed are recent ones. See, for example, *Dial.* 3.16.11, SC 260:336: "Facta haec placent, quia mira, et multum, quia recentia"; and *Dial.* 3.31.8, SC 260:390: "Res mira et nostris stupenda temporibus." For a different view, however, see de Vogüé, *Introduction*, p. 91: "Loin de poser a priori que les miracles sont rares de nos jours, les Dialogues s'efforcent au contraire de montrer qu'ils sont fréquents, et le contraste de l'âge apostolique avec le nôtre fait place à des rapprochements."

[59] The idea often takes on ecclesiological implications, being tied to Gregory's protests over the assumption by the Patriarchs of Constantinople of the title of ecumenical or universal patriarch. In a letter of May 599 to several bishops of the eastern church he calls the Patriarchs John and Cyriacus harbingers of the Antichrist because of their use of the hateful title. See *Ep.* 9.157, CCL 140A:714-716 at 715: "huius mundi termino propinquante in praecursione sua paravit humani generis inimicus, ut ipsos, qui ei contradicere bene atque humiliter vivendo debuerunt, per hoc superbiae vocabulum praecursores habeat sacerdotes. ..." Cf. his letters of June 595 to John (*Ep.* 5.44, CCL 140:329-337 at 332), of June 597 to Cyriacus (*Ep.* 7.28, CCL 140:486-487 at 487), and of June 595 to Eulogius, Patriarch of Alexandria, and to Anastasius, Patriarch of Antioch (*Ep.* 5.41, CCL 140:320-325 at 323-324).

Fridrichsen maintains that there was a connection between the eschatological hopes of the early Christians and their openness to miracle.[60] Gregory's thought reveals precisely the reverse. Just before the appearance of the Antichrist, Gregory declares, the power of miracles will be withdrawn from the church. It will not disappear entirely, but it will be greatly reduced. The reward of the good, who venerate the church, not because of present signs, but in the hope of things eternal, will thereby be increased; and the true nature of the reprobate, who neglect invisible truths unless they are supported by visible signs, will be made more apparent:

> By the fearful order of a hidden arrangement, before Leviathan appears in that accursed man whose form he will assume, the signs of virtue will be withdrawn from Holy Church. For prophecy will be hidden, the grace of cures be removed, the virtue of more extended abstinence be diminished. The words of learning will grow silent; prodigies and miracles (*miraculorum prodigia*) will be taken away. The supernal dispensation will by no means withdraw these blessings completely, but it will not manifest them openly and in various ways as in previous times. Nevertheless, this will happen by a wondrous arrangement, so that from one divine deed piety and justice may be fulfilled at the same time. For while (the virtues of signs having been withdrawn) Holy Church will appear as though it were more lowly, the reward of the good, those who revere her for the hope of heavenly things and not on account of present signs, will increase. Conversely, the intent which the evil habour against her, those who neglect to embrace the invisible things which she promises unless they are charmed by visible signs, will be revealed more quickly. ... First the riches of miracles will be withdrawn from the faithful, and then their ancient enemy will be revealed through manifest prodigies, so that the more he is exalted through signs, the more firmly and the more laudably may he be overcome by the faithful without the benefit of signs. Although even the faithful will not lack signs in this contest, his will be so great that ours may seem to be little or nothing. But the virtue of the faithful will come to prevail over all signs (*omnibus signis fit potior*), when it crushes under the heel of inner steadfastness everything which it beholds him dreadfully accomplishing.[61]

In the background to this discussion is the question of why modern miracles occur at all. Is the work of evangelization not complete, or are there other purposes, purposes different from those that prevailed in New Testa-

---

[60] A. Fridrichsen, *The Problem of Miracle in Primitive Christianity* (Minneapolis, 1972), pp. 58-59.

[61] *Mor.* 34.3.7, CCL 143B:1737-1738: "Terribili quippe ordine dispositionis occultae, priusquam Leviathan iste in illo damnato homine quem assumit appareat, a sancta Ecclesia virtutum signa subtrahuntur. ..." Gregory uses the present tense throughout this passage.

ment times, that miracles now serve? We shall turn to this question in the next chapter. But this much at least should have been established: Gregory advanced a relatively clear and completely consistent position on the history of miracle in the Christian church. At one time miracles were more numerous than they are now, but they are still a constant of Christian experience.

2

The Purpose of Miracle

Those who approach the New Testament expecting to find one clear and consistent idea of miracle should be prepared for disappointment, for there are tensions in the Biblical doctrine that may not admit of reconciliation. As Van Uytfanghe puts it: "Le miracle fût, dès le début, un 'signe de contra-diction'."[1] One of the central elements in the Biblical doctrine is that faith is an essential precondition for miracles. When Christ cured the blindness of Bartimaeus, he announced the cure by saying to him: "Go your way; your faith has made you well." This man believed in Christ, and it was precisely because of his belief that he could receive such a favour from the hand of the Saviour.[2] The unbelieving citizens of Christ's own home town, on the other hand, were unresponsive to his message, and as a result "he could do no mighty work there, except that he laid his hands upon a few sick people and healed them. And he marvelled because of their unbelief."[3] Belief seems to have been an absolute requirement on the part of the beneficiaries of Christ's miracles. Hence Christ exercised his supernatural powers only when faith was at least implicit in the requests or search for his help.[4]

However, this is only part of the story, for once these miracles had been performed, they served to authenticate Christ's message, and hence were instrumental in encouraging others to believe. Christ himself acknowledged this when he cast the legion of devils out of the demoniac and into the herd of swine. The man begged that he be allowed to remain with the Saviour, but

[1] M. Van Uytfanghe, "La controverse biblique et patristique autour du miracle, et ses répercussions sur l'hagiographie dans l'Antiquité tardive et le haut Moyen Age latin," *Hagiographie, cultures et sociétés, IVe-XIIe siècles* (Paris, 1981), pp. 205-231 at 209.

[2] Mark 10:52. Cf. Matt. 8:5-13; 9:18-22, 27-30; 14:22-33; 15:21-28; Mark 5:25-34; Luke 8:43-48; 17:11-19; 18:35-43; Acts 14:7-9.

[3] Mark 6:5-6.

[4] See Van Uytfanghe, "La controverse biblique," pp. 207-208; and A. Fridrichsen, *The Problem of Miracle in Primitive Christianity* (Minneapolis, 1972), pp. 77-84.

Christ refused, saying, "Go home to your friends and tell them how much the Lord has done for you, and how he has had mercy on you." The apologetic function of miracles is even clearer in the case of the apostles. When Christ charged them to "go into all the world and preach the gospel to the whole creation," he promised that their preaching would be accompanied by miraculous signs verifying the truth of their claims. Hence they "went forth and preached everywhere, while the Lord worked with them and confirmed the message by the signs that attended it."[5]

Like St Augustine before him, Gregory was particularly struck by the apologetic value of Scriptural miracles, although neither would have endorsed a strict evidentialism. Just as people respond in different ways to the preaching of the Gospel, so the New Testament indicates that they responded differently to miracles, some with belief, others with unbelief.[6] Hence neither Augustine nor Gregory would have maintained that the miracles reported in Scripture possessed an objective, probative value independent of the motions of grace. Scriptural miracles functioned as signs; rather than compelling assent, they summoned a response of faith.[7] But to both church fathers their apologetic purpose was still their most striking feature. For Augustine, just as the miracles related in the Old Testament were intended to support the worship of the one true God, those in the New Testament were designed to stimulate belief in the Gospel. Their effect was such that even the kings of the earth who were wont to persecute the Christians were brought into subjection to the name of Christ.[8] Because men generally fail to be impressed by the wonders of nature which God performs on a regular basis, miracles were necessary to rouse them from their spiritual torpor.[9] Hence Christ's

---

[5] For the demoniac, see Mark 5:19; however, cf. Matt. 9:27-31, where Christ directs the two blind men he healed to keep their cure a secret. For the apostles, see Mark 16:15-20; cf. Acts 9:36-42; 13:6-12; Heb. 2:3-4. See also Van Uytfanghe, "La controverse biblique," pp. 207-208; and Fridrichsen, *The Problem of Miracle*, esp. pp. 56-59.

[6] *Mor.* 27.21.41, CCL 143B:1361-1362: "Unum ergo idemque miraculum quod aliis lumen fidei praebuit, alios per invidiae tenebras a lumine mentis excaecavit." Cf. *Enar. in Psalmos* 87.10, CCL 39:1214-1216. Augustine and Gregory refer frequently to Jewish unresponsiveness to the miracles of Christ and the apostles: cf. *De catechizandis rudibus* 23.42, CCL 46:166-167; *De div. quaest. ad Simplicianum* 1.2.14, CCL 44:38-39; *In Iohannis Evangelium* 16.3, CCL 36:167; with *Hom. in Evan.* 1.10.2, PL 76:1111; 1.18.5, PL 76:1153; *In 1 Reg.* 1.30, CCL 144:71. See also D.P. de Vooght, "La théologie du miracle selon saint Augustin," *RTAM* 11 (1939): 197-222, esp. pp. 218-220.

[7] Cf. J. Grange, *Le miracle d'après saint Augustin* (Brignais, 1912), esp. pp. 73ff.

[8] On Old Testament miracles, see *De civitate Dei* 10.9, CCL 47:281; *Epist.* 111.5, CSEL 34.2:651; cf. *De catechizandis rudibus* 21.37, CCL 46:161. On New Testament miracles, see *De vera religione* 25.47, CCL 32:216-217; *De catechizandis rudibus* 27.53, CCL 46:176.

[9] *In Iohannis Evangelium* 8.1, CCL 36:81-82; 9.1, CCL 36:90-91; 24.1, CCL 36:244. Cf. *Enar. in Psalmos* 110.4, CCL 40:1623.

miracles were performed so that mankind would believe in him; and the apostles' miracles were performed to corroborate the truth of the Gospel they preached.[10] Gregory's perspective is fundamentally the same. When he speaks in general terms about the miracles of the New Testament, he almost always conceives them as adjuncts to evangelization, as aids in the process of conversion.[11]

In the time of the apostolic church, says Gregory, the Christian faith was like a tender plant that needed to be watered by the grace of miracles until its roots had become firmly established. The preaching of the apostles alone would not have sufficed, for words can be understood without having any influence on the hearer. Miracles were necessary to move the minds of men, to penetrate their mental darkness and make them responsive to the Gospel.[12] When Christ commissioned the apostles to go out and proclaim that the Kingdom of Heaven was at hand (Matthew 10:5-8), he entrusted them with miraculous powers. They would be able to heal the sick, raise the dead, cleanse lepers, cast out demons, powers which were essential if their message was to receive a serious audience. The present ruin of the world makes it relatively easy for us now to believe that its end is near, and that another kingdom is at hand. But such a belief could not be embraced so readily when the apostles were sent out. The early evangelists were therefore entrusted with miraculous powers to substantiate the truth of their message: "miracles were associated with the holy preachers, so that virtue displayed might give credence to their words, and so that those who proclaimed extraordinary things might do extraordinary things."[13] Miracles were performed for the sake of unbelievers, not believers. When Saint Paul was preaching at Troas, a young man by the name of Eutychus, who was sitting in the window, was overcome by sleep and fell to his death three stories below. For the benefit of this Eutychus and the other unbelievers who were

---

[10] On Christ's miracles, see *De utilitate credendi* 14.32, CSEL 25.1:40-41; *In Iohannis Evangelium* 49.1, CCL 36:419-420; 49.6, CCL 36:422; 49.11, CCL 36:426; *Sermo* 88.1.1, PL 38:539, ed. P.-P. Verbraken, "Le sermon LXXXVIII de saint Augustin sur la guérison des deux aveugles de Jéricho," *RBén.* 94 (1984): 71-101 at 75. Augustine frequently claims, somewhat more specifically, that Christ's miracles were designed to demonstrate his divinity: see *De civitate Dei* 18.46, CCL 48:644; *De vera religione* 16.31, CCL 32:206; *In Iohannis Evangelium* 8.12, CCL 36:90; 17.1, CCL 36:169-170. On the apostles' miracles, see *De civitate Dei* 22.5, CCL 48:811-812; *Enar. in Psalmos* 64.12, CCL 39:834; *Epist.* 185.6.24, CSEL 57:23.

[11] Cf. C. Dagens, *Saint Grégoire le Grand. Culture et expérience chrétiennes* (Paris, 1977), p. 225; and A. de Vogüé, *Grégoire le Grand, Dialogues* 1: *Introduction, bibliographie et cartes* (Paris, 1978), p. 91.

[12] See *Hom. in Evan.* 2.29.4, PL 76:1215; *Mor.* 30.2.6, CCL 143B:1494; *Mor.* 27.11.20, CCL 143B:1345.

[13] *Hom. in Evan.* 1.4.2-3, PL 76:1090-1091 at 1090.

there, Paul revived him by the power of prayer. When he visited Malta, an island he knew to be full of unbelievers, he healed the father of Publius, who was sick with fevers and dysentery. However, Timothy, his own companion and helper, was not cured by such miraculous means, but rather advised simply to take a little wine for his frequent ailments. Already a Christian, Timothy did not receive a miracle; the unbelievers did, so that through external miracles they might be moved to conversion.[14]

Gregory frequently maintains that miracles performed in the apostolic church served to subdue the proud and the powerful who persecuted the church in its infancy, and at times he seems to regard these miracles not so much as instruments for effecting the conversion of the persecutors as a means of securing the protection of the apostles. Miracles enabled the apostles to defend themselves, for they encouraged their opponents to accord them some respect, even if they remained unmoved by the preaching of the Gospel.[15] However, this is a minor theme. When speaking of the subjection of the persecutors, Gregory thinks primarily in terms of their conversion,[16] and it was here that miracles played their most important role. The proud and the mighty who had initially rejected Christ were both astonished and frightened by them; they came to dread in miracles the sanctity they had despised in precepts.[17] Miracles in the primitive church served primarily apologetic purposes, by encouraging belief in the Gospel of Christ which was being proclaimed.

Given the insistence with which Gregory emphasizes their apologetic role in the New Testament church, it comes as no surprise to discover that miracles can play the same role in the contemporary world. This was a view

---

[14] *Ibid.* 1.4.3, PL 76:1091; cf. *Mor.* 27.18.37, CCL 143B:1358-1359. The Biblical references are Acts 20:7-12, 28:8; 1 Tim. 5:23.

[15] Cf. *Mor.* 9.10.11, CCL 143:463-464; 27.18.36, CCL 143B:1358; 31.2.2, CCL 143B:1550-1551; and see *Mor.* 30.2.6, CCL 143B:1494: "Sancti enim praedicatores verbis suis quasi quibusdam iaculis adversarios feriunt; armis vero, id est miraculis semetipsos tuentur; ut et quantum sint audiendi, sonent per impetum iaculorum, et quantum sint reverendi, clarescant per arma miraculorum."

[16] Cf. *Mor.* 31.2.2, CCL 143B:1550: "In ipsis vero initiis nascentis Ecclesiae, dum contra illam divitum se potestas extolleret, atque in eius nece immensitate tantae crudelitatis anhelaret; dum tot cruciatibus anxia, tot persecutionibus pressa succumberet, quis tunc credere potuit quod illa erecta et aspera superborum colla sibi subiceret, et iugo sancti timoris edomita, mitibus fidei loris ligaret?"

[17] *Mor.* 31.1.1, CCL 143B:1549. Cf. *Mor.* 30.25.75-76, CCL 143B:1543-1544, where Gregory claims that the miracles performed by the martyrs after their deaths frightened the persecutors into leaving the church in peace. He states quite clearly that these miracles were sufficient to effect the conversion of the persecutors: "dum mortuorum martyrum corpora miraculis coruscare conspiciunt, luce veritatis fracti, quod impugnaverunt, crediderunt."

that Augustine came to emphasize only towards the end of his life. The young Augustine, on occasion at least, seems to have thought that miracles cannot serve to verify the claims of the true church. Rather, the truth is the other way around. It is the faith of the true church that serves to establish the authenticity of miracles.[18] In Augustine's mature thought, however, the apologetic value of contemporary miracles is clearly acknowledged: "God, who made visible the heaven and earth, does not disdain to work visible miracles in heaven and on earth, so that by these he may arouse the soul hitherto preoccupied with visible things to the worship of his invisible self."[19] It is given even more emphasis by Gregory the Great. The miracles recorded in Scripture can still serve to confirm the faith, of course. But at least equally significant is the continued efficacy of modern miracles in this regard.[20] On more than one occasion Gregory acknowledges the role that they played in the conversion of the Anglo-Saxons in particular. In a celebrated passage of the *Moralia* he rejoices over the success with which God has crowned the preaching and miracles of the apostles and their modern successors, for with the conversion of the *Angli* virtually the whole world has been brought to the Christian faith: "Omnipotens enim Dominus ... emicantibus praedicatorum miraculis, ad fidem etiam terminos mundi perduxit."[21]

---

[18] See, for example, *Epist. ad catholicos de secta Donatistarum* 19.50, CSEL 52:297-298, esp. 298: "quaecumque talia [mirabilia] in catholica fiunt, ideo sunt approbanda, quia in catholica fiunt, non ideo ipsa catholica manifestatur, quia haec in ea fiunt." Cf. P. Courcelle, *Recherches sur les Confessions de Saint Augustin* (Paris, 1950), p. 147; G. Bardy, "Les miracles contemporains dans l'apologétique de saint Augustin," in *La Cité de Dieu, livres XIX-XXII*, Oeuvres de Saint Augustin 37 (Paris, 1960), pp. 825-831, esp. 828-829.

[19] *De civitate Dei* 10.12, CCL 47:287; trans. H. Bettenson (Harmondsworth, 1972), p. 390 (slightly revised). Cf. *Ibid.* 22.10, CCL 48:828, where he refers explicitly to the miracles being produced at the shrines of the martyrs: "faciunt autem ista ... ut fides illa proficiat, qua eos non deos nostros esse, sed unum Deum nobiscum habere credamus." In *Conf.* 13.21.29-30, CCL 27:258, and 13.27.42, CCL 27:267, Augustine argues that, although miracles are not necessary for the faithful, the same cannot be said for "homines idiotae atque infideles, quibus initiandis atque lucrandis necessaria sunt sacramenta initiorum et magnalia miraculorum." Cf. Grange, *Le miracle*, pp. 78ff; Bardy, "Les miracles contemporains," p. 830; V. Saxer, *Morts, martyrs, reliques en Afrique chrétienne aux premiers siècles* (Paris, 1980), p. 269.

[20] See *Hom. in Ezech.* 2.3.23, CCL 142:255, where he says of the Biblical saints: "Hi itaque quam vera de Deo dixerint testantur miracula, quia talia per illum non facerent, nisi de illo vera narrarent. ... Si igitur de fide tentamur, quam ex illorum praedicatione concepimus, loquentium miracula conspiciamus, et in fide quam ab eis accepimus confirmamur." Cf., on modern miracles, *Hom. in Ezech.* 1.5.14, CCL 142:64-65; *In 1 Reg.* 5.117, CCL 144:492; *Mor.* 26.18.32, CCL 143B:1289-1290.

[21] *Mor.* 27.11.21, CCL 143B:1346. See also, for example, *Ep.* 11.36, CCL 140A:925-929 at 926.

On occasion Gregory suggests that contemporary saints are entrusted with
the power of miracles for their own protection, and therefore that, rather than
contributing directly to the conversion of unbelievers, they simply create the
atmosphere in which the preaching of the saints can have its proper effect.[22]
But as was the case with regard to the apostles, his primary emphasis in such
passages is on the role that miracles play in the conversion process itself.
Miracles have an important role to play because they corroborate the truth
of Catholic doctrine. In a letter of July 597 to Domnica, the wife of one of
his curial officials, Gregory rejoices that she has returned to the unity of the
faith, but points out that this step ought to have been taken earlier. The truth
of the Catholic faith is confirmed, not only by the multitude of believers in
the bosom of the church, but also by the miracles performed at the tombs
of the saints.[23] More specifically, however, the role of miracles in the
conversion process is to make people conscious of their sinful condition and
fearful of the judgment to come. Miracles, together with preaching, first bring
people to repentance, and then the words of preaching hold out before them
the consolation of the joys of heaven.[24]

It is conceivable that Gregory regarded the continued efficacy of miracles
for the purposes of conversion as the principal reason for their occurrence
in the modern church. Despite his joyful proclamation that with the
conversion of the *Angli* the very ends of the earth had been brought to the
Christian faith, he was acutely conscious of the fact that the work of
evangelization was by no means finished. Paganism remained a serious
problem for the church of the sixth century, as the *Dialogues* themselves and
some of Gregory's other works eloquently testify.[25]

---

[22] See, for example, *Hom. in Ezech.* 1.5.14, CCL 142:64-65.

[23] *Ep.* 7.34, CCL 140:497-498 at 498.

[24] *Mor.* 27.12.22, CCL 143B:1346-1347. Cf. *Mor.* 27.17.33, CCL 143B:1355, where Gregory
comments further on the two steps of the conversion process: "Auditio igitur vocis Dei prius
in terrore fit, ut post vertatur in dulcedinem, quia ante nos districti iudicii timore castigat, ut
iam castigatos supernae dulcedinis consolatione reficiat." Cf. Augustine, *De catechizandis
rudibus* 5.9, CCL 46:129.

[25] The same can be said of the works of Caesarius of Arles, Martin of Braga and Gregory
of Tours. On Gregory of Tours, for example, see M. Vieillard-Troiekouroff, *Les monuments
religieux de la Gaule d'après les oeuvres de Grégoire de Tours* (Paris, 1976), p. 389; and M.
Weidemann, *Kulturgeschichte der Merowingerzeit nach den Werken Gregors von Tours* (Bonn,
1982), 2:157-161. More generally, see C.E. Stancliffe, "From Town to Country: The
Christianization of the Touraine, 370-600," in *The Church in Town and Countryside* (Oxford,
1979), pp. 43-59; and R. Manselli, "Resistenze dei culti antichi nella pratica religiosa dei laici
nelle campagne," in *Cristianizzazione ed organizzazione ecclesiastica delle campagne nell'alto
medioevo: Espansione e resistenze* (Spoleto, 1982), pp. 57-108.

Le Goff has pointed out that it is misleading to speak merely of the survival of paganism in the period between the fifth and the eighth centuries, for there were in fact two kinds of paganism: the paganism of folklore, of long duration and deeply embedded in the countryside; and the more cultivated and not quite so firmly established official paganism of Greco-Roman origin. In general, Christian authors of late antiquity and the early Middle Ages did not distinguish between these two forms of paganism as clearly as we would like, and they tended to concentrate their efforts on combatting what we would call the more official version.[26] In this Gregory is not an exception. The paganism he expressly acknowledges, often identifying it with the worship of demons, is usually paganism of Greco-Roman origin.

In book two of the *Dialogues* Gregory records that, when Saint Benedict moved to Monte Cassino, he discovered at the summit of the mountain "a very old temple, in which the ignorant country people still worshiped Apollo as their pagan ancestors had done, and went on offering superstitious and idolatrous sacrifices in groves dedicated to various demons." Benedict consecrated the pagan monument to Christian purposes by establishing a chapel dedicated to Saint Martin within the precincts of the temple, and by erecting a chapel in honour of Saint John the Baptist at the very spot where the altar of Apollo had stood.[27] Official paganism appears to be expressly mentioned later in the same book, where Gregory relates Benedict's conversion of the inhabitants of a nearby village from the worship of idols. Book three, however, provides a clear example in the story of Bishop Andrew of Fondi. We shall discuss this story at some length in chapter five. Suffice it to say here that one of the central characters is a Jew who takes shelter for the night in a temple of Apollo delivered over to a throng of evil spirits, and that at the end of the story Andrew transforms the pagan temple into a chapel in honour of Saint Andrew the Apostle.[28]

[26] J. Le Goff, "Culture cléricale et traditions folkloriques dans la civilisation mérovingienne," *Annales E.S.C.* 22 (1967): 780-791 at 785n.

[27] *Dial.* 2.8.10, Zimmerman 74, SC 260:168. Slightly further on (*Dial.* 2.10, SC 260:170-172) Gregory tells us that Benedict's monks subsequently managed to unearth a bronze idol. They tossed it, somewhat carelessly, into their kitchen, where it created the illusion that the entire place was burning down, until Benedict himself finally dispelled the phantasm through the power of prayer. Laporte maintains that the idol in question was probably Dionysos, for the episodes that follow appear to bear a Dionysian stamp, and the cults of Dionysos and Apollo were customarily found together. Cf. J. Laporte, "Saint Benoît et les survivances du paganisme," in *Etudes Ligériennes d'histoire et d'archéologie médiévales* (Auxerre, 1975), pp. 233-246 at 241-243. Whatever its specific identity, however, it seems clear that the idol was somehow or other associated with the Apollo cult that prior to Benedict's arrival had dominated the scene.

[28] See *Dial.* 2.19, SC 260:194-196; and 3.7, SC 260:278-284.

Although the *Dialogues* also illustrate the survival of the paganism of folklore, the relevant examples tend not to be as clear as those just given. In fact, the only obvious example is a story in the first book in which local magicians partly cure a woman possessed of an evil spirit by immersing her in the waters of a river, before she is finally delivered of her affliction by Bishop Fortunatus of Todi.[29] However, if we probe a little more deeply, at least one other example comes to light.

In the second book Gregory writes that, while Benedict was still at Subiaco, the success that he had with the people of the area aroused the enmity of the priest Florentius: "envious as the wicked always are of the holiness in others which they are not striving to acquire themselves, he denounced Benedict's way of life and kept everyone he could from visiting him." After trying in vain to poison Benedict, Florentius decided to take aim at the souls of his disciples. He sent "seven depraved women" into the garden of Benedict's monastery, where "they joined hands and danced together for some time within sight of his followers, in an attempt to lead them into sin." The story ends happily enough and Benedict is triumphant. However, the dance performed by the seven women is worth noting. Laporte maintains that Gregory was loath to give too much publicity to the enemy, and so disguised its character somewhat, presenting it as the gamboling of a group of prostitutes. In all likelihood, says Laporte, it was a pagan fertility rite.[30]

Paganism in slightly disguised form may lurk beneath other incidents in the *Dialogues* as well, although convincing proof has not yet been provided.[31]

---

[29] *Dial.* 1.10.1-5, SC 260:92-96. Cf. C. Ginzburg, "Folklore, magia, religione," in *Storia d'Italia* 1: *I caratteri originali* (Torino, 1972), pp. 601-676 at 605; and S. Boesch Gajano, "Dislivelli culturali e mediazioni ecclesiastiche nei *Dialogi* di Gregorio Magno," in *Religioni delle classi popolari*, ed. C. Ginzburg, *QS* 41 (1979): 398-415 at 404.

[30] *Dial.* 2.8.1, 4, Zimmerman 70, 71, SC 260:160, 162. See Laporte, "Saint Benoît," pp. 238-240. Cf. Boesch Gajano, "Dislivelli culturali," p. 405; and R. Grégoire, "Il contributo dell'agiografia alla conoscenza della realtà rurale," in *Medioevo rurale* (Bologna, 1980), pp. 343-360 at pp. 355-356.

[31] Laporte, "Saint Benoît," pp. 243-244, detects sympathetic magic at work when Scholastica's tears produce a downpour that prevents her brother from returning to his monastery (*Dial.* 2.33, SC 260:230-234). Boesch Gajano, "Dislivelli culturali," p. 405, concurs with this judgment. We shall examine this incident in greater detail in the Epilogue. Suffice it to say that, although Laporte's interpretation does deserve to be taken seriously, it has not been universally well received. Cf. A. de Vogüé, "La rencontre de Benoît et de Scholastique. Essai d'interprétation," *RHSp.* 48 (1972): 257-273 at 258-259.

Boesch Gajano detects another example in the wonder that was performed by the anonymous holy man of Mount Argentaro (*Dial.* 3.17.1-5, SC 260:336-340). This holy man used to come down from the mountain once every year to visit the Church of Saint Peter, and to enjoy the hospitality of Quadragesimus, a subdeacon of the church from whom Gregory

But further evidence for the survival of paganism can be found in abundance in Gregory's register. Many of his letters express concern about the idolatry of those who worship trees and stones. The problem seems to have been particularly acute in Sardinia. As Richards argues, "uncivilized, mountainous and backward, Sardinia had clung to the old religion and the old gods with

---

heard the story. One of his visits happened to coincide with the death of a resident of the neighbourhood, and the holy man was much moved by the grief of the poor widow. Therefore, taking Quadragesimus with him, he went into the church to pray. Then, gathering up some dust from the base of the altar, he proceeded to the spot where the dead man had been laid out. After kneeling there in prayer for some time, he removed the cloth that covered the dead man's head with his left hand, and with his right hand he rubbed the dust of the altar on the face of the deceased, continuing his massage until life gradually returned to his limbs. Boesch Gajano is struck by the widow's reaction to the unveiling of the face of her dead husband. She objected strenuously, a reaction, says Boesch Gajano, "che va probabilmente collegata al valore attribuito al velo come mezzo di separazione dal mondo." Boesch Gajano is even more impressed by what took place after the wonder had been accomplished. The mysterious holy man directed the joyful woman not to reveal what he had done; and after explaining that the miracle was to be attributed to Christ rather than to any virtue he may have possessed, he disappeared from view, never to be seen again. Says Boesch Gajano: "A me sembra che l'episodio vada visto come esempio di sussunzione di un miracolo di matrice e contesto non cristiano nella religione ufficiale, quasi che un miracolo così importante come la resurrezione di un morto dovesse essere necessariamente attribuito a Dio" (p. 406).

However, the story possesses two additional features that should be emphasized. First, Gregory has a first-hand source, Quadragesimus himself, whose veracity he respects. Second, the anonymous saint who performed the miracle is clearly identified as a man of God: "vir ... venerabilis vitae, qui habito monachi, quem praetendebat specie, moribus explebat." Taken together, these factors suggest that this particular miracle is as Christian in its character as any other miracle recorded in the *Dialogues*. There is nothing particularly puzzling in the woman's initial reaction to the raising of the veil, for as Gregory himself tells us, she protested as she did simply because she didn't know what the holy man intended: "contradicere vehementer coepit, et mirari quid vellit facere." Nor is there anything untoward in the holy man's desire to keep the miracle secret, or in his desire to have it credited to Christ's account and not his own, and his subsequent disappearance from the scene. For the former Christ himself provided the precedent in Matthew 9:27-31, a precedent followed by several other early medieval saints as well (see, for example, Sulpicius Severus, *Dial.* 2.4, CSEL 1:184; Eugippius, *Vita S. Severini,* chaps. 13, 16, CSEL 9.2:31, 34; and *Vita patrum Jurensium* 1.41, SC 142:284). For his withdrawal from human view we have a perfectly plausible explanation in the humility of the mysterious holy man: "temporalem namque honorem fugiens, egit ut ab his, a quibus visus in tanta virtute fuerat, numquam in hac vita iam videretur." There are, of course, the odd maneuvers that were performed to bring the deceased back to life; but ultimately they reduce themselves to applying dust from the saint's altar, a common medieval practice for procuring miraculous remedies, as Boesch Gajano herself would acknowledge. Moreover, Christ himself also performed strange actions on occasion—in Mark 7:31-37, for example—although, of course, these too have been regarded as quasi-magical. Cf. Morton Smith, *Jesus the Magician* (New York, 1978), esp. pp. 126-129.

considerable tenacity."[32] Gregory wrote repeatedly to Januarius of Cagliari, the rather ineffectual metropolitan, urging him to take action, and to several other prominent individuals as well, including the Empress Constantina.[33]

The letter to Constantina is of particular interest. It expresses Gregory's horror that paganism not only continued to thrive on the island, but did so with the connivance of the imperial administration. Gregory had come to learn that the Sardinian pagans had been expected to pay bribes for permission to sacrifice to idols. Even worse, the extortion had continued to be practised even on former pagans who had converted to the true faith. When the judge in question had been rebuked for not only permitting paganism to prosper but profiting from it, he had replied that he had promised so large a *suffragium* on his appointment that he would not have been able to make it up without this income. But if it was a particular problem in Sardinia, the contagion of paganism was by no means isolated to that one rather remote locale. Gregory's register contains evidence of its survival, not only in Anglo-Saxon England, but in Gaul, Corsica and Sicily as well, and even on his doorstep in Campania. Clearly, the problem much preoccupied Gregory, and so it is quite conceivable that, to his mind, miracles continued to take place, and were worth recording in the *Dialogues*, precisely to help effect the conversion of the remaining pagan population.[34]

It is equally possible that Gregory's principal concern was not so much the conversion of pagans as the conversion of the Lombard heretics.[35] The *Dialogues* themselves attest that pagan elements still persisted in the Lom-

---

[32] J. Richards, *Consul of God: The Life and Times of Gregory the Great* (London, 1980), p. 234.

[33] To Januarius: see *Ep.* 4.26, CCL 140:244-246 at 245-246, written in May 594; *Ep.* 4.29, CCL 140:247-248, written in June 594; *Ep.* 9.205, CCL 140A:763-765 at 764, written in July 599. To Constantina: see *Ep.* 5.38, CCL 140:312-314 at 312, written in June 595. See also his letter of May 594 to the nobles and proprietors (*nobilibus ac possessoribus*) in Sardinia (*Ep.* 4.23, CCL 140:241-242), and his letter of the same date to Hospito, Duke of the Barbaricini (*Ep.* 4.27, CCL 140:246).

[34] See Gregory's letters: of September 597 to Brunichild, Queen of the Franks (*Ep.* 8.4, CCL 140A:518-521, esp. 521); of September 597 to Peter, Bishop of Corsica (*Ep.* 8.1, CCL 140A:513-514, esp. 513); of August 593 to Eutychius, Bishop of Tyndaris (*Ep.* 3.59, CCL 140:207-208); and of April 598 to Agnellus, Bishop of Terracina (*Ep.* 8.19, CCL 140A:539). Cf. E. Auerbach, *Literary Language and its Public in Late Latin Antiquity and in the Middle Ages* (London, 1965), pp. 96-97; and Dagens, *Saint Grégoire le Grand*, pp. 229-230. Auerbach maintains that the conversion of pagans was one of Gregory's principal objectives in the *Dialogues*; Dagens considers it as a possibility, without, however, committing himself.

[35] Cf. Auerbach, *Literary Language*, p. 101; and Richards, *Consul of God*, pp. 261-262. The possibility is also considered by de Vogüé, *Introduction*, pp. 40, 92.

bard population,[36] chiefly in the duchy of Benevento. But, for the most part, the Lombards were Arians, militant Arians: King Autharis had forbidden the sons of Lombards to be baptized according to the Catholic rite. Although it is difficult to generalize about Gregory's attitude toward the Lombards, an attitude that seems to have changed significantly throughout his career in the papal office,[37] in the light of most recent scholarship his dealings with them seem to have been primarily political, and in the final analysis not very successful. There were periodic victories, but long-term success eluded him, and at the end of his pontificate the Lombards remained as much a threat to the security of Rome as they had been at its outset.[38] However, until recently, the conventional view on the subject was that, of course, Gregory was concerned about the Lombards' spiritual status as well; and if that indeed was the case, it is at least conceivable that the *Dialogues* were designed to help in their conversion.

The principal feature of Gregory's plan would have been to rely on the efforts of the Lombard queen, Theodelinda. Theodelinda was a supporter of the "Three Chapters" schism. But she was a Catholic, and she was in an influential position, having been the wife first of King Autharis, and later of his successor, Duke Agilulf of Turin. It was probably on account of her influence that in 603 the son she bore to Agilulf, Adaloald, was baptized as a Catholic Christian, thus abrogating the policy of Agilulf's predecessor. Since Gregory sent Theodelinda a copy of the *Dialogues*, it is at least possible that the miracles recorded there were intended to play a role in the conversion of her husband and his subjects. De Vogüé's comments are salient: "Dialogues en main, la catholique Théodelinde pourra faire entendre à son royal époux et aux Lombards ariens ce qu'il en coûte, ici-bas et dans l'éternité, de persécuter l'Eglise de Dieu."[39]

[36] See *Dial.* 3.27-28.1, sc 260:372-374, where Gregory relates two episodes that took place about fifteen years before the *Dialogues* were written. They have to do with two groups of Christians who, having been taken prisoner by the Lombards, chose martyrdom rather than participate in their idolatrous worship. Cf. R. Manselli, "Gregorio Magno e due riti pagani dei Longobardi," in *Studi storici in onore di Ottorino Bertolini*, 2 vols. (Pisa, 1972), 1:435-440. Manselli argues that these stories are quite authentic, although he also maintains that in one particular the pagan practices related in the second episode seem to have been misunderstood by their Christian observers.

[37] See V. Paronetto, "I Longobardi nell'epistolario di Gregorio Magno," in *Atti del 6° congresso internazionale di studi sull'alto medioevo* (Spoleto, 1980), 2:559-570. From the evidence of Gregory's register, Paronetto argues for a gradual softening in his attitude.

[38] Richards, *Consul of God*, esp. pp. 191-192.

[39] De Vogüé, *Introduction*, p. 40. The possibility is firmly denied by G. Vinay, *Alto medioevo latino* (Napoli, 1978), p. 17: "I Longobardi erano per lui, in primo luogo, i nemici della Chiesa e non v'è traccia nella sua opera (o sbaglio di grosso) dell'opinione che avessero

Recent scholarship on Gregory's relationship to the Lombards, however, suggests that Gregory may in fact have been too pressed by other matters concerning them to have given their conversion a very high priority.[40] His register indicates that, at the outset of his pontificate, Gregory showed the same enthusiasm for the conversion of the Lombards that he showed for the conversion of the Anglo-Saxons. In January 591 he addressed a letter to all the bishops of Italy, encouraging them to make every effort to bring the Lombards into the family of the true faith.[41] However, as Bertolini points out,[42] Gregory quickly discovered that his dealings with the Lombards were complicated by two political and religious factors not present in his relationship with the Anglo-Saxons: first, the Lombards were conquerors on Italian soil who represented a constant and serious threat to the peace; second, the "Three Chapters" schism had ruptured communion between Rome and most of the churches of northern Italy. The religious difficulties were exacerbated when, largely for political reasons on the part of Agilulf, and for more genuinely spiritual reasons on the part of Theodelinda, the schismatics won the sympathy and support of the Lombard court.

Before any systematic attempt to convert the Lombards to orthodox Christianity could have had much chance of success, these political and religious problems had to be addressed, and they were so difficult of solution that they occupied Gregory's attention up to the very end of his pontificate. Hence, despite his original enthusiasm for their conversion, Gregory's conduct toward the Lombards was governed by two other objectives that were more immediately pressing, the achievement of which occupied his mind to the end of his life: the neutralization of the schismatics, and the stabilization of a lasting peace between Lombards and Romans. His strategy was indeed to rely on the good offices of Theodelinda, and it seems that it did pay dividends in strengthening the influence of the orthodox Christian faith. But that was not his main objective, and it seems unlikely that it could have been in the forefront of his mind when he sent Theodelinda a copy of the *Dialogues*. Gregory's principal aim was to wean Theodelinda from the "Three Chapters" schismatics under whose influence she had fallen; and

---

un'anima, nonostante Teodolinda." It is Paul the Deacon, *Historia Langobardorum* 4.5, MGH, SRL, p. 117, who speaks of Gregory sending a copy of the *Dialogues* to Theodelinda.

[40] See O. Bertolini, "I papi e le missioni fino alla metà del secolo VIII," in *La conversione al cristianesimo nell'Europa dell'alto medioevo* (Spoleto, 1967), pp. 327-363, esp. pp. 328-343. Bertolini's views are endorsed by S. Boesch Gajano, "Missione, cristianizzazione, conversione. In margine à un recente convegno," *RSCI* 21 (1967): 147-166 at 151.

[41] *Ep.* 1.17, CCL 140:16-17.

[42] Bertolini, "I papi e le missioni," esp. pp. 341-342.

when he encouraged her to do more, it was to work for peace between Lombards and Romans rather than engage in a process of evangelization.

Since the *Dialogues*, which were written in 593/594, date from the early years of Gregory's pontificate, Bertolini concedes that they may well have been intended to exert a religious influence—to make "un'impressione ... esemplare, salvatrice e sanatrice"—on any Lombard readers they may have found. The circumstances in which the *Dialogues* were written, however, makes this rather unlikely. It was precisely in the fall and winter of 593/594 that Agilulf's siege of Rome took place. Gregory himself gave eloquent expression to the horrors to be witnessed at that time in a letter of June 595 to the emperor Maurice; and one suspects that under the conditions there described the conversion of the Lombard marauders would have been the last thing on Gregory's mind.[43]

It is possible that the *Dialogues* might have been intended to facilitate, if not the conversion of the Lombards, at least a more modest purpose. The miracle stories they contained may have been designed to strike terror into the hearts of these superstitious people, and hence to exert a mitigating influence on their behaviour towards the representatives of a religion so blessed by the gifts of Providence. But the specific portrait of the Lombards in the *Dialogues* makes even this unlikely. They are systematically presented as being unresponsive to the world of Christian sanctity. The *Dialogues* portray both the Goths and the Lombards as fearsome savages, but the traits that tend to soften and humanize somewhat the portrait of the Goths are entirely lacking in the case of the Lombards. As Boesch Gajano suggests: "Il miracolo li spaventa, li allontana, impedisce loro di nuocere, ma non ha, salvo in un caso, un effetto positivo su di loro, non li induce alla moderazione, al pentimento, alla venerazione: spiritualmente insensibili alla santità ne subiscono solo la *virtus* punitiva."[44] If Gregory really had addressed the

---

[43] See Bertolini's comments in the discussion that follows "I papi e le missioni," pp. 537-553 at p. 548. See also *Ep.* 5.36, CCL 140:304-307, esp. 306: "plaga gravior fuit adventus Agilulfi, ita ut oculis meis cernerem Romanos more canum in collis funibus ligatos, qui ad Franciam ducebantur venales."

[44] See Boesch Gajano, "Dislivelli culturali," pp. 400-402, esp. 401; and A. Vitale-Brovarone, "Latini e Germani nei *Dialoghi* di Gregorio Magno," in *Atti del 6° congresso internazionale di studi sull'alto medioevo*, 2:717-726, esp. 722-726. For the incident, or rather incidents, to which Boesch Gajano refers, see *Dial.* 3.37.1-3, 8-20, SC 260:410-414, 416-426. See also P. Boglioni, "Spoleto nelle opere di Gregorio Magno," in *Atti del 9° congresso internazionale di studi sull'alto medioevo* (Spoleto, 1983), 1:267-318 at 292-293. Boglioni points to the large influence that refugees from Lombard persecution had on the composition of the *Dialogues*, seeing in this state of affairs a reason why the *Dialogues* present such a dark picture of the Lombards.

Dialogues to the Lombards, presumably he would have softened their brutal features to some extent. The weight of the evidence, therefore, does not support the notion that the *Dialogues* were written as part of Gregory's answer to the problems the Lombards presented, although the possibility cannot be dismissed altogether. One piece of evidence for the contrary argument, as de Vogüé suggests, is the strong anti-heretical theme of the *Dialogues*, which is particularly evident in the series of miracles in book three designed to demonstrate the victory of Christian truth over Arianism.[45]

In fact, neither of the possibilities we have discussed can be dismissed. Ultimately, Gregory could have had either pagans or heretics in mind when he wrote his *Dialogues*. Not only was there ample precedent in the hagiographical literature for such a view of the purpose of modern miracles,[46] but some of Gregory's own statements about the apologetic purpose of miracles in the early church strongly suggest that contemporary miracles must have a similar function. They must be designed to effect the conversion of *someone*. At first glance at least there seems to be little room for any other

---

[45] De Vogüé, *Introduction*, pp. 40, 92. See *Dial.* 3.29-32, sc 260:376-392. The theme of showing the divine condemnation of the Arian heresy even leads Gregory to depart from his established terms of reference. Hence at *Dial.* 3.30.8, sc 260:382-384, Gregory says to Peter: "Quamvis sola quae in Italia gesta sunt narrare decreveram, visne tamen ut pro ostendenda eiusdem arrianae hereseos damnatione transeamus verbo ad Hispanias, atque inde per Africam ad Italiam redeamus?" Peter, of course, replies that he would be quite happy to follow wherever Gregory might care to lead him. See also *Dial.* 4.22-24, sc 265:78-82, where the evils done by the Lombards are occasions for miracles. Here, however, the Lombards are not presented as Arians or even as heathens, but simply as murderers and marauders.

[46] Perhaps the best example is provided by Sulpicius Severus. See E. Delaruelle, "La spiritualité des pèlerinages à Saint-Martin de Tours du Ve au Xe siècle," in *Pellegrinaggi e culto dei santi in Europa fina alla Ia crociata* (Todi, 1963), pp. 199-243, esp. pp. 203-208. As Delaruelle points out, in many of the miracles about which Sulpicius Severus informs us, Martin's actions are shown to have been instrumental in the conversion of barbarians, whether Arians or pagans. In fact, this is a prominent theme in the *Vita S. Martini*: see, for example, chap. 13, sc 133:280-282; chap. 14, sc 133:282-284; chap. 17, sc 133:288-290; and cf. *Dial.* 2.4, CSEL 1:185. Delaruelle remarks: "Les miracles de saint Martin ne seront donc pas seulement une réponse au besoin de merveilleux des foules, mais une prédication" (p. 208). It is perhaps doubtful that Sulpicius himself had a similar work of evangelism in mind when committing these miracles to paper. In all likelihood, he intended his work to be directed in the first instance at least to an audience of Christian ascetics, to encourage them in the Christian life (see below, n. 71). However, see J. Fontaine, *Sulpice Sévère. Vie de Saint Martin*, vol. 1 (Paris, 1967), pp. 74-75, who maintains that the *Life of St Martin* was also addressed to a larger audience. Indeed, "Sulpice l'a d'emblée voulue comme une oeuvre 'ad extra', intelligible et séduisante pour des païens." A monastic audience was the primary audience of St Athanasius in his *Life of St Antony* as well, and yet Athanasius also clearly envisaged the possibility of his work being read to unbelievers; cf. *Vita S. Antonii*, chap. 94, PG 26:975.

alternative. Miracles are for unbelievers, not believers, says Gregory. Hence today they are not as frequent as they once were, because the number of the faithful has grown considerably.[47] The case is strengthened, as Dagens shows, when we note that the miracles recorded in the *Dialogues* are the equivalent of those recorded in the Gospels or the Acts of the Apostles,[48] and therefore seem to be aids divinely established to complete the work of evangelization. On balance, however, I am inclined to agree with de Vogüé and maintain that, although Gregory attributed an apologetic purpose to modern miracles, and although he may have had pagans and heretics in mind during the composition of the *Dialogues*, these elements belong to the background of his thought.[49] More can be claimed for them only by overlooking the fact that Gregory is addressing an audience of Catholic Christians.

Until quite recently there seems to have been a broad consensus among scholars that the *Dialogues* of Gregory were populist in conception.[50] One

[47] *Hom. in Evan.* 1.4.3, PL 76:1091; *Mor.* 27.18.36, CCL 143B:1358. Cf. Isidore of Seville, *Sententiae* 1.24.1-4, PL 83:591-592. Similar thoughts can be found in Augustine; cf. *Conf.* 13.21.29-30, CCL 27:258, where Augustine maintains that in the contemporary world miracles are for the faithless, not for believers; and *De utilitate credendi* 14.32, CSEL 25.1:40-41, where he maintains that Christ's miracles were intended exclusively to stimulate belief: "quid enim aliud agunt tanta et tam multa miracula, ipso etiam dicente illa fieri non ob aliud, nisi ut sibi crederetur?"

[48] Dagens, *Saint Grégoire le Grand*, p. 229.

[49] De Vogüé, *Introduction*, p. 92.

[50] See, for example, P. Batiffol, *Saint Gregory the Great* (London, 1929), pp. 181-182. Batiffol argues that "the *Dialogues* were *The City of God* re-written for the simple." Lambot endorses this judgment, and applies it specifically to book two of the *Dialogues*, the Life of Saint Benedict. See C. Lambot, "La vie et les miracles de saint Benoît racontés par saint Grégoire-le-Grand," *RMon.* 143 (1950): 49-61 at 50: "La vie de S. Benoît est 'un livre populaire, délibérément populaire,' destiné principalement à édifier des lecteurs simples, insatiablement avides de merveilleux, comme on l'était communément à l'époque de S. Grégoire." For similar views see L. Weber, *Hauptfragen der Moraltheologie Gregors des Grossen* (Freiburg in der Schweiz, 1947), pp. 11, 26-27; J.H. Wansbrough, "St. Gregory's Intention in the Stories of St. Scholastica and St. Benedict," *RBén.* 75 (1965): 145-151 at 150; R. Gillet, "Grégoire le Grand," *DSp.* 6:872-910 at 878; and R. Manselli, *Gregorio Magno* (Torino, 1967), p. 161. Ginzburg, "Folklore, magia, religione," p. 605, also maintains of the *Dialogues* that "un senso elementare, popolaresco del miracoloso affiora, per quanto filtrato e esorcizzato, in queste pagine."

Recently, however, the notion that the *Dialogues* were essentially a popular work has come under attack. See, for example, A. Vitale-Brovarone, "La forma narrativa dei *Dialoghi* di Gregorio Magno: problemi storico-letterari," *AAST.M* 108 (1974): 95-173, esp. 95; J.M. Petersen, *The Dialogues of Gregory the Great in their Late Antique Cultural Background* (Toronto, 1984), esp. pp. 21-22; and L. Cracco Ruggini, "Gregorio Magno, Agostino e i quattro Vangeli," *Augustinianum* 25 (1985): 255-263, esp. 262-263. See also de Vogüé, *Introduction*, p. 31ff; and Dagens, *Saint Grégoire le Grand*, pp. 94, 229. For Dagens, the idea of the popular audience of the *Dialogues* can be defended only with certain reservations.

suspects that in many cases the miracle stories themselves were enough to prompt such a judgment. Miracles, it could be thought, address their appeal, not to the more sophisticated members of society, but to the less enlightened masses.[51] However, a brief glance through the register of Gregory's correspondence is sufficient to disabuse oneself of this notion. As we have already seen, miracle stories occur there with some frequency, and in letters addressed to distinguished citizens of the Empire. As de Vogüé observes: "il n'est pas d'esprit à l'époque, du plus petit au plus grand, qui n'apprécie hautement les faits miraculeux. Remplir un livre de ceux-ci, ce n'est nullement le disqualifier, comme ce serait le cas de nos jours, aux yeux des hommes cultivés."[52]

It may still be argued that Gregory could have regarded miracle stories as particularly appropriate for a popular work, even if their appeal was not restricted to the uncultivated and simple-minded. Gregory did not separate literary genres as effectively as many of his predecessors had done,[53] but he did distinguish between his works on the basis of their intended audiences. Whereas his *Homilies on the Gospels* were preached on public occasions before presumably mixed congregations, the *Moralia* were intended for a more restricted and more sophisticated readership; and so Bishop Marinianus of Ravenna had to bear the brunt of Gregory's wrath for making the mistake of having them read publicly at vigils.[54] Gregory was aware of and

---

[51] See, for example, Ginzburg, "Folklore, magia, religione," p. 609, who argues that the rejection of pagan folklore by the representatives of clerical culture had to be accompanied by certain concessions to the popular mentality, and that one such concession was the emphasis on the miraculous found in hagiographical literature. Cf. Le Goff, "Culture cléricale," pp. 785-786.

[52] De Vogüé, *Introduction*, pp. 41-42. Far from being simply an expression of popular religiosity, throughout the entire Middle Ages belief in the miracles of the saints was common to all ranks of society. On the later Middle Ages, see, for example, J. Paul, "Miracles et mentalité religieuse populaire à Marseille au début du XIVe siècle," in *La religion populaire en Languedoc du XIIIe siècle à la moitié du XIVe siècle* (Toulouse, 1976), pp. 61-90, esp. pp. 86-89; and A. Vauchez, *La sainteté en Occident aux derniers siècles du Moyen Age* (Rome, 1981), esp. pp. 557, 580-581, 626.

[53] Dagens, *Saint Grégoire le Grand*, p. 435.

[54] On the *Homilies*, see *Hom. in Evan.*, Praef., PL 76:1075-1077. Gregory explains that he was able to deliver only the last twenty of these sermons himself; the others were dictated in advance and read by a *notarius*. He also tells us that at least one was subsequently revised to remove ambiguity. But there is no doubt that they were read before a public and probably mixed audience: "quarumdam quidem dictata expositio, *assistente plebe*, est per notarium recitata; quarumdam vero explanationem *coram populo* ipse locutus sum." The same can be said for the *Homilies on Ezechiel*, although these sermons seem to have been more systematically reworked. Cf. *Hom. in Ezech.*, Praef., CCL 142:3: "Homilias, quae in beatum Hiezechihelem prophetam, ita ut coram populo loquebar, exceptae sunt, multis curis irruenti-

even emphasized the fact that exhortation has to be suited to the audience addressed.[55] Hence, given that of all Gregory's works the *Dialogues* find their closest parallel in the *Homilies on the Gospels*, which also contain many stories of contemporary miracles; and given that the *Dialogues* contain more of this edifying material than any of the other works, it might be supposed that they were intended for an even more popular audience than the sermons. As Gregory himself tells us, although the wise are most readily converted by arguments from reason, the unlearned are often more effectively moved by the force of examples;[56] and what better examples can there be than those of saints resplendent in their miracles?

The argument, although plausible, is weak. Despite the miracle stories, in their content the *Dialogues* are indissolubly linked with Gregory's other works. As we shall see in detail in chapter four, the doctrinal issues raised in the *Dialogues* are frequently handled at the same level of sophistication found in works like the *Moralia*.[57] All of this makes it inherently unlikely that the *Dialogues* were intended in the first instance for audiences any more popular than those Gregory addressed elsewhere. As Gregory himself points out, deep matters of the faith should not be discussed before the multitude of simple believers, but rather should be reserved to those who are mature in the faith.[58]

Although it may be difficult to distinguish between the *Dialogues* and Gregory's other works on the basis of their content, it has also been argued that distinctions can be made on stylistic grounds. The prose of the *Dia-*

---

bus in abolitione reliqueram. Sed post annos octo, petentibus fratribus, notariorum schedas requirere studui, easque favente Domino transcurrens, in quantum ab angustiis tribulationum licuit, emendavi. ..." However, the *Homilies on Ezechiel* may have been directed to a more specialized congregation—at least in their final form. Although they too are described as having been preached *coram populo*, the fact that they were reworked *petentibus fratribus* may add some weight to Dagens' judgment, *Saint Grégoire le Grand*, p. 94: "Familier et concret dans ses *Homélies sur l'Evangile*, qui s'adressaient pour la plupart à l'ensemble des fidèles, Grégoire approfondit le sens allégorique ou anagogique dans les *Moralia* ou les *Homélies sur Ezéchiel*, qu'a écoutées sans doute un cercle plus restreint composé surtout de moines." Cf. Gillet, "Grégoire le Grand," col. 878.

On the *Moralia*, see *Ep.* 12.6, CCL 140A:974-977 at 975. Gregory informs Marinianus: "non est illud opus populare et rudibus auditoribus impedimentum magis quam provectum generat."

   [55] See *Mor.* 1.20.28, CCL 143:40; and especially *Past.* 3 Prol., PL 77:49. All of part 3 of the *Pastoral Care* is devoted to demonstrating the different approaches to be taken towards different kinds of people.

   [56] *Past.* 3.6, PL 77:57.

   [57] Cf. de Vogüé, *Introduction*, pp. 32-33.

   [58] *Past.* 3.39, PL 77:124.

logues, it is said, is much simpler than that found elsewhere in the corpus. According to Auerbach, Gregory himself declares in the introduction his intention to depart from the norms of classical Latin. His account, he says, will be based on what he has learned from others, and to alleviate the doubts of his readers he will indicate his authority for each episode. He then adds: "Hoc vero scire te cupio quia in quibusdam sensum solummodo, in quibusdam vero et verba cum sensu teneo, quia si de personis omnibus ipsa specialiter et verba tenere voluissem, haec rusticano usu prolata stilus scribentis non apte susciperit."

According to Auerbach, this refers to Gregory's desire to reproduce common speech as much as possible, except when it cannot be reproduced in written Latin. However, this interpretation is not very compelling. Rather than contrasting the common speech of his sources and the minimal requirements of correct Latin, Gregory seems to be thinking in terms of common speech and the norms of proper style, informing his readers that when the two come into conflict he will allow himself to be governed by the prescriptions of the latter. Zimmerman captures Gregory's meaning more faithfully when he translates as follows: "You should bear in mind, however, that in some instances I retain only the substance of the original narrative; in others, the words as well. For if I had always kept to the exact wording, the crude language used by some would have been ill suited to my style of writing."[59]

Auerbach goes on to say that a comparison of the *Dialogues* and Gregory's other works reinforces his contention that, in the *Dialogues*, Gregory "did his best ... to remain close to the popular tongue." According to Auerbach, the "theological works and letters are written in a very different, far more literary style; [Gregory] still had the power to vary his manner, as the classical tradition prescribed, according to the nature and purpose of the work in hand. For the *Dialogues* he chose the most popular form of which, to his mind, written Latin was capable."[60] However, a quite different consensus has emerged from more recent scholarship on the issue. The result

---

[59] *Dial.* 1 Prol. 10, Zimmerman 6, sc 260:16-18. Contrast Auerbach's comments on style in *Literary Language*, p. 100n with de Vogüé's in *Introduction*, p. 35. Vitale-Brovarone, "La forma narrativa," p. 172, offers a third possibility, although it is advanced only tentatively: "I termini di maggior interesse sarebbero dunque *prolata* e *apte*, che ritengo usati in senso proprio: il primo come 'pronunciate', il secondo come 'in modo aderente': in altre parole Gregorio constaterebbe una certa disparità fra il sistema fonetico dell'*usus rusticanus* e il sistema grafico tradizionale, decidendo quindi di normalizzare la parlata rustica."

[60] Auerbach, *Literary Language*, pp. 100n, 103. Cf. Gillet, "Grégoire le Grand," col. 879.

of Tateo's investigations, for example, is that there is no fundamental difference in style between the *Dialogues* and Gregory's other works.[61]

The prevailing consensus on Gregory's style in general is that, although he was quite familiar with and used the customary rhetorical devices, on balance his prose must be considered relatively simple when judged by classical standards. If his works were often praised by medieval authors precisely on stylistic grounds, one suspects, like Dufner, that the explanation is to be sought in their veneration of Gregory himself rather than in the literary merits of his writing.[62] But the *Dialogues* are not qualitatively different from the other works in the corpus in this regard, especially once allowances are made for the fact that they are somewhat distinctive in being largely narrative in form. They are not written in a style that is particularly humble or "popular" in comparison with the others. Rhetorical devices used elsewhere are found in the *Dialogues* as well. In fact, Gregory's rhetorical power is at its height when he narrates miracles, in order to highlight the exceptional nature of these events. Gregory did, of course, on occasion wish to capture the flavour of spoken language to enhance his narrative. But whether even this amounts to a simplification of his prose is problematic. To achieve the effect he desired he availed himself of generally acknowledged rhetorical devices like *annominatio* or *iteratio*.[63]

The attitude of medieval authors toward the style and audience of the *Dialogues* is probably not without significance. In general, they do not seem to have regarded the *Dialogues* as occupying a different cultural level than Gregory's other works. The Venerable Bede, for example, thought that the *Dialogues* naturally complemented Gregory's exegetical works—the relationship between them was one of *veritas* to *exemplum*—but did not insist on their popular nature. If Bede did not see any fundamental differences in audience or style between the *Dialogues* and Gregory's other works, there probably were in fact no such differences. As Vitale Brovarone puts it, "l'alta cultura non rifiutava le semplici narrazioni dei *Dialoghi*."[64]

---

[61] F. Tateo, "La struttura dei Dialoghi di Gregorio Magno," *VetC* 2 (1965): 101-127; cf. Vitale-Brovarone, "La forma narrativa," esp. pp. 150-173.

[62] G. Dufner, *Die Dialoge Gregors des Grossen im Wandel der Zeiten und Sprachen* (Padua, 1968), p. 16. However, cf. F. Gastaldelli, "Teologia e retorica in San Gregorio Magno. Il ritratto nei 'Moralia in Iob'," *Salesianum* 29 (1967): 269-299.

[63] Tateo, "La struttura," pp. 112-114. Cf. de Vogüé, *Introduction*, pp. 33-34, who maintains that, "loin d'appartenir à une catégorie littéraire inférieure, notre ouvrage se fait remarquer au contraire par sa tenue, qui l'apparente aux productions dont Grégoire pouvait être le plus satisfait."

[64] Bede, *Historia ecclesiastica* 2.1, ed. and trans. B. Colgrave and R.A.B. Mynors (Oxford, 1969), p. 128; Vitale-Brovarone, "La forma narrativa," p. 101.

Gregory's use of terms taken from vulgar speech, which are introduced to add some colour to the narrative, is particularly significant.[65] The *Homilies on the Gospels* were composed for a genuinely mixed audience, and so contain at least one passage in which we find the author translating the language of Sacred Scripture into a more popular idiom so that the humbler members of the congregation could understand it.[66] In the *Dialogues*, however, his procedure seems to be the precise opposite. We find instances of what appear to be translations from the language of popular speech—the language in which various episodes were originally conveyed to him—into traditionally more correct Latin. If Gregory really had been writing for a popular audience, such translations would not have been required, nor would it have been necessary for him to explain in detail, as we find him doing on occasion, the meaning of agricultural terminology with which a popular audience presumably would have been quite familiar.[67] This suggests that if any of Gregory's works can be called "popular," then it is the *Homilies on the Gospels*, which were originally presented orally. The *Dialogues*, which were designed to be read,[68] seem to have been written in the first instance at least for a more highly refined and educated audience. Indeed, in view of the chasm that separated the literate members of society and the illiterate masses during the sixth century, it is highly unlikely that any genuinely popular audience could have been reached directly by a literary work like the *Dialogues*.[69]

[65] Cf. de Vogüé, *Introduction*, pp. 34-35.

[66] *Hom. in Evan.* 2.38.4, PL 76:1283-1284: "Quia enim vulgo loquor, etiam ipsa me necesse est verba evangelicae lectionis explanare. Altilia enim saginata dicimus; ab eo enim quod est alere, altilia quasi alitilia vocamus."

[67] See, for example, *Dial.* 2.6.1, SC 260:156: "ferramentum ... quod a falcis similitudine falcastrum vocatur"; *Dial.* 3.14.6, SC 260:306: "ferramenta, quae usitato nos nomine vangas vocamus." The best example of translations from popular speech is probably at *Dial.* 2.18, SC 260:194: "lignea vascula, quae vulgo flascones vocantur." Thereafter Gregory uses the word *flasco*. It seems fairly certain, therefore, that his initial explanation was for the benefit of readers accustomed to more formally correct Latin. Cf. *Dial.* 3.14.3, SC 260:304: "hunc simulatorem dicere et verbo rustico coepit inpostorem clamare." The other relevant examples are not quite as clear; taken on their own, they could equally be interpreted as translations from correct Latin into the language of common discourse for the benefit of less sophisticated readers. Cf. *Dial.* 1.12.1, SC 260:112: "In eo etiam loco Interorina vallis dicitur, quae a multis verbo rustico Interocrina nominatur"; *Dial.* 2.2.1, SC 260:136: "nigra parvaque avis, quae vulgo merola vocatur"; and *Dial.* 2.11.2, SC 260:174: "in psyatio, (quod vulgo matta vocatur)."

[68] See *Dial.* 1 Prol. 10, SC 260:16, and 3.7.1, SC 260:278, where Gregory refers explicitly to his readers, *legentes*.

[69] For what follows, see A. Petrucci, "Scrittura e libro nell'Italia altomedievale," *SM* 3rd. ser. 14 (1973): 961-1002.

The cultural changes experienced in sixth-century Italy were substantially the same as those experienced in the rest of western Europe: increasing social polarization between the uneducated masses and an educated elite led to a virtual monopoly of literary culture by the church.[70] In the case of Italy the precipitating cause seems to have been the Lombards. Although some members of the Lombard population undoubtedly were able to read and write Latin, for the most part the ruling classes were illiterate. Of course, Italy had suffered this kind of indignity before, and so at the time of Cassiodorus the Roman aristocracy was transformed into a bureaucracy which became an essential component of the Gothic state. But instead of delegating administration to educated Romans, the Lombards chose to retain power in their own hands. On those relatively few occasions on which writing was necessary for coins, inscriptions or perhaps even documents, they were content to draw on the services of simple artisans. The Lombards were not hostile to the world of learning, but it was not part of their experience, and the net result was a significant impoverishment of schools, libraries, indeed of the whole literary culture that was a bequest of antiquity. Since that culture, such as it was, became largely a preserve of the clergy and a few members of the highest levels of lay society, the *Dialogues* could hardly have been addressed to a popular audience. The audience was almost certainly clerical; indeed, Gregory himself provides the evidence that confirms the fact.

In a letter of July 593 to Bishop Maximian of Syracuse, in which he asks for information about the Abbot Nonnosus, Gregory tells us that he undertook the writing of the *Dialogues* at the urging of the brethren who lived with him. It is not entirely clear whether Gregory means his brethren from the monastery of St Andrew, or rather his episcopal *familia*, the monastic brethren with whom he surrounded himself in the papal curia. His use of the present tense—"fratres mei, qui mecum familiariter vivunt"—would suggest the latter. But, whatever the case, there cannot be much doubt that Gregory followed a well established hagiographical precedent, and that, initially at least, the *Dialogues* were intended for a monastic audience.[71]

---

[70] Cf. Le Goff, "Culture cléricale," p. 783.

[71] See *Ep.* 3.50, CCL 140:195-196 at 195. Cf. Athanasius, *Vita S. Antonii*, Prooemium, PG 26:838; chap. 94, PG 26:974-975; Palladius, *Historia Lausiaca*, Prooemium, ed. E.C. Butler (Cambridge, 1898-1904), 2:3; Rufinus, *Historia monachorum*, Prol., PL 21:387-388. Given the fact that the *Life of St Martin* was dedicated to Desiderius, a member of the same ascetic circle to which Sulpicius himself belonged, the hagiographical work of Sulpicius Severus was probably intended, in the first instance at least, for a monastic audience as well. Confirmation may be found at *Vita S. Martini* 27.6, SC 133:316: "Illud facile confido, *omnibus sanctis opusculum istud gratum fore*"; and in the words of Postumianus at *Dial.* 2.8, CSEL 1:189:

However, rather than address himself exclusively to monks, Gregory also had a larger clerical audience in mind. In this regard the *Dialogues* themselves are instructive. There are two occasions on which Gregory addresses his readers directly. The first is not all that helpful for our immediate purposes, although it does indicate that some of the members of Gregory's audience might have been doubtful of the truth of what he was about to say. To remove any reason for disbelief on the part of his readers, Gregory declares that he will give the authority on which each of his miracle stories is based, a promise which, for the most part, he is faithful in keeping. The second occasion, however, is more revealing; it occurs in the chapter, alluded to already, that tells us of the wonderful mercy God showed to Bishop Andrew of Fondi: "I earnestly pray that the account of it may influence my readers at least to this degree, that if they have dedicated their lives to chastity they may no longer presume to have women living in their homes, for ruin creeps into the mind all the more readily when the object desired is present to minister to sinful inclinations." As de Vogüé points out, Gregory has the clergy at large in mind in this particular passage, probably prelates above all others.[72]

Additional confirmation is provided by the fact that, although laymen are not entirely lacking, for the most part the saints portrayed in the *Dialogues* are clerics in the broad sense, either monks or secular clergy. Clerics of high rank, i.e. abbots and bishops, tend to dominate.[73] We should probably resist

---

"Praeclare, inquit Postumianus, nostros istos, ut Martini non egrediantur exemplum, tua constringit oratio." Cf. C. Stancliffe, *St. Martin and His Hagiographer* (Oxford, 1983), p. 72.

[72] See *Dial.* 1 Prol. 10, SC 260:16-18; 3.7.1, Zimmerman 120 (slightly revised), SC 260:278; and de Vogüé, *Introduction*, p. 42. Stancliffe, *St. Martin*, p. 75, maintains that Sulpicius Severus addressed a similar extended audience in his *Life of St Martin*, an audience that included not only prelates of the church in Gaul, but "those compatriots whose loyalties to Christianity were still torn by their love for the classical culture in which they had been nurtured."

[73] S. Boesch Gajano, "La proposta agiografica dei 'Dialogi' di Gregorio Magno," *SM* 3rd. ser. 21 (1980): 623-664, esp. 628. For a different view see G. Cracco, "Uomini di Dio e uomini di chiesa nell'alto medioevo (per una reinterpretazione dei 'Dialogi' di Gregorio Magno)," *RSSR* n.s. 12 (1977): 163-202. Cracco does not deny that most of the heroes of the *Dialogues* are clerics, but he argues that this is incidental to the main point. What is distinctive about them, says Cracco, has nothing to do with their official status but rather with the charismatic authority that all of Gregory's saints share, whether clerics or not: "ciò che conta, per Gregorio, non è il fatto che un tale sia prete o vescovo, ma il fatto che sia 'uomo di Dio' e quindi capace di miracoli. ..." (p. 199) Rather than being men of the church, the heroes of the *Dialogues* are men of God who possess the authority and power of the Holy Spirit: "essi posseggono la vera autorità, la vera potenza, quella dello Spirito, davanti alla quale si ritirano le piccole autorità e i fragili poteri degli uomini, anche quelli dello stesso papa"

the temptation of thinking that Gregory privileges one particular version of the spiritual life, as if he were using the *Dialogues* to argue for the primacy of the monastic life, or of the pastoral function of the bishop, or of some balanced version of the mixed life in which active and contemplative elements conjoin harmoniously.[74] Gregory of Tours may have shown a marked predilection for examples of holy bishops in his writings, but with Gregory the Great a comparable preferred order of sanctity is not so easily identified. As Boesch Gajano remarks, "Voler trovare il 'modello' di santità significa stringere i *Dialogi* in uno schema che lascerebbe fuori troppi e troppo importanti 'elementi secondari'; tendenza pericolosa."[75] However, not sur-

---

(p. 193). Cracco has developed his thesis further in "Chiesa e cristianità rurale nell'Italia di Gregorio Magno," in *Medioevo rurale* (Bologna, 1980), pp. 361-379; in "Gregorio Magno interprete di Benedetto," in *S. Benedetto e otto secoli (xii-xix) di vita monastica nel Padovano* (Padova, 1980), pp. 7-36; and in "Ascesa e ruolo dei 'Viri Dei' nell'Italia di Gregorio Magno," in *Hagiographie, cultures et sociétés*, pp. 283-296. Cf. L. Cracco Ruggini, "Potere e carismi in età imperiale," *SStor*. 20 (1979): 585-607, esp. 604.

[74] On the monastic life, see B. Calati, "I dialoghi di S. Gregorio Magno (Tentativo di indagine di spiritualità monastica)," *VMon*. 11 (1957): 61-70, 108-116, who claims that the *Dialogues* champion monastic values. His analysis concentrates almost exclusively on St Benedict, but he doesn't limit his claims to book two. Rather, he maintains that the fundamental theme of the *Dialogues* as a whole is "the return to Paradise", a return made possible by the monastic vocation.

For the pastoral function of the bishop, see Vitale-Brovarone, "La forma narrativa," esp. p. 149. Vitale-Brovarone argues that there is a precise structure behind the fragmentary appearance of the *Dialogues*; and after a long analysis of the settings for the episodes as they shift from book one through to the end of book four, he refers to "la strada che conduce dal monastero alla diocesi, dalla campagna alla città, dal mondo a Roma. ..."

The mixed life is often represented as Gregory's highest ideal; see, for example: F. Lieblang, *Grundfragen der mystischen Theologie nach Gregors den Grossen Moralia und Ezechielhomilien* (Freiburg, 1934), pp. 160-170; R. Gillet, Introduction to *Grégoire le Grand, Morales sur Job, Livres 1 et 2*, sc 32 (Paris, 1952), p. 16; "Spiritualité et place du moine dans l'église selon saint Grégoire le Grand," in *Théologie de la vie monastique* (Paris, 1961), pp. 323-351, esp. pp. 346-351; "Grégoire le Grand," coll. 881-888; and Dagens, *Saint Grégoire le Grand*, pp. 135-163. Both Gillet and Dagens acknowledge that, in an absolute sense, the life of contemplation takes pride of place over the active life in Gregory's thought. They also observe that, personally, Gregory was deeply attached to a monastic, contemplative kind of spirituality. However, they maintain that Gregory developed as his highest ideal a mixed life combining both contemplative and active elements, although neither claims that specifically this ideal is championed in the *Dialogues*. This general view has been endorsed recently by J. Fontaine, "Un fondateur de l'Europe: Grégoire le Grand (590-604)," *Helmantica* 34 (1983): 171-189 at 184-186; and by G.R. Evans, *The Thought of Gregory the Great* (Cambridge, 1986), esp. pp. 105-111.

[75] Boesch Gajano, "La proposta agiografica," p. 636. On Gregory of Tours, cf. A. Monaci Castagno, "Il vescovo, l'abate e l'eremita: tipologia della santità nel Liber Vitae Patrum di Gregorio di Tours," *Augustinianum* 24 (1984): 235-264.

prisingly, saints who are also laymen are relatively rare in the *Dialogues*, and the few who are to be found there tend to be persons from the highest levels of the social order.[76] The peasant population is generally portrayed as not being profoundly influenced by the world of sanctity. Indeed, one example appears to reveal a real estrangement: the case of the simple *rusticus* who lost his load of grain when, "without consideration or respect for the renowned saint," he carelessly deposited it on the tomb of Equitius.[77] More usually the peasantry makes its appearance in Gregory's narrative simply to acknowledge the miraculous powers of some saint, and perhaps be the beneficiary of those powers, and then drop out of sight.[78]

[76] Boesch Gajano, "Dislivelli culturali," p. 399. Apart from the phenomenon of the sainted king, sanctity seems to have been primarily a clerical phenomenon throughout the Middle Ages. J.-C. Poulin, *L'idéal de sainteté dans l'Aquitaine carolingienne d'après les sources hagiographiques (750-950)* (Québec, 1975), esp. pp. 81-98, argues that a new model of lay sanctity made its appearance in the tenth century with Odo of Cluny's biography of Gerald of Aurillac. On this matter, however, cf. M. Heinzelmann, "Sanctitas und 'Tugendadel'. Zu Konzeptionen von 'Heiligkeit' im 5. und 10. Jahrhundert," *Francia* 5 (1977): 741-752. Even in the later Middle Ages, when many of those who were venerated as saints were in fact drawn from the laity, the notion of lay sanctity would remain problematic. See, for example, Vauchez, *La sainteté*, pp. 410-448; and R. Kieckhefer, *Unquiet Souls: Fourteenth-Century Saints and their Religious Milieu* (Chicago and London, 1984), pp. 14-15.

Along with clerical status, noble lineage was an equally important requirement of sanctity throughout the Middle Ages. On the Merovingian period, for example, see F. Prinz, "Zur geistigen Kultur des Mönchtums im spätantiken Gallien und im Merowingerreich," *ZBLG* 26 (1963): 29-102, esp. 82-88; *Frühes Mönchtum im Frankenreich* (München and Wien, 1965), esp. pp. 496-501; "Heiligenkult und Adelsherrschaft im Spiegel merowingischer Hagiographie," *HZ* 204 (1967): 529-544. On the Carolingian period, see Poulin, *L'idéal de sainteté*, esp. pp. 45-48, 127. On the later Middle Ages, see A. Murray, *Reason and Society in the Middle Ages* (Oxford, 1978), esp. pp. 337-341; Vauchez, *La sainteté*, esp. pp. 185-186, 204-220, 324-326; M. Goodich, *Vita Perfecta: The Ideal of Sainthood in the Thirteenth Century* (Stuttgart, 1982), pp. 69-81; D. Weinstein and R.M. Bell, *Saints and Society: The Two Worlds of Western Christendom, 1000-1700* (Chicago and London, 1982), pp. 194-219.

[77] *Dial.* 1.4.20, Zimmerman 24, sc 260:56.

[78] Boesch Gajano, "Dislivelli culturali," p. 403. Cf. de Vogüé, *Introduction*, pp. 36-37. However, for a different point of view, see S. Mazzarino, "L'"èra Costantiniana' e la 'prospettiva storica' di Gregorio Magno," in *Passaggio dal mondo antico al medio evo* (Rome, 1980), pp. 9-28 at 21; and L. Cracco Ruggini, "Il miracolo nella cultura del tardo impero: concetto e funzione," in *Hagiographie, cultures et sociétés*, pp. 161-202 at pp. 171-172. See also Cracco, "Chiesa e cristianità rurale," esp. pp. 367-368, where Cracco points to the humble social and economic circumstances of the clerics (bishops, priests and monks) in the *Dialogues*. Honoratus, abbot of Fondi, was a former *colonus*; his successor, Libertinus, was a freed slave. Because of the modest origins of the heroes of the *Dialogues*, and because of the role that he attributes to them in the evangelization of the countryside, Cracco does not detect any estrangement between Gregory and the peasant population. What he does note is a basic incompatibility between sanctity and nobility in the *Dialogues*: "un nobile che se vuole farsi santo deve rinnegare *in toto* e senza compromessi la propria matrice sociale" (p. 365).

It should be emphasized, however, that, in addressing the *Dialogues* to clerics, Gregory almost certainly did not intend them to use the work only for their own personal edification. Interesting results might be forthcoming from a systematic study of the typology of the miracles. The various types of miracle could conceivably tell us something further about the intended audience.[79] But even a cursory view is sufficient to indicate that Gregory also hoped to reach the lay community. In de Vogüé's judgment, Gregory was addressing an elite, if not necessarily a religious elite, certainly a social elite. This may well be true; one can certainly detect on occasion implicit admonition of the nobility.[80] But behind the primary audience of clerics Gregory envisaged a secondary lay audience as well, possibly of all social classes.[81] It was Gregory's intention that, rather than using the *Dialogues* only for their own benefit, his clerical readers would draw on them in their ministry to others, most probably in their own sermons.[82]

From this perspective, and with the reservations mentioned above, the *Dialogues* can indeed be regarded as a popular work. They were intended to be an instrument of evangelization which, when placed in the hands of the clerics who were their primary audience, could reach a secondary audience composed of the lay population. As remarked above, Gregory may have given some thought to reaching those who were still pagans. But it is more likely that the lay audience he had in mind was one of Catholic Christians whose grasp on the faith was tenuous at best, "un public," Dagens calls it, "composé de croyants encore proches du paganisme et dont la foi demande à s'intérioriser."[83] The modern miracles recorded in the *Dialogues* were very probably intended in some way or other to deepen the faith of those who were already baptized Christians. The precedent for miracles of this kind was to be found in the New Testament itself. In his more theoretical passages Gregory seems to restrict himself to an apologetic purpose for the miracles of the early church, as if miracles were intended strictly for unbelievers. But

[79] Cf. J.-L. Derouet, "Les possibilités d'interprétation sémiologique des textes hagiographiques," *RHEF* 62 (1976): 153-162, esp. 162. On the dividends to be derived from this kind of research, cf. S. Boesch Gajano, "La tipologia dei miracoli nell'agiografia altomedievale. Qualche riflessione," *Schede medievale* 5 (1983): 303-312.

[80] De Vogüé, *Introduction*, pp. 42-43. See, for example, *Dial.* 2.23.1-5, sc 260:204-208, where the nobility is encouraged to practise humility.

[81] See *Dial.* 4.19, sc 265:72-74, which contains an admonition directed potentially to all parents on the proper upbringing of their children.

[82] S. Boesch Gajano, "'Narratio' e 'expositio' nei Dialoghi di Gregorio Magno," *BISIAM* 88 (1979): 1-33 at 33. Cf. her "Dislivelli culturali," pp. 407-409; and Petrucci, "Scrittura e libro," pp. 980-981.

[83] Dagens, *Saint Grégoire le Grand*, p. 230.

a rather different picture emerges from his comments on the individual miracles of Christ.

In his commentary on the first book of Kings, Gregory tells us that the miracles that Christ performed were incomparably greater than the miracles of the Old Testament saints. Moses was able to divide the waters of the sea; but Christ was able to walk on them. Moses could act only as an instrument of the divine power; but Christ could perform miracles in virtue of his own divine authority.[84] More important, however, Gregory tells us that Christ performed miracles to teach us the truth: his miracles were proof of his claim to divinity, and of his claim to be able to forgive sins. Indeed, they were such a clear demonstration of the truth of what he said that those who refused to believe and conspired instead to slay him achieved only their own greater damnation.[85] All of this is generally in accord with the apologetic purpose that Gregory usually attributes to miracles in the primitive church. Christ's miracles are here seen as aids to conversion, which served to substantiate his claims. However, when Gregory focuses on the individual miracles that Christ performed, he seems to imply that they were designed to do more than induce a state of belief. Indeed, one could infer from his remarks that Christ's miracles were aimed at those who already were believers, and that they were intended to deepen their faith.[86] Thus Christ's raising of Lazarus from the dead (John 11:38-44) contains a lesson in ecclesiastical discipline;[87] his healing of the deaf mute (Mark 7:31-37), his expulsion of the evil spirit from the young boy (Mark 9:13-28), and his healing of the official's son (John 4:46-53) illustrate important moral lessons;[88] and his healing of the woman who had been bent over for eighteen years (Luke 13:11-13), his healing of the blind man on the road to Jericho (Luke 18:35-43), his transformation of water into wine at Cana (John 2:1-11), and his production of the

---

[84] *In 1 Reg.* 1.93, CCL 144:108-109.

[85] *Ibid.* 1.10, CCL 144:61-62; 1.90, CCL 144:106-107; 1.93, CCL 144:108; 2.48, CCL 144:147-148.

[86] Cf. P. Boglioni, "Miracle et nature chez Grégoire le Grand," in *Cahiers d'études médiévales* 1: *Epopées, légendes et miracles* (Montreal and Paris, 1974), pp. 11-102 at pp. 89-92. Boglioni emphasizes the pedagogical value that Gregory attributes to the miracles of Christ, but fails to appreciate the apologetic role that he also attributes to them: "Grégoire n'est pas sensible à la valeur proprement apologétique des miracles du Christ par rapport aux vérités qu'il prêche, ni à leur aspect de bienfait ou de lutte contre les diverses formes du mal, deux thèmes qui avaient principalement retenu l'attention des premiers apologistes. Ils lui apparaissent plutôt comme théophanie d'un côté, pédagogie de l'autre" (p. 91).

[87] *Hom. in Evan.* 2.26.6, PL 76:1200.

[88] *Hom. in Ezech.* 1.10.20, CCL 142:153-154; *Mor.* 10.30.50, CCL 143:572-573; *Hom. in Evan.* 2.28.1, PL 76:1211.

miraculous draught of fishes when he appeared to the disciples by the Sea of Tiberias (John 21:1-14) all encompass important doctrinal lessons from which only those who already were believers could have benefited.[89]

Since Gregory usually speaks only of the significance that these miracles have for *us*, it is conceivable that the purpose they served at the time they were performed was different from the purpose they serve now. His discussion of the healing of the blind man on the road to Jericho (Luke 18:35-43) strongly suggests the possibility: "Opera quippe ejus et per potentiam aliud ostendunt, et per mysterium aliud loquuntur." Immediately before this episode the Evangelist says that Christ tried to explain to the disciples what the future had in store (cf. verses 31-34). He told them that they were going up to Jerusalem, where everything that the prophets had written about the Son of Man would be fulfilled. He told them that he would be delivered over to the Gentiles, would be mocked, scourged and finally put to death, but that on the third day he would rise from the tomb. The disciples, however, understood none of these things, and so recourse was had to miracle. Says Gregory:

> Forseeing that the minds of the disciples would be disturbed on account of his passion, our Redeemer prophesied to them long beforehand both the punishment of this same passion and the glory of his resurrection, so that when they perceived him to be dying, as had been foretold, still they might not doubt that he was to rise again. But because his fleshly-minded (*carnales*) disciples still were in no way able to comprehend his words of mystery, a miracle came to pass (*venitur ad miraculum*). Before their eyes a blind man regained his sight, so that divine deeds might strengthen the faith of those who did not comprehend the words of divine mystery.[90]

This understanding of the event would be plausible if the miracle served in any way to clarify what Christ had meant. However, it does not. It does contain a spiritual message that Gregory takes pains to explain to his readers, but not one that casts direct light on the specific points Christ had been trying to explain: the necessity of his death and resurrection.[91] Hence when he claims that the disciples had not been able to grasp what Christ had said, what Gregory means is that they had not been able to *believe* it. For the disciples, the miracle on the road to Jericho was designed to induce belief

---

[89] On the crippled woman, see *Hom. in Evan.* 2.31.2, PL 76:1228; 2.31.6, PL 76:1230. On the other miracles, see respectively *ibid.* 1.2.1, PL 76:1082; *Hom. in Ezech.* 1.6.7, CCL 142:70; and *Hom. in Evan.* 2.24.3, PL 76:1185.

[90] *Hom. in Evan.* 1.2.1, PL 76:1082.

[91] Gregory tells us that the blind man here is to be taken as a representative of humanity in general, whose spiritual blindness is illuminated by the presence of the Redeemer.

by corroborating the authority of Christ's words. For Gregory's Christian congregation, and for us, the miracle contains a theological lesson about the fall of man and the redemptive work of the Saviour.

This situation may apply with all the Biblical miracles mentioned above: at the time of their performance they may have served to encourage or strengthen belief, as they still do; but for those who are believers they now provide other lessons in morals or doctrine. However, Gregory's treatment of Christ's appearance by the Sea of Tiberias after his resurrection (John 21:1-14) suggests otherwise. Whether the disciples saw the same significance Gregory does in the miraculous draught of fishes that was produced on that occasion, or in Christ's subsequent sharing of a meal of broiled fish and bread with them, Gregory does not say. But he does say that they were intended to derive the same lesson from the fact that, on this occasion, Christ chose to remain on the shore, whereas earlier (in Matthew 14:25) he had walked on the water; and this was a theological lesson designed for those who had already accepted the truth of the resurrection, not for those who needed to be convinced that it had taken place. The disciples did need convincing, of course, and Gregory points out elsewhere how the proofs that served to allay their doubts can allay ours.[92] But here he treats the disciples who saw the risen Christ and his present Christian hearers as though belief in the resurrection were firm in each case, and dwells instead on the doctrinal message implicit in the event for both, an important truth about the nature of Christ's risen body:

> What indeed does the sea signify if not the present age, which beats itself with the storms of trials and the waves of a perishable life? What is represented by the solidity of the shore if not that perpetuity of eternal rest? Because, therefore, the disciples were still upon the waves of mortal life, they worked on the sea. But because our Redeemer had already left behind the corruption of the flesh, after his resurrection he stood on the shore, *as if in these things he were to explain* (loqueretur) *to his disciples the very mystery of his resurrection, saying: "Now I do not appear to you* (nobis: vobis?) *on the sea, because I am not in the waves of confusion with you."*[93]

In view of this passage we may legitimately wonder if Gregory seriously intends to say that the miracles of Christ served strictly apologetic purposes, even at the time of their performance. Moreover, even if we could distinguish between the purpose Christ's miracles served then (to induce belief) and the purpose they serve now (to induce belief in some cases, but primarily to

---

[92] *Hom. in Evan.* 2.29.1, PL 76:1213.
[93] *Ibid.* 2.24.2, PL 76:1184-1185. The emphasis has been added.

deepen the faith of believers), we would still be left with the fact that, at least for Gregory's Christian audience, miracles performed in New Testament times are systematically interpreted as serving more than strictly apologetic purposes. Despite the fact that the miracles performed then were supposed to be for unbelievers, not believers, Gregory interprets them with present believers in mind. They serve to deepen faith, which is precisely what Gregory expects of contemporary miracles as well.

The contradiction implied here is only apparent; it disappears when the perspective that Gregory adopts on the church of his own day is considered. Although Gregory speaks of his own time as one in which virtually everyone has been converted to Christianity, he also observes that many profess to be Christians only because it is the fashion: if the Christian faith were not generally held in such high renown, the church would not have nearly as many members.[94] These people call themselves Christians only because almost everyone else does. At heart they are not what they claim to be, and although the verbal profession of their faith may be sufficient to disguise their real nature from the sight of men, God sees them for what they are. If the present relative tranquillity of the church were replaced by the winds of persecution, these false Christians would be separated from the genuine faithful like chaff from wheat, for they have not experienced any kind of conversion at all. Far from seeking the good which is invisible, they do not even believe in its existence.[95]

Although these faithless seem mere opportunists, Gregory may also have been thinking of those whom Bonner has called "paganised Christians": baptized Christians who were serious enough in their profession of the faith, but who still had not given up pagan beliefs.[96] In a letter of September 597 to Brunichild, Queen of the Franks, Gregory expresses his horror on learning that many who had been baptized had not abandoned the worship of demons, and he exhorts Brunichild to do her utmost to prevent those subject to her authority from sacrificing to idols or worshipping trees. In a letter to him of the same date, Peter, Bishop of Corsica, is directed to correct the offenders in his jurisdiction by imposing a penance of a few days' duration, so that they might bewail their guilt and in the future hold all the more firmly to the true faith. By July 599, a couple of years later, Gregory seems to have

---

[94] *Ibid.* 2.32.5, PL 76:1236.

[95] *Mor.* 25.10.26, CCL 143B:1251-1252; *Hom. in Evan.* 2.32.6, PL 76:1237: "sunt nonnulli qui Christianitatis nomine censentur, sed Christianitatis non habent fidem. Sola esse visibilia aestimant, invisibilia non appetunt, quia nec esse suspicantur."

[96] G. Bonner, "The Extinction of Paganism and the Church Historian," *JEH* 35 (1984): 339-357, esp. 348.

lost the moderation for which he is justly famous. A letter to Januarius of Cagliari shows him willing to countenance more severe measures against baptized Christians who nevertheless continue to be worshippers of idols. If these false Christians are unwilling to give up their pagan practices, Januarius is to chastise the slaves among them with blows and the freemen with strict confinement, so that those who refuse to listen to salutary words recalling them from the peril of death might be brought back to the desired sanity of mind by physical coercion.[97]

However, in addition to such pseudo-Christians, who are really either simple opportunists or pagans at heart, Gregory tells us that there are many others who are in only slightly less jeopardy, not because of failure of belief on their part, but because of their failure to lead Christian lives. Although there is a difference between those who are simply wicked (*iniqui*) and those who are genuinely faithless (*impii*),[98] people who are notorious because of the wickedness of their lives can be likened to infidels, because they proclaim their faith with their voices only to deny it in practice.[99] In fact, those whose failure is one of practice rather than belief often by a divine judgment lose the faith that they possess. Since they persist in their evil ways in apparent disregard of the punishment to come, they cannot be said really to believe in the divine judgment at all.[100]

Gregory emphasizes that the failures of belief or practice he describes are committed by baptized Christians who are Christians in name only. In the church, they are not of it; they have undergone no real conversion, or the process of conversion is incomplete in their case, and they are in imminent danger of losing their already tenuous grasp on the Christian faith. Those whom Gregory describes as patent unbelievers or covert pagans may have been extreme cases. But his concern about them, and about those whose failure was one of practice, is significant nonetheless. Despite the fact that the world had, superficially at least, been Christianized, it was Gregory's view that much of this Christianization was a veneer, and that for many people the

---

[97] *Ep.* 8.4, CCL 140A:518-521 at 521; *Ep.* 8.1, CCL 140A:513-514 at 513; *Ep.* 9.205, CCL 140A:763-765 at 764.

[98] *Mor.* 18.6.12, CCL 143A:892: "Impius namque pro infideli ponitur, id est a pietate religionis alienus; iniquus vero dicitur, qui pravitate operis ab aequitate discordat, vel si fortasse christianae fidei nomen portat." Cf. *Mor.* 25.10.25, CCL 143B:1250, where the contrast is between the *impius* and the *peccator.* "Peccator enim dici etiam qui in fide pius est potest. ... Impius vero proprie dicitur qui a religionis pietate separatur."

[99] *Mor.* 18.6.12, CCL 143A:892; cf. *Mor.* 25.10.25, CCL 143B:1251.

[100] *Mor.* 25.10.27, CCL 143B:1252-1253.

reality underneath had not been significantly altered.[101] The task of changing this reality, of making Christianity a living force to those who professed it, was the ultimate end of his labours.

It is generally acknowledged that Gregory was not a great speculative thinker, and that it is pointless to look for a theological or philosophical system in his writings.[102] Rather than choosing to deepen a purely theological understanding of Christian dogma, for the most part Gregory limited himself to making doctrine as widely accessible as possible, so that Christians could have a firm grasp on what they were required to believe. He has, with justification, been regarded as one of the great masters of the contemplative life. But he no more contented himself with addressing a spiritual elite than he did an intellectual one. His greatest efforts were expended in clarifying the nature of ordinary Christian life as it ought to be lived from day to day, for it was his fundamental conviction that intellectual assent without practice was empty.[103] A genuine understanding of Scripture necessarily involved implementing its precepts. Dagens puts it concisely:

> C'est la *conversio morum* qui devient peu à peu une priorité absolue, car la foi continue à coexister avec des pratiques trop 'séculières'. ... On a remarqué que la morale tenait très peu de place dans la culture d'Augustin. Il en va tout autrement pour l'auteur des *Moralia*. Pour lui, toute son oeuvre l'atteste, la foi chrétienne est orientée vers la pratique et la culture chrétienne ne vise pas d'abord à acquérir des notions abstraites, mais à permettre à l'homme de vivre toujours davantage sa relation à Dieu.[104]

From Gregory's point of view what the church required was as much a work of evangelization as the preaching of the apostles in the early church

---

[101] Similar complaints about the multitudes of pseudo-Christians who continued to adhere to elements of paganism, or who failed to practice the precepts of the Christian life, run through the works of Augustine: see, for example, *De catechizandis rudibus* 25.48, CCL 46:171-172; *De civitate Dei* 20.9, CCL 48:718; *Enar. in Psalmos* 30.2.2.2, CCL 38:203; 30.2.3.3, CCL 38:213-214.

[102] See, for example, the judgments of Batiffol, *Saint Gregory the Great*, p. 133; and Dagens, *Saint Grégoire le Grand*, pp. 21-22.

[103] See Dagens, *Saint Grégoire le Grand*, pp. 22-23. The contrast between intellectual assent and practical denial was one of Gregory's favourite themes; see, for example, *Past.* 1.2, PL 77:15: "Et sunt nonnulli qui solerti cura spiritalia praecepta perscrutantur, sed quae intelligendo penetrant, vivendo conculcant; repente docent quae non opere, sed meditatione didicerunt; et quod verbis praepicant [praedicant?], moribus impugnant." Cf. Weber, *Hauptfragen*, p. 68.

[104] Dagens, *Saint Grégoire le Grand*, p. 20. On the implications of a genuine understanding of Scripture, see *Hom. in Ezech.* 1.10.20, CCL 142:153-154; cf. P. Catry, "Lire l'écriture selon Saint Grégoire le Grand," *CCist.* 34 (1972): 177-201, esp. 191-193.

or the recent mission to the *Angli*, and if it was to prosper it too was in need of the *gratia miraculorum*. We might recall that in his adherence to the principle that "tongues are a sign not for believers but for unbelievers" (1 Cor. 14:22), Saint Paul chose not to favour Timothy with a miraculous cure. But Timothy was a devout Christian whose profession of faith had been accompanied by an interior transformation: *iam totus intus vivebat*.[105] Gregory would probably say that many of those in the flock of which he was shepherd should probably be compared instead with Eutychus, or with the father of Publius, whom Paul did favour with miracles. The father of Publius was an unbeliever, and they of course were baptized Christians. But they shared the need for conversion, a conversion which would go beyond the first steps of external observance and capture their hearts. For this process the miracles of the New Testament were still necessary; so were the miracles of the modern saints with which God continued to bless them.

[105] *Mor.* 27.18.37, CCL 143B:1359.

3

Miracles and Sanctity

To grasp the purpose that Gregory attributes to contemporary miracles, we must come to terms with the connection between miracles and sanctity. Whatever else we might know about them, miracles are performed by saints. However, Gregory makes it clear that the connection is not rooted in the essence of sanctity itself. Throughout the New Testament considerable importance is attached to the performance of miracles, especially for apologetic purposes; yet in the final analysis, miracles are significantly less important than a life of virtue. When the disciples are given to rejoicing that even demons were subject to them, Christ declares that they should rather rejoice in the fact that their names are written in heaven. Elsewhere he says that on the Day of Judgment many will come to him seeking a claim on his mercy because of the wonders that they have performed in his name, only to suffer his rejection: "Not every one who says to me, 'Lord, Lord,' shall enter the kingdom of heaven, but he who does the will of my Father who is in heaven."[1] The import of these and similar passages was not lost on Gregory. He consistently maintains that it is the life of virtue, not miracles, that can provide the real test of sanctity.[2]

In the *Dialogues* Gregory tends to be very indulgent of Peter, whose appetite for wondrous tales is virtually insatiable. Yet at the same time, and from the very beginning of their conversation, he frequently finds ways of reminding Peter that, ultimately, the miracles about which he is so anxious

---

[1] See Luke 10:17-20, esp. 20; and Matthew 7:21-23, esp. 21. Cf. 1 Cor. 13:1-13, where Saint Paul proclaims the absolute priority of charity.

[2] The point has been widely acknowledged. See, for example, F.H. Dudden, *Gregory the Great: His Place in History and Thought* (1905; repr. New York, 1967), 2:357; P. Boglioni, "Miracle et nature chez Grégoire le Grand," in *Cahiers d'études médiévales* 1: *Epopées, légendes et miracles* (Montreal and Paris, 1974), pp. 11-102 at 80-81; and C. Dagens, *Saint Grégoire le Grand. Culture et expérience chrétiennes* (Paris, 1977), pp. 227-228.

to hear pale in significance when compared to a virtuous life. When, early in the account, Peter presses for details about the miracles of Libertinus of Fondi, Gregory responds by pointing out that, great though these may be, the virtue of patience they exemplify is even greater. When, after having already heard of several, Peter asks for additional miracles of Abbot Equitius, Gregory's answer is even more pointed: "Why do you look for more deeds," he says, "when the purity of his life was as remarkable as the fervour of his preaching?" His clearest statement on the issue comes near the end of book one: "one cannot conclude that there are no great saints just because no great miracles are worked. The true estimate of life, after all, lies in acts of virtue, not in the display of miracles."[3] Peter had probably grasped the point even earlier, but this time Gregory's vigorous insistence produces the clear admission that "vita et non signa quaerenda sunt."[4]

Unfortunately, Peter's conviction is not strong enough to prevent lapses, and so, throughout the *Dialogues*, there are occasions on which he continues to demonstrate a fascination with miracles for their own sake. But by the end of the very first book Gregory's own perspective on these matters is clear. It was shared by many other authors of late antiquity and the early Middle Ages as well, from St Athanasius and John Cassian to Hilary of Arles and Sulpicius Severus, for example.[5] Augustine also was familiar with it, and it was summed up admirably by Isidore of Seville: "In the apostles themselves the wonderful virtue of [good] works was greater than the virtue of signs. Hence even now in the church it is a greater thing to live well than to perform miracles."[6] The primacy of virtue was not grasped clearly by all early medieval

---

[3] *Dial.* 1.2.8, sc 260:30; 1.4.9, Zimmerman 19-20, sc 260:46; 1.12.4, Zimmerman 51, sc 260:116.

[4] *Dial.* 1.12.6, sc 260:118. See *Dial.* 1.5.6, sc 260:62, where Peter says of Constantius, sacristan of the church of Saint Stephen the Martyr: "Ut agnosco, vir iste magnus foris fuit in miraculis, sed maior intus in humilitate."

[5] See Athanasius, *Vita S. Antonii,* chap. 38, pg: 26:898-899; John Cassian, *Coll.* 15.2, csel 13:428; 15.7, csel 13:433; Hilary of Arles, *Sermo de vita S. Honorati* 37.1-2, sc 235:168-170. Cf. B. Steidle, "'Homo Dei Antonius'. Zum Bild des 'Mannes Gottes' im alten Mönchtum," in *Antonius Magnus Eremita* = *SAns.* 38 (1956): 148-200, esp. 158; and O. Chadwick, *John Cassian,* 2nd. ed. (Cambridge, 1968), p. 100. Sulpicius Severus, *Dial.* 1.10, csel 1:162, tells a story of two young monks who had managed miraculously to subdue a serpent, only to fall victim to the sin of pride by boasting of their accomplishments to their brethren. Given that the offending monks were appropriately disciplined by their abbot, and that the general point of the story is that pride is to be avoided and humility preserved at all times, the priority of the life of virtue seems to be acknowledged. However, Sulpicius nowhere provides as clear and unqualified a statement of the relationship between miracles and virtue as found in the work of Gregory the Great.

[6] Augustine, *De div. quaest. octoginta tribus* 79.3, ccl 44a:228; *In Iohannis Evangelium* 13.17, ccl 36:139-140; Isidore, *Sententiae* 1.24.1, pl 83:591.

hagiographers,[7] and was largely ignored by many of their successors. The typical attitude was largely governed by the more popular conception of sanctity, according to which miracles were of central importance.[8] However,

[7] Gregory's earliest biographer, the Anonymous of Whitby, could be cited as a case in point. Cf. *Vita S. Gregorii*, chaps. 3-4, ed. and trans. B. Colgrave (Lawrence, Kansas, 1968), pp. 76-78. Although he was aware of and reports Gregory's position, he also endorses a very different point of view: "Multi igitur a miraculis vitam quidem sanctorum solent considerare, atque a signis sancta illorum merita metiri, et hoc nec inmerito" (chap. 3, p. 76). An even clearer example is provided by Gregory of Tours, for whom miracles are of the essence. Cf. S. Boesch Gajano, "Il santo nella visione storiografica di Gregorio di Tours," in *Gregorio di Tours* (Todi, 1977), pp. 27-91, esp. pp. 89-90; O. Giordano, "Sociologia e patologia del miracolo in Gregorio di Tours," *Helikon* 18-19 (1978-1979): 161-209, esp. 167; and F.E. Consolino, *Ascesi e mondanità nella Gallia tardoantica* (Napoli, 1979), p. 79. As Consolino puts it: "in Gregorio il miracolo si fa prova imprescindibile di santità, e il santo può definirsi tale soltanto se ha al suo attivo una intensa attività miracolistica."

H. Delehaye, *Sanctus. Essai sur le culte des saints dans l'antiquité* (Brussels, 1927), pp. 243-244, argues that, at one point at least, Gregory acknowledges that miracles are not necessary for sanctity. Cf. *Liber vitae patrum* 2.1-2, MGH, SRM 1.2, pp. 219-220. Gregory begins by telling us of the only known miracle that St Illidius, Bishop of Clermont, performed during his life; and he then goes on to consider the objection that one miracle is hardly sufficient to establish sanctity: "Non potest hic habere inter sanctos pro unius tantum operatione miraculi." His initial approach to the objection is quite promising, for he attempts to counter it by quoting the words of the Saviour in Matthew 7:22-23. He does not, however, deal with the problem by arguing that miracles are not essential to sanctity. Instead, he says, the lesson to be derived from the Gospel is that any miracles the saint may have produced while he was alive would pale in comparison to those produced at his tomb: "magis proficit ad laudem virtus egressa de tumulo, quam ea quae quisquam vivens gessit in mundo; quia illa labem habere potuerunt per assidua mundanae occupationis impedimenta, haec vero omnem labem ad liquidum caruerunt." The rest of the chapter is then devoted to the recounting of a post-mortem miracle.

[8] On the popular conception of sanctity, see E. Demm, "Zur Rolle des Wunders in der Heiligkeitskonzeption des Mittelalters," *AKG* 57 (1975): 300-344, esp. p. 325: "das Volk hat den Heiligen in erster Linie als Thaumaturgen erfahren, in der Volksfrömmigkeit blieb das Wunder das primäre Kriterium der Heiligkeit." Cf. D. Weinstein and R.M. Bell, *Saints and Society: The Two Worlds of Western Christendom, 1000-1700* (Chicago and London, 1982), pp. 208-209; A.J. Gurevich, *Categories of Medieval Culture* (London, 1985), p. 179. However, see also B. Ward, *Miracles and the Medieval Mind* (Philadelphia, 1982), esp. pp. 127-131, where she discusses the conditions that were necessary to ensure the success of a cult. Ward points out that "miracles in themselves were not enough to set up and maintain a shrine in popular esteem" (p. 127).

On the hagiographical tradition, see, for example, F. Graus, *Volk, Herrscher und Heiliger im Reich der Merowinger. Studien zur Hagiographie der Merowingerzeit* (Praha, 1965), esp. pp. 56-57; J.-C. Poulin, *L'idéal de sainteté dans l'Aquitaine carolingienne d' après les sources hagiographiques (750-950)* (Québec, 1975), esp. p. 109; and P.-A. Sigal, *L'homme et le miracle dans la France médiévale (XIe-XIIe siècle)* (Paris, 1985), p. 293. However, Poulin goes on to explain (esp. pp. 113-115) that to speak only of a popular conception of sanctity

Gregory's endorsement of the preeminence of the life of virtue was probably in itself sufficient to ensure that the idea exerted a very great influence on the course of medieval thought as a whole, and that, after a period of relative eclipse, a significantly increased emphasis on the life of the saint came to characterize the mature, late medieval canonization procedures.[9] As far as Gregory is concerned, to dwell on the external miracles of a saint rather than his virtues is to have one's priorities badly disordered. It is the latter alone that are properly constitutive of sanctity.[10]

For Gregory, sainthood is essentially a matter of the heart. Hence he would have had little sympathy for the ideal of sanctity found in the lives of some of the desert fathers, whose extreme asceticism seems to have been practised virtually for its own sake. Palladius offers as a model for our edification a monk who "reached such a high degree of mortification and so wasted away his body that the sun shone through his bones." Rufinus is pleased to relate for our instruction the example of John the Hermit, who began his life in the desert by standing under a rock for three years, his only source of nourishment being the communion which he received from the priest on Sundays. As Festugière remarks, it often seems that sanctity resides in the heroic act of self-denial itself.[11] Gregory acknowledges the importance of disciplining the body and bringing it into subjection, but he would have had none of this.[12]

---

dominating the hagiographical tradition is inadequate. He refers to two complementary points of view: a learned one, according to which virtue was of central importance, and a popular one, according to which miracles were the fundamental requirement. These two points of view influenced one another, and both were reflected in the work of the hagiographers. Cf. L. Zoepf, *Das Heiligen-Leben im 10. Jahrhundert* (1908; repr. Hildesheim, 1973), pp. 181-186; G. Penco, "Significato e funzione dei prologhi nell'agiografia benedettina," *Aevum* 40 (1966): 468-476, esp. 475-476.

[9] Cf. A. Vauchez, *La sainteté en Occident aux derniers siècles du Moyen Age* (Rome, 1981), esp. pp. 583-590.

[10] Cf. A. de Vogüé, "La mention de la 'regula monachorum' à la fin de la 'Vie de Benoît' (Grégoire, Dial. II, 36). Sa fonction littéraire et spirituelle," *RBenS* 5 (1976): 289-298. De Vogüé argues that, in part at least, the mention of the Rule of Saint Benedict at the end of the second book of the *Dialogues* is designed to illustrate Gregory's conviction that sanctity of life is of greater import than miracles. However, for a fundamentally different assessment, see G. Cracco, "Gregorio Magno interprete di Benedetto," in *S. Benedetto e otto secoli (xii-xix) di vita monastica nel Padovano* (Padova, 1980), pp. 7-36, at pp. 13-14.

[11] A.-J. Festugière, *Les moines d'Orient* 1: *Culture ou sainteté* (Paris, 1961), pp. 59-74. Cf. Palladius, *Historia Lausiaca*, chap. 48, ed. E.C. Butler (Cambridge, 1898-1904), 2:143, trans. R.T. Meyer (Westminster, Md., 1965), p. 131; Rufinus, *Historia monachorum*, chap. 15, PL 21:433-434.

[12] Cf. R. Gillet, "Spiritualité et place du moine dans l'église selon saint Grégoire le Grand," in *Theologie de la vie monastique* (Paris, 1961), pp. 323-351 at 335-338.

Of course, this is not true of all the literature of the desert. Hence the *Vitae patrum* clearly endorse the rule of moderation, and Cassian teaches that ascetic practices are of little value without purity of heart.[13] Its excesses notwithstanding, the literature on the desert fathers is not without a moral dimension. Palladius includes stories of monks who, flattering themselves because of their accomplishments, inevitably succumb to the sin of pride. These episodes clearly show that external acts of mortification are of little value if the heart is not properly disposed.[14] The moral basis of the *Historia monachorum* is even more evident. There the mastery over the passions and appetites through ascetic practice is valuable only if accompanied by genuine humility. Rufinus says that the holy man Apollo warned against conspicuous self-denial that sought the approval of men rather than of God.[15] Ultimately, as Ward remarks, "it is not the exercise of asceticism in itself which is fundamental to this way of life, but repentance, *metanoia*, the turning from the cultivation of the ego, the eradication of self-will".[16] This is a position with which Gregory could indeed have sympathized, although the cultivation of humility does not seem to have been quite as central to Gregory's thought.

Some commentators have stressed the importance of humility in Gregory's scale of values as the virtue on which all others depend. According to Dagens, for example, "l'humilité est pour lui la première des vertus, la qualité indispensable à tout prédicateur. Si bien que la charge pastorale est définie comme un véritable *magisterium humilitatis*."[17] If such indeed were the case, there would be a perfect symmetry in Gregory's thought, for he does maintain that pride is the root of all sin.[18] However, when Gregory wishes to

---

[13] See, for example, *Vitae patrum* 5.10.72, PL 73:924-925, where the dangers of excessive fasting are exposed: "Semper enim quod sine mensura est, corruptibile est" (col. 925); and John Cassian, *Coll.* 1.6, CSEL 13:12: "unde liquido conprobatur perfectionem non statim nuditate nec privatione omnium facultatum seu dignitatum abiectione contingi, nisi fuerit caritas illa cuius apostolus membra describit, quae in sola cordis puritate consistit." Cf. J.-C. Guy, *Jean Cassien. Vie et doctrine spirituelle* (Paris, 1961), p. 50; P. Christophe, *Cassien et Césaire. Prédicateurs de la morale monastique* (Gembloux and Paris, 1969), pp. 26-27.

[14] Cf. *Historia Lausiaca*, chaps. 25, 47, Butler 2:80, 138-139.

[15] *Historia monachorum*, chap. 7, PL 21:419. Cf. *Vitae patrum* 5.10.91, PL 73:928-929.

[16] B. Ward, *The Lives of the Desert Fathers* (Oxford and Kalamazoo, 1981), p. 33. Cf. B. Flusin, *Miracle et histoire dans l'oeuvre de Cyrille de Scythopolis* (Paris, 1983), pp. 107-108.

[17] Dagens, *Saint Grégoire le Grand*, p. 93. See also A. Vitale-Brovarone, "Forma narrativa dei *Dialoghi* di Gregorio Magno: prospettive di struttura," *AAST.M* 109 (1975): 117-185 at 147.

[18] *Mor.* 31.45.87, CCL 143B:1610. Cf. F. Gastaldelli, "Prospettive sul peccato in San Gregorio Magno," *Salesianum* 28 (1966): 65-94. The idea is a commonplace in the thought of St Augustine as well: see, for example, *Enar. in Psalmos* 1.4, CCL 38:2-3; 7.4, CCL 38:39; 18.1.14, CCL 38:104-105; 18.2.15, CCL 38:112; *De Genesi ad litteram* 11.5, CSEL 28:338; *De*

emphasize that it is a virtuous life that makes the saint rather than miracles, it is usually charity he singles out as being of paramount importance. As Christ himself said in John 13:35: "By this all men will know that you are my disciples, if you have love for one another."[19]

More generally, however, the essence of sanctity lies in the imitation of Christ, and hence ultimately involves the exercise of all the virtues. It is to the deeds of the Saviour, Gregory argues, that we should look for the correct norms of our conduct: "Propositae regulae nostrae actioni sunt facta veritatis."[20] The point is illustrated in the parallels between the lives of the saints and the life of the Redeemer in the *Dialogues*.[21] It is developed further in the commentary on the first chapter of Ezechiel. There the four creatures having the form of man represent in the first instance the four Evangelists, and then through them the entire company of the saints (*perfectorum omnium numerus*); and the man whose form they possess is Christ. Gregory continues:

> So that they might be able to rise to the virtue of holiness, these creatures (*haec animalia*) strive after imitation of this man. Indeed, they would not be holy if

---

civitate Dei 14.13, CCL 48:434. Occasionally Augustine conceives of charity as being pride's opposite and therefore the fundamental virtue. Cf. *De Genesi ad litteram* 11.15, CSEL 28:347. Elsewhere, however, he argues that, since pride is the root of all sin, it is humility which is to be regarded as the beginning of blessedness. Cf. *De sermone Domini in monte* 1.1.3, CCL 35:4; *In Iohannis Evangelium* 25.15-16, CCL 36:256. The humility that heals our swollen pride is the humility of Christ: "Si ergo initium omnis peccati superbia; unde sanaretur tumor superbiae, nisi Deus dignatus esset humilis fieri? ... Ideo in omnibus Dominus Christus humiliari dignatus est, praebens nobis viam: si tamen dignemur ambulare per eam" (*Sermo* 123.1.1, PL 38:684). Cf. *Enar. in Psalmos* 35.17, CCL 38:334; *Epist.* 140.28.68, CSEL 44:215.

[19] See *Ep.* 11.36, CCL 140A:925-929 at 928; and *Mor.* 20.7.17, CCL 143A:1016: "veros Dei famulos non miracula, sed sola charitas probat." Cf. P. Catry, "L'amour du prochain chez saint Grégoire le Grand," *SMon.* 20 (1978): 287-344. Cf. also John Cassian, *Coll.* 15.2, CSEL 13:428; 15.7, CSEL 13:433; Chadwick, *John Cassian*, p. 100.

[20] *Dial.* 3.21.4, SC 260:354. Cf. Delehaye, *Sanctus*, pp. 236, 240, 245-247; A.-J. Festugière, *La sainteté* (Paris, 1942), p. 114.

[21] See, for example, *Dial.* 3.1.8, SC 260:264, where Gregory tells us of Paulinus of Nola, who surrendered himself into slavery in order to lead a great multitude to freedom, "illum videlicet imitatus, qui formam servi adsumpsit, ne nos essemus servi peccati. Cuius sequens vestigia Paulinus ad tempus voluntarie servus factus est solus, ut esset postmodum liber cum multis." See also *Dial.* 3.31.8, SC 260:388-390, where Gregory explains how the example and influence of the martyred King Hermenegild was instrumental in bringing the Visigoths to the true faith: "Qua in re considerandum nobis est, quia totum hoc agi nequaquam posset, si Herminigildus rex pro veritate mortuus non fuisset. Nam, sicut scriptum est: 'nisi granum frumenti cadens in terra mortuum fuerit, ipsum solum manet; si autem mortuum fuerit, multum fructum adfert,' hoc fieri videmus in membris, quod factum scimus in capite. In Wisigotharum etenim gente unus est mortuus, ut multi viverent, et dum unum granum fideliter cecidit ad obtinendam fidem, animarum seges multa surrexit."

they did not possess his likeness. Whatever they possess of the heart of piety, of gentleness of spirit, of the zeal of righteousness, of the care of humility, of the fervour of charity, this they have drawn from the very fountain of mercy, from the very root of gentleness, from the very virtue of justice, that is, from the Mediator between God and men. ...

Sanctity consists of being conformed to the image of Christ, which in turn requires a life in imitation of his.[22]

It should be stressed, however, that it is the virtues of the Redeemer which must be imitated, and not necessarily his miracles, for "there are many ... who, without performing miracles, are not at all inferior to those who perform them."[23] The examples of Saint Peter and Saint Paul illustrate the point nicely. Their merits, says Gregory, allow them to share equally in the rewards of heaven, although in their ability to perform miracles the one far surpassed the other: "Peter walked on the water, whereas Paul was shipwrecked on the high seas. In the very same element, then, where Paul was unable to proceed on board ship, Peter could go on foot."[24] Moreover, even when the grace of miracles *is* granted, it is not necessarily bestowed permanently.

---

[22] *Hom. in Ezech.* 1.2.18-19, CCL 142:27-29, esp. 28-29. As Gregory also states: "Sanctus etenim quisque in tantum ad similitudinem huius hominis ducitur, in quantum vitam sui Redemptoris imitatur." On the centrality of the idea of the imitation of Christ in Gregory's thought, see P. Hale, "L'imitazione di Cristo come ritorno in S. Gregorio Magno," *VMon.* 20 (1966): 30-42, 89-99. On its significance in the hagiographical tradition, see G. Penco, "L'imitazione di Cristo nell'agiografia monastica," *CCist.* 28 (1966): 17-34; and most recently, M. Van Uytfanghe, "Modèles bibliques dans l'hagiographie," in *Le Moyen Age et la Bible* (Paris, 1984), pp. 449-488, esp. pp. 457, 469ff.

[23] *Dial.* 1.12.4, Zimmerman 51, SC 260:116. Cf. *Hom. in Evan.* 1.4.3, PL 76:1091; *Ep.* 11.36, CCL 140A:925-929 at 926. Cf. also Augustine, *De div. quaest. octoginta tribus* 79.3, CCL 44A:228; *In Iohannis Evangelium* 13.17, CCL 36:139-140; *Sermo* 90.5, PL 38:562.

[24] *Dial.* 1.12.5, Zimmerman 52, SC 260:116. Sulpicius Severus also compares Saints Peter and Paul, but to very different effect. See his *Epist.* 1.6, SC 133:318-320, where he maintains that "omnes fere sanctos magis insignes periculorum suorum fuisse virtutibus. Video quidem Petrum, fide potentem, rerum obstante natura mare pedibus supergressum et instabiles aquas corporeo pressisse vestigio. Sed non ideo mihi minor videtur gentium praedicator, quem fluctus absorbuit et post triduum totidemque noctes emergentem e profundo unda restituit. Atque nescio an paene plus fuerit vixisse in profundo an supra maris profunda transisse." Conceivably, however, something has fallen out of Sulpicius's text at this point. The reference to three days and three nights in the deep suggests Jonas rather than Paul: cf. Matt. 12.40; and 2 Cor. 11.25. His source may well have been Pseudo-Augustine, *Sermo* 203.3, PL 39:2123: "Petrus ambulare super aquas debita soli Deo potestate praesumpsit, et rerum obstupescente natura per insueti itineris novas vias pendulum inferens gressum, tumentia maris dorsa calcavit: sed non minor Paulus, qui, sicut ipse de se dicit, nocte et die in profundo maris fuit. Non minor, inquam, Paulus, quem velut Novi Testamenti Jonam, die ac nocte per maris profunda jactatum absorbuit fluctus, et reddidit, quasi sacrum depositum violare non audens, quasi famulo eum sinu unda custodiens illaesum populorum praedicationibus reservabat."

The saints enjoy permanent possession of only those gifts of the Holy Spirit necessary for salvation, not any others they might have. Hence, as a lesson in humility, the grace of miracles is sometimes withdrawn from those to whom it has been entrusted.[25] The clear implication of all this is that the power of performing miracles cannot be considered a necessary condition of sanctity. At best, it is simply a sign of sanctity, a means by which the essential internal virtue is made manifest to others. Indeed, miracles cannot be considered a sufficient condition of sanctity either. Not only are there some saints who cannot perform them, but some of the people who *can* perform them are not saints.

In a letter of June 601 to Augustine of Canterbury, who was distinguished by the accomplishment of many miracles in the conversion of the *Angli*, Gregory observes that we can be instructed in the true value of miracles by the example of Moses.[26] Moses performed astonishing wonders (*mira signa*) as he led the children of Israel out of Egypt towards the promised land. But at the end of the journey, he was told that he could not enter because of the fault he had committed thirty-eight years earlier when he had doubted his ability to draw water from the rock. How formidable is the judgment of Almighty God! says Gregory. If God's chosen servant suffered judgment for his sins, with what fear ought we to tremble who do not even know whether we are among the elect? Miracles themselves provide no assurance of ultimate standing with God. Although Augustine should rejoice because of the role that his miracles have played in the conversion of the Anglo-Saxons, he should also tremble lest they become an occasion for vainglory. Presumption is deplorable: miracles, Gregory reminds us elsewhere, can be performed by evil men, by hypocrites, heretics, and the reprobate, as well as by the good.[27] In Matthew 7:22-23 Christ himself, through the words of the Evangelist, tells us that on the Day of Judgment many will come to him proclaiming that they have performed mighty works in his name, only to receive, by way of reply, a sentence of damnation: "I never knew you; depart from me, you evildoers."

Above all among Gregory's predecessors, St Augustine addressed this issue systematically, especially with regard to the miracles that had been attributed to classical pagan deities or their agents.[28] Augustine frequently

---

[25] *Mor.* 2.56.91, CCL 143:113.

[26] *Ep.* 11.36, CCL 140A:925-929 at 927-928.

[27] *Hom. in Evan.* 2.29.4, PL 76:1216. Cf. John Cassian, *Coll.* 15.6, CSEL 13:431-432; Sulpicius Severus, *Vita S. Martini*, chaps. 23-24, SC 133:302-308; Augustine, *De div. quaest. octoginta tribus* 79.3, CCL 44A:228; *Contra litteras Petiliani*, 2.55.126, CSEL 52:91; *Epist.* 187.12.36, CSEL 57:113-114.

[28] Cf. J. Grange, *Le miracle d'après saint Augustin* (Brignais, 1912), pp. 29-32; D.P. de Vooght, "La théologie du miracle selon saint Augustin," *RTAM* 11 (1939): 197-222 at

refers to these miracles in passing, without commenting explicitly on their ontological status, although arguing that miracles performed in pagan temples or by pagan magicians cannot be compared with those that take place at the shrines of the martyrs.[29] However, given his conception of the nature of the pagan deities, he had no doubt whatever of their ability to produce genuine wonders.

The objects of pagan worship, Augustine says, are not simply insensate idols. Would that that were true! Although such idols would not help their worshippers, they would not do them any real harm either. The situation is really much worse. Cultivated pagans will sometimes maintain that their idols have merely symbolic significance, and that their worship is really directed at the invisible deity or deities that the visible symbols represent. However, the spiritual forces behind pagan idolatry are really demonic, rather than divine. In the customary veneration they pay to idols the pagans fall victim to the stratagems of Satan.[30] Occasionally Augustine endorses the widely accepted view first proposed by Euhemerus, maintaining that the pagan gods were originally men who came to be accorded divine honours after their death. But this ultimately leads to the same result: the cults of these dead heroes were fostered by evil spirits in order to delude the minds of men.[31] In the final analysis, Augustine's view of the pagan gods represents a clear endorsement of the teaching of the Apostle himself. The gods of the pagans are really demons,[32] to whose supernatural power the performance of wonders of various kinds would represent no difficulty.

Although he sometimes seems to imply that the miracles of the pagan gods were mere demonic illusions,[33] Augustine was convinced that at least some

---

212-214; F.M. Brazzale, *La dottrina del miracolo in S. Agostino* (Rome, 1964), pp. 55-57. On Augustine's treatment of pagan worship in general, see M.D. Madden, *The Pagan Divinities and their Worship as Depicted in the Works of Saint Augustine* (Washington, 1930); and A. Mandouze, "Saint Augustin et la religion romaine," *RAug.* 1 (1958): 187-223.

[29] *De civitate Dei* 10.16, CCL 47:290; 22.10, CCL 48:828; *Epist.* 138.4.20, CSEL 44:147.

[30] *Enar. in Psalmos* 85.12, CCL 39:1186; 96.11, CCL 39:1362-1363. Cf. *Epist.* 102.3.18, CSEL 34.2:559-560.

[31] *De civitate Dei* 6.8, CCL 47:178; 7.18, CCL 47:200. See also *De civitate Dei* 8.26, CCL 47:246 (cf. 18.8, CCL 48:598-599); *De consensu Evangelistarum* 1.23.32, PL 34:1056-1057; *Sermo* 273.3.3, PL 38:1249.

[32] Cf. 1 Cor. 10:20 with Ps. 95:5 and *De civitate Dei* 4.1, CCL 47:98. See also *De civitate Dei* 2.29, CCL 47:64; 4.16, CCL 47:112; 4.27, CCL 47:121; 5.12, CCL 47:142; 6 Praef., CCL 47:163-164; *Enar. in Psalmos* 49.6, CCL 38:580; 95.5, CCL 39:1347; *Epist.* 102.3.18, CSEL 34.2:559. This was a view that was generally held in the early church: cf. E.R. Dodds, *Pagan and Christian in an Age of Anxiety* (Cambridge, 1965), p. 117. The result, says Dodds, was that "fear of evil spirits was an ever-present source of anxiety to Christian minds" (p. 117n).

[33] *De civitate Dei* 4.19, CCL 47:113; 7.35, CCL 47:215-216; 18.5, CCL 48:597; 18.18, CCL 48:608; *Epist.* 102.3.18, CSEL 34.2:559-560; 102.6.32, CSEL 34.2:572. There was precedent

of them really occurred, even if they cannot be compared with the miracles
of the people of God. Augustine takes the wonders recorded by the ancient
historians quite seriously. The images of the Penates, carried from Troy by
Aeneas, did move themselves from one place to another; Tarquinius did cut
a whetstone with a razor; the serpent from Epidaurus did accompany
Aesculapius on his voyage to Rome; and the vestal virgin who was under
suspicion of having violated her vows did succeed in carrying water from the
Tiber in a sieve.[34] The same is true more generally. Miracles performed by
evil men through demonic forces—miracles of which Christ himself warned
us—are real, and not just apparent.[35]

Augustine sometimes seems to conceive of them as pure trickery, the
equivalent of theatrical spectacles. He seems to imply that the miracles of
Pharaoh's magicians fell into the same category of demonic slight-of-hand.[36]
But this is not the main thrust of his thought. In Augustine's view, wonders
performed through the agency of demons are illusions and deceptions, not
because they are false (although some of them are indeed that), but primarily
because they are designed to lead us into error. We cannot deny the reality
of such miracles without denying the truth of Sacred Scripture itself.[37] Hence
the miracles performed by Pharaoh's magicians were everything they seemed
to be. The power of these magicians was limited, but it was quite real; and
they possessed it on divine licence.[38] It is part of the design of Providence,

---

for such a view in the thought of Tertullian, for example. Cf. H. Remus, "'Magic or Miracle'?
Some Second-Century Instances," *The Second Century* 2 (1982): 127-156, esp. 148-149.

[34] *De civitate Dei* 10.16, CCL 47:290. On Augustine's attitude toward the last of these
examples, see H. Silvestre, "Le 'plus grand miracle' de Jésus," *ABoll* 100 (1982): 1-15 at 8.
Silvestre maintains that Augustine would attribute this particular miracle to the true God rather
than demonic forces, for it functioned to confirm the virgin's innocence.

[35] Matt. 24:23-25; *De sermone Domini in monte* 2.25.84-85, CCL 35:184-185.

[36] *Epist.* 137.4.13, CSEL 44:115. Cf. *De civitate Dei* 10.8, CCL 47:280; *De trinitate* 4.11.14,
CCL 50:179. See also *Vita S. Martini* 23.11, SC 133:306, where Sulpicius Severus tells us of
the wonders performed by the false monk Anatolius. Sulpicius regards them as mere Satanic
illusions that could not deceive Martin: "Unde quis dubitet hanc etiam Martini fuisse virtutem,
ut fantasiam suam diabolus, cum erat Martini oculis ingerenda, dissimulare diutius aut tegere
non posset."

[37] *De doctrina christiana* 2.23.35, CCL 32:57-58; *De civitate Dei* 21.6, CCL 48:767.

[38] *De sermone Domini in monte* 2.25.85, CCL 35:185; *De trinitate* 3.7.12, CCL 50:138-139.
Cf. *De trinitate* 3.7.13, CCL 50:139-141; 3.8.16-17, CCL 50:143-144, where Augustine
explains that evil spirits have no genuine creative power. All things that are generated in
corporeal or visible fashion have their origin in the *rationes seminales* God implanted in
creation. It is by virtue of their superior natures and their superior intelligence that the evil
spirits can perform the wonders they do, but they do so only by actualizing the potential that
God has infused in the natural realm. For further discussion, see below, chapter 8. The fact
remains, however, that their wonders are more than mere appearances. For Augustine, the

says Augustine, that evil men be allowed to perform genuine wonders through the agency of evil spirits. Such miracles serve God's purposes by deceiving the deceitful, warning the faithful, and testing the patience of the just.[39]

Unfortunately, Gregory is not as explicit, and to a certain extent one has to read between the lines to assess his attitude towards the miracles of evildoers. Because of Gregory's alleged disinterest in dealing with the problem of miracles on the ontological level, Boesch Gajano maintains that he uses only moral criteria to distinguish between the miracles of the saints and the miracles of evildoers. Here she seems to be following Boglioni, whose view is fundamentally the same.[40] According to Boglioni, Gregory is apparently ready to acknowledge that heretics, for example, can perform real miracles, but the "reality" of these miracles is never explored. It functions rather as an unexamined postulate to his thought:

> L'absence de définition théorique, tout autant pour la structure ontologique du fait miraculeux que pour les limites exactes des charismes extraordinaires, le conduit à accepter sans problèmes apparents la réalité historique des miracles des hérétiques ou des réprouvés: ce qui les distingue n'est pas une fausseté 'ontologique', ... mais une fausseté 'morale', c'est-à-dire leur intégration différente dans la vie.[41]

There is some truth in this, of course, for Gregory underlines an important moral distinction between the miracles of evildoers and the miracles of the just. The miracles that the elect perform out of charity, the reprobate perform out of pride, and the miracles that saints perform as a manifestation of Christian virtue, heretics perform out of a desire for praise. Clearly the two

---

miracles performed by good and bad angels are indistinguishable, except that demons are not as powerful: cf. *De Genesi ad litteram* 11.29, CSEL 28:362.

[39] *De trinitate* 3.7.12, CCL 50:138-139: "Neque enim parva visibilium miraculorum potentia Iob cuncta quae habebat amisit et filios et ipsam corporis sanitatem" (p. 139).

[40] S. Boesch Gajano, "La proposta agiografica dei 'Dialogi' di Gregorio Magno," *SM* 3rd. ser. 21 (1980): 623-664 at 647n; cf. Boglioni, "Miracle et nature," pp. 100-101.

[41] Boglioni, "Miracle et nature," p. 102. This conclusion reveals tensions in Boglioni's thought. He maintains that, because Gregory is not very interested in exploring the ontological structure of miracle, he is inclined to conceive of the nature of miracle in terms of its moral/pedagogical function: "On dirait que, pour lui, la finalité d'un événement en définit la nature. ... S'ils possèdent une particulière fonction pédagogique ou morale d'avertissement, de prémonition, de consolation, de condamnation, pourquoi dès lors ne pas leur attribuer une particulière origine divine et donc un caractère miraculeux?" (p. 75) However, if this is correct, Gregory's reaction to the miracles of evildoers should have been quite different than what Boglioni suggests it is: because of their defective moral character, Gregory should have been inclined to regard them as false or apparent miracles only.

classes of miracle rest on different moral foundations, and for all practical purposes, this is the only way we can tell them apart.[42] However, Gregory is also aware that questions about the ontological status of these miracles are legitimate. His treatment is not as systematic as one would prefer, but only because he is taking a good deal for granted. If he is read carefully, his view turns out, in the final analysis, to be identical to Augustine's.

In many of the passages that refer to the miracles of evildoers, Gregory offers no comment on their ontological status at all. But these same passages often contain references to Matthew 7:22-23, where Christ says that on the Day of Judgment he will not recognize many who have performed wonders in his name; and usually Christ's words are offered without comment, as if their meaning were obvious. Gregory clearly thinks, therefore, that the miracles in question are quite genuine.[43] His letter of August 598 to the ex-consul Leontius points to this conclusion as well. The reprobate Judas, he observes, performed miracles along with the other apostles. Although he does not expressly say so, Gregory clearly implies that the miracles of Judas were as genuine as those of the other eleven.[44]

Elsewhere Gregory is more explicit. For example, he observes that hypocrites can occasionally perform quite genuine wonders because of the grace they possess. At first glance this is somewhat surprising. Beneath their appearance of sanctity, there is a fundamental evil which will become manifest on the Day of Judgment. True saints concern themselves with both their outward actions and the inner life of their souls, for they seek to provide proper examples to their brethren and to be irreproachable in the sight of God; hypocrites concentrate only on external matters, on putting forth the

---

[42] *Hom. in Ezech.* 2.5.22, CCL 142:292; *Mor.* 20.7.17, CCL 143A:1016. The same can be said of Augustine. Cf. Grange, *Le miracle*, p. 72: "Augustin distingue les vrais miracles de leur contrefaçons démoniaques par leur valeur de signification religieuse. Les vrais miracles sont liés à la seule doctrine religieuse cohérente et morale: le monothéisme; les prodiges païens sont liés à un culte détestable où se mêlent la magie et l'immoralité."

[43] See, for example, *Past.* 1.1, PL 77:15; *Hom. in Evan.* 2.40.3, PL 76:1305; *Ep.* 11.36, CCL 140A:925-929 at 928. The miracles of evil-doers of various kinds are mentioned at several points in the Gospels. See, for example, Matthew 12:22-28; Matthew 24:23-24; and Mark 13:21-22. The significance of these passages is discussed by M. Van Uytfanghe, "La controverse biblique et patristique autour du miracle, et ses répercussions sur l'hagiographie dans l'Antiquité tardive et le haut Moyen Age latin," in *Hagiographie, cultures et sociétés, IVe-XIIe siècles* (Paris, 1981), pp. 205-231 at 208-209: "Le miracle et le merveilleux sont inhérents à la *Weltanschauung* de l'Antiquité biblique comme de l'Antiquité païenne. Dans les Ecritures judéo-chrétiennes, ils sont intégrés dans l'histoire du salut qui est elle-même théocentrique et providentialiste. Mais en même temps, les prodiges qui se font en dehors de ce contexte, et notamment ceux de 'faux prophètes', sont reconnus comme réels."

[44] *Ep.* 8.33, CCL 140A:557-559 at 557-558.

appearance of sanctity to attract the praise of men.[45] They perform miracles for their own glory rather than the greater glory of God, and abuse their divine gift only to achieve their greater damnation. But despite their moral failures, these hypocrites are not without grace, and so the miracles that they sometimes perform are perfectly genuine, even if they are corrupted by their evil purposes.[46]

If hypocrites sometimes perform miracles through the power God has granted them, other evildoers can perform miracles equally genuine, but through Satanic rather than divine influence. In the first book of the *Dialogues* Gregory tells of a noblewoman from Tuscany whose daughter-in-law had been possessed by an evil spirit. Despite the fact that the recently married young woman had indulged in marital relations the night before, she had had the temerity to accompany her mother-in-law to the dedication of the church of Saint Sebastian; her presumption was duly punished when she was seized by an evil spirit at the very moment the relics of the martyr were brought into the chapel. Misguided relatives took her to the local magicians, who successfully cast out the devil; but God immediately sent a whole legion of devils into her, causing wild agitation, until Bishop Fortunatus of Todi, after several days and nights of fervent prayer, finally delivered her from their power.

It is significant that, although the woman's afflictions were not ended until she was brought to the saint, the pagan magicians *were* successful in driving out the first demon. Their influence was not as great as his, but they were capable of working genuine wonders nonetheless by means of the Satanic power (*perversa arte*) that they possessed.[47] The *Dialogues* contain at least one other example of this kind of Satanic power in the more sophisticated magic of Basilius.[48] But for Gregory the clearest instance of such power will

---

[45] *Mor.* 8.46.76, CCL 143:441. Cf. Dagens, *Saint Grégoire le Grand*, p. 197.

[46] *Mor.* 8.42.66, CCL 143:433: "hypocritarum vita ad bona opera infusionem quidem superni muneris percipit; sed in cunctis quae agit exteriores laudes appetens, a fructu perceptae infusionis inanescit. Saepe namque mira signorum opera faciunt, ab obsessis corporibus spiritus pellunt et per prophetiae donum ventura quaeque sciendo praeveniunt; sed tamen a largitore tot munerum cogitationis intentione divisi sunt, quia per eius dona non eius gloriam, sed proprios favores quaerunt. Cumque per accepta bona in sua laude se elevant, ipsis muneribus contra largitorem pugnant. Inde quippe contra dantem superbiunt unde ei amplius humiles esse debuerunt. Sed eo eos postmodum districtior sententia percutit, quo nunc superna bonitas et ingratos largius infundit."

[47] *Dial.* 1.10.1-5, SC 260:92-96, esp. 96.

[48] *Dial.* 1.4.3-6, SC 260:38-42; cf. S. Boesch Gajano, "Dislivelli culturali e mediazioni ecclesiastiche nei *Dialogi* di Gregorio Magno," in *Religioni delle classi popolari*, ed. C. Ginzburg, QS 41 (1979): 398-415 at 404. When magicians were being arrested in Rome, Gregory says, this Basilius disguised himself as a monk, and sought refuge in the monastery

be provided by the Antichrist: the splendour of his wonders will be such as
to eclipse the miracles of even the most celebrated of the saints.[49]

Some of Gregory's statements seem to suggest that the Antichrist will
perform false or counterfeit miracles only. In the thirty-second book of the
Moralia, for example, he describes the different stratagems the Antichrist will
employ on his different victims:

> Indeed, he will then be raised up not by power alone, but will be supported by
> a display of miracles as well. Hence David also says: "He lies in wait secretly,
> just as a lion in his den." In order to make manifest his power, it would have
> been sufficient for him to be a lion, even if he had not been lying in wait.
> Conversely, to account for his hidden acts of cunning, it would have sufficed
> for him to snatch away his victims in ambush, even if he were not a lion. But
> because this ancient enemy will be unchecked in all his forces, he will be
> allowed to rage in both ways, so that in his contest against the elect he may be
> set loose in both his deceit and his virtue: his virtue by means of power, his
> deceit by means of signs. Quite rightly, therefore, is he called both a lion and
> one who lies in ambush: the latter through the appearance of miracles, the
> former through secular strength. Indeed, in order to entice those who are
> openly wicked, he will display secular power; but in order to deceive even the
> just, he will feign holiness with signs. To the former he will commend the
> exaltation of his greatness; the latter he will deceive with a display of sanctity.[50]

The miracles of Antichrist may simply be trickery, for Gregory refers to
the *appearance* of miracles (*miraculorum species*), which he describes as
being a product of cunning (*versutia*) and deceit (*fraus*). However, *species*
is an ambiguous term. Rather than meaning the outer appearance as opposed

---

of the Abbot Equitius. However, Equitius saw him for what he was, and drove him out.
Ultimately, says Gregory, Basilius was burned to death in Rome. Gregory describes him as
a man whose magical powers were unsurpassed: "in magicis operibus primus fuit" (sc
260:38-40). But instead of relating any genuine wonders that Basilius performed, Gregory tells
us only of his claims: "dixit frequenter se cellam Equitii magicis artibus in aera suspendisse,
nec tamen eius quempiam laedere potuisse" (sc 260:42).

[49] For a general overview of the medieval doctrine of the Antichrist, see R.K. Emmerson,
Antichrist in the Middle Ages: A Study of Medieval Apocalypticism, Art and Literature (Seattle,
1981), especially the first three chapters; the range of opinion in medieval thought on the
nature of Antichrist's miracles is discussed on pp. 93-94.

[50] *Mor.* 32.15.25, CCL 143B:1648: "Non enim sola tunc potestate erigitur, sed etiam
signorum ostensione fulcitur. ..." (I have frequently found it necessary to translate Gregory's
present tenses with the English future.) See also *Mor.* 33.27.48, CCL 143B:1714-1716; and
34.18.33, CCL 143B:1757: "sive per se, seu per ministros suos quolibet prodeat, *mendacibus
signis* coruscat"; cf. 2 Thess. 2:8-10. Augustine also refers to the coming persecution of
Antichrist "qua nihil est periculosius, quoniam et violenta et fraudulenta erit. Vim habebit in
imperio, dolum in miraculis" (*Enar. in Psalmos* 9.27, CCL 38:70).

to the reality within, here it more likely means simply the outer appearance or form, that which can be seen. If that is indeed the case, Gregory is not referring to what are only the *apparent* miracles of Antichrist, but rather to his *visible* miracles. His miracles will be quite real, and they will be the products of deceit, not because he will only seem to do what he does, but rather because he will use his wonders for deceitful purposes.[51] In this passage, as elsewhere, Gregory tells us that the Antichrist will use his miraculous powers to give himself the veneer of sanctity: *signis sanctitatem simulat.* But whereas the miracles of the saints are signs of true sanctity, manifestations of the virtue possessed within, the miracles of Antichrist will only appear to be miracles of sanctity. In actuality they will be miracles of false sanctity that disguise his consummate evil and serve only to substantiate his lies.[52]

His campaign of deceit will be successful, for the Antichrist will be resplendent with such great miracles that, were it possible, even the elect would falter.[53] Indeed, he is already having some success, for the contest has already begun. His minions are even now among us, and as their master will do when he ultimately appears, they cover their iniquity with a veil of sanctity: "isti praedicatores antichristi ... sanctitatis sibi speciem arrogant, sed tamen opera iniquitatis exercent."[54] In order to distinguish between genuine virtue and vice disguised as virtue, Gregory tells us that we must become spiritual money-changers. When we are confronted with the miracles of men unknown to us, we must first test the gold, lest what appears to be the product of genuine virtue later turn out to have been corrupted by the bronze of evil intention. We must then check the impression, to ensure that the spiritual coinage we are offered does not bear the mark of error, but rather the seal

---

[51] It seems fairly certain that this was Augustine's view. See *De civitate Dei* 20.19, CCL 48:732-733, where he explicitly considers the alternatives mentioned above. Although he does not commit himself, the reference to Job's afflictions with which he closes clearly indicates a preference: "Non enim quando de caelo ignis cecidit et tantam familiam cum tantis gregibus pecorum sancti Iob uno impetu absumpsit et turbo inruens et domum deiciens filios eius occidit, phantasmata fuerunt; quae tamen fuerunt opera satanae, cui Deus dederat hanc potestatem."

[52] *Mor.* 15.58.69, CCL 143A:793-794: "tantis signis et prodigiis *in sanctitatis ostensione* se elevat, ut argui ab homine eius facta non valeant; quia cum potestate terroris adiunguntur etiam *signa ostensae sanctitatis*"; *Mor.* 32.15.22, CCL 143B:1646: "antichristus ... modo honoribus saeculi, modo signis et prodigiis *fictae sanctitatis* in tumore potentiae elevare permittitur"; *Mor.* 32.15.26, CCL 143B:1649: "Quod enim fallendo dicit, hoc mira faciendo asserit; nam quicquid mendax lingua simulat, hoc quasi verum esse manus operis ostentat." The emphasis has been added.

[53] *Mor.* 33.32.56, CCL 143B:1722.

[54] *Mor.* 33.35.59, CCL 143B:1724.

of the ancient fathers. We must finally test for weight, lest the imperfect be accepted for the perfect, to the undoing of him who receives it. These are tests that the precursors of Antichrist cannot pass:

> How can the preachers of the Antichrist possess the true nature of the [spiritual] coin, they who know not the force of a right intention in these things that they do, because through these things they seek not the heavenly kingdom but the heights of temporal glory? How can they not differ from the form of [true spiritual] money, they who are at variance with all the piety of the just by persecuting the just? How can they display the weight of integrity in themselves? Not only have they in no way pursued the perfection of humility, but they have not reached its very first door. From this, therefore, from this the elect may learn how they may despise their signs, the signs of those whose action truly assails all that memory records as having been done by the holy fathers.[55]

At the coming of Antichrist himself, however, the trials of the faithful will be much greater than they are at present, for just before his appearance the saints will discover their own power of miracles greatly diminished. They will not be deprived of the grace of miracles entirely, but in comparison with those of the Antichrist the miracles of the saints will seem insignificant. All this will fulfill the marvelous dispensation of God. It will work both to manifest the depravity of the evil, who regard everything the church represents as of no account if it is not buttressed by visible signs, and to augment the reward of the good, who venerate the church, not because of miracles, but because of the hope of things celestial.

The virtue of the faithful will ultimately prove stronger than all the wonders of the Antichrist; and in overcoming him without the benefit of miracles of their own, their victory will be all the more secure, all the more praiseworthy.[56] But the temptation they will suffer on the road to their final triumph will be severe. Even the elect will be seriously shaken by doubt, suffering what Gregory calls a darkening of vision, although the wiles of Antichrist will be of no avail in the end against those predestined for salvation.[57] The miracles

---

[55] *Mor.* 33.35.60, CCL 143B:1724-1726, esp. 1725-1726. The imagery of the spiritual money-changer is derived from Cassian, although Cassian employs it to somewhat different purpose; cf. *Coll.* 1.20-22, CSEL 13:29-34.

[56] *Mor.* 34.3.7, CCL 143B:1738.

[57] On the temptation of the faithful, see *Mor.* 32.15.24, CCL 143B:1648: "Pensemus ergo quae erit humanae mentis illa temptatio, quando pius martyr et corpus tormentis subicit, et tamen ante eius oculos miracula tortor facit. Cuius tunc virtus non ab ipso cogitationum fundo quatiatur, quando is qui flagris cruciat signis coruscat?" On the elect, see *Mor.* 33.35.60, CCL 143B:1726: "ipsi quoque electi dum tot signa conspiciunt ... quoddam dubietatis nubilum in corde patiuntur; quia dum se per prodigia illius malitia elevat, in istis aliquatenus visus certior caligat." Cf. *Mor.* 33.36.61, CCL 143B:1726: "Fumus ergo de eius naribus procedere dicitur,

of Antichrist will have this effect because they will be perfectly genuine. If Gregory at times calls them false, it is not because they will lack reality, but is rather because they will be designed to lead men astray. Indeed, they will be effected by Satan who, despite his fall, has lost none of his supernatural power; although it is now restrained by the dispensation of God, it will then be loosed in the person of his servant.[58]

The miracles to which Gregory devotes most of his attention are, of course, the miracles of the saints. Unlike the miracles of all evildoers, these are performed with divine blessing; God does not merely permit them to occur for the achievement of his purposes, but actively sponsors them, and so they can be regarded as signs of divine favour. But because physical miracles that are perfectly genuine can be performed by both the good and the wicked, Gregory emphasizes that the miracles of greatest import are miracles of the spiritual order—miracles of conversion, for example.[59] The preeminent importance of miracles of this sort is unequivocally stated for Peter's benefit in the *Dialogues*. When Peter declares that, as far as he is concerned, the greatest miracles are those in which the dead are revived, Gregory replies that this is undoubtedly true when we consider only visible reality. "But if we consider the invisible, then it becomes evident that to convert a sinner by preaching the word of God to him and aiding him with our prayers is a greater miracle than raising to life the physically dead. For in the latter case the flesh is brought back to life, only to die again; in the former, the soul is brought to life for all eternity."[60]

---

quia de miraculorum eius insidiis ad momentum caligosa dubietas etiam in electorum corde generatur." On their final triumph, see *Mor.* 33.36.61, CCL 143B:1726.

[58] *Mor.* 32.15.22, CCL 143B:1646-1647. On the relationship between Antichrist and Satan, see H. Savon, "L'Antéchrist dans l'oeuvre de Grégoire le Grand," in *Grégoire le Grand*, Chantilly, 15-19 septembre 1982 (Paris, 1986), pp. 389-404.

[59] He refers to one of these miracles in his letter of August 599 to Reccared (*Ep.* 9.229, CCL 140A:805-811 at 805-806). Here Gregory rejoices over the conversion of the Visigoths, calling it a new miracle in our days: "Audita quippe *novi diebus nostris* virtute *miraculi*, quod per excellentiam tuam cuncta Gothorum gens ab errore haereseos Arrianae in fidei rectae soliditate translata est, exclamare cum propheta libet: 'Haec est immutatio dexterae excelsi.'" The emphasis has been added. Cf. *In 1 Reg.* 5.118, CCL 144:492-493.

[60] *Dial.* 3.17.7, Zimmerman 147, SC 260:340. Cf. *In 1 Reg.* 5.34, CCL 144:441. Augustine had earlier made the same point (cf. *Enar. in Psalmos* 9.2, CCL 38:59; *In Iohannis Evangelium* 49.2, CCL 36:420; *Sermo* 98.1.1, PL 38:591); and it was later repeated by Gregory's earliest biographer (cf. *Vita S. Gregorii*, chap. 6, Colgrave 82). However, the perspective of Sulpicius Severus was significantly different; cf. *Dial.* 1.24, CSEL 1:177, where Sulpicius argues that Martin was undoubtedly greater than the saints of the desert precisely because he was able to raise a dead man to life.

This idea is developed in the twenty-ninth homily on the Gospels, where
Gregory preaches on Mark 16:15-18. Christ enjoins the disciples to go out
and preach the Gospel to the whole creation, promising that those who
believe will be entrusted with miraculous powers: "In my name they will cast
out demons; they will speak in new tongues; they will pick up serpents, and
if they drink any deadly thing, it will not hurt them; they will lay their hands
on the sick, and they will recover." Lest any of his congregation falter in their
faith because they are incapable of performing such wonders, Gregory points
out that today the Holy Church often performs spiritually the miracles the
apostles performed corporeally. When priests lay their hands upon believers
in the sacrament of exorcism, what are they doing but driving out demons?
When the faithful abandon the worldly discourse of the old life and offer up
their voices in praise of their Creator, what are they doing but speaking in
new tongues? When by their exhortation they remove the evil in the hearts
of others, they, as it were, pick up serpents; when they are exposed to evil
counsel but do not yield to the temptation, they drink in a poisonous
substance, but it does them no harm; and when by their good example they
strengthen those who are stumbling in their efforts to live the Christian life,
like the apostles they lay their hands upon the sick and are the instruments
of their recovery. By the grace of God, Gregory continues, such spiritual
miracles are within the power of every Christian, and indeed are greater than
any physical miracles that might be performed, because by them not simply
bodies but souls are revived.[61]

Although one of the spiritual miracles here discussed is a function of
sacramental power, the others, which presumably are within the power of all
the faithful, consist simply of living a life of Christian virtue. It is these
miracles of virtue that the faithful should desire. Although they may not win
renown among men, they are rewarded in heaven. These are the miracles
essential to sanctity; physical miracles merely demonstrate it: "corporalia illa
miracula ostendunt aliquando sanctitatem, non autem faciunt; haec vero
spiritalia, quae aguntur in mente, virtutem vitae non ostendunt, sed faciunt."
Physical miracles do not have any intrinsic value; they are simply outward
manifestations of the virtue the saints possess within.[62] As Marc Doucet puts

---

[61] *Hom. in Evan.* 2.29.4, PL 76:1215-1216. Cf. Augustine, *Sermo* 88.3.3, PL 38:540, ed.
P.-P. Verbraken, "Le sermon LXXXVIII de saint Augustin sur la guérison des deux aveugles de
Jéricho," *RBén.* 94 (1984): 71-101 at 76; Caesarius of Arles, *Sermo* 168.5, CCL 104:690;
John Cassian, *Coll.* 12.12, CSEL 13:353-356, esp. 355; 15.8, CSEL 13:434. See also F. Heiler,
"Vom Naturwunder zum Geisteswunder. Der Wandel des primitiven Wunderglaubens in der
hohen Religion," in *Festschrift Walter Baetke* (Weimar, 1966), pp. 151-166.
[62] See *Dial.* 1.12.6, SC 260:118, where Peter confesses that "vita et non signa quaerenda
sunt. ... ipsa signa quae fiunt, bonae vitae testimonium ferunt." See also *Hom. in Ezech.* 2.5.22,

it: "ce sont des signes et ce ne sont que des signes ... d'une realité qui, elle seule, importe au fond: la réalité intérieure de sainteté."[63]

CCL 142:292, where Gregory says of the miracles of the saints: "de eis foris ostenditur quales apud omnipotentem Dominum intus habeantur"; and 2.3.23, CCL 142:255, where he says of the Biblical saints, and in a context that clearly establishes that he has their miracles in mind: "quam pii, quam humiles, quam benigni exstiterint, eorum testantur operationes."

[63] M. Doucet, "Pédagogie et théologie dans la 'Vie de saint Benoît' par saint Grégoire le Grand," *CCist.* 38 (1976): 158-173 at 166. Cf. Dagens, *Saint Grégoire le Grand*, p. 231, where he speaks of "la théorie grégorienne des miracles: l'extérieur est ... le signe efficace de l'intérieur; il est signe puisqu'il invite à prendre en considération ce qui est invisible et se déroule au-dedans de l'homme." Dagens notes that the frequency and diversity of context of expressions of interiority and exteriority—adjectives like *interior/exterior*, or adverbs like *intus/foris, interius/exterius, intrinsecus/extrinsecus*—suggest a fundamental structural element in Gregory's thought: "Ne s'agit-il pas là d'une véritable 'structure', antérieure à tout contenu théologique particulier et qui se prête à de multiples applications dans des domaines très divers?" (p. 133) See also P. Aubin, "Intériorité et extériorité dans les Moralia in Job de saint Grégoire le Grand," *RSR* 62 (1974): 117-166.

4

Miracles and Virtue

The demonstrative role Gregory assigns to miracles—"miracula ostendunt aliquando sanctitatem, non autem faciunt"[1]—has caused many scholars to argue that miracles in the *Dialogues* serve primarily, if not exclusively, to emphasize the importance of sanctity of life and to encourage its pursuit. Thus, while acknowledging Peter's role in bringing out the spiritual significance of the miracle stories, Dagens says:

> La fonction de Pierre, et, par suite, l'intention de Grégoire, consistent à ménager une transition entre le miracle, en tant qu'événement extérieur, et les réalités intérieures, dont il est le signe. ... On devine qu'en fin de compte, le but de Grégoire est plus que celui d'un hagiographe, qu'il est plutôt celui d'un moraliste, d'un auteur spirituel, qui n'a entrepris de raconter les hauts faits des Pères d'Italie que pour inciter ceux qui l'écoutent à rentrer en eux-mêmes et à progresser sur le chemin de l'intériorité, en méditant ces *exempla* de sainteté.[2]

The miracles of the saints provide graphic illustrations of the central patterns of Christian sanctity, which Gregory hopes his readers can be encouraged to emulate. Hence the purpose of miracle stories would be similar to the purpose Gregory attributes to the lives of the saints in general. These also are models, as he explains in his *Homilies on Ezechiel*, that help us to advance in the virtues.[3]

---

[1] *Hom. in Evan.* 2.29.4, PL 76:1216.

[2] Cl. Dagens, *Saint Grégoire le Grand. Culture et expérience chrétiennes* (Paris, 1977), p. 230. Cf. F. Tateo, "La struttura dei Dialoghi di Gregorio Magno," *VetC* 2 (1965): 101-127 at 127; B. de Gaiffier, "Miracles bibliques et vies de saints," in his *Etudes critiques d'hagiographie et d'iconologie* (Brussels, 1967), pp. 50-61 at p. 55; P. Boglioni, "Miracle et nature chez Grégoire le Grand," in *Cahiers d'études médiévales* 1: *Epopées, légendes et miracles* (Montreal and Paris, 1974), pp. 11-102 at pp. 95-97; A. de Vogüé, *Grégoire le Grand, Dialogues* 1: *Introduction, bibliographie et cartes* (Paris, 1978), pp. 48, 86.

[3] *Hom. in Ezech.* 2.5.21, CCL 142:291. Cf. M. Doucet, "Pédagogie et théologie dans la 'Vie de saint Benoît' par saint Grégoire le Grand," *CCist.* 38 (1976): 158-173 at 158.

By Gregory's time of writing this was a quite traditional view of the purpose of hagiography,[4] although at first glance at least Gregory's endorsement of it seems incongruous. It was obviously appropriate to hagiographers writing about essentially clerical or monastic saints for an essentially clerical or monastic audience. But it does not seem quite so appropriate for Gregory, who, as we have already seen, did not wish the *Dialogues* to be limited to such a restricted readership. Precisely how, we might ask, could the lay audience that Gregory hoped to reach possibly be expected to imitate the saintly heroes of the *Dialogues*, most of whom were clerics, and clerics of the highest stature?[5] Even when allowances are made for the layman's very different mode of life, we are still left with the fact that, by definition, the saint is an individual of exceptional merit, whom the average Christian might well venerate, but would probably despair of ever being able to imitate.[6]

In view of these difficulties, it should be no surprise that, in the *Dialogues*, Gregory retreats a little from the idea of imitation. He points out explicitly, for example, that Honoratus of Fondi cannot serve as a model of education in the spiritual life. Honoratus was blessed by the indwelling of the Holy Spirit, made manifest both in his miraculous powers and in his remarkable humility. He therefore had no need of any human instruction whatever, but was taught the principles of the monastic life directly by the Holy Spirit himself. If lesser men, in the vain presumption that they too were filled with the Holy Spirit, were to attempt to follow his example, instead of reaching heights of sanctity they might become teachers of error. Honoratus, therefore, is to be venerated, not imitated, for his case was a clear exception to the rule that normally applies.[7]

The exceptional character and life of Abbot Equitius also could not be imitated, not even by his own monks. While he was a young man Equitius

---

[4] Cf. Athanasius, *Vita S. Antonii*, Prooemium, PG 26:838; chap. 89, PG 26:967; Sulpicius Severus, *Vita S. Martini* 1.6-9, SC 133:252-254; Rufinus, *Historia monachorum*, Prol., PL 21:387-388; Palladius, *Historia Lausiaca*, Prooemium, ed. E.C. Butler (Cambridge, 1898-1904), 2:3; Gregory of Tours, *Liber vitae patrum*, Praef., MGH, SRM 1.2, p. 212.

[5] J.-C. Poulin, *L'idéal de sainteté dans l'Aquitaine carolingienne d'après les sources hagiographiques (750-950)* (Quebec, 1975), pp. 119-125, points out that similar difficulties arose for the hagiographers of the Carolingian period, some of whom explicitly renounced the idea that the lives of the saints are offered for the general imitation of the faithful.

[6] H. Delehaye, *Sanctus: Essai sur le culte des saints dans l'antiquité* (Brussels, 1927), p. 236. On the prevalence of the imitation-topos in early medieval hagiography and its problematic nature, cf. F. Graus, *Volk, Herrscher und Heiliger im Reich der Merowinger. Studien zur Hagiographie der Merowingerzeit* (Praha, 1965), pp. 446-448.

[7] *Dial.* 1.1.6, SC 260:22. As Gregory explains: "Usus quidem rectae conversationis est, ut praeesse non audeat qui subesse non didicerit, nec oboedientiam subiectis imperet, quam praelatis non novit exhibere."

suffered severely because of temptations of the flesh. But one night he experienced a vision of his being made a eunuch, and from then on the temptations ceased, never to return again. "Relying on this virtue, which God had helped him to acquire," says Gregory, "he took upon himself the guidance of communities of women just as he had done of monks. Yet he warned his disciples to be distrustful of themselves and not to be too eager to follow his example, for they would be the cause of their own downfall in trying to do what God had not given them the power to do."[8]

Unlike Christ's actions, then, the actions of the saints cannot be imitated in detail.[9] However, we *can* draw inspiration from the general tenor of their lives, the pattern of sanctity revealed in their day-to-day experience. Their example can spur to action those on whom mere precept and admonition are often wasted.[10] In the *Dialogues* Peter maintains that the lives of the saints can have a twofold effect. They can be humbling: if we have too high an opinion of our own worth, it is salutary to learn of others who have done better. However, they can also offer positive encouragement: when we compare ourselves with the saints who have gone before, their example can fill us with a longing for the future life.[11]

Essentially the same view is detailed in the *Moralia*. There Gregory explains that the lives of the saints can bring us to self-knowledge, to a realization of our sinful nature, which otherwise is difficult to obtain. Any attempt to examine the condition of our own souls without the lives of the saints to instruct us will fail to grasp our real sinfulness. We need to measure ourselves against the standards they represent to realize how far short we have fallen from the good.[12] Elsewhere in the *Moralia* Gregory remarks that an awareness of the good deeds of others is often accompanied by increased concern about our own possible damnation. The lives of the saints, who were frequently afflicted with torments during their earthly pilgrimage, can make us more aware of the punishment that might be ours if we fail to make amends. If God could inflict such trials on the saints whom he undoubtedly

---

[8] *Dial.* 1.4.2, Zimmerman 16, sc 260:38.

[9] *Dial.* 1.9.7, sc 260:80: "Redemptor noster per mortale corpus omne quod egit, hoc nobis in exemplum actionis praebuit, ut pro nostrarum virium modolo eius vestigia sequentes, inoffenso pede operis praesentis vitae carpamus viam."

[10] Gregory frequently emphasizes the efficacy of good examples. See, for example, *Past.* 2.3, pl 77:28: "Sit rector operatione praecipuus, ut vitae viam subditis vivendo denuntiet, et grex qui pastoris vocem moresque sequitur, per exempla melius quam per verba gradiatur."

[11] *Dial.* 1 Prol. 9, sc 260:16.

[12] *Mor.* 24.8.15, ccl 143b:1197-1199. Cf. *Dial.* 3.37.22, sc 260:426: "numquam peccatores ad lamentum paenitentiae redirent, si nulla essent bonorum exempla quae eorum mentem traherent."

loved, what sort of punishment is in store for us, who have much less claim on his mercy? But in the same passage Gregory also observes that the lives of the saints do not leave us paralyzed before the prospect of eternal torment. In offering us examples of good actually accomplished, by illustrating that the demands of the Christian life *can* be fulfilled, the saints also incite us to good action.[13]

The miracles of the saints function in the same way: as *exempla*, as signs of virtue that have been granted to stimulate others to good works. Peter makes the point at the very outset of the *Dialogues*: interrupting the study of Scripture for miracle stories should not be a matter of grave concern, for "the amount of edification to be gained from a description of miracles is just as great. An explanation of holy Scripture teaches us how to attain virtue and persevere in it, whereas a description of miracles shows us how this acquired virtue reveals itself in those who persevere in it."[14] When the *Dialogues* are examined against this background, and when we remember that their author, along with Origen, has been considered one of the two great masters of the tropological sense,[15] the most striking feature of many of the miracles there recorded, their moral content, is no longer surprising. Miracles are signs of sanctity, containing implicit instruction on the nature of the Christian life for the edification of Gregory's readers.

Boglioni believes that Gregory's failure to make clear the precise connection between *miraculum* and *aedificatio* causes difficulties:

> Il existe donc dans les miracles une valeur d'édification qui provient du fait que s'ils ne constituent pas la sainteté, toutefois ils la révèlent et ont en eux une capacité de stimulation psychologique que la sainteté à elle seule ne possède que pour un cercle restreint de personnes. Nulle part Grégoire ne décrit avec quelque précision *comment* se produit concrètement ce processus d'influence psychologique et sociale, c'est-à-dire quel est le lien entre les *exempla virtutum* (ou *miracula*) et l'*aedificatio* qui en procède, mais il semble qu'il pense aux miracles comme à une théophanie qui ouvre à l'homme, à travers l'expérience de la puissance divine, une trouée sur la Jérusalem céleste: "Magna aedificatio vitae est videre viros mira facientes, atque in civibus suis Hierusalem coelestem in terra conspicere."[16]

---

[13] *Mor.* 9.59.89-90, CCL 143:520. Cf. Delehaye, *Sanctus*, pp. 260-261.

[14] *Dial.* 1 Prol. 9, Zimmerman 6, SC 260:16. Cf. *Hom. in Ezech.* 2.5.22, CCL 142:292: "plerumque Sanctis etiam et in locis sublimioribus positis, ut ad bona opera alii provocentur, virtutes et signa dantur."

[15] H. de Lubac, *Exégèse médiévale. Les quatre sens de l'Ecriture*, part 1, vol. 2 (Paris, 1959), p. 558.

[16] Boglioni, "Miracle et nature," p. 96. Boglioni quotes *Dial.* 3.35.6, SC 260:406.

However, this makes things unnecessarily difficult. The simple fact of the matter is that on a number of occasions the moral import of Gregory's story is clearly discernible. In the first book of the *Dialogues*, for instance, we read that, while he was still a young man living at home, Boniface of Ferentis often used to give away even the clothes on his back to those in need, although in so doing he suffered the rebukes of his mother: "By divesting his body in this way, he wished to clothe his soul in the sight of God with merits for heaven." One day his mother went to the granary and was distressed to discover that Boniface had given away almost all the wheat that had been set aside that year. But God rewarded this generosity; in answer to his servant's prayer he replaced the wheat that had been given away by wheat in even greater abundance.[17] The lesson in Christian charity this episode contains is so obvious that Gregory does not even comment on it.

In the same first book of the *Dialogues* Gregory tells the story of how the Abbot Equitius, who was remarkable for his humility, subdued the proud and sometimes insolent men who were disdainful of his simple manner and jealous of what they regarded as a threat to their prerogatives. Although he was not ordained, Equitius received a private vision authorizing him to preach the Gospel in the countryside surrounding his monastery. When this raised the hackles of curial officials in Rome, the pope (probably Agapitus I [535-536][18]) agreed to have Equitius summoned to his court to give an account of himself. But Equitius never made the journey. His humble manner vanquished the pride of those who had been dispatched to fetch him. Indeed, heaven itself came to his defence by sending the pontiff a terrifying vision, which led to the cancellation of the order. Again, the moral point is sufficiently clear in the story itself, but Gregory, as usual, takes pains to ensure that Peter has grasped it:

> Now mark well, Peter, how those who have learned to despise themselves in this life enjoy the protection of God. Since they are not ashamed to accept dishonour among men, they receive a spiritual rank among most honorable citizens. On the other hand, God sees how truly despicable those men are who, moved by a desire for the empty glory of this life, plume themselves with greatness in their own and in their neighbours' eyes. It is to such that Christ, the Truth, says: "You are always courting the approval of men, but God sees

---

[17] *Dial.* 1.9.16-17, Zimmerman 40, sc 260:90.

[18] A. de Vogüé, "Le pape qui persécuta saint Equitius. Essai d'identification," *ABoll.* 100 (1982): 319-325. However, the identification is not certain. J.M. Petersen, *The Dialogues of Gregory the Great in their Late Antique Cultural Background* (Toronto, 1984), p. 79, maintains that the pope in question was probably John III (561-574).

your hearts; and what is highly esteemed among men is an abomination in God's sight."[19]

It is interesting that the *Dialogues*, especially when compared with the work of Gregory's famous contemporary Gregory of Tours, devote relatively little attention to miracles that transpire at the tombs of the saints. As de Vogüé suggests: "Autant l'oeuvre de Grégoire de Tours abonde en histoires de ce genre, autant les Dialogues en sont pauvres."[20] Gregory does mention both the many wonders being worked at the tomb of Fortunatus of Todi and the miracles Saint Benedict continued to perform in the cave at Subiaco. Several passages in the *Dialogues* also refer in general to the miraculous powers of holy bodies, or to the miracles performed by martyrs for the faith both at their tombs and elsewhere.[21] Indeed, in book four Gregory argues that miracles that occur at the tombs of the martyrs provide a *prima facie* case for the immortality of the soul.[22] But the number of specific miracles credited to the influence of saints who have departed this life is really quite small.[23] This is probably no more than we should expect if the primary purpose of miracles is to illustrate virtue. The miracles of living saints can provide vivid demonstration of how God honours specific virtues, such as charity in the case

---

[19] *Dial.* 1.4.9-18, Zimmerman 19-23 at 23, SC 260:46-54 at 54.

[20] De Vogüé, *Introduction*, p. 94. The contrast has frequently been noted; see, for example, Petersen, *The Dialogues*, esp. pp. 140-141. Petersen also argues that it was primarily authors who were influenced by Eastern Christendom who chose to emphasize the miracles of living saints, whereas those more clearly in the Western Christian tradition tended to emphasize the miracles that occurred at the tombs of the saints. However, she admits that no hard and fast distinction is possible on this basis. Cf. also her "Dead or Alive? The Holy Man as Healer in East and West in the Late Sixth Century," *JMH* 9 (1983): 91-98.

[21] See, for example, *Dial.* 2.38.3, SC 260:246-248; 3.21.5, SC 260:354-356; and 4.21, SC 265:78. On Fortunatus and Benedict, see *Dial.* 1.10.18, SC 260:108-110; and *Dial.* 2.38.1, SC 260:246.

[22] *Dial.* 4.6.1-2, SC 265:40. Cf. Gregory of Tours, *Liber in gloria confessorum*, chap. 52, MGH, SRM 1.2, p. 329.

[23] A catalogue of the more striking of these miracles would include two at the tomb of Equitius (*Dial.* 1.4.20-21, SC 260:56-58), and one each at Saint Benedict's cave at Subiaco (*Dial.* 2.38.1, SC 260:246), the tomb of a pious priest of Valeria (*Dial.* 3.22, SC 260:356-358), the tomb of the holy abbot of St Peter's at Palestrina (*Dial.* 3.23, SC 260:358-360), and the bier of the deacon Paschasius (*Dial.* 4.42.2, SC 265:152). To this list we should probably add Gregory's account of the miraculous properties of the cloak of Euthicius (*Dial.* 3.15.18, SC 260:326), and the episode in which Libertinus of Fondi raises a dead child to life by means of the sandal of his former abbot, Honoratus (*Dial.* 1.2.5-7, SC 260:28-30). In the latter case, however, Gregory explains that the miracle must be credited to both Libertinus and Honoratus, and to the faith of the dead child's mother as well. For a more complete list, see de Vogüé, *Introduction*, p. 94.

of Boniface of Ferentis, or humility in the case of the Abbot Equitius. But generally speaking the miracles of dead saints cannot. They might confirm that the general tenor of their earthly lives conformed to the saintly pattern. Indeed, as Gregory explicitly acknowledges, the fact that God continues to honour them through their miracles implies as much.[24] But since these miracles usually are not linked to specific human actions by the saints, they cannot serve to demonstrate the specific virtues with which they might have been endowed.

It is also noteworthy that the *Dialogues* reveal a curious ambivalence in Gregory's use of the term *virtus*. *Virtus/virtutes* appears for the first time in the prologue to book one, in Peter's declaration:

> Non valde in Italia aliquorum vitam *virtutibus* fulsisse cognovi. Ex quorum igitur conparatione accenderis ignoro. Et quidem bonos viros in hac terra fuisse non dubito, signa tamen atque *virtutes* aut ab eis nequaquam factas existimo, aut ita sunt hactenus silentio suppressa, ut utrumne sint facta nesciamus.

In the first line of this passage the virtues Gregory has in mind are clearly moral virtues, and so Zimmerman quite properly translates: "I do not know of any persons in Italy whose lives give evidence of extraordinary spiritual power." In line four, however, *virtutes* is linked with *signa*, and is qualified by the passive participle *factas*, indicating that it is miracles Gregory intends. Zimmerman correctly translates: "... but to my knowledge no signs or miracles have been performed by any of them; or, if they have been, they were till now kept in such secrecy that we cannot even tell if they occurred."

This ambivalence persists in another of Peter's statements a few lines later:

> Vellem quaerenti mihi de eis aliqua narrares, neque hoc pro re interrumpere expositionis studium grave videatur, quia non dispar aedificatio oritur ex memoria *virtutum*. In expositione quippe qualiter invenienda atque tenenda sit *virtus* agnoscitur, in narratione vero signorum cognoscimus inventa ac retenta qualiter declaratur.

The context clearly establishes that, in this passage, *virtutum* means "miracles," whereas *virtus* means "virtue." In Zimmerman's translation: "... the amount of edification to be gained from a description of *miracles* is just as great. An explanation of holy Scripture teaches us how to attain *virtue* and

---

[24] See *Dial.* 1.4.20, SC 260:56, where one of the wonders that occurred at the tomb of Equitius is described as having taken place "ut palam cuncti cognoscerent quanti esset meriti is cuius illic corpus iacerit." See also *Dial.* 3.15.19, SC 260:326, where, after describing the miraculous rain-making qualities of the cloak of Euthicius, Gregory says: "Ex qua re patuit eius anima quid virtutis intus, quid meriti haberet, cuius foris ostensa vestis iram conditoris averteret."

persevere in it, whereas a description of miracles shows us how this acquired virtue reveals itself in those who persevere in it."[25]

Boesch Gajano maintains that such ambivalent terminology reveals Gregory's conceptual uncertainty, but this is improbable. It was simply a linguistic matter, and it is highly unlikely that it betrays any fundamental confusion. Rather than being distinctive to Gregory's usage, the play on the word *virtus* can be found in other authors as well, and none of them betrays any lack of awareness of the difference between external miracle and internal virtue. Although several writers were capable of using the same term to mean now the one and now the other, nothing suggests that they were unaware of the differences in possible meaning.[26]

Nevertheless, this ambiguity introduces an uncertainty about the precise relationship between miracles and virtue. Does it serve to minimize the significance of miracles, in which case they are to be considered simply as signs of virtue? Or does it rather serve to enhance their independent value, in which case miracles are to be regarded as virtues in and of themselves?[27] In Gregory's case the weight of the evidence suggests the former alternative. The ambiguous use of the word *virtus* serves to underline the important connection between miracle and moral virtue. It provides lexical reinforcement for a central fact: above all a miracle is an *ostensio* or *declaratio virtutis* that can awaken those who are privileged to witness it to the fundamental importance of Christian virtue,[28] and hence be productive of a genuine inner transformation. We must be careful to avoid precipitate judgment, however. That Gregory considers a miracle primarily an *ostensio virtutis* is undeniable; whether this can be said of all of the miracles he records is another matter entirely.

It is abundantly clear that, for Gregory, miracles cannot be gratuitous wonders. He was compulsively interested in the larger religious significance that his miracle stories possessed. In this respect the difference between Gregory the Great and Gregory of Tours could scarcely have been wider.[29]

---

[25] *Dial.* 1 Prol. 7, 9, Zimmerman 5-6, SC 260:14, 16. The emphasis has been added.

[26] See, for example, Sulpicius Severus, *Dial.* 1.10, CSEL 1:161-162; and John Cassian, *Coll.* 15.6, CSEL 13:431-432. Cf. S. Boesch Gajano, "La proposta agiografica dei 'Dialogi' di Gregorio Magno," *SM* 3rd. ser. 21 (1980): 623-664 at 640.

[27] Cf. Poulin, *L'idéal de sainteté*, pp. 113-115.

[28] Cf. de Vogüé, *Introduction*, p. 48; Boglioni, "Miracle et nature," p. 102.

[29] See Dagens, *Saint Grégoire le Grand*, pp. 278-280; and S. Boesch Gajano, "'Narratio' e 'expositio' nei Dialoghi di Gregorio Magno," *BISIAM* 88 (1979): 1-33, esp. p. 19. However, cf. G. Cracco, "Uomini di Dio e uomini di chiesa nell'alto medioevo (per una reinterpretazione dei 'Dialogi' di Gregorio Magno)," *RSSR* n.s. 12 (1977): 163-202. Cracco acknowledges that, beginning with the earliest commentators, the religious significance of the

Gregory the Great was obviously very concerned that his stories be accepted as factually true, and so throughout the *Dialogues* he insists on their factual credibility by citing qualified witnesses. This is an issue to which we shall return in chapter five. But he was equally concerned about religious credibility. There are very few miracles that are not supported by reference to their witnesses; there are also very few that are not accompanied by an explanation or interpretation designed to bring out their religious significance. As Boesch Gajano puts it, "Il 'fatto' miraculoso presente nella realtà del suo tempo è accettato e narrato solo spiegandolo, rendendolo credibile a livello religioso ufficiale, attribuendogli una precisa funzione pedagogica e inserendolo organicamente nella sfera della riflessione teologica e morale."[30] Throughout the *Dialogues* narratives of miracles constantly alternate with passages of edification, the importance of which is established, not only by their number, but by the care invested in their composition.[31] Even if, as Boesch Gajano suggests, no less an authority than the Venerable Bede conceived of the *Dialogues* as a simple collection of wonder tales,[32] a cursory examination is sufficient to convince one of the inadequacy of such a view. Rather, they must be considered an integral part of Gregory's pastoral function.[33] Whenever

---

Dialogues has been thought to be of primary importance (pp. 169-170). But he maintains that the *Dialogues* have been systematically, and perhaps perversely, misinterpreted (p. 202), for it is the miracles themselves that are important, as manifestations of God's direct intervention in human affairs.

   For the most part, Gregory of Tours is content to celebrate the miracle-working powers of the saints he exalts; unlike Gregory the Great, he seems largely unaware of any larger spiritual significance of their miracles. Cf. S. Boesch Gajano, "Il santo nella visione storiografica di Gregorio di Tours," in *Gregorio di Tours* (Todi, 1977), pp. 27-91, esp. 89-90; O. Giordano, "Sociologia e patologia del miracolo in Gregorio di Tours," *Helikon* 18-19 (1978-1979): 161-209, esp. 165. However, see also E. Delaruelle, "La spiritualité des pèlerinages à Saint-Martin de Tours du Ve au Xe siècle," in *Pellegrinaggi e culto di santi in Europa fino alla Ia crociata* (Todi, 1963), pp. 199-243, esp. pp. 215-220; J. Schlick, "Composition e chronologie des *De virtutibus sancti Martini* de Grégoire de Tours," *SPatr.* 7 (1966): 278-286; C.E. Stancliffe, "From Town to Country: The Christianisation of the Touraine, 370-600," in *The Church in Town and Countryside* (Oxford, 1979), pp. 43-59, esp. pp. 56-57.

   [30] Boesch Gajano, "La proposta agiografica," p. 645.

   [31] Tateo, "La struttura," p. 117.

   [32] Boesch Gajano, "'Narratio' e 'expositio'," p. 1. It seems clear, however, that Boesch Gajano does not do Bede full justice. Cf. *Historia ecclesiastica* 2.1, ed. B. Colgrave and R.A.B. Mynors (Oxford, 1969), p. 128: "Libros etiam Dialogorum IIII fecit, in quibus rogatu Petri diaconi sui virtutes sanctorum, quos in Italia clariores nosse vel audire poterat, ad exemplum vivendi posteris collegit ut, sicut in libris expositionum suarum quibus sit virtutibus insudandum edocuit, ita etiam descriptis sanctorum miraculis quae virtutum earundem sit claritas ostenderet."

   [33] Hence Puzicha can emphasize "die grundlegend pastorale Funktion der Wunder-erzählungen," and Boesch Gajano can refer to the *Dialogues* as a whole as "il capolavoro del

Gregory indulges in miracle stories, whether in the *Dialogues* or in his *Homilies on the Gospels*, he intends them to edify, a task at which they can be particularly effective for those who are moved more by examples than by words.[34]

One of the clearest illustrations of Gregory's concern with edification is a story that occurs in the first book of the *Dialogues*.[35] Bishop Fortunatus of Todi, famous for his extraordinary power over evil spirits, had one day successfully exorcised a demon. But instead of quitting the region entirely, the evil spirit masqueraded as a pilgrim, and paraded up and down the streets complaining that Fortunatus had thrown him out of his lodging and left him without shelter for the night. One of the citizens of the town who heard his complaint invited the stranger into his own home, and while they were talking the evil spirit suddenly seized his little boy and cast him into the hearth, where he was consumed by the flames.

Our immediate reaction to this story, like Peter's, is one of puzzlement. It scarcely seems appropriate material for Christian edification. The unfortunate man who was the victim of the devil's spite had demonstrated the charity due to strangers, as was his Christian duty, only to suffer an enormous crime against his family. Gregory is able to find a lesson nonetheless. He explains, with the full benefit of hindsight, that the man lost his son because of his misguided intention. Not a desire to show mercy, but rather an interest in defaming the bishop had motivated him: "He wished to appear more righteous than the bishop, by receiving a person whom the bishop had rejected." The lesson of the episode is plain: "many things are good only in appearance but not in reality, because they do not flow from good motives...."

---

genio pastorale di Gregorio Magno." See Boesch Gajano, "'Narratio' e 'expositio'," p. 33; and M. Puzicha, "*Vita iusti* (Dial. 2.2). Grundstrukturen altkirchlicher Hagiographie bei Gregor dem Grossen," in *Pietas. Festschrift für Bernhard Kötting* (Münster-en-W., 1980), pp. 284-312 at 290.

[34] See *Hom. in Evan.* 2.38.15, PL 76:1290, where Gregory introduces the story of his three aunts, Tharsilla, Gordiana and Aemiliana, by saying: "Sed quia nonnumquam mentes audientium plus exempla fidelium quam docentium verba convertunt, volo vobis aliquid de proximo dicere, quod corda vestra tanto formidolosius audiant, quanto eis hoc de propinquo sonat." Cf. *Hom. in Evan.* 2.39.10, PL 76:1300; *Dial.* 4.7, SC 265:40-42. Clearly, Gregory's miracle stories are intended to move the hearts of readers who might otherwise remain unaffected by mere preaching. However, G. Cremascoli, '*Novissima hominis' nei 'Dialogi' di Gregorio Magno* (Bologna, 1979), p. 52, goes too far when he refers to "la volontà dell'autore di scuotere ad ogni costo gli animi con la drammaticità degli eventi narrati, anche a prezzo di accogliere nella vicenda elementi che contrastano con la genuinità del dogma cristiano." This would have vitiated the whole enterprise.

[35] *Dial.* 1.10.6-7, SC 260:96-100.

An act which results from an evil intention becomes bad in itself, though outwardly it may still appear good."[36]

Another story, about Bishop Boniface of Ferentis, which appears in the immediately preceding chapter of the *Dialogues*, seems even less promising in its power to edify. Boniface had been invited to dine at the home of Fortunatus, a nobleman of the city. But they had no sooner approached the table than they were disturbed by a minstrel who appeared at the door, and in his annoyance the holy man pronounced a curse upon the intruder: "'Alas! That poor wretch is dead! He is dead, I say. I come to table and, before I have opened my mouth to pray, this man with a monkey at his side is already playing cymbals.'" Boniface encouraged his host to be charitable to the wretched man, and so Fortunatus received him into his home and gave him bread and wine. But the curse was not lifted. True to the words of the holy man, the minstrel's end was near. On his way out of the house he was mortally wounded by a large stone that fell from the roof.[37] It might be tempting to think that Gregory tells this story simply because it is entertaining, or because he is caught up in the act of story-telling itself. The conduct of the bishop appears distinctly uncharitable, particularly in view of the fact that he was a guest in another man's home. The outburst directed at the minstrel was more than a prophecy, "an instance of some kind of clairvoyant gift," as Petersen would have it.[38] It was a death sentence: *secundum viri Dei sententiam funditus finivit vitam.* And although the bishop could have been provoked by the less than honourable profession of the minstrel, his own words indicate that what really upset him was the fact that he had been disturbed before he could even begin his meal. What possible lesson, we might ask, could be hidden behind this example of pique?[39]

---

[36] *Dial.* 1.10.7, Zimmerman 44, sc 260:98, 100. A careful reading of the story shows that Gregory's explanation is not entirely without foundation. Earlier Gregory had said: "Tunc quidam in hospitio cum uxore sua et parvulo filio ad prunas sedebat, qui, vocem eius [i.e. maligni spiriti] audiens et *quid ei episcopus fecerit requirens*, hunc invitavit hospitio, sedere secum iuxta prunas fecit" (*Dial.* 1.10.6, sc 260:98; emphasis added). However, it is still difficult to see the justice in the event unless, like Peter, we reason that the unfortunate ending of the story in itself demands impure motives on the part of the unfortunate man. After hearing Gregory's explanation, Peter says: "Ut dicitur ita est. Nam finis operis probat quod munda intentio in operatione non fuerit" (*Dial.* 1.10.7, sc 260:100).

[37] *Dial.* 1.9.8-9, Zimmerman 37-38, sc 260:82-84.

[38] Petersen, *The Dialogues*, p. 48.

[39] Cf. Cremascoli, '*Novissima hominis*', pp. 41-42, who points to incongruous elements in both this episode and the one involving Fortunatus of Todi, particularly the fact that in each case a just relationship between guilt and punishment is difficult to discern. Cf. also S. Boesch Gajano, "Dislivelli culturali e mediazioni ecclesiastiche nei *Dialogi* di Gregorio Magno," in *Religioni delle classi popolari*, ed. C. Ginzburg, *QS* 41 (1979): 398-415 at 402-403. Boesch

Nothing indicates more convincingly Gregory's didactic concern than the fact that even such distinctly unpromising material can be turned to spiritual purposes. The context of the episode clearly establishes the personal holiness of this "very saintly man," this "true bishop in every respect."[40] The stories that immediately precede and follow demonstrate respectively his remarkable humility and his charity. All of this serves to remind us that Boniface was a man of God, whose conduct, therefore, must of necessity have been honourable. Hence, Gregory would have us understand that the saintly bishop's anger was fully justified because the minstrel failed to pay him the respect to which he was entitled. The lesson of the episode, Gregory explains to Peter, is that "great reverence is due to holy men because they are the temples of God. When a holy man is provoked to anger, no less a person is angered than He who dwells in that temple. We must, therefore, fear the anger of the just from a firm conviction that the One who is present in them has full power to inflict whatever vengeance He may choose."[41] We are left with the impression that Gregory is determined to turn the miracle stories of the *Dialogues* to edifying purpose, even if the material with which he has to work remains recalcitrant and at times requires considerable imagination and dexterity.

However, if the miracles recorded in the *Dialogues* always edify, they do not always do so in the same way. Never mere wonders, they have what Dhanis calls "transcendance séméiologique."[42] They function as signs invested with divine meaning. However, to understand Gregory correctly, we have to be open to the possibility of several different kinds of meaning. The episodes just discussed give some sense of the variety to be encountered. In particular they show that the miracles of the *Dialogues* do not always demonstrate some saintly virtue that the faithful are advised to emulate.

Gajano maintains that the episode with which we are here concerned indicates not only religious estrangement between the saint and the minstrel, but social and cultural estrangement as well.

[40] *Dial.* 1.9.1, Zimmerman 34, SC 260:76.

[41] *Dial.* 1.9.9, Zimmerman 38, SC 260:84. Such punitive miracles are relatively rare in the *Dialogues*. However, they are prominent in some other examples of early medieval hagiography, the *Vita Ambrosii* of Paulinus of Milan, for example, and they play an important role in later hagiographical tradition. Cf. E. Lamirande, *Paulin de Milan et la 'Vita Ambrosii'* (Montreal and Paris, 1983), pp. 119-125; P.-A. Sigal, "Un aspect du culte des saints: le châtiment divin aux XIe et XIIe siècles d'après la littérature hagiographique du Midi de la France," in *La religion populaire en Languedoc du XIIIe siècle à la moitié du XIVe siècle* (Toulouse, 1976), pp. 39-59; *L'homme et le miracle dans la France médiévale (XIe-XIIe siècle)* (Paris, 1985), pp. 276-282.

[42] E. Dhanis, "Qu'est-ce qu'un miracle?" *Gregorianum* 40 (1959): 201-241 at 202-203.

Indeed, sometimes the meaning Gregory discerns is much more modest, and his thought thus much closer to the mainstream of the hagiographical tradition. Despite Gregory's acknowledgment that miracles in themselves are never conclusive proof of sanctity,[43] over the next several pages it will be argued that, at times, his miracle stories serve the rather limited objective of establishing that the saintly hero in question was indeed a saint.

* * *

In Vitale-Brovarone's discussion of the various narrative techniques used by Gregory to link one episode of the *Dialogues* to another, or to link dialogue to narrative, one in particular stands out. An example is provided by the opening words of the second book, where the life and miracles of Saint Benedict are introduced in the following terms: "Fuit vir vitae venerabilis, gratia Benedictus et nomine, ab ipso pueritiae suae tempore cor gerens senile."[44] What is significant about the passage is the prominence given to the qualifications of the saint: the very first statement made about Benedict is that he was a man of saintly life. Vitale-Brovarone suggests that this technique, distinctive to Gregory, is appropriate if miracles exemplify virtue: "La qualificazione si pone come condizione essenziale del *signum*: la *vita* del santo deve aderire ad un certo modello, e il *signum* poi viene da sé."[45] However, despite the importance of the moral qualities of his heroes in Gregory's scheme of things, Vitale-Brovarone himself would admit that Gregory's descriptions of them are usually less than satisfying. Like most of the medieval authors of saints' lives, his efforts at characterization are often weak and superficial.

Although Delehaye is probably quite correct in suggesting that true sanctity does not suppress individuality, scholars frequently maintain that the point was lost on the vast majority of medieval hagiographers, who were much more interested in ideal types than they were in individual personalities.[46] Individual characteristics disappear entirely behind the uniform, stereo-

---

[43] Cf. *Dial.* 1.1.6, sc 260:22: "Mens autem quae divino Spiritu impletur habet evidentissime signa sua, virtutes scilicet et humilitatem, quae, *si utraque in una mente perfecte conveniunt, liquet quod de praesentia sancti Spiritus testimonium ferunt.*" The emphasis has been added.

[44] *Dial.* 2 Prol. 1, sc 260:126.

[45] A. Vitale-Brovarone, "Forma narrativa dei *Dialoghi* di Gregorio Magno: prospettive di struttura," *AAST.M* 109 (1975): 117-185 at 164.

[46] Delehaye, *Sanctus*, p. 240. On medieval hagiographers, see, for example, G. Strunk, *Kunst und Glaube in der lateinischen Heiligenlegende* (München, 1970), p. 11; J. Leclercq, *The Love of Learning and the Desire for God*, 2nd. ed. (New York, 1977), pp. 200-201; and R. Boyer, "An Attempt to Define the Typology of Medieval Hagiography," in *Hagiography*

typed portraits of the holy martyr, the holy monk, the holy bishop and perhaps three or four other major types, with the result that the specific features of many individual lives are virtually interchangeable. From the hagiographers' perspective the lives of the saints are static. Not being real individuals, they undergo no real development; no single stage of the saint's life represents a higher degree of perfection than any other. This is particularly evident in the case of the sainted infant, who, possessed of all the attributes of his calling at the outset of his earthly pilgrimage, is no further along the road to perfection at the end of his life than he was at the beginning. The only real difference is that at his life's end his saintly character is more widely known, having been demonstrated most effectively by his wondrous powers.[47]

If this is an accurate characterization of the work of the medieval hagiographer, it probably should not be applied to Gregory without a few reservations. Gregory's portraits are not mere stereotypes; they possess some individuality. His saints are not simple paragons of Christian virtue; he often

---

and *Medieval Literature* (Odense, 1981), pp. 27-36, esp. pp. 29-31. On early medieval hagiography, see Graus, *Volk, Herrscher und Heiliger*, p. 62; B. de Gaiffier, "Hagiographie et historiographie. Quelques aspects du problème," in *La storiografia altomedievale* (Spoleto, 1970), 1:139-166, esp. 157-158; and Poulin, *L'idéal de sainteté*, pp. 99-100. On the hagiography of the eleventh century, see de Gaiffier, *Etudes critiques*, pp. 461-463. On the hagiography of the later Middle Ages, see R. Kieckhefer, *Unquiet Souls: Fourteenth-Century Saints and their Religious Milieu* (Chicago and London, 1984), pp. 7-8. One of the few dissenting voices is that of L. Zoepf, *Das Heiligen-Leben im 10. Jahrhundert* (1908; repr. Hildesheim, 1973), esp. pp. 151-155. Although he admits that stylization in terms of standard archetypes was an essential feature of the hagiographer's task, Zoepf still maintains that the hagiographers of the tenth century captured many of the individual features of their subjects.

Closely related to the medieval hagiographer's partiality for stereotyped heroes is the alleged lack of awareness of autonomous individuality in the medieval period in general. This is a very large issue, which we cannot take the time to examine in detail here. But see, for example, A.J. Gurevich, *Categories of Medieval Culture* (London, 1985), pp. 300-310. It is frequently maintained—for example, by C. Morris, *The Discovery of the Individual, 1050-1200* (London, 1972)—that by the late eleventh and twelfth centuries various sources reveal an awakening interest in the distinctive individual personality. Although this is an issue that has not yet been fully resolved—for recent discussion, see the exchange between C.W. Bynum and C. Morris, *JEH* 31 (1980): 1-17, 195-206—B. Ward, *Miracles and the Medieval Mind* (Philadelphia, 1982), pp. 171-184, argues for the greater biographical value of such twelfth-century *vitae* as Eadmer's *Life of St Anselm* and Walter Daniel's *Life of Aelred of Rievaulx*. On Eadmer specifically, cf. R.W. Southern, *Saint Anselm and his Biographer* (Cambridge, 1963), esp. pp. 320-336. For late medieval examples in which "hagiographic stereotypes paled under the vivid imprint of powerful individual personality," see D. Weinstein and R.M. Bell, *Saints and Society: The Two Worlds of Western Christendom, 1000-1700* (Chicago and London, 1982), pp. 36-37.

[47] Cf. Poulin, *L'idéal de sainteté*, pp. 101-102, 107-108.

tells us quite candidly of their human failings as well. Of course, the type of the sinful saint was itself to become a well-established feature of medieval hagiography, and Gregory exerted a formative influence on its development. The basic type as described by Dorn was simply a variation on the general stereotyping tendencies of medieval hagiography noted above. It did not portray saints who possessed flaws, but sinners who first renounced their sinful behaviour, and only then became saints. Hence, common to the legends Dorn discusses is a three-stage development from sin, through repentance to the achievement of saintly status.[48] In his frank admission that even the saint can possess flaws, Gregory is fundamentally different.

His treatment of Isaac of Spoleto is a case in point. "In spite of the fact," says Gregory, "that the saintly Isaac was endowed to a unique degree with the virtue of abstinence, contempt for worldly goods, the spirit of prophecy and steadfastness in prayer, he had one trait that seemed reprehensible—at times he gave way to extreme joviality. On such occasions, anyone who did not know of his great virtues would never have believed that he possessed them in abundant measure." The presence of such a flaw in a man of otherwise unimpeachable character is explained in the following terms:

> Almighty God shows wonderful providence in distributing His blessings. Frequently, by denying lesser gifts to those whom He has favored with great virtues, He offers an opportunity for self-reproach. When they find themselves unable to reach the perfection they aspire to and see themselves struggling in vain for a mastery of virtues not granted them, they are not likely to pride themselves on the gifts they have received.[49]

Eleutherius of Spoleto "was well known for his simplicity and compunction of heart, and undoubtedly through his tears this humble, childlike soul obtained many favors from almighty God."[50] But he was once pierced by the sin of pride after he had successfully delivered a young boy from the torment of an evil spirit: his boasts were no sooner uttered than the Devil took possession of the boy once again. For Gregory, pride seems to be the one sin to which the saints are most vulnerable. Eventually Eleutherius was able successfully to exorcize the demon, but only by prostrating himself in prayer together with all his monks.[51]

---

[48] See E. Dorn, *Der sündige Heilige in der Legende des Mittelalters* (München, 1967), pp. 117, 148, 122. Dorn says that we cannot speak of any genuine development in the personalities of these saints (pp. 122-123).

[49] *Dial.* 3.14.10, 12, Zimmerman 133-134, SC 260:310-312.

[50] *Dial.* 3.33.1, Zimmerman 170-171, SC 260:394.

[51] *Dial.* 3.33.2-6, SC 260:394-396.

That these are not isolated cases can be confirmed by the example of the saintly monk Florentius, whose anger once unleashed horrifying consequences that he spent the rest of his life lamenting, and also by the example of Paschasius.[52] Gregory explicitly acknowledges the intellectual accomplishments and the personal piety of this celebrated deacon of the Roman church. Indeed, the sanctity of his life was such, says Gregory, that his death was marked by a miraculous cure. However, Paschasius was also a notorious schismatic who to the very end of his life stubbornly adhered to his own opinions in defiance of the judgment of the universal church. Hence after his death he had to undergo a period of purgation in the baths of Angulus, where he was seen by Germanus, Bishop of Capua. Clearly, the saints of the *Dialogues* are not simple stereotypes. In many cases at least, they are recognizable individuals presented to us warts and all.[53]

The fact remains, however, that Gregory was not primarily interested in biography.[54] Although the distinctive characters of his saints are not always totally subordinated to his didactic ends, they are hardly complete, well-rounded individuals. Rather than focusing on the personality of the saint as a whole, he tends to concentrate on individual virtues or individual actions. Not even the treatment of Saint Benedict, whose life occupies the entire second book of the *Dialogues*, is an exception to this rule.[55] Because of the space devoted to Benedict, we know a good deal more about him than is

---

[52] *Dial.* 3.15.2-8, SC 260:314-320; 4.42-43, SC 265:150-156.

[53] C. Stancliffe, *St. Martin and His Hagiographer* (Oxford, 1983), pp. 315-327, makes similar claims on behalf of Sulpicius Severus. Sulpicius's portrait of Martin is not a highly stereotyped presentation that obscures all individuality; there are many passages "where the particular is portrayed at the expense of general principles, where a historical incident has taken precedence over a timeless ideal" (p. 322).

[54] The point has often been made: see, for example, Boesch Gajano, "La proposta agiografica," pp. 636-638; and Cracco, "Uomini di Dio," pp. 182-183.

[55] Gregory's treatment of St Benedict has inspired radically different assessments. Puzicha, " *Vita iusti*," regards it as an example of typical, stereotyped hagiography. In Gregory's portrait of Benedict "tritt das Individuelle zurück hinter dem allgemein Spirituellen, das Typische gewinnt Vorrang vor dem Subjektiven" (p. 287). However, a very different view is offered by C. Lambot, "La vie et les miracles de saint Benoît racontés par saint Grégoire-le-Grand," *RMon.* 143 (1956): 49-61; 144 (1956): 97-102; 145 (1956): 149-158. Lambot acknowledges that Gregory "n'avait pas l'intention de composer une biographie complète au sens où nous l'entendons aujourd'hui" (p. 54). However, he still maintains that the *Dialogues* reveal a personal portrait of Benedict: "Le rôle que Benoît joue dans les récits de miracles n'est pas celui d'un personnage inconsistant, mais d'un homme en chair et en os, chez qui telle attitude, tel geste, telle parole sont autant de traits bien individuels. Rapprochés l'un de l'autre, ils révèlent une personnalité" (p. 151). Lambot sketches this personality for us on pp. 151-156.

usually the case, and in all likelihood Gregory's narrative covers at least the principal events in his life. Yet, instead of writing a biography that would attempt to do justice to Benedict's life as a whole, Gregory sets for himself a much more modest objective. His intention is to record some of the miracles of Benedict, and in conformity with this design it is a miracle of some kind that forms the central focus for each chapter.[56] The result is that much of Benedict's life and character remain shrouded in mystery, as Gregory himself seems to acknowledge. If we want to know more, he says, we should consult Benedict's *Rule*, remarkable for both its discretion and its clarity, "for his life could not have differed from his teaching."[57]

Gregory's tendency to avoid a genuinely biographical treatment of his saintly heroes seems to have been quite deliberate, and not the result of mere lack of information. He knew a great deal about the priest Sanctulus, to whom he devotes an extensive section of the *Dialogues*.[58] He explains that Sanctulus was known personally both to himself and to Peter, his interlocutor; that it was the custom of Sanctulus to spend a few days every year visiting him in Rome; and that the clerics of Sanctulus' neighbourhood had given him much additional information about his life. Indeed, Gregory tells us, Sanctulus himself was an important source for the *Dialogues*.[59] Yet although he was strategically placed to give us a well-rounded portrait of the man, Gregory chooses to tell us remarkably little about him. It may be a slight exaggeration to say that he does not even see fit to tell us who Sanctulus was,[60] for we are informed that he was a priest from Nursia, and that, although uneducated, he was remarkable for his charity.[61] But beyond these few facts we know virtually nothing about the man, except, of course, for the many miracles he performed. We know even less about most of the characters in the *Dialogues*. A perhaps more typical example of Gregory's efforts at characterization can be seen in the chapter devoted to Frigdianus, Bishop of Lucca.[62] Gregory tells us simply that he was a man of "marvelous virtue," as

---

[56] See *Dial.* 1.12.7, sc 260:118, where Gregory introduces the material of book two by saying to Peter: "Vellem tibi in laudibus redemptoris de viri venerabilis Benedicti miraculis aliqua narrare. ..." Hence A. de Vogüé, "La mention de la 'regula monachorum' à la fin de la 'Vie de Benoît' (Grégoire, Dial. II, 36)," *RBenS* 5 (1976): 289-298 at 297, can describe the life of saint Benedict as "une grande biographie qui n'est qu'une enfilade de miracles." Cf. W. von den Steinen, "Heilige als Hagiographen," *HZ* 143 (1931): 229-256 at 232.

[57] *Dial.* 2.36, Zimmerman 107, sc 260:242.

[58] *Dial.* 3.37.1-20, sc 260:410-426.

[59] *Dial.* 3.37.1, sc 260:410-412; 3.15.1, sc 260:314.

[60] This is claimed by Boesch Gajano, "La proposta agiografica," p. 636.

[61] *Dial.* 3.15.2, sc 260:314; 3.37.1, sc 260:410-412; 3.37.18-19, sc 260:424.

[62] *Dial.* 3.9, sc 260:286-288.

evidenced by a "most unusual miracle" much talked about by the inhabitants of the town. There then follows directly an account of the miracle in question, a miracle in which, by the power of prayer alone, Frigdianus managed to solve the town's problem of flooding by diverting the course of the river Serchio.

If external miracles are always to be understood as manifestations of inner sanctity, this is a somewhat puzzling episode. Boesch Gajano maintains that, in a case like this, sanctity of life is not so much described as asserted, and that, rather than being manifested by miracle, it tends to be resolved into miracle. The distinction between virtue and miracle becomes blurred. This may be something of an overstatement, but she is clearly right in cautioning us against a one-dimensional reading of the miracle stories of the *Dialogues*, as if Gregory tells them *only* because miracles are manifestations of virtue. The fact of the matter is that the connection between a miracle and the virtue of which it is supposedly a manifestation is often very difficult if not impossible to discern.[63] In the case of Frigdianus one wonders what specific virtues he possessed (he is referred to simply as *mirae virtutis vir*), and what virtues in particular were manifested in his miracle. It is, of course, conceivable that he was a master of all the virtues, and that somehow they are revealed together for the edification of Gregory's readers in the miraculous diversion of the river. But a miracle that manifests all the virtues does not really manifest any of them. At most, it demonstrates that, because Frigdianus was distinguished by sanctity of life, such wonders were within his power: that sanctity was the cause, miracles the effect.

The relationship between virtue and miracle that this episode suggests underlies much of the hagiographical tradition Gregory inherited. The miracles recorded in the *Historia Lausiaca*, for example, are not manifestations of some particular virtue, but only signs that the heroic acts of self-denial performed by Palladius's heroes met with divine approval. Any connection between the ability to perform miracles and a life of virtue is purely external. Miracles may confirm *that* a holy man is possessed of virtue, but they do not demonstrate the virtue itself. The same can be said of the *Historia monachorum*, the *Vita S. Antonii*, and both the *Collations* and the *Institutes* of John Cassian.[64] Cassian, who addresses the issue perhaps most clearly of all, believes that miracles in themselves provide no spiritual

---

[63] Boesch Gajano, "La proposta agiografica," pp. 637-638, 640. Cf. Vitale-Brovarone, "Forma narrativa," p. 147.

[64] For a different assessment of the *Historia monachorum*, see B. Ward, *The Lives of the Desert Fathers* (Oxford and Kalamazoo, 1981), p. 44. Ward seems to suggest that the imagery of its miracle stories conveys spiritual truths.

instruction whatsoever. In the preface to his *Institutes* he announces that he will omit them from his account and concentrate instead on the institutions and rules of the monastic life, as well as its principal faults and their remedies. Miracles may confirm the sanctity of a particular form of life, but they provide no specific edification, and satisfy the reader only with simple astonishment.[65]

Sulpicius Severus would appear to suggest a somewhat different view. Occasionally in the *Dialogues* Postumianus conceives of miracles as providing specific examples we ought to emulate.[66] Ultimately, however, even Sulpicius is not an exception. Although the *life* of Saint Martin serves as an example of virtue that should be emulated, generally his miracles do not: they serve to confirm *that* Martin was a man of virtue, rather than to illustrate the specific virtues he possessed. The same can be said of Gregory's account of the miracle performed by Frigdianus. This miracle demonstrates sanctity only by being the result of it. Unlike the miracle of abbot Equitius discussed earlier, it cannot function as an object lesson in Christian morality.

The interpretation suggested here is confirmed by Gregory himself in the comments he appends to other miracle stories of similar general structure. In the first book of the *Dialogues* he speaks of Constantius, sacristan of the church of St Stephen the Martyr near Ancona, a man "known far and wide for his sanctity. Having renounced the things of this world completely, he directed his soul heavenward with all the powers of his mind." Contenting himself with this generalized description, Gregory goes on to claim that once, when his church's oil supply ran out, Constantius was able to make the

---

[65] *Inst.* Praef., CSEL 17:6: "legentibus praeter admirationem [mirabilia] nihil amplius ad instructionem perfectae vitae conferunt." Cf. *Coll.* 18.1, CSEL 13:506-507, where Cassian explains why he cannot take the time to relate the miracles of the abbot Piamun: "non enim de mirabilibus dei, sed de institutis studiisque sanctorum quaedam quae reminisci possibile est nos spopondimus memoriae tradituros, ut necessariam tantum perfectae vitae instructionem, non inutilem absque ulla emendatione vitiorum ac supervacuam admirationem legentibus praeberemus."

[66] Cf. *Dial.* 1.18, CSEL 1:170: "Duo vobis referam incredibilis oboedientiae admodum magna miracula, licet suppetant plura recolenti: sed ad incitandam virtutum aemulationem, cui pauca non sufficiunt, multa non proderunt"; and *Dial.* 1.22, CSEL 1:175: "haec vos de virtutibus Domini, quae in servis suis vel imitanda operatus est vel timenda, scire sufficiat." There is an element of ambiguity in these comments, for miracles could show us what to imitate and what to dread simply by confirming the general pattern of life of those who were able to perform them. In that case, their lives would provide the examples, and miracles would function only to establish that these lives were indeed exemplary. However, Postumianus does tell a couple of stories, neither about Saint Martin, that illustrate virtue in a more profound sense by conveying quite specific moral points. See *Dial.* 1.20, CSEL 1:172-173; and *Dial.* 1.22, CSEL 1:174-175. He introduces the two by saying: "Duo vobis adhuc praeclara memorabo: quorum unum egregium erit adversus inflationem miserae vanitatis exemplum, alterum adversus falsam iustitiam non mediocre documentum."

lamps in the church burn on mere water instead. Like the miracle of Frigdianus, this miracle can be considered a manifestation of virtue only in a very general sense. Any connection between the miracle and any specific virtue Constantius may have possessed is difficult to perceive. It was evidently difficult for Gregory as well, and so in his remarks to Peter he chooses to treat the miracle only as evidence that Sanctulus was in fact a saint. "Try to imagine," says Gregory, "how great must have been the merits of the man who, when necessity required it, could change the nature of a physical element."[67]

Gregory also gives only brief, very general descriptions of the characters of Severus and Martin in books one and three of the *Dialogues* before passing on immediately to tell of the wonders they performed.[68] Hence in neither case would he have us understand that the miracles are supposed to demonstrate *in concreto* the sanctity of life by which these men were distinguished. In each case he seeks only to show that their miracles establish clearly their saintly credentials. After recording how God provided water for Martin's daily needs from the stone of the cave he had inhabited, Gregory comments: "Through this miracle almighty God showed how carefully He watched over His saint, for in imitation of the ancient miracle He provided him in the wilderness of his retreat with cool water from a hard rock." Of Satan's unsuccessful attempt to drive Martin away by taking on the form of a serpent, Gregory says only: "Consider, then, my dear Peter, on what spiritual heights the man of God stood who for three years was unafraid to lie down to sleep with this serpent at his side." When the grief-stricken Severus raises a dead man to life in the one miracle attributed to him, Gregory's remarks clearly show that the miracle does not demonstrate the saint's virtue. It demonstrates only that he was a man whose personal sanctity, simply stated rather than described, made him much beloved of God.[69]

The miracles reported in book two of the *Dialogues*, the Life of Saint Benedict, are generally of much the same sort.[70] If they accomplish more, it

---

[67] *Dial.* 1.5.2, Zimmerman 25 (slightly revised), SC 260:58-60.

[68] See *Dial.* 1.12.1, SC 260:112: "vir vitae valde admirabilis, nomine Severus"; and *Dial.* 3.16.1, SC 260:326: "vir valde venerabilis, Martinus nomine."

[69] See *Dial.* 3.16.2, Zimmerman 141, SC 260:328; 3.16.4, Zimmerman 142, SC 260:330; and 1.12.3, SC 260:114: "Perpende, quaeso, hunc de quo loquimur Severum quam dilectum Dominus adtendit, quem contristari nec ad modicum pertulit."

[70] See, for example, the first miracle story of book two (*Dial.* 2.1.1-2, SC 260:128-130), in which we learn how Benedict repaired by means of prayer the tray that had been broken by his nurse. Like the episodes just considered, this miracle does not demonstrate the possession of any particular virtue, but simply the possession of virtue in general. It shows simply that Benedict was a saint, and therefore that the reputation for holiness he acquired

is not by demonstrating Benedict's virtue, but by establishing that he possessed some particular spiritual power. This is the significance, for example, of the story about the monks who committed the fault of accepting food and drink while they were away on the business of the monastery, only to discover on their return that, if Benedict had been absent from them in body, he had been present with them in spirit, and hence was fully aware of their guilt.[71] The miracle does not demonstrate virtue, merely the possession of an extraordinary gift.

The representative nature of this miracle lends support to one very recent analysis of the Life of Saint Benedict, in which the episodes of the life are referred to as *pre-exempla*, to distinguish them from the *exempla* that became deeply rooted in medieval spiritual life from the twelfth century on. In the *pre-exemplum* it is the hero of the story who is exemplary in some way or other; in the *exemplum* that role is assumed by the story itself. But this gives rise to another contrast between the two genres that is equally as significant:

> Dans le premier, il s'agit de montrer le pouvoir, *potestas*, du héros au moyen d'un récit où il fait merveille. ... le *pre-exemplum* a donc tendance à se confondre dans le *miraculum* dont le rôle est de persuader l'auditeur (ou le lecteur) du pouvoir d'un saint et de l'amener à en tirer les conséquences, c'est-à-dire de devenir un dévot du saint. L'*exemplum* conduit à une morale implicite ou explicite que l'auditeur (ou le lecteur) peut et doit mettre lui-même en pratique.[72]

Be this as it may, however, this much at least is clear. Although miracles can exemplify virtue and teach others to emulate it, this explains only some of them. Gregory's miracle stories serve a variety of purposes, most of which have yet to be determined.

*
* *

---

at the very outset of his monastic life was richly deserved. Gregory puts it thus: "Quae res in loco eodem a cunctis est agnita, atque in tanta admiratione habita, ut hoc ipsum capisterium eius loci incolae in ecclesiae ingressu suspenderent, quatenus et praesentes et secuturi omnes agnoscerent, Benedictus puer conversationis gratiam a quanta perfectione coepisset."

[71] *Dial.* 2.12, sc 260:174-176.

[72] J. Le Goff, "'Vita' et 'pre-exemplum' dans le 2e livre des 'Dialogues' de Grégoire le Grand," in *Hagiographie, cultures et sociétés, IVe-XIIe siècles* (Paris, 1981), pp. 105-117 at pp. 110-111. Further on, however, Le Goff points to elements in the Life of Saint Benedict which require him to qualify his thought: "A la fin du chapitre VII Pierre dit à Grégoire: *Magna sunt valde quae narras, et multorum aedificationi profutura.* Ici ce n'est pas seulement le pouvoir miraculeux de Benoît qui est donné comme bénéfice de l'oeuvre, ce n'est pas seulement en tant qu'exemple vivant, en sa personne, que Benoît est présenté comme modèle profitable, ce sont les histoires racontées elles-mêmes qui apparaissent comme les instruments de l'édification" (p. 115). Cf. C. Bremond *et al.*, *L'exemplum'* (Turnhout, 1982), pp. 49-50.

To achieve a more adequate understanding of the variety of purpose that Gregory attributes to contemporary miracles, we should perhaps consider the various kinds of meaning he attributes to Biblical miracles, especially the miracles of Christ. Not unexpectedly, his view reflects his concern for moral issues. For example, the significance of Christ's miraculous healing of the official's son in John 4:46-53 is brought out by comparing it with the healing of the centurion's servant in Matthew 8:6-7. Christ's willingness to go to the centurion's servant, but not to the son of the official, shows that men should be honoured because they are made in the image of God, not because of any outward distinctions or riches they may possess.[73]

Sometimes Gregory sees a lesson in ecclesiastical discipline rather than Christian life and practice in Christ's example. Hence the raising of Lazarus from the dead (John 11:38-44) provides instruction on the proper exercise of the power of binding and loosing. It was only after he had first revived Lazarus and called him forth that Christ permitted the disciples to loosen the bandages with which he had been bound. "Causae ... pensandae sunt, et tunc ligandi atque solvendi potestas exercenda," Gregory declares. Therefore, those who exercise pastoral authority must take care to ascertain the nature of the sinner's fault, and the depth of any penance performed, so that the sentence of absolution may be granted only to those whom God has already revived spiritually by visiting them with the grace of compunction.[74]

In one sense, the lesson in this last example is moral as well, although it pertains to the proper conduct of those consecrated to God's service rather than to Christian life and practice in general. Quite different are miracles containing doctrinal lessons. Christ's healing of the woman who had been bent over for eighteen years (Luke 13:11-13) contains an important lesson on humankind's fall from grace. This woman, like the fig tree in the immediately preceding parable in the Gospel, represents human nature. Like both the fig tree and the woman, human nature was originally created whole. But just as the fig tree is now barren and the woman now deformed, so human nature has been corrupted. Having fallen into sin of its own free will,

---

[73] *Hom. in Evan.* 2.28.1, PL 76:1211. For additional examples of this kind of moral interpretation, see *Mor.* 10.30.50, CCL 143:572-573, where Gregory comments on Christ's expulsion of the evil spirit from the young boy (Mark 9:13-28); and *Hom. in Ezech.* 1.10.20, CCL 142: 153-154, where he comments on Christ's healing of the deaf mute (Mark 7:31-37). The first episode is meant to teach us that those who successfully repress earthly desires are virtually dead in the eyes of worldly men. Among other things, the second episode apparently contains the lesson that hearing the words of the Lord means living them in practice.

[74] *Hom. in Evan.* 2.26.6, PL 76:1200. Augustine also interpreted this miracle as having reference to the sacrament of penance: cf. *Enar. in Psalmos* 101.2.3, CCL 40:1440; *In Iohannis Evangelium* 49.24, CCL 36:431; *Sermo* 98.6.6, PL 38:595.

it has forfeited its original stature of rectitude and no longer bears the fruit of good works.[75] A similar doctrinal lesson is contained in Christ's healing of the blind man on the road to Jericho (Luke 18:35-43), for he also represents the human race in general. Cast out of paradise because of the sin of its first parents, humankind suffers the darkness of its damnation in total ignorance of the clarity of the supernal light. Yet the presence of the Redeemer can illumine its spiritual blindness, enable it to take the steps of good works in the pathway of life, and through desire at least, to contemplate the joys of the eternal light.[76]

The miraculous draught of fishes produced by the risen Christ (John 21:1-14), when compared with the analogous miracle Christ performed before his passion (Luke 5:4-7), reveals an instructive contrast between the church militant and the church triumphant. In the first episode Christ tells Simon simply to lower his nets, and Gregory assumes that they are lowered on both sides of the boat. In the second Christ specifies that the net is to be cast on the right side. Since the right side signifies good, and the left evil, the miraculous draught of fishes obtained from both sides signifies the present church, which contains both good and evil persons, whereas the draught of fishes produced from the right side alone signifies the church of the elect, from which evil has been expelled. In the first episode so many fish are caught that the nets are broken, because, in addition to the elect, the present church contains many reprobate who shatter the unity of the faith with their heresies. In the second episode, however, the net remains intact, despite the fact that many fish, and many great fish, are caught; for unlike the present church, the church of the elect is not rent by schism.[77]

Several other examples could be adduced,[78] but the point is sufficiently

---

[75] *Hom. in Evan.* 2.31.2, PL 76:1228. Cf. Augustine, *Enar. in Psalmos* 37.10, CCL 38:389; *Sermo* 110.1.1-2.2, PL 38:638-639.

[76] *Hom. in Evan.* 1.2.1, PL 76:1082. Gregory's exposition of the allegory continues at some length. Cf. *In Iohannis Evangelium* 44.1, CCL 36:381; and *Sermo* 135.1.1, PL 38:746, where Augustine provides a similar interpretation of the healing of the man born blind (John 9:1-7). Gregory himself does the same in *Mor.* 8.30.49, CCL 143:420-421. Cf. also *Sermo* 88.10.9, PL 38:544, ed. P.-P. Verbraken, "Le sermon LXXXVIII de saint Augustin sur la guérison des deux aveugles de Jéricho," *RBén.* 94 (1984): 71-101 at 83, where Augustine treats the blindness of the two blind men of Matt. 20:29-34 as a figure for spiritual blindness.

[77] *Hom. in Evan.* 2.24.3, PL 76:1185. Cf. Augustine, *In Iohannis Evangelium* 122.7, CCL 36:671-672; *De diversis quaestionibus octoginta tribus* 57.2, CCL 44A:101.

[78] Hence Gregory informs us that the meal which the risen Christ shared with the disciples, immediately after having produced the miraculous draught of fishes (John 21:12-13), contains a sophisticated lesson in Christology (*Hom. in Evan.* 2.24.5, PL 76:1186-1187); and that his choosing to remain on the shore, whereas previously he had walked on the water, illustrates the nature of his resurrected body (*Ibid.* 2.24.2, PL 76:1184-1185). For further examples see

clear. The miracles of Christ edify us with lessons both moral and doctrinal, teaching us of the life that we should live as well as instructing us about the truth we should believe. Not surprisingly, then, contemporary miracles display similar variety of purpose: they inculcate Christian virtue, but they also instruct us in ecclesiastical discipline or in some fundamental doctrine of the church.

The miracle stories in Gregory's *Homilies on the Gospels* usually serve to make a moral point. The story of Martyrius, *vitae valde venerabilis monachus*, who met Christ in the form of a poor leper on whom he had compassion, provides a lesson in Christian charity.[79] Given its occurrence in a homily on the parable of Dives and Lazarus, the story of the wondrous death of Romula, the saintly disciple of Redempta, appropriately instructs us on the worthlessness of wealth and worldly honour:

> As long as she lived in the body, who held her in honour? She seemed unworthy to everyone, despised by all. Who thought it worthwhile to approach her, who to look on her? But a pearl of God lay hidden in the dung-heap. A dung-heap, brethren, is what I call this very corruptibility of the body; a dung-heap is the name I give to the lowliness of poverty. Therefore, the pearl that lay in the dung-heap has been taken up, and, having been placed in the ornament of the heavenly King, now shines among the celestial citizens, now gleams among those glowing jewels of the eternal diadem. Oh you who either believe yourselves to be wealthy in this world or indeed are, compare, if you can, your false riches to the true riches of Romula. ... Therefore, learn, brethren, to despise all temporal things; learn to have contempt for transitory honour, to love eternal glory. Honour the paupers whom you see, and those whom you perceive to be the despised of the present day outwardly, reckon them to be friends of God inwardly. Share what you have with these, so that by this they might deign at some time to share what they have with you.[80]

The story of Gregory's three aunts, Tharsilla, Gordiana and Aemiliana, two of whom died wondrous deaths and were received into heaven, while the

---

Hom. in Ezech. 1.6.7, CCL 142:70, where Gregory discusses the miracle at Cana (John 2:1-11); *Hom. in Ezech.* 2.9.22, CCL 142:375-376, where he comments on the miracle of the loaves and fishes (Mark 8:1-10); and *Hom. in Evan.* 2.30.4-6, PL 76:1222-1224, where he discusses the miracle of Pentecost (Acts 2:1ff). The first of these miracles is a lesson on the interpretation of Scripture; the second contains important teaching on the process of conversion; the third helps us to explicate the different gifts of the Holy Spirit. See also *Mor.* 4.27.52, CCL 143:196-197, where Gregory refers to the three resurrections performed by Christ, all of which illustrate how the soul which is dead in sin can be brought to life again. Cf. Augustine, *In Iohannis Evangelium* 49.3, CCL 36:420-421; *Sermo* 98.3.3-6.6, PL 38:592-595; 128.12.14, PL 38:720.

[79] *Hom. in Evan.* 2.39.10, PL 76:1300-1301.

[80] *Ibid.* 2.40.11-12, PL 76:1310-1312, esp. 1312.

third, Gordiana, was unable to remain true to her spiritual vocation, reinforces the Biblical doctrine that many are called but few are chosen (Matthew
22:14). This same lesson is illustrated by the story of the miraculous
eleventh-hour conversion of a worldly brother in Gregory's own monastery
of St Andrew, and is stressed when the fate of this monk is contrasted with
Gordiana's fall from grace: "Behold, my brethren, Gordiana," says Gregory,
"of whom I spoke earlier. From the eminence of her religious habit she fell
into torment. And yet this brother, about whom I have related these things,
returned to eternal life from the very point of death. No one, therefore, knows
what may be done with regard to himself in the secret judgments of God;
because 'many are called, but few are chosen.'"[81] However, Gregory's
concern with Christian life and practice is not far beneath the surface of both
stories. Hence we are exhorted not to attribute any good works we perform
to our own strength, for we do not know what the morrow may bring.
Because we can have no assurance of our own salvation, our confidence
ought not to be placed in ourselves, but only in the divine mercy.[82]

In the *Dialogues* the balance is somewhat different, especially in book four,
where miracles serve primarily to demonstrate points of doctrine about the
afterlife. Indeed, Gregory is so concerned with doctrinal issues in the final
book of the *Dialogues* that many chapters are completely devoted to their
exposition, and contain no miracles at all.[83] Of principal importance is a
series of stories Gregory offers to confirm the doctrine of the immortality of
the soul. They contain examples of individuals who, through the power of a
spiritual vision purified by acts of faith and prayer, were able to witness the
souls of the departed leaving their bodies and ascending into heaven.[84] Of
similar import are stories like the *Dialogues*' account of the death of the
saintly Romula. Those who were present did not actually see her soul ascend
to heaven, but they did smell the sweet odor that accompanied her death, and
they both saw and heard the heavenly choir that had come to usher her out
of this world.[85]

---

[81] *Ibid.* 2.38.15, 16, PL 76:1290-1292, 1292-1293, esp. 1293.

[82] *Ibid.* 2.38.15, PL 76:1292; 2.38.16, PL 76:1293.

[83] See especially *Dial.* 4.44-47, SC 265:156-168. Cf. *Dial.* 4.1-7, SC 265:18-42; 4.21, SC
265:78; 4.25-26, SC 265:82-86; 4.29-30, SC 265:98-102; 4.34, SC 265:112-116; 4.39, SC
265:138; 4.41, SC 265:146-150; 4.43, SC 265:154-156; 4.50-52, SC 265:172-176; 4.60-62,
SC 265:200-206.

[84] *Dial.* 4.8-11, SC 265:42-48. After beginning the fourth book with an extensive discussion
of the issue, Gregory introduces this series of miraculous visions with the following words:
"mihi nunc necesse est vel qualiter egredientes animae visae sint, vel quanta ipsae, dum
egrederentur, viderint enarrare, quatenus fluctuanti animo, quod plene ratio non valet, exempla
suadeant" (*Dial.* 4.7, SC 265:40-42).

[85] *Dial.* 4.16, SC 265:62-68, esp. 66-68.

Gregory's accounts of contemporary miracles are intended to help us understand specific details of the afterlife as well. When Peter asks him whether burial in church can be of any benefit to the souls of the departed, Gregory answers:

> Those not burdened with mortal sin benefit from being buried in church because, whenever their friends and relatives come to church, they see the burial place and are reminded to pray to God for their dear ones. Those who die in the state of mortal sin do not obtain pardon by being buried in church; instead, they incur an even worse condemnation. I can bring this point out more clearly by telling you briefly of events that took place in our lifetime.[86]

Gregory then tells four illustrative stories,[87] the first of them a particularly gruesome tale about a nun who, although otherwise faultless, used to indulge in vain and foolish chatter. She was buried in a church. But the night after her interment, the sacristan had a vision of her being led to the altar. There she was cut in two, and while the one part of the corpse was preserved intact, the other was consumed by fire. The events of the following morning substantiated the vision, for the marble floor in front of the altar was found to have been scorched, just as if the nun had actually been burned there. In Gregory's opinion, this incident establishes conclusively that burial in a holy place will not help the unrepentant sinner escape full judgment.[88]

Among other things, in book four Gregory also records miracles designed to prove that masses can be of benefit to the souls of the departed, provided their sins are such as to be pardonable in the afterlife.[89] Of course, he takes pains to bring out the moral significance these stories contain as well. The efficacy of the mass notwithstanding, he adds that it is preferable not to have

---

[86] *Dial.* 4.52, Zimmerman 263 (slightly revised), sc 265:176.

[87] *Dial.* 4.53-56, sc 265:178-184.

[88] *Dial.* 4.53, sc 265:178. See especially Gregory's concluding comment: "Ex qua re aperte datur intellegi quia hii, quibus dimissa peccata non fuerint, ad evitandum iudicium sacris locis post mortem non valent adiuvari."

[89] *Dial.* 4.57, sc 265:184-194. See in particular Gregory's comment after the first incident in this chapter, the story of the priest of the diocese of Centumcellae, who met one of the shades of the departed at the hot springs of Tauriana, and secured his release from the penance he was performing by offering prayers and masses on his behalf: "Qua ex re quantum prosit animabus immolatio sacrae oblationis ostenditur, quando hanc et ipsi mortuorum spiritus a viventibus petunt, et signa indicant quibus per eam absoluti videantur." Cf. J. Ntedika, *L'évocation de l'au-delà dans la prière pour les morts* (Louvain and Paris, 1971), pp. 105-110. Gregory records incidents proving that masses can work for the benefit of the living as well: cf. *Dial.* 4.58-59, sc 265:194-200. However, at the end of the series he states: "Idcirco credo quia hoc tam aperte cum viventibus ac nescientibus agitur, ut cunctis haec agentibus atque nescientibus ostendatur, quia si insolubiles culpae non fuerint, ad absolutionem prodesse etiam mortuis victima sacrae oblationis possit" (*Dial.* 4.59.6, sc 265:200).

to rely on masses that we hope others will offer for us after our death: "It is better to make one's exit a free man than to seek liberty after one is in chains. We should, therefore, despise this world with all our hearts as though its glory were already spent, and offer our sacrifice of tears to God each day as we immolate His sacred Flesh and Blood."[90] Gregory also underlines the moral significance of the story of Reparatus, whose "journey to hell, ... return and description of what he had seen, and ... subsequent death, indicate that all this did not happen for [his] own benefit, but as a warning for us that we should use the opportunities given us to correct our evil ways."[91] Given the emphasis Gregory places on sanctity of life, his attention to the moral significance of contemporary miracles is unsurprising. But like the miracles of Christ, contemporary miracles instruct us not only in the life of Christian virtue, but also in substantive matters of the faith. By the time he reaches the end of the *Dialogues*, this has become Gregory's fundamental concern. Symptomatic is the fact that, despite its moral value, the story of Reparatus is one of a series designed primarily to illustrate that the souls of the reprobate are punished by the corporeal flames of hell.[92]

---

[90] *Dial.* 4.60.1, Zimmerman 272, sc 265:200.

[91] *Dial.* 4.32.5, Zimmerman 229, sc 265:108.

[92] *Dial.* 4.31-33, sc 265:104-112. That this is the point of these miracles is clear from the fact that, immediately after having discussed with Peter this very problem of how incorporeal souls could be punished by corporeal fire, Gregory begins the series by stating: "Postquam laboriose credidisti, operae praetium credo, si ea quae mihi a viris fidelibus sunt digesta narravero. ..."

5

Miracles: Fact or Fiction?

In the third book of the *Dialogues* Gregory tells us that once, while he was still living in the monastery of St Andrew, the pain from the illness that afflicted his intestines was so severe he thought death was near. Had his fellow monks not fed him regularly in small amounts, he almost certainly would have died. What pained him even more was the fact that Easter Sunday was approaching, and he was unable to observe the fast. In his distress he asked the holy abbot Eleutherius of Spoleto to pray on his behalf; and wonderful to relate, the prayer was no sooner said than Gregory found strength returning to his weakened body, his anxiety banished. Not only was he able to keep the fast, he says, but in his restored condition he could have prolonged it to the next day had he so desired.[1]

The incident is unique in the *Dialogues*, because it is the only one in which Gregory was himself the beneficiary of a miracle. His famous Frankish contemporary, Gregory of Tours, experienced the miraculous healing power of St Martin on several occasions. Indeed, in one place he seems to imply that he called upon Martin's personal intercession frequently, and for a wide variety of ailments.[2] However, this was a grace that seems to have been denied Gregory the Great. Like both St Augustine and Gregory of Tours, he may have *witnessed* a few other miracles himself, although this is not always

---

[1] *Dial.* 3.33.7-9, SC 260:396-398.

[2] Gregory of Tours, *De virtutibus S. Martini* 1.32-33, MGH, SRM 1.2, pp. 153-154; 2.1, p. 159; 2.60, pp. 179-180; 4.1-2, pp. 199-200. Cf. *Ibid.* 3.1, p. 182, where Gregory tells us how St Martin once came to his rescue when a fishbone had become lodged in his throat; and 3 Praef., MGH, SRM 1.2, p. 182, where he speaks of Martin's many intercessions on his behalf. Not surprisingly, he experienced directly the miraculous benefits of other saints as well. See, for example, *Liber vitae patrum* 2.2, MGH, SRM 1.2, p. 220, where we learn that, when he was a boy, Gregory was cured of a fever at the tomb of St Illidius.

entirely clear.[3] But in the vast majority of cases he was forced to rely on information provided by others. Gregory explains all this at the very outset of the *Dialogues*, where he defends his practice by appealing to the example of the Evangelists. What he is doing, he says, is no different from what Mark

---

[3] Gregory of Tours claims to have witnessed a number of miracles in addition to the ones he experienced in his own person. See, for example, *De virtutibus S. Martini* 2.5, MGH, SRM 1.2, p. 161; 2.14, p. 163; *Historia Francorum* 4.32, MGH, SRM 1, p. 166; *Liber in gloria martyrum*, chap. 5, MGH, SRM 1.2, p. 40; *De passione et virtutibus S. Iuliani*, chap. 24, MGH, SRM 1.2, pp. 124-125. In the last of these passages he gives us an eyewitness account of the miraculous cure of his brother, Peter, from a serious fever. See also the more general claims made in *Historia Francorum* 5.6, MGH, SRM 1, p. 203; and *Liber in gloria confessorum*, chap. 6, MGH, SRM 1.2, p. 302: "Sed nos, qui cotidie, indigni quidem, eius miracula cernimus ad sepulchrum. ..."

Augustine, too, claims to have witnessed at least some of the miracles he reports in *De civitate Dei* 22.8, CCL 48:815-827. See, for instance, his accounts of the healing of Innocentius (p. 816) and of Paulus and Palladia (pp. 825-827). Cf. V. Saxer, *Morts, martyrs, reliques en Afrique chrétienne aux premiers siècles* (Paris, 1980), pp. 270-275. In *Conf.* 9.7.15-16, CCL 27:141-142, Augustine describes the miracles that took place in Milan in 386, on the occasion of the discovery and translation of the bodies of the martyrs Protasius and Gervasius. It would seem, however, that he was not an eyewitness. See P. Courcelle, *Recherches sur les Confessions de Saint Augustin* (Paris, 1950), pp. 148-151.

According to Moricca (pp. xxii-xxiii), there are three additional places in the *Dialogues* where Gregory the Great reports miracles confirmed by his own first-hand experience: (1) *Dial.* 3.35.3-5, SC 260:404-406, where he tells us of the miraculous cure of a madman by the priest Amantius, whom he had placed in a hospital to test his miraculous powers. However, Gregory makes it clear that he did not witness the cure himself, but rather was informed of it later by Bishop Floridus and by the young man who was in charge of the patients in the hospital that night. (2) *Dial.* 4.49.1-7, SC 265:168-172, where Gregory describes the visions of Antony, Merulus and John, three monks of his own monastery in Rome. But there is no real indication, except perhaps in the last instance, that Gregory heard of their visions from their own lips rather than from other members of the community. And even if he did, he did not really experience any miracle himself. (3) *Dial.* 4.57.8-17, SC 265:188-194, where Gregory tells us of the punishment he inflicted on the monk Justus, and of how the sacrifice of the mass was instrumental in accomplishing his eventual salvation. However, although Gregory was involved in the events he relates, and describes his role, he seems to have been informed of their miraculous aspects only by others, most likely the prior, Pretiosus, and Copiosus, a lay physician and brother of Justus. Several other possible instances are mentioned in more recent scholarship on the issue. See, for example, A. de Vogüé, *Grégoire le Grand, Dialogues* 1: *Introduction, bibliographie et cartes* (Paris, 1978), p. 125; and S. Boesch Gajano, "Dislivelli culturali e mediazioni ecclesiastiche nei *Dialogi* di Gregorio Magno," in *Religioni delle classi popolari*, ed. C. Ginzburg, *QS* 41 (1979): 398-415 at 399. Of these the likeliest is *Dial.* 4.17, SC 265:68-70, where Gregory may wish us to understand that he himself witnessed the miraculous death of his aunt, Tharsilla. But even this is doubtful. The same story is found in greater detail in *Hom. in Evan.* 2.38.15, PL 76:1290-1292, and there Gregory implies that all his information came from others: "Neque enim res longe ante gestas dicimus, sed eas de quibus testes existunt, eisque interfuisse se referunt, memoramus" (col. 1290).

and Luke did when they composed their Gospels, not as eyewitnesses of the
events they recorded, but on the word of others. The second-hand nature of
his account is prey to doubt, he realizes, and may tempt some to think he
is writing pious fiction. But to remove any ground for such suspicion, he
promises to reveal the sources on which his account rests,[4] a promise he
observes quite faithfully in the four books that follow.

As several commentators have observed,[5] Gregory provides witnesses for
almost all the miracles reported in the *Dialogues*, and he never tires of
insisting on their reliability. There is only a handful of episodes for which no
source is given, and most of these allow of some kind of explanation.[6] Some

---

[4] *Dial.* 1 Prol. 10, sc 260:16-18. For the comparison with the Evangelists, cf. Theodoret,
Histoire des moines de Syrie (Histoire Philothée) Prol. 11, sc 234:143.

[5] See, for example, Moricca, pp. xxi-xxii; de Vogüé, *Introduction*, pp. 124-125; the studies
of Boesch Gajano, "Dislivelli culturali," p. 399; "'Narratio' e 'expositio' nei Dialoghi di
Gregorio Magno," *BISIAM* 88 (1979): 1-33 at 9; "La proposta agiografica dei 'Dialogi' di
Gregorio Magno," *SM* 3rd. ser. 21 (1980): 623-664 at 641.

[6] There are only nineteen such episodes in the *Dialogues*: two in book one, two in book
three, and fifteen in book four; and all but five or six can be accounted for. Both of the episodes
in book one (*Dial.* 1.6, sc 260:62-64; 1.8.1-4, sc 260:70-72) admit of an explanation. For
the first of these Gregory would possibly have us understand that his source is the anonymous
bishop on whom he draws in *Dial.* 1.5.1-3, sc 260:58-60 (the fact that the episode centres
in Ancona suggests as much); for the second his source is probably the monk Laurio,
mentioned in *Dial.* 1.7.1, sc 260:64-66. At least one of the two episodes in book three (*Dial.*
3.28.1, sc 260:374; 3.36, sc 260:408-410), the second of the two, admits of an explanation
as well. Here Gregory's source is undoubtedly Maximian, Bishop of Syracuse and former
Abbot of St Andrew's. Of the fifteen episodes in book four, at least ten can be explained. Four
of these episodes (*Dial.* 4.19, sc 265:72-74; 4.27.1-3, sc 265:86-88; 4.37.7-16, sc
265:128-134; 4.38.1, sc 265:136) deal with events of a Roman provenance from the recent
past, and so may be offered as common knowledge. Events generally well known would not,
of course, have required specific witnesses. Hence elsewhere, where Gregory contents himself
with anonymous sources, the same reasoning often seems to apply. See, for example, *Dial.*
3.26.1-2, sc 260:366, where, with reference to Menas, the subject of the story, Gregory says:
"De cuius operis narratione unum auctorem non infero, quia paene tot mihi in eius vita testes
sunt, quot Samnii provinciam noverunt." See also *Dial.* 4.59.2-6, sc 265:196-200, where
Gregory refers only to faithful and devout men: "fideles ... ac religiosi viri" (p. 196). Peter
subsequently confesses to having heard the same story when he was in Sicily (p. 198).
However, if this is a satisfactory explanation for the four episodes just mentioned, six others
(*Dial.* 4.27.4-5, sc 265:88-90; 4.40.1-5, sc 265:138-142; 4.49.1-3, sc 265:168-170;
4.49.4-5, sc 265:170; 4.49.6-7, sc 265:170-172; 4.57.8-17, sc 265:188-194) can be
accounted for in somewhat different terms. These all deal with events that transpired at
Gregory's own monastery of St Andrew, and so are probably based on information which he
obtained from the monks. Indeed, two of these latter cases may allow of further precision. In
one of them (*Dial.* 4.49.6-7, sc 265:170-172) Gregory may have learned of the miraculous
vision in question directly from John, the monk who experienced it. In the other (*Dial.*
4.57.8-17, sc 265:188-194) his informants were probably the prior, Pretiosus, and Copiosus,

of Gregory's informants remain anonymous, but at least half of them are
identified by name;[7] and although reasonable conjecture must play a role in
assigning responsibility in many cases, named sources still account for a clear
majority of the episodes he relates.[8] Gregory's witnesses are also usually

---

a lay physician and brother of the monk, Justus. This leaves only five episodes in book four
unexplained (*Dial.* 4.17, sc 265:68-70; 4.24, sc 265:80-82; 4.48, sc 265:168; 4.58, sc
265:194-196; 4.59.1, sc 265:196), and for one of these (*Dial.* 4.17, sc 265:68-70) Gregory
himself may have been the source, although that appears unlikely. See above, n. 3.

[7] For a list of the sources identified by name in the *Dialogues*, see Appendix A. It contains
the names of thirty-nine people, of whom thirty-five are mentioned specifically by Gregory as
being his informants. Although the remaining four are not so identified by Gregory himself,
they can reasonably be assumed to have been among his informants from the various contexts
in which they appear. For a list of the anonymous sources in the *Dialogues*, see Moricca, pp.
xxiii-xxvi. There are thirty-seven entries in Moricca's list, although the total needs to be
corrected to thirty-eight. Moricca misses two examples which should have been included, and
lists one other which is questionable. The missing examples occur at *Dial.* 1 Prol. 10, sc
260:18: "Seniorum valde venerabilium didici relatione quod narro"; and at *Dial.* 4.37.3, sc
265:126: "quidam Illiricianus monachus, qui in hac urbe mecum in monasterio vivebat, mihi
narrare consueverat. ..." The questionable entry is the reference to the disciples of St Benedict
at *Dial.* 4.9.1, sc 265:42. These disciples are identified by name at *Dial.* 2 Prol. 2, sc 260:128.

[8] For an analysis of the sources on which Gregory drew for the various episodes related
in the *Dialogues*, see Appendix B. It provides a detailed breakdown for books one, three and
four, omitting book two because of its rather distinctive character. Gregory's normal practice
is to cite a source for every episode, or every few episodes. However, in book two he departs
from this practice. In the prologue (sc 260:128) he mentions four sources on whom his
account of the life of St Benedict is based: Constantine, Benedict's successor as abbot of Monte
Cassino; Valentinian, Abbot of the Benedictine monastery at the Lateran; Simplicius,
Benedict's second successor as abbot of Monte Cassino; and Honoratus, the current abbot of
Subiaco. Thereafter he does not mention specific sources except on three occasions: *Dial.*
2.15.4, sc 260:184 (Honoratus, Abbot of Subiaco); *Dial.* 2.26, sc 260:214 (Aptonius, *vir
inlustris*); and *Dial.* 2.27.1, sc 260:214 (Peregrinus, Benedict's disciple). If the miracles
recorded in book two were to be included in our calculations, the preponderance of episodes
for which there are named sources would be even more pronounced. Gregory clearly implies
that everything he knows about Benedict is to be credited to the four individuals mentioned
in the prologue and the two additional informants referred to later. However, the general
situation is clear enough from an analysis of the episodes in the other three books. A certain
amount of reasonable conjecture is necessary, for Gregory often names two sources for a series
of miracles, leaving it unclear how the responsibility is to be divided; and he often refers to
his source only at the beginning of a series of episodes, making it difficult to determine how
far into the series he would have us understand the authority of the source extends. However,
even when allowances are made for a margin of error, the preponderance of episodes for which
we have clearly named sources is still clear. By my reckoning, the total number of such
episodes for all three books is seventy-five, roughly 52% of the total, whereas the total number
of episodes dependent on anonymous sources is fifty-one. As noted above, the total number
of episodes for which no source of any kind is given is a mere nineteen, most of them in book
four. In book one the preponderance of episodes for which there are named sources is even

eyewitnesses, or at the very least members of the immediate entourage of the saints; and they tend to be persons of substance or reputation. Boesch Gajano has analyzed their social status, and the results of her investigation, on balance, have been confirmed by my own.[9] Clerical sources in the broad sense of the term are clearly prominent,[10] and the representatives of the monastic clergy dominate those of the secular clergy.[11] Abbots and priors have a larger role than simple monks;[12] and if we include the one pope

---

more pronounced. They outnumber episodes dependent on anonymous sources by twenty-six to eight, and there are only two episodes for which no source is given. In books three and four, however, the situation is somewhat different. In book four episodes for which there are named sources do outnumber those dependent on anonymous sources, and they do so significantly, by twenty-one to twelve. But there are fifteen more episodes for which no source is identified. In book three episodes dependent on anonymous sources actually outnumber episodes for which we have named sources by thirty-one to twenty-eight, and there are two more episodes for which no source is given.

[9] Boesch Gajano, "La proposta agiografica," pp. 641-643; "Dislivelli culturali," pp. 399-400. Cf. Moricca, pp. xxvii-xxxii. Here as well reasonable conjecture is sometimes necessary; and frequently we have to suspend judgment. Gregory's tendency to describe anonymous sources simply as *religiosi viri* provides a case in point. The term can be used to refer to clerics, religious men in the technical sense (e.g. *Dial.* 2.31.1, SC 260:222). However, it can also refer to religious laymen (e.g. *Dial.* 4.38.1, SC 265:136). Cf. de Vogüé's note at *Dial.* 1.1.4, SC 260:21. Unless the context provides some indication, the status of these witnesses must remain indeterminate. Despite difficulties of this sort, however, the evidence is clear enough to permit at least some general conclusions.

[10] The basis for a detailed analysis can be found in Appendices A and B. Of the sources listed in Appendix A, the sources of whom Gregory chooses to inform us by name, by my calculations roughly 74% are clerics, whereas only 26% are laymen. Of all the episodes in Appendix B that can be attributed to identifiable sources, 69% come from clerical sources, whereas only 31% come from laymen and other sources. Appendix B, of course, omits the episodes in book two, and the total percentage to be attributed to clerical sources would be even higher if they were taken into account. But the basic pattern is sustained in each of the other three books as well. Clerics dominate by 69% to 31% in book one, by 70% to 30% in book three, and by 68% to 32% in book four.

[11] Of the sources Gregory identifies by name, 46% come from the monastic clergy, whereas only 28% come from the secular clergy. Of all the episodes in Appendix B whose sources can be identified, 36% come from the monastic clergy, and 33% from the secular clergy. Here once again the pattern would be more pronounced if book two were taken into consideration. Monastic clergy dominate secular clergy by 54% to 14% in book four. In books one and three, however, their roles are reversed. Secular clergy dominate by 36% to 33% in book one, and by 47% to 23% in book three.

[12] Abbots and priors are more likely to be identified by name. Hence of the named sources who clearly come from monastic circles, abbots and priors outnumber simple monks by two to one. Of all the episodes in Appendix B that can be identified as coming from monastic clergy, 56% come from abbots and priors, and 44% from their brethren. Once again the prominence of higher ranking members of the monastic clergy would be much more striking

Gregory mentions, bishops are clearly more conspicuous than simple priests or minor clerics.[13] Laymen play a relatively small role, but those on whose information Gregory does draw are frequently members of society's highest ranks.[14]

In view of Gregory's own aristocratic, clerical and monastic background, none of this is particularly surprising. But it is also important to note that, if Gregory insists on providing witnesses for his stories, witnesses who are usually identified by name, and who are usually people of stature, he does so to enhance their credibility.[15] Of course, this could also have been achieved by illustrating the meaning of the miracles, by establishing that, rather than being simple marvels, they have a divinely-established significance; indeed, we have already remarked on Gregory's efforts to demonstrate the point. But he does not seem to have thought that sufficient. Hence he appeals to witnesses, witnesses of distinction, to convince the reader that the stories he tells are factually true, even if he cannot attest to them by his own personal

---

if book two were taken into account. In books one and three abbots and priors dominate significantly by a ratio of 70% to 30%. In book four, however, the roles are reversed by a ratio of 57% to 43%.

[13] Of the named sources who are clearly members of the secular clergy, bishops dominate all others by a ratio of 64% to 36%. Of all the episodes in Appendix B that can be identified as coming from the secular clergy, bishops account for 56%, whereas priests and minor clerics account for only 44%. Once again this pattern is sustained in two of the three books: in book three, where the ratio is 57% to 43%, and in book four where it is a striking 82% to 18%. The exception is book one, where priests and minor clerics dominate by 56% to 44%.

[14] Laymen constitute only 26% of Gregory's named sources, and they are responsible for only 18% of all the episodes in Appendix B that can be attributed to identifiable sources, although another 12% come from common report where their influence might be discerned. They account for 31% of the episodes in book one, 11% of the episodes in book three, and 15% of the episodes in book four, although in books three and four another 16% and 17% respectively can be attributed to common report. When Gregory does draw on lay sources, he shows a marked predilection for laymen of high rank. At least these are the individuals whom he is most likely to identify by name. In the list of named sources they outnumber more humble laymen by 8 to 2. However, they account for only 48% of all the episodes in Appendix B that can be attributed to lay sources. They clearly dominate in book four, where they are responsible for over 80% of such episodes. However, in books one and three their responsibility slips to 36% and 30% respectively.

[15] Cf. Boesch Gajano, "La proposta agiografica," p. 660. Boesch Gajano sees here a desire on Gregory's part to distance his own work from the fantastic tales of the Gesta martyrum Romanorum. On the relationship between Gregory and the Gesta, cf. J.M. Petersen, The Dialogues of Gregory the Great in their Late Antique Cultural Background (Toronto, 1984), pp. 56-89. Petersen argues that any positive influence they might have had on Gregory was slight, certainly less than has sometimes been thought, and that "his own spiritual formation owes little or nothing to them" (p. 88).

experience. If they really are pious fiction, it seems clear that that is not what Gregory would have us believe.

Presumably Gregory had at least moderate success with his medieval readers, especially if there is any substance to the frequent complaints one hears about the credulity of his contemporaries. This is an issue to which we shall return in the last chapter. But whatever the reaction of late sixth-century readers might have been, Gregory has been rather less than successful in convincing modern scholars, many of whom have tended to be sceptical of the historical value of the *Dialogues*. Moricca, for example, was troubled by miracles in general: before such events a modern observer can express only disbelief. For him, the miracles reported by Gregory cannot be genuine; their historical value is limited to what they reveal of the spirit of the times in which they were written. They cannot be accepted as truthful accounts of actual events, Moricca argues, but there may be genuine historical significance in the background material introduced almost unconsciously into the narrative.[16] More recent scholars have come to similar conclusions, not so much because of a refusal in advance to accept the possibility of the kind of story that Gregory relates (although that certainly plays a part), but rather because a critical examination of these stories betrays a kind of artfulness in their composition that casts doubt on their historicity.

Much of the most recent research has focused on the second book of the *Dialogues*, the life of Saint Benedict, and has concentrated on the literary background that is supposed to have shaped Gregory's account. Courcelle, for example, has argued that the story of Benedict's temptation is dependent on imagery that reaches back to classical authors. He sees a precedent for the black bird, which in Gregory's story functions as an omen for impending death of the soul, in Virgil's *Aeneid*, where it portends physical death; and he finds precedents for the thorns and nettles, into which Benedict hurls himself to quell the desires of the flesh, in Horace, where thorns represent the passions, and in Juvenal, where nettles represent sexual desire. Although he does not pronounce on the matter categorically, Courcelle does confess his difficulty in accepting the historicity of the episode, choosing to regard it as in all likelihood the product of Gregory's creative imagination working with the materials of the preceding literary tradition.[17] He comes to similar conclusions in his analysis of the story of Benedict's vision, the purpose of which, he says, is to represent "le caractère merveilleux de la contemplation, et de presenter Benoît comme le type du saint contemplatif." Once again the

---

[16] Moricca, pp. lxiv-lxv; cf. p. xxxiv.

[17] *Dial.* 2.2.1-4, SC 260:136-140. See P. Courcelle, "Saint Benoît, le merle et le buisson d'épines," *JS* (July-September 1967), 154-161.

historicity of the episode is open to doubt, here because of Gregory's dependence on an antecedent philosophical tradition of the cosmic vision, represented by authors such as Cicero, Seneca, Macrobius and Boethius.[18]

Courcelle's analysis of Benedict's vision has been criticized by Recchia, who argues for the basic historicity of the episode, maintaining that, although Gregory was influenced by his cultural background, this background was shaped primarily by Scripture rather than classical literature.[19] However, Courcelle's reservations about the historical value of Gregory's account of Saint Benedict have been pressed home by others. According to Cusack, there can be "no question of historical truth" in the story of Benedict's temptation, for Gregory was dependent on a variety of even more recent literary precedents than those Courcelle identified, his principal source being the *Vita S. Pachomii*, which had been translated into Latin during Benedict's own lifetime by Dionysius Exiguus. With regard to the story of Benedict's encounter with Totila, Cusack again concludes that "the historicity of the whole event must be called in question." Indeed, he claims to have discovered "an embarrassingly large number of literary precedents," although he also maintains that Gregory's immediate inspiration was the similar encounter between Saint Martin and the Emperor Maximus recorded in the *Vita Martini* of Sulpicius Severus.[20]

Gregory's account of St Benedict's meeting with his sister, Scholastica, is perhaps one of the most troublesome of all the stories in the *Dialogues*, and one that has received considerable attention. Recent discussion began with Wansbrough, who, without denying the historical existence of Scholastica, tends to treat her as an abstraction, a personification of the virtue of

---

[18] *Dial.* 2.35, SC 260:236-242. See P. Courcelle, "La vision cosmique de Saint Benoît," *REAug.* 13 (1967): 97-117, esp. 117. Cf. Th. Delforge, "Songe de Scipion et vision de saint Benoît," *RBén.* 69 (1959): 351-354; and B. Steidle, "Die kosmische Vision des Gottesmannes Benedikt," *EuA* 47 (1971): 187-192, 298-315, 409-414, esp. 413-414. Whereas Steidle endorses Courcelle's conclusions, Delforge (whose work preceded that of Courcelle) limits himself to the possible influence of the *Somnium Scipionis*, and offers considerably more modest conclusions. In his judgment, Gregory "avait été trop profondément impressionné par la plus sublime page de prose latine sortie d'une plume païenne pour ne pouvoir relater la vision d'un mystique chrétien sans retomber, peut-être inconsciemment, dans les images et les termes retenus parmi les souvenirs littéraires" (p. 354).

[19] V. Recchia, "La visione di S. Benedetto e la 'compositio' del secondo libro dei 'Dialoghi' di Gregorio Magno," *RBén.* 82 (1972): 140-155, esp. 142-143, 147.

[20] P.A. Cusack, "The Temptation of St. Benedict: An Essay at Interpretation through the Literary Sources," *ABR* 27 (1976): 143-163, esp. 158. The meeting with Totila (*Dial.* 2.14-15, SC 260:180-184) is discussed by Cusack in "Some Literary Antecedents of the Totila Encounter in the Second Dialogue of Pope Gregory I," *SPatr.* 12 (1975): 87-90; see esp. pp. 90, 87.

contemplation. To de Vogüé, who does not expressly deny her existence either, Scholastica represents, not contemplation, but the virtue of charity. Her role is modelled on the sinful woman of Luke 7:36-50; both women are blessed by God because of the greatness and depth of their love. Cusack, however, goes further. He admits that there is some historical foundation to Gregory's story, for independent archaeological evidence confirms the existence of a deeply rooted tradition of devotion to a St Scholastica, somehow connected with Monte Cassino. But he maintains that we can no more draw historical inferences from this story than we can from others in the second book of the *Dialogues*: "they are all themes, not facts." Cusack claims that Gregory drew on several sources of inspiration in addition to the Gospel account mentioned by de Vogüé, and although it is impossible to determine them precisely, they very likely included the *Vita S. Pachomii* and the *Vitae patrum*. These different elements, he continues, are woven together to form a composite picture in which Scholastica fulfills the traditionally necessary role of herald of death.[21]

Fundamental to most of these critiques is the notion that Gregory not only drew upon an already existing literary tradition, but also shaped that tradition to meet his own theological or pastoral purposes. The historicity of the life of Saint Benedict has been compromised, not only by Gregory the literary scholar, but also by Gregory the theologian. Similar claims have been made by Dagens, Doucet and Gross. In his analysis of the story of Benedict's conversion, Dagens claims no desire to deny the historical value of Gregory's account. But he also maintains that it has been coloured by recurring themes and expressions of Gregory's theology of the spiritual life, and even by Gregory's own conversion. The conversion of Benedict is invested with an ideal perfection that contrasts sharply with Gregory's own hesitant, much-delayed withdrawal from the world.[22] Doucet's analysis of Benedict's temp-

---

[21] *Dial.* 2.33, SC 260:230-234. See J.H. Wansbrough, "St. Gregory's Intention in the Stories of St. Scholastica and St. Benedict," *RBén.* 75 (1965): 145-151; A. de Vogüé, "Le rencontre de Benoît et de Scholastique. Essai d'interprétation," *RHSp.* 48 (1972): 257-273; P.A. Cusack, "St Scholastica: Myth or Real Person?" *DR* 92 (1974): 145-159, esp. 157.

[22] *Dial.* 2 Prol. 1, SC 260:126. See C. Dagens, "La 'conversion' de Saint Benoît selon Saint Grégoire le Grand," *RSLR* 5 (1969): 384-391. Dagens repeats this judgment in *Saint Grégoire le Grand. Culture et expérience chrétiennes* (Paris, 1977), pp. 303-305. A. de Vogüé, "Benoît, modèle de vie spirituelle d'après le Deuxième Livre des Dialogues de saint Grégoire," *CCist.* 38 (1976): 147-157, endorses Dagens' interpretation (p. 150n), and goes on to suggest that, rather than being limited to this one episode, the influence of Gregory's own personal experience may extend throughout the whole life of St Benedict (pp. 156-157). Indeed, de Vogüé has recently suggested that the *Dialogues* in their entirety can be seen as a spiritual autobiography. Cf. "De la crise aux résolutions: les *Dialogues* comme histoire d'une âme," in *Grégoire le Grand*, Chantilly, 15-19 septembre 1982 (Paris, 1986), pp. 305-314. G. Vinay,

tation reaches a similar conclusion: "ce court récit de la tentation de saint Benoît nous révèle finalement plus la théologie du biographe en matière de combat spirituel et de tentation qu'il ne nous livre la figure elle-même du héros du second livre des Dialogues."[23] In his treatment of Benedict's death scene, Gross makes no comment on the historicity of the account at all. But his analysis of its individual features is designed to illustrate their traditional nature. The scene, he says, has been enriched by Scriptural echoes, by theological reflection, and most important, by the preceding hagiographical tradition, in which precedents for many of its elements, Benedict's prediction of his own death, for example, or his dying in an attitude of prayer with his hands outstretched to heaven, can be found.[24]

The effect of these studies has been to deal the historicity of the life of St Benedict a severe blow. As de Vogüé points out, there cannot be much doubt about the historical existence of Benedict himself, or about the authenticity of the principal events of his life; yet there apparently may be some doubt about the historicity of many of the individual episodes recorded in the Dialogues.[25] Doucet believes even the design of the biography as a whole may be called into question. Any genuinely historical elements in the life are difficult to disentangle because of the overarching primacy of Gregory's spiritual purpose, a purpose which, in addition to influencing the account of individual episodes, imposes itself on the structure of the life as a whole. What Gregory offers in the second book of the Dialogues is a description of the essential stages of the spiritual life—"d'abord, Benoît rentre en lui-même, ensuite il habite avec lui-même, enfin il est élevé par la contemplation au-dessus de lui-même"—that parallels the theological doctrine developed in his other works. Rather than being a biography proper, the life of St Benedict is "un *exemplum* longuement développé."[26]

Alto medioevo latino (Napoli, 1978), pp. 33-35, also speaks of the Dialogues in their entirety as being autobiographical in a large sense, as a kind of unconscious objectification of internal spiritual needs.

[23] M. Doucet, "La tentation de Saint Benoît: Relation ou création par saint Grégoire le grand?" CCist. 37 (1975): 63-71, esp. 71.

[24] Dial. 2.37, SC 260:242-244. See K. Gross, "Der Tod des hl. Benedictus. Ein Beitrag zu Gregor d. Gr., Dial. 2, 37," RBén. 85 (1975): 164-176.

[25] A. de Vogüé, La règle de saint Benoît 1: Introduction et texte (Paris, 1972), p. 153; "Benoît, modèle de vie spirituelle," p. 149. Cf. J. Le Goff, "'Vita' et 'pre-exemplum' dans le 2e livre des 'Dialogues' de Grégoire le Grand," in Hagiographie, cultures et sociétés, IVe-XIIe siècles (Paris, 1981), pp. 105-117 at 106, who argues that the genuinely biographical elements in the life of St Benedict represent, at most, ten percent of the total.

[26] M. Doucet, "Pédagogie et théologie dans la 'Vie de saint Benoît' par saint Grégoire le Grand," CCist. 38 (1976): 158-173 at 160, 173.

In the final analysis, the historicity of both the life of St Benedict and the *Dialogues* as a whole is not something I would care to defend,[27] and it is not of central importance for our present purposes. What *is* important is that recent research has cast doubt, not only on the historical accuracy of Gregory's work, but also on his veracity: all his claims to truthfulness notwithstanding, it would appear that Gregory was not really engaged in the writing of something designed to be historically accurate at all. According to Wansbrough, rather than writing history in his life of St Benedict, Gregory "was engaged upon the 'cura pastoralis' for which he gave up his ideal of monastic life." According to Puzicha, questions about the historical reliability of the life of St Benedict are irrelevant. Gregory aimed at a work that would demonstrate Benedict's sanctity, and to that end he used thoroughly tradition-al hagiographical themes and *topoi* throughout.[28]

Other scholars have argued in a similar way about the *Dialogues* as a whole. Dufner reminds us that they were used as an historical source throughout the Middle Ages, in particular by Bede in his ecclesiastical history, and by Paul the Deacon in his history of the Lombards. But he also maintains that Gregory's primary concern for edification so transformed whatever historical elements the *Dialogues* may have contained that the modern scholar can have confidence only in those untouched by his pedagogical purpose and introduced unconsciously into the narrative.[29] Both Hallinger and Bolton argue that the author of the *Dialogues* was not concerned with historical truth but was interested only in providing a framework for the lessons he wanted to teach. Questions about historical veracity or its lack only obscure the more important meaning of the miracle stories in the *Dialogues*. For Gregory, Bolton claims, "the historical form and chronology of an event are its least significant characteristic." Hence "the

[27] Cf. B. de Gaiffier, "Les héros des Dialogues de Grégoire le Grand inscrits au nombre des saints," *ABoll.* 83 (1965): 53-74, who points out that many of the saints of the *Dialogues* commemorated in medieval and early modern martyrologies were included on the strength of the *Dialogues* alone, without the corroborating evidence of a cult.

[28] Wansbrough, "St. Gregory's Intention," p. 151; M. Puzicha, "*Vita iusti* (Dial. 2,2). Grundstrukturen altkirchlicher Hagiographie bei Gregor dem Grossen," in *Pietas. Festschrift für Bernhard Kötting* (Münster-en-Westfalen, 1980), pp. 284-312, esp. pp. 311-312.

[29] G. Dufner, *Die Dialoge Gregors des Grossen im Wandel der Zeiten und Sprachen* (Padua, 1968), pp. 28, 30. The argument is similar to Moricca's (see above, n. 16). Cf. Bede, *Historia ecclesiastica* 2.1, ed. and trans. Bertram Colgrave and R.A.B. Mynors (Oxford, 1969), pp. 122-134; and Paul the Deacon, *Historia Langobardorum* 1.26, 3.23, 4.17, MGH, SRL, pp. 63-64, 104, 122. Gregory's earliest biographer, the anonymous monk of Whitby, also clearly conceived of the *Dialogues* as an historical work: cf. *Vita S. Gregorii*, chap. 28, ed. B. Colgrave (Lawrence, Kansas, 1968), p. 124.

historian who concentrates on peripheral details in Gregorian hagiography, to the neglect of the supra-historical sense, is taking chaff for grain."[30] For his part, Hallinger goes even further. When we read the *Dialogues* carefully, he says, we find that even Gregory himself admits that his stories are not to be taken as factually true.

Although it is conceivable that his protestations of truthfulness were designed simply to provide an atmosphere of verisimilitude to his narrative, it would be very surprising if Gregory were to break the mood himself. In fact, he does not. Throughout the *Dialogues* he insists on the truthfulness of what he relates. Hallinger claims that Gregory clearly did not believe the story in book four about Theodoric the Great being hurled into hell through the mouth of the volcano, because a few chapters later he remarks that he spoke of the Sicilian volcanoes only to illustrate the frightful punishments of the next world.[31] However, Hallinger overlooks an important fact: the venerable hermit's story of Theodoric being cast into the abyss by Pope John and the patrician Symmachus is the report of a *vision*, not an actual event. It is the account of a spiritual experience that Gregory would have us believe really occurred.

Gregory notes that it was singularly appropriate: "Because he [Theodoric] had killed Pope John with the hardships of imprisonment and had executed the patrician Symmachus with the sword, it seems very proper that the vision should show these two men hurling Theodoric into hell, since he had condemned both of them unjustly." If the gateway to hell appeared as the mouth of a volcano, it was not because *Gregory* chose this image for illustrative purposes, but was rather, as Gregory carefully explains, because *God* had made the realms of torment visible to convince the unbelievers. Hence with regard to the dying man, Eumorphius, who had a vision of a ship

---

[30] K. Hallinger, "Papst Gregor der Grosse und der hl. Benedikt," *SAns.* 42 (1957): 231-319, esp. 243; W.F. Bolton, "The Supra-Historical Sense in the Dialogues of Gregory I," *Aevum* 33 (1959): 206-213, esp. 211, 213. Cf. R. Gillet, "Spiritualité et place du moine dans l'église selon saint Grégoire le Grand," in *Théologie de la vie monastique* (Paris, 1961), pp. 323-351 at p. 324n; G. Cremascoli, '*Novissima hominis*' nei '*Dialogi*' di Gregorio Magno (Bologna, 1979), pp. 34, 43; M. Van Uytfanghe, "La controverse biblique et patristique autour du miracle, et ses répercussions sur l'hagiographie dans l'Antiquité tardive et le haut Moyen Age latin," in *Hagiographie, cultures et sociétés*, pp. 205-231 at p. 219; Petersen, *The Dialogues*, pp. xvi-xvii, 17-18, 20, 54. The idea is frequently encountered in the less specialized scholarly literature as well; for a recent example, see J.B. Russell, *Lucifer: The Devil in the Middle Ages* (Ithaca and London, 1984), p. 156.

[31] *Dial.* 4.31, SC 265:104-106. Hallinger, "Papst Gregor der Grosse," p. 243, refers to *Dial.* 4.36.12, SC 265:122: "ut mentes infidelium ... tormentorum loca videant, quae audita credere recusant."

being prepared to transport him to Sicily, Gregory says: "That he should sail to Sicily is best explained by recalling that in the islands around Sicily there are more open pits burning with fires from hell than in any other region. ... God made these fires appear on the surface of the earth in order to correct the minds of men. Unbelievers who had heard of the torments of hell and still refused to believe were to see these realms of torture with their own eyes." Of course, Hallinger maintains that Gregory is again speaking only metaphorically, and admits as much when Peter questions him about the episode. But what Gregory actually does is simply explain the man's vision; he provides us with no reason to doubt that it was real: "The soul has no need of a conveyance," he says. "But it is not surprising that in the vision a man of flesh and blood saw an object which was physically real to him, and through it was given to understand where his soul was to be transported spiritually."[32]

Hallinger is also mistaken in his analysis of the anonymous soldier's experiences in the other world, as reported in the same fourth book of the *Dialogues*. According to Hallinger, these cannot be taken seriously either. When Peter asks him about the house being made of bricks of gold, Gregory replies that the soldier's statement is not literally true. But Hallinger fails to notice that the soldier's story is again a story of a vision Gregory would have us understand really took place. The vision itself was a genuine spiritual experience. However, because it was a vision, its individual elements do not have to be regarded as literally true descriptions of the other world, but rather are to be appreciated for their spiritual significance.[33]

Similar confusions can be found in Wansbrough. In the second book of the *Dialogues* Gregory reports that Benedict saw the soul of his sister Scholastica leave her body and ascend to heaven in the form of a dove; in the fourth book he speaks of the similar experience of the brethren of the Abbot Spes, who saw a dove leave his body at the moment of death and ascend to heaven through the open roof of the oratory. According to Wansbrough, all this cannot be taken literally, for elsewhere in the *Dialogues* Gregory seems to deny the possibility of events of this kind. Thus, when Peter

---

[32] *Dial.* 4.31.4, Zimmerman 228, SC 265:106; 4.36.11-12, Zimmerman 235-236 (slightly revised), SC 265:122.

[33] *Dial.* 4.37.7-16, SC 265:128-134. See Hallinger, "Papst Gregor der Grosse," p. 244n. At *Dial.* 4.37.15-16, SC 265:134, Peter asks: "Quid est hoc, quaeso te, quod in amoenis locis cuiusdam domus laterculis aureis aedificari videbatur? Ridiculum est valde, si credimus quod in illa vita adhuc metallis talibus egeamus." Gregory replies: "Quis hoc, si sanum sapit, intellegat? Sed ex eo quod illic ostensum est, quisquis ille est cui mansio ista construitur, aperte datur intellegi quid est quod hic operatur."

expresses some scepticism about the reality of the soul (he was once present at the sudden death of a monk, and failed to notice any soul leaving his body), Gregory explains that "the soul is invisible by nature and remains invisible whether it is in the body or departing from it."[34] However, further on Gregory clears up the matter, explaining that although the soul is invisible to corporeal vision, it can be seen by spiritual vision. It cannot be seen by the eye of the body, but those who have purified themselves by acts of faith and much prayer can see it through the eye of the soul.[35]

For Wansbrough, spiritual vision is no real vision at all, and therefore reports of these experiences are to be regarded merely as literary conventions adopted to express the sanctity of people like Spes and Scholastica. But this kind of reductionism does violence to the thought of Gregory, who, like Augustine before him and countless mystics after, acknowledged the reality of spiritual vision as a divinely bestowed gift. It enabled its recipients to "see" through bodily images spiritual realities invisible to naked corporeal vision.[36] Hence neither here nor elsewhere in the *Dialogues* does Gregory admit that anything is to be taken *simply* allegorically. He takes pains to explain to his readers the deeper significance of the events he records, but this significance is written into the structure of events he would have us accept as factually true. Indeed, there seems every reason to believe that he accepts them as factually true himself.

That Gregory's pedagogical purpose is so transparent need not imply literary invention, and may indicate nothing more than that he was selective. Gregory did not tell miracle stories for their own sake. He wanted to edify his readers, and it should hardly be surprising that he included stories best suited to that purpose. The existence of literary antecedents for Gregory's stories, too, cannot conclusively establish that the events described are fictions. Indeed, the research that claims to have uncovered such parallels is uneven in quality; some of it, not very good, is quick to leap to conclusions on the slightest evidence. Even the more substantial studies have not clearly

---

[34] *Dial.* 2.34.1, sc 260:234; 4.11.4, sc 265:48. See Wansbrough, "St. Gregory's Intention," pp. 147-148. On Peter's scepticism, see *Dial.* 4.5.2, Zimmerman 196-197, sc 265:34.

[35] *Dial.* 4.7, sc 265:40.

[36] Augustine analyzes the various forms of vision at some length in book 12 of *De Genesi ad litteram.* According to their primary meanings, corporeal vision is vision of corporeal objects through the bodily senses; spiritual vision is vision by means of bodily images of corporeal objects not immediately present to the senses; and intellectual vision is the direct apprehension of non-material, intelligible realities. However, the category of spiritual vision also includes vision of non-material, spiritual realities through bodily images. For Augustine's discussion of this kind of spiritual vision of the soul, see *De Genesi ad litteram* 12.33, CSEL 28:428.

demonstrated that Gregory's stories are pious invention. That some of the stories share elements with other accounts does not mean that Gregory borrowed from those accounts. The borrowing, if indeed there were such, may have been done by Gregory's sources, and perhaps not even they were borrowing consciously.[37] Most of the texts suggested were well known to the members of the sixth-century intelligentsia from which Gregory's witnesses for the most part were drawn, and we are certainly familiar enough by now with the manner in which minds can be influenced by what they have read or by what they have heard elsewhere to reshape unconsciously the material of memory. To base arguments of literary dependence on loose analogies is a perilous undertaking. Before we accuse Gregory of pious invention, clear textual evidence of borrowing is required, and precisely this kind of evidence has not been provided for any of the episodes discussed above.[38]

However, before drawing firm conclusions, we should consider de Vogüé's treatment of the issue, to my knowledge the most thorough. De Vogüé points to some potentially significant facts: that several of the miracles of St Benedict duplicate one another; that some of the miracles of St Benedict duplicate the miracles of other saints reported in the *Dialogues*; that miracles in other books of the *Dialogues* duplicate one another; and that, in addition to the literary antecedents already discussed, Scriptural and other sources can be found for many other stories in the *Dialogues*.[39] In the pages that follow we shall try to consider these points systematically.

*
* *

[37] Hence Courcelle, "La vision cosmique," p. 117, admits that the sources he discovered for the tradition of the cosmic vision do not justify the conclusion that Gregory invented the story of Benedict's vision with their help. Gregory could still have received the story, as he claims, from the disciples of St Benedict: "Benoît et ses disciples adoptaient, selon toute vraisemblance, les mêmes modes de représentation et d'expression de la vision cosmique, puisque Boèce emploie, presque à la même date, une imagerie analogue."

[38] Cusack, "Some Literary Antecedents," esp. p. 87, argues that at one point Gregory borrowed from the *Vita Martini* of Sulpicius Severus, even though by his own admission "the actual text does not betray much evidence of dependence." The lack of clear evidence does not disturb him, however, for "this is usually the case with Gregory." But given his contention that one can identify "an embarrassingly large number of literary precedents" for the incident under consideration, Cusack's procedure seems reckless in the extreme. In "The Temptation of St. Benedict," esp. p. 153, Cusack claims that there *is* textual evidence of Gregory's dependence on Dionysius Exiguus, but he is not very convincing. Although he contends that Gregory "betrays himself in his phraseology," at the most he demonstrates only that Gregory "lets an odd phrase stray into his text from his [alleged] source."

[39] De Vogüé, *Introduction*, pp. 126-138. Cf. idem, "Un cinquantenaire: l'édition des Dialogues de saint Grégoire par Umberto Moricca," *BISIAM* 86 (1976-1977): 183-216 at 185-198.

There is nothing very disturbing about the duplications that fall into the first category, as an analysis of two examples de Vogüé gives will make clear. The first concerns the duplication of a story from the eleventh chapter of the life of St Benedict in another from the thirtieth. In the first episode Gregory tells us that the Devil appeared to Benedict in his cell one day and announced that he was on his way to visit the brethren, who were working on one of the walls of the monastery. Benedict sent them a warning, but just as it was received the Devil overturned the wall and crushed a young monk beneath the ruins. Benedict prevailed, however, by reviving him through the power of prayer. In the second episode Gregory tells us that one day the Devil met Benedict while he was on his way to the oratory of St John on the summit of the mountain. The Devil, this time disguised as a veterinarian (*mulomedicus*), announced that he was taking some medicine to the brethren. Benedict continued on his way. But after he had finished saying his prayers he hurried back to the monks, where he discovered that the Devil had possessed one of them, an older monk whom he had found drawing water, and had thrown him to the ground in a violent convulsion. Again, however, Benedict was triumphant. He cured the monk by giving him a slap on the cheek (*alapa*), thus driving out the evil spirit once and for all.[40]

The similarities are obvious. In both stories the Devil warns Benedict in advance of an impending attack, makes such an attack, and is finally overcome by the virtues of the saint. But there are important differences as well. In the one story the Devil approaches Benedict in his cell; in the other he approaches him out of doors, and in disguise. In the one story he attacks a young monk; in the other his target is an older monk. In the one story Benedict raises an apparently dead monk to life through the power of prayer; in the other he cures a brother of demonic possession by a variation of the laying on of hands. The stories are not really similar enough to justify the suspicion that one has been copied from the other. We have here simply two different occasions on which Benedict made use of the same or similar spiritual gifts.[41]

---

[40] *Dial.* 2.11, SC 260:172-174; 2.30, SC 260:220-222.

[41] Cf. M. Mähler, "Evocations bibliques et hagiographiques dans la Vie de Saint Benoît par Saint Grégoire," *RBén.* 83 (1973): 398-429 at 418. Mähler sees a prototype for the second of the two episodes just considered in a story about the abbot Macarius in *Vitae patrum* 5.18.9, PL 73:981-982. Like Benedict, Macarius too saw Satan, although we are told simply that he was disguised as a man. He was wearing what appeared to be an old linen tunic filled with holes, through each of which a small flask was suspended. When Macarius asked him where he was going, he replied that he was going to visit the brethren, to tempt them to sample the contents of his flasks. As in Gregory's case, Satan was successful with only one of the brethren, a monk by the name of Theoctistus. But rather than taking physical possession of him, Satan

The same conclusion emerges from another example mentioned by de Vogüé, concerning stories that occur in the fourth and twenty-fifth chapters of the second book of the *Dialogues*. The first episode concerns a monk in one of Benedict's monasteries who refused to remain with the rest of the monastic community for prayer. He was rebuked by his abbot and by Benedict himself, but to no effect. Taking the matter firmly into his own hands, Benedict visited the monastery, and noticed that it was a little black boy pulling at the edge of his habit who was drawing the restless monk outside at the time of prayers. Neither the abbot, Pompeianus, nor the monk, Maurus, who had accompanied Benedict, was able to see what was happening. But after the three of them had prayed together for three days, Maurus was able to discern what was taking place, although the abbot still could not. The next day, when Benedict found the offending monk loitering outside after prayers, he beat him with his staff, and this finally solved the problem. From that time on the monk remained quietly at prayer with the others, and was not tempted any further by the Devil.

The cognate episode concerns one of Benedict's monks who had set his heart on abandoning the monastery. He was finally given permission to depart, but had no sooner left the monastery grounds than he found his way blocked by a dragon, and in his fright he returned to the monastery where he promised to remain for ever thereafter. This dragon, which had been visible to the monk, was not visible to the brethren who responded to his cries for help, for only by virtue of Benedict's prayer was the discontented monk able to see the evil one who had been leading him astray. This story is really quite different from the earlier episode. The only feature the two stories hold in common is that they both exemplify Benedict's ability to enhance, through the power of prayer, the spiritual sight of those who came within his sphere of influence, a gift that quite conceivably could have been manifested on several other occasions as well.[42]

---

succeeded only in tempting him by illicit thoughts. And rather than slapping the target of Satan's wiles as Benedict did, Macarius skilfully brought the monk in his care to the point of confessing his fault. He so strengthened the monk by his spiritual counsel that, on his return, Satan was unable to have any further success with him. There are similarities between the two stories, to be sure, but also significant differences; there are no verbal parallels between them at all.

[42] *Dial.* 2.4, sc 260:150-152; 2.25, sc 260:212. On the imagery of the black boy in ancient and early medieval monastic literature, cf. B. Steidle, "Der 'schwarze kleine Knabe' in der alten Mönchserzählung. Beitrag zu St. Gregor, Dial. 2,4," *BenM* 34 (1958): 339-350; and G. Penco, "Sopravvivenze della demonologia antica nel monachesimo medievale," *SMon.* 13 (1971): 31-36 at 34-36.

De Vogüé is more concerned by the miracle stories in the second of the four categories mentioned above: the miracles of Benedict that appear to duplicate the miracles of other saints. However, most of these are no more problematic than the instances just considered. One example links Benedict with Bishop Boniface of Ferentis. In book one of the *Dialogues* Gregory says that Boniface once gave some poor people begging for alms twelve gold coins that his nephew, the priest Constantius, had received from the sale of his horse and had deposited in his treasure chest. Later Boniface prayed to the Virgin, and miraculously received from her hand twelve new coins to appease the anger of his nephew. In the second book of the *Dialogues* Gregory tells us that Benedict also was able to obtain money miraculously by means of prayer. But whereas Boniface displayed his charity to the poor, Benedict came to the relief of a man heavily in debt and tormented by his creditor; and whereas Boniface removed twelve gold coins from his nephew's treasure chest, and later received the same amount from the Virgin, Benedict received thirteen gold pieces, of which twelve were to be given to the creditor, while the other was to be kept by the debtor himself for his own needs. The stories are certainly similar, but different enough that one need not depend on the other. In the final analysis the only feature that they share is the fact that they both demonstrate how the charity of the two saints was divinely blessed and supported. Moreover, both stories are reasonably well attested.[43]

Scarcely more troubling are the parallels between Benedict and Sabinus of Canosa. In the second book of the *Dialogues* we read that the wayward monks of Vicovaro, resenting the harsh discipline Benedict imposed upon them, tried to assassinate him by offering him a glass pitcher containing poisoned wine. Their attempt came to naught, however, for the pitcher shattered as soon as Benedict made the sign of the cross over it. In the next book Gregory tells us that Sabinus also survived a murderous plot, one hatched by his archdeacon, an ambitious man impatient to take over the episcopal see. This archdeacon conspired with one of the bishop's servants to poison him. But when Sabinus made the sign of the cross over the poisoned cup the servant offered him, and drank its contents, it was the

---

[43] *Dial.* 1.9.10-13, SC 260:84-88; 2.27.1-2, SC 260:214-216. The story of Boniface of Ferentis was obtained from the priest, Gaudentius, who was still alive at Gregory's time of writing. See *Dial.* 1.9.1, SC 260:76: "Huius [Bonifatii] multa miracula is qui adhuc superest Gaudentius presbiter narrat. Qui in eius obsequio nutritus, tanto valet de illo quaeque veracius dicere, quanto eis hunc contigit et interesse." The source for the story about Benedict was Benedict's disciple, Peregrinus, who seems to have been deceased. See *Dial.* 2.27.1, SC 260:214: "Neque illud taceam, quod eius [i.e. Benedicti] discipulus, Peregrinus nomine, narrare consueverat."

archdeacon who died: Sabinus himself suffered no ill effects. Although the details of the stories differ, in both cases the sign of the cross was sufficient to protect these men of God from attempts at poisoning on the part of their enemies.[44]

Gregory also observes that Benedict and Sabinus both possessed prophetic powers, and were able to foil Totila's attempts to test them. Totila tried the virtue of Benedict by disguising one of his retainers as the king of the Goths, sending him off to meet Benedict in his place. He attempted to test Sabinus by assuming himself the role of a servant. Sabinus, we are told, had become blind in his old age. When, therefore, he invited Totila to dine with him, Totila took the opportunity to verify his spiritual powers by intercepting the servant who was about to offer the bishop his cup, and by presenting it to the bishop himself. Both deceptions were detected, however: Benedict recognized the retainer for an imposter, and Sabinus realized that it was the hand of royalty that had proffered him his cup.[45]

The saints' actions are certainly similar in both pairs of episodes, and the witnesses cited in their support are not identified as precisely as we would like.[46] But the similarities are limited, and there is no reason to doubt that Gregory availed himself of independently circulating stories of Benedict and Sabinus. It is hardly surprising that the saints had enemies; or that they used the sign of the cross as a defence against evil, a well-attested practice in the hagiographical literature. Moreover, if Benedict and Sabinus both possessed the gift of farsightedness, so did many other saints; and if Totila was tempted to test this gift in one of their cases, there is no reason why he could not have done so in the other, especially since the specific details of the two tests are quite different.[47]

Perhaps more troubling, at least at first glance, are the parallels in the deaths of Spes, Scholastica and Benedict to which de Vogüé refers. But, when

[44] *Dial.* 2.3.1-5, SC 260:140-142; 3.5.3-4, SC 260:274-276.

[45] *Dial.* 2.14, SC 260:180-182; 3.5.1-2, SC 260:272-274.

[46] Gregory mentions no specific source for these stories of Benedict, and so would have us understand that he was dependent on the four disciples mentioned at *Dial.* 2 Prol. 2, SC 260:128, at least one of whom, Honoratus, was still alive at his time of writing. As his source for the stories of Sabinus Gregory mentions only some *religiosi viri* well known in the province of Apulia. See *Dial.* 3.5.1, SC 260:272: "Quidam etenim religiosi viri Apuliae provinciae partibus cogniti, hoc quod apud multorum notitiam longe lateque percrebuit, de Sabino Canusinae urbis episcopo testari solent."

[47] On the sign of the cross, see Athanasius, *Vita S. Antonii*, chap. 35, PG 26:894; Sulpicius Severus, *Vita S. Martini* 13.8, SC 133:282; 22.1, SC 133:300. Several of the fathers of the desert could read the hearts of their brethren and had the gift of prophetic insight: the Abba Helle, for example. See Rufinus, *Historia monachorum*, chap. 11, PL 21:430-431.

examined carefully, these yield similarly inconclusive results. Benedict saw
the soul of his sister leave her body and ascend to heaven in the form of a
dove; the brethren of the Abbot Spes had a similar experience on the death
of their spiritual father. But what Benedict witnessed at a distance, the
brethren of Spes saw at first-hand and in greater detail: at the moment of their
abbot's death they saw a dove leave his body through his mouth, and ascend
to heaven through the open roof of the oratory.[48]

The similarities in the deaths of Spes and Benedict are more striking, and
have been noted by other scholars as well. But once again the details differ.
In his last year Benedict informed a number of his disciples of the day of his
death. Six days before he died he ordered his tomb to be opened, and he was
seized by a violent fever that grew steadily worse thereafter. On the day of
his death his disciples carried him into the oratory, where he received the
Body and Blood of the Lord. Then, supported by the arms of his brethren,
he stood with his hands raised in prayer to heaven; and as he prayed, he died.
That same day two monks, one at the monastery, the other some distance
away, received an identical revelation. They both saw a road, covered with
rich carpeting (*strata palliis*) and glittering with innumerable lights, stretch
eastward from the monastery in a straight line until it reached heaven. A man
of majestic appearance told them that this was the route travelled by
Benedict.

In a number of important respects the death of Spes is similar, but it is by
no means identical. Gregory says that after forty years of blindness God
restored the Abbot's sight, revealing that the day of his death was near, and
urging him to go out and preach in the surrounding monasteries. After fifteen
days of preaching Spes returned to his monastery, where he received the
Body and Blood of the Lord. While the monks were chanting the Psalms,
Spes became fixed in prayer and died. As we have already noted, all those

---

[48] *Dial.* 2.34, sc 260:234; 4.11.4, sc 265:48. Apart from the motif of the dove, there is
nothing particularly noteworthy in the fact that Benedict and the brethren of the Abbot Spes
shared a similar experience. The hagiographical literature provides many parallel examples.
St Benedict also witnessed the soul of Germanus of Capua ascend to heaven (*Dial.* 2.35.3-4,
sc 260:238); St Antony saw the souls of both Amoun of Nitria and St Paul the Hermit make
a similar journey (Athanasius, *Vita S. Antonii*, chap. 60, pg 26:930-931; Jerome, *Vita S.
Pauli*, chap. 14, pl 23:27); and the holy man Paphnutius had much the same kind of
experience when he saw the soul of a man he had converted to the monastic life rise to its
heavenly reward (Rufinus, *Historia monachorum*, chap. 16, pl 21:438). Sulpicius Severus tells
us that he himself had a similar vision of the soul of the blessed Martin (*Epist. 2 ad Aurelium
diaconum*, csel 1:142-143). Of all these examples, Benedict's vision of Germanus of Capua
and Antony's vision of Amoun of Nitria probably have the most in common, but scarcely
enough to establish any strict dependence.

present saw his soul ascend into heaven in the form of a dove. Like Benedict, Spes was granted advance knowledge of his death. Again like Benedict, he died in his own monastery, in an attitude of prayer, having been fortified by the holy sacrament. These similarities have aroused de Vogüé's suspicions, which conceivably could be strengthened by Gregory's failure again to name his witnesses. But there are also important differences between the two accounts, and the similarities that remain are precisely those elements that could have been incorporated into independently established legends to decorate the deaths of their heroes.[49]

Of all the miracles of Benedict said to duplicate those of other saints, the most problematic links Benedict with Isaac of Spoleto. In the second book of the *Dialogues* we learn that, while still a boy, the monk Exhilaratus was instructed by his master to take two flasks of wine to Saint Benedict. Exhilaratus delivered only one, and hid the other along the way. But Benedict was aware of his dishonesty, and after he had thanked the boy for the flask he had delivered, he warned him about a serpent that had crawled into the other one. Virtually the same story is told in the third book. According to this version, an unidentified young servant was sent to Isaac, not with two flasks of wine, but with two baskets of food. But like Exhilaratus in the earlier story, he delivered only one of the baskets, concealing the other; and like Benedict, Isaac thanked the servant for the one basket he received, and then warned him of a serpent that had crawled into the one he had concealed. As de Vogüé points out, the identity of the two episodes is virtually complete, and so in all likelihood the miracle of one of these saints has been transferred to the other.[50]

But was the transfer effected by Gregory, or had it already taken place at some earlier stage? Either alternative is possible. 'Doublets' of this sort are a common feature of orally-transmitted material, and do not necessarily imply conscious duplication on the part of the author who committed the

---

[49] *Dial.* 2.37, SC 260:242-244; 4.11.3-4, SC 265:46-48. In addition to de Vogüé, see Gross, "Der Tod des hl. Benedictus," esp. p. 170. De Vogüé, *Introduction*, p. 127, maintains that Gregory sought to conceal the similarities in the deaths of Spes, Scholastica and Benedict. He points to the fact that, at the beginning of book four, before recounting the death of Spes, Gregory does not mention the deaths of the two other saints, although the examples would have served to strengthen his thesis.

Gregory mentions no specific source for Benedict's vision of the death of Scholastica, or for his account of Benedict's own death. Again, we should understand that these stories were obtained from the four disciples mentioned at *Dial.* 2 Prol. 2, SC 260:128. His source for the death of Spes is an unidentified *vir venerabilis*: "Adhuc in monasterio meo positus, cuiusdam valde venerabilis viri relatione cognovi quod dico" (*Dial.* 4.11.1, SC 265:44).

[50] *Dial.* 2.18, SC 260:194; 3.14.9, SC 260:310. See de Vogüé, *Introduction*, p. 126n.

oral tradition to written form.[51] The fact that the identity of these two episodes extends even to some verbal similarity might incline one to suspect that Gregory himself was responsible.[52] But he may simply have lapsed unconsciously into the same language because of the striking uniformity of the tales. To complicate matters, the two stories are among the best attested, although neither witness was alive when Gregory wrote the *Dialogues*. No specific source for the first story is mentioned, but the Exhilaratus whom it concerns had probably been a monk in Gregory's own monastery of St Andrew, and was known to Peter: "Exhilaratus noster, quem ipse conversum nosti." Gregory's source for the second story was the saintly Eleutherius, who had been Abbot of the monastery of St Mark the Evangelist in Spoleto, but had spent his later years with Gregory at his monastery in Rome.[53] Since Gregory was writing for an audience that included his own brethren, would he have attempted to disguise a case of conscious duplication by pointing to two monks who had been known to them? I think not, although it is difficult to argue conclusively one way or the other.

When the enquiry is expanded to include other instances of duplication in the *Dialogues*, one encounters cases equally as striking as the one just discussed, with results, unfortunately, equally as inconclusive. One of them is of particular interest in the pre-history of the doctrine of Purgatory. In book four of the *Dialogues* Gregory tells us a story concerning Germanus, Bishop of Capua, who went to the baths one day and found there the deacon, Paschasius, who had died some time before, acting as an attendant. Asked what he was doing in such a place, Paschasius replied that he was there because he had endorsed the party of Lawrence against Pope Symmachus in the papal schism. He asked Germanus to pray for him, and told him that

---

[51] Cf. C. Stancliffe, *St. Martin and his Hagiographer* (Oxford, 1983), pp. 168-169. Stancliffe makes the point while considering the issue of variant versions of the same story in Sulpicius's Martinian work.

[52] Gregory's descriptions of the thefts perpetrated by Exhilaratus and the unnamed boy are very similar: compare "unum [flasconem] detulit, alterum vero pergens in itinere abscondit" with "unam [sportam] ... subripuit atque in itinere abscondit, unam vero ad Dei hominem detulit."

[53] Cf. *Vie de saint Benoît* (Bégrolles-en-Mauges, 1982), p. 122, where de Vogüé argues that Exhilaratus was a *conversus*, "c'est-à-dire un chrétien engagé dans une vie quasi religieuse au milieu du monde"; and *Introduction*, p. 159n, where he claims that he is probably to be identified with a curial official mentioned in Gregory's Register and still alive in 593. If de Vogüé is correct, it is surprising that Gregory does not identify Exhilaratus more precisely. Moreover, Gregory's language clearly implies he was deceased.

On the source for the story of Isaac, see *Dial.* 3.14.1, sc 260:302: "Multa autem de eodem viro, narrante venerabili patre Eleutherio, agnovi, qui et hunc familiariter noverat, et eius verbis vita fidem praebebat." See also *Dial.* 3.33.1, sc 260:392-394.

when he returned and found him no longer there, Germanus would know that his prayers had been answered. Germanus did pray for him, and when he came back to the baths a few days later, Paschasius was nowhere to be found.

This episode is remarkably similar to a story of a priest of the diocese of Centumcellae that Gregory tells a few chapters later. This priest, who was the pastor of the church of St John in Tauriana, used to bathe in the hot springs of that city. One day he found a stranger acting as an attendant at the baths, an experience which was repeated several times. Because the attendant was always helpful, the priest offered him two loaves of bread (*duas oblationum coronas*) as an expression of his appreciation. The attendant declined the gift, however. He explained that during his lifetime he had been the owner of the establishment, but that now he was required to act as a servant there to do penance for his sins. He asked the priest to offer the bread to God to make intercession for him, and told him that when he came back and found him no longer there, he would know that his prayers had been heard. The priest spent an entire week in prayer and tearful supplication, offering masses daily. When he then returned to the baths, the mysterious man had disappeared.[54]

Although there are some minor differences between the two accounts, the parallels extend even to matters of detail. Indeed, as de Vogüé observes, "Un parallèle aussi exact et aussi suivi suggère irrésistiblement qu'un des récits a été copié sur l'autre, à moins qu'ils ne reproduisent tous deux le même modèle."[55] It is possible that Gregory was responsible for the conflation of the stories, for only the second is well attested. Gregory's source there was Bishop Felix of Porto, who was still alive at the time of Gregory's writing; Felix had heard it from the priest himself, who was still alive two years earlier. As his source for the story about Germanus and Paschasius, Gregory can cite only some unidentified elders from whom he had heard it while he was still a young layman.[56] He could have decided to modify slightly the story he had received from Felix, and to use it a second time in his account of the encounter between Germanus and Paschasius, concealing his tracks with a vague reference that could not be verified. However, there is no real evidence that this is in fact what he did, and it is equally possible that a legend originally attached to Paschasius and Germanus, and which Gregory heard

---

[54] *Dial.* 4.42.2-4, sc 265:152; 4.57.3-7, sc 265:184-188. Cf. J. Le Goff, *La naissance du Purgatoire* (Paris, 1981), pp. 121-131, esp. pp. 125-129.

[55] De Vogüé, *Introduction*, p. 128.

[56] *Dial.* 4.42.1, sc 265:150: "Nam cum adhuc essem iuvenculus atque in laico habitu constitutus, narrari a maioribus atque scientibus audivi quod Pascasius huius apostolicae sedis diaconus. ..."

while he was still a young man, was claimed for his own benefit by the priest
of Centumcellae and later reported to Gregory in precisely the way Gregory
describes.

An even more puzzling case of duplication occurs in the same fourth book
of the *Dialogues*. On the authority of his friend Deusdedit, who was known
for his honesty and his cordial relations with the Roman nobility (*honestus
senex, ... valde huius urbis nobilibus amicus*), Gregory tells us that, during the
time of the Goths, a prominent Roman (*spectabilis vir*) by the name of
Reparatus had died and then suddenly come back to life. Reparatus immediately asked that a messenger be sent to the church of St Lawrence the Martyr
to enquire about the priest Tiburtius, a man with a reputation for dissolute
living. After the messenger had set out on his way, Reparatus told those
attending him that during his visit to the next world he had seen an enormous
funeral pyre whose summit towered to the sky, and more important, that he
had also seen a second pyre upon which Tiburtius was being consumed by
the flames. Having said this, he died once again; when the messenger arrived
at the church of St Lawrence the Martyr, he discovered that Tiburtius had
died as well. The story of Stephen, a man of high rank who, on a trip to
Constantinople, became ill and died, and was conducted into the regions of
hell, is quite similar. However, when his case was brought before the infernal
court, it was dismissed, for the man who had been ordered to appear there
was not this Stephen at all, but rather Stephen the smith (*ferrarius*), his
neighbour. Eventually the administration of eternal justice was righted. No
sooner had the noble Stephen been ordered to return to earth than Stephen
the smith passed out of this life.[57]

The similarity between these stories is obvious, but it is even more striking
that both of them, especially the story of Stephen, share many features with
a tale related by Augustine. A man named Curma, a minor curial official
(*curialis pauper*) at Tullium, near Hippo, fell ill and lapsed into unconscious-
ness. After several days he woke up, and asked immediately that someone go
to the house of Curma the smith (*faber ferrarius*) to see if anything had
happened there. When enquiries were made, it was found that the smith had
died at the precise moment the official had regained consciousness. The
curialis pauper explained that it was not his time that had come but that of
the *faber ferrarius*, who therefore had been summoned to the other world.[58]

In some respects the stories of Stephen and Reparatus have more in
common with one another than either has with the story of Curma. Stephen
and Reparatus were both men of prominence, and they both died and later

---

[57] *Dial.* 4.32, sc 265:106-108; 4.37.5-6, sc 265:128.
[58] Augustine, *De cura pro mortuis gerenda* 12.15, csel 41:644-647.

came back to life. Curma was a minor official, and he simply fell into a coma from which he subsequently awakened. But the Reparatus narrative shares with the story of Curma the device of the messenger, and the account of Stephen shares with it the theme of mistaken identity in which a smith (*ferrarius* or *faber ferrarius*) figures prominently. As de Vogüé points out, this strongly suggests that Augustine's story of Curma was the source for both of Gregory's stories,[59] although it would seem that the story of Stephen is more dependent on Augustine than the story of Reparatus.

Important differences between the stories of Stephen and Curma of course remain. Unlike Stephen, Curma had a vision of Paradise as well as a vision of Hell. While he was in Paradise, he was admonished to be baptized, and after his revival he received the sacrament from the hand of Augustine himself. Moreover, each story has a different purpose: Gregory's point is primarily moral, Augustine's metaphysical.[60] But according to de Vogüé, the connection between the stories, indeed their dependence, is clear, and is confirmed by a number of additional facts: (1) that Peter alludes to Augustine's story at the beginning of the chapter; (2) that the vision of the anonymous soldier that immediately follows the story of Stephen seems to be an expanded version of what is claimed in general terms for Curma; and (3) that Gregory offers only his own word to testify to the truth of the story of Stephen, which takes place far away from Rome, at Constantinople, and at an indeterminate date. It is, says de Vogüé, a clear case of Gregory borrowing directly from his predecessor: "Cette fois, Grégoire ne s'est pas donné beaucoup de peine pour masquer son emprunt. Visiblement, son histoire des deux Etienne n'est qu'un remploi de celle des deux Curma."[61]

---

[59] De Vogüé, *Introduction*, p. 130.

[60] At the beginning of the chapter containing the story of Stephen Gregory tells us that, because words alone are not always sufficient to induce belief in the torments of hell, God has allowed some people to die and then come back to life so that they might properly fear these punishments for having seen them with their own eyes (*Dial.* 4.37.2, SC 265:126). Presumably their stories are worth telling to others for the same reason. This seems particularly clear from the details of the story of the anonymous soldier who, like Stephen, died, had a vision of hell, and then returned to tell of his experience (*Dial.* 4.37.7-16, SC 265:128-134). They illustrate the virtues by means of which heaven might be won and hell avoided. Augustine's main point, however, is to emphasize that the persons seen by Curma in his vision were mere appearances. He points out that Curma saw not only persons who were dead at the time, but those who were still alive and had no awareness of the events he reported of them. He also saw places where he assuredly could not have been. Hence all of the people seen in the vision, both those who were dead at the time and those who were still alive, and all of the places as well, were seen in appearance only and not in reality.

[61] De Vogüé, *Introduction*, pp. 134-135. Cf. Petersen, *The Dialogues*, pp. 87-88. Augustine's story itself was not without precedent. Indeed, there are some striking parallels between

That the story of Stephen, and possibly the story of Reparatus, can be traced back ultimately to Augustine is undeniable. Indeed, the case for Gregory's direct dependence on Augustine is a strong possibility as well, for neither story is particularly well attested. As we have seen, Gregory's source for the story of Reparatus is a certain Deusdedit, otherwise unknown, who appears to have been dead at Gregory's time of writing. The source for the story of Stephen, he claims, was Stephen himself, whom Peter is said to have known quite well, and who died three years earlier in the plague that devastated Rome.[62] But at least both sources are identified by name; and whatever we might think of Deusdedit, it is unlikely that Stephen at least was a product of Gregory's imagination, given the fact that Peter had apparently known him. De Vogüé's case needs corroboration, and, unfortunately, the evidence that he adduces is inadequate to the task.

At the beginning of the chapter containing the story of Stephen, Peter does ask his master how it is that some people die as it were by mistake, and then come back to life again claiming they had heard that it was not they but someone else who had been summoned.[63] De Vogüé claims that this is an unequivocal allusion to the story of Curma. In fact, however, there is no reason for believing that it is any more than an appropriate introduction to Gregory's own story of Stephen. Curma, after all, did not really die. De Vogüé points out that, according to Augustine, Curma saw various people, some of whom he had known while they were alive, judged according to their merits; and he maintains that this general assertion is amplified in Gregory's account of the anonymous soldier. But the vision of the soldier is remarkably detailed. Although it may have been suggested directly by Augustine's brief statement, it is more likely to be attributed to the source of the soldier's story. The soldier did, after all, journey to the other world.

Gregory declares that the soldier died during the plague that devastated Rome three years earlier, but came back to life shortly thereafter and told of what had happened to him. He had seen a river of dark waters, covered by vapors that gave off a horrible stench. Spanning the river was a bridge that led to grassy meadows, dotted with fragrant flowers, on the other side. People in white robes gathered there, and each of them had a dwelling of brilliant light. One house, still under construction, was being built of bricks of gold.

---

his tale of Curma and stories to be found in Lucian and elsewhere. Conceivably Augustine too could be accused of literary borrowing. On this matter, however, see M. Dulaey, *La rêve dans la vie et la pensée de saint Augustin* (Paris, 1973), pp. 205-210; and Stancliffe, *St. Martin*, pp. 198-200.

[62] *Dial.* 4.37.5-7, SC 265:128-130.
[63] *Dial.* 4.37.1, SC 265:124-126.

The bridge was a testing place for souls of the departed: the unjust would fall into the filthy waters; the just would cross over without incident. The soldier saw one of the damned, an overseer of the church (*ecclesiasticae familiae maior*) named Peter, loaded down with heavy chains and mired in the foulness beneath the bridge. His torment was a punishment for the spirit of cruelty rather than justice with which he had administered punishment in this world. The soldier also had a clear vision of one of the elect, a priest from some foreign country who crossed the bridge without difficulty, and of one whose status had not as yet been determined, the Stephen of the previous story, who had been allowed to return to this life. The lower half of his body was dangling over the edge of the bridge, and some fiends from the waters below were trying to drag him down; but some good spirits arrayed in white were striving to haul him back to safety. Although Stephen had been guilty of evil deeds of the flesh, Gregory explains, he had also been liberal in giving alms; before his eternal fate could be decided, he had to undergo this trial of the competing good and evil tendencies within him. Unless this detailed account was provided by his source, Gregory must have invented it out of whole cloth, or else pieced it together from a variety of literary sources. There is nothing in the story of Curma to suggest any of it, other than the very brief mention that Curma saw people being judged according to their merits.[64]

---

[64] *Dial.* 4.37.7-16, SC 265:128-134. Gregory does not mention a source for this story. Since it took place three years earlier in Rome and became known to many, it was probably received simply on common report. Conceivably, however, Gregory would have us understand that he heard it from the soldier himself.

Petersen, *The Dialogues*, p. 87, suggests that Gregory's account may have been influenced by the apocryphal *Apocalypse of Peter*, which was written in the first half of the second century, or the apocryphal *Apocalypse of Paul*, written in the late fourth or early fifth century. Cf. E. Hennecke, *New Testament Apocrypha*, ed. W. Schneemelcher, English translation ed. R.McL. Wilson, 2 vols. (London, 1963-1965), 2:663-683, 755-798. Of the two, she says, Gregory was more likely influenced by the *Apocalypse of Paul*, which was available in Latin translation. Moreover, the *Apocalypse of Paul* speaks of a horrible river in hell (Hennecke, p. 779), a more exact analogue of what is found in Gregory's story than the horrible lake referred to in the earlier account (pp. 672, 676). In the final analysis, however, the differences between both of these texts and Gregory's account are such that it is not very likely that Gregory was dependent on either of them.

A stronger candidate would be the sixth book of the *Aeneid.* Cf. P. Courcelle, "Les Pères de l'Eglise devant les enfers virgiliens," *AHDLMA* 22 (1955): 5-74 at 31n, 33n; *Connais-toi toi-même, de Socrate à saint Bernard*, 2 vols. (Paris, 1974-1975), 2:465-466n. Although Courcelle detects some verbal similarity, the parallels are not striking enough to suggest direct dependence. But Virgilian influence may be discernible nonetheless. Particularly noteworthy is the fact that the geographical relationship between the Styx and the fields of Elysium seems to be repeated in the soldier's story. Although the river of the soldier's story is very different than the Styx, it may owe something to Virgil's description of the Tartarean Phelegethon, the

Hence Gregory's direct dependence on Augustine is far from certain. Clear textual evidence that would put the matter beyond doubt is completely lacking; there are no verbal parallels between Augustine's and Gregory's stories at all.

The case for Gregory's direct dependence on Augustine in the episode of Stephen is no stronger than the case for his direct dependence on Sulpicius Severus at another point in the *Dialogues*. Yet de Vogüé maintains that Gregory probably received this latter story substantially in the manner he reports. In the first book of the *Dialogues* Gregory tells us that once, while he was travelling through Samnium on the business of his monastery, Libertinus of Fondi was robbed of his horse by some soldiers under the command of Darida, the Goth. Far from showing resentment, Libertinus offered them his riding whip as well, and then gave himself over to prayer. The soldiers made off with the stolen horse. But when they came to the Volturno river, their own horses would go no further, even after repeated beatings. At length one of them remarked that they were being punished for the wrong they had inflicted upon the man of God, and so they turned back to find Libertinus still on his knees in prayer. After the horse had been returned to its rightful owner, the soldiers set out on their way once again, and this time they were able to cross the Volturno without incident.[65]

In its general outline this story is strikingly similar to a story of Saint Martin in the *Dialogues* of Sulpicius Severus. Once, when Martin was riding his donkey along the public highway, carefully keeping to the side of the road, the sight of the saint, who was attired in a shabby tunic covered with a flowing black pallium, frightened the mules pulling a wagon under the command of some armed officials of the imperial treasury, and the traces of the animals became hopelessly tangled. The enraged officials jumped down from the wagon and subjected Martin to a savage beating. However, after they had spent their anger and had returned to their wagon to resume their

---

burning river of Hell. Perhaps the strongest parallel to Gregory's story is provided by Gregory of Tours, *Historia Francorum* 4.33, MGH, SRM 1, p. 166. Cf. M.P. Ciccarese, "Alle origini della letteratura delle visioni: il contributo di Gregorio di Tours," *SSR* 2 (1981): 251-266, esp. 261-266. Gregory of Tours describes a vision of a river (although a river of flame) in which sinners are immersed to varying degrees; and he also supplies the motif of a bridge, similarly conceived as a testing place. But once again there are significant differences, perhaps most importantly the fact that the grassy meadows and dwellings on the other side of the river have been replaced by a single white mansion. What all of this suggests, therefore, is that by the sixth century many of the elements in the soldier's story had entered the realm of folklore, from which they were retrieved by Gregory's source. It does not prove that Gregory himself was the creator of the story, although that remains a possibility.

[65] *Dial.* 1.2.1-3, SC 260:24-26.

journey, the mules would not move, not even after repeated lashing. When the officials learned from some passers-by that the victim of their abuse had been Saint Martin, it became clear to them that they were being held back because of the way they had treated the man of God. So they set out after Martin, who by this time had been discovered by his companions and taken away. When they caught up to him, they pleaded for his forgiveness; once it was granted, they were free to go on their way.[66]

The general similarity in the shapes of the two stories in itself is probably enough to suggest that Sulpicius must have been the source for the story about Libertinus. But the parallels between Gregory and Sulpicius are more extensive. After a brief episode, Gregory continues with a story about a miraculous cure effected by Libertinus. While he was journeying to Ravenna, Libertinus met a mother carrying her dead son in her arms, and the woman implored him to restore her child to her. Libertinus was torn between the demands of humility and the demands of compassion:

> One can readily imagine [Gregory says] the struggle that went on in his heart where the habitual humility of his life now came face to face with the devotedness of a mother. Fear kept him from attempting to fulfill a request so unusual, while a feeling of compassion kept urging him to help the mother in her bereavement. But, thanks be to God, the pious mother was victorious in this struggle, and the saint, in being overcome, gave proof of real strength. For, if the devotion of the mother had not been able to conquer his heart, how could he have been a man of true virtue?

Libertinus dismounted, knelt in prayer, and, placing on the breast of the dead child the sandal of Honoratus which, out of veneration for his saintly master, he carried with him wherever he went, he brought the child back to life.[67]

A comparison with the story in Sulpicius Severus that follows directly on the account of Martin's beating by the officers of the state is especially revealing. On his way to Chartres with his companions, Martin stopped to preach the Word of God to a crowd of village people. A woman whose son had just died approached him and implored him to revive her child. Martin knelt and prayed over the body, and after his prayer was finished, handed back to the mother a child completely restored to life.[68]

The cumulative effect of the parallels is to make the Sulpician inspiration for Gregory's stories undeniable. It is reinforced by the fact that the theme of humility, which plays such a prominent role in the second story of

---

[66] Sulpicius Severus, *Dial.* 2.3, CSEL 1:183-184.
[67] *Dial.* 1.2.5-7, SC 260:26-30, esp. 1.2.6, Zimmerman 11, SC 260:28.
[68] Sulpicius Severus, *Dial.* 2.4, CSEL 1:184-185.

Libertinus, is equally prominent in the corresponding story about Martin. But even if Sulpicius Severus is the ultimate source for these stories of Libertinus of Fondi, it is not at all clear that Gregory drew directly on Sulpicius, as de Vogüé himself acknowledges. Although he is aware that the parallels between Gregory and Sulpicius extend to two pairs of stories, de Vogüé restricts his analysis to the first pair, and concludes that Gregory was probably simply retelling a story that he got either from Lawrence, the *vir religiosus* whom he mentions specifically as his source, or from general report, a story that in the course of the telling had been conflated with one of the very popular stories of Saint Martin.[69] But if a conclusion of Gregory's non-dependence on Sulpicius is justified here, a similar conclusion of his non-dependence on Augustine for the Stephen episode discussed earlier could be justified as well. The textual evidence is the same in the two cases. It is sufficient to indicate that Sulpicius Severus was clearly the ultimate source for the stories of Libertinus, and that Augustine was the ultimate source for the story of Stephen; but in neither case is there the kind of textual evidence that would clearly indicate Gregory's direct dependence on his literary predecessor.

De Vogüé would argue that the stories of Libertinus are slightly better attested than the story of Stephen, for in the former Gregory can point to a living witness, Lawrence, the *vir religiosus* who had known Libertinus at Fondi; his source for the story of Stephen, Stephen himself, is now deceased. But we should be careful not to make too much of this. In both cases the source is identified by name and is eminently qualified to attest to the story in question. If one of them is now deceased, there is nothing inherently implausible about that fact, and we can be reasonably sure that he was more than a figment of Gregory's imagination, since he is said to have been well known to Peter. There are several specific details in the first of the Libertinus stories that, as de Vogüé points out, serve to localize and date the episode: the references to Samnium, the Volturno river, and Darida, details that are missing in the story of Stephen.[70] But Stephen's story does, I think, contain all the specificity that one could reasonably expect, and it can be located with considerable precision in space and time. We are told that Stephen's

---

[69] De Vogüé, *Introduction*, p. 131. De Vogüé maintains that, although he would have us understand that he drew particularly on Lawrence, Gregory does not exclude a recourse to common report. However, Gregory's language makes it clear that Lawrence was indeed his source: "De quo [Libertino] quamvis virtutes multas plurimorum narratio certa vulgaverit, praedictus tamen *Laurentius* religiosus vir, qui nunc superest et ei ipso in tempore familiarissimus fuit, *multa mihi de illo dicere consuevit. Ex quibus ea quae recolo pauca narrabo*" (*Dial.* 1.2.1, SC 260:24; emphasis added).

[70] De Vogüé, *Introduction*, p. 131.

experience occurred in the recent past, since he died only three years earlier, and that it took place after an illness in Constantinople. In point of fact, to conclude that Gregory was not dependent on the literary source would be unwarranted in either case. Skilful plagiarism on Gregory's part remains a possibility. But it is a possibility only, not a fact. In neither case can Gregory's direct dependence on a literary source be clearly established.

Perhaps the most interesting example of the duplication of an earlier literary source has to do with Gregory's account of an incident in the life of Bishop Andrew of Fondi, which closely parallels stories in the *Collations* of John Cassian and in the *Vitae patrum*. Andrew of Fondi was a virtuous man. But because he was unwilling to dismiss from his episcopal residence a holy woman whom he kept as a servant, the Devil began to tempt him with sinful thoughts. One day a Jew who was travelling along the Appian Way from Campania to Rome had managed to reach as far as Fondi when night fell. Unable to find any other lodging, he decided to stay in the temple of Apollo, although (somewhat implausibly) he first took the precaution of protecting himself from possible evil with the sign of the cross. The dreadful solitude of the place weighed on him, and he was still wide awake at midnight, when there suddenly appeared a crowd of evil spirits parading before their leader. The chief spirit had sat down in the middle of the temple and begun a formal investigation of the accomplishments of his subalterns, when one of them jumped up and reported the success he had had in tempting Bishop Andrew. Just on the previous evening Andrew had been induced to give the woman in his household a caressing pat on the back. Eventually the Jew was spotted; but when, on the orders of their leader, the spirits approached him to find out who he was, they noticed that he was marked with the sign of the cross, and their whole troop suddenly disappeared. The frightened man hurried off to the bishop, whom he finally persuaded to confess his fault. Andrew dismissed the woman from his service, and converted the temple of Apollo into a chapel in honour of St Andrew the Apostle. The whole experience was not without its salutary effect on the Jew as well, who was converted to the Christian faith and baptized.[71]

In Cassian the story concerns, not a Jew, but a monk journeying in the desert. When night fell he took shelter in a cave, where he said his evening office; he was still singing the Psalms when midnight passed. After he had finished, he suddenly saw crowds of demons gathering together on all sides. When their prince began his investigation of their actions, one spirit reported that he had finally been successful in tempting a very well-known monk

---

[71] *Dial.* 3.7.1-9, sc 260:278-284.

whom he had been attacking for fifteen years: that very night he had impelled
the monk to commit adultery with a consecrated maid. At the break of day
the whole swarm of demons vanished, and the monk, thinking to test the
claims of this spirit, made his way to the monastery at Pelusium, where his
offending brother resided. When he questioned the monk, he learned that the
night before he had indeed left his monastery, gone into town, and committed the sin of which the demon had accused him.[72]

In the *Vitae patrum* the story appears in two versions. Following Petersen,
we shall label the longer one Version A and the shorter one Version B.[73] In
Version B the story concerns a monk who had gone out at mealtime to draw
some water. When he accidentally overturned his water vessel, he decided to
go into the desert to consult with the *seniores* about the significance of the
mishap. At nightfall he took refuge in a pagan temple, where he overheard
some demons claiming that that very night they had successfully tempted a
monk to commit fornication. When he sought out the offending monk on the
pretext of discussing with him the overturned water vessel, the monk
voluntarily confessed his sin. Although he was about to withdraw from the
monastic life, the other monk persuaded him to resist the temptation of the
devil, and to dismiss the woman with whom he had sinned instead.[74]

Version A of the story again concerns a monk, but a monk who was the
son of a pagan priest. When he was a young boy he used to sit in the temple
and see his father enter and offer sacrifices to the idol. Once he entered the
temple after him secretly, and saw Satan sitting there attended by all his
demons. One of them came up to his leader and reported the success he had
had fomenting wars and disturbances, with much shedding of blood; but
because he had taken thirty days to accomplish these ends, the Devil had him
flogged. A second demon approached Satan and reported that he had been
at sea, where he had stirred up storms and sunk ships, killing many; but
having taken twenty days to produce this mayhem, he was sent out to be
whipped as well. A third demon came up to Satan and reported that he had
been in the city, where he had managed to stir up contention at a wedding,
leading to great shedding of blood and even the death of the bridegroom. But
because he had taken ten days for these meager accomplishments, he too was
sent out for scourging. A fourth demon, however, escaped this punishment,
and indeed received a rich reward, even though it had taken him forty years
to accomplish his objective. For he had been in the wilderness where he had
been attacking a certain monk, and just that very night he had finally

---

[72] John Cassian, *Coll.* 8.16, CSEL 13:231-233.
[73] Cf. Petersen, *The Dialogues*, pp. 170-174.
[74] *Vitae patrum* 5.5.24, PL 73:879-880.

prevailed over him and induced him to commit the sin of fornication. When the Devil heard this, he rose from his seat, kissed the demon, placed his own crown on the demon's head, and invited him to join him on his throne, proclaiming that his accomplishment was indeed a great one.[75]

These four stories clearly serve a variety of purposes. Cassian's narrative provides a lesson in demonology.[76] The stories in the *Vitae patrum* are ostensibly concerned with the sin of fornication, although Version A is principally a celebration of the strength of the monastic order.[77] Gregory's version seems to have more in common with Version B, for as he declares at the outset, his main purpose is to show those who have dedicated their lives to chastity the dangers that can ensue from presuming to have women living in their homes. (A minor theme of the story is mentioned at the end, where Gregory notes that "in saving his neighbor this son of Abraham attained his own salvation. Through God's providence it so happened that the preservation of the one from sin became the occasion for the other's conversion."[78]) But despite their different purposes, all four stories share a striking similarity in subject matter, particularly the narratives of Gregory and Cassian. Hence Hallinger, for example, has concluded that what we have here is a clear case of borrowing on Gregory's part. Hallinger argues that, when these literary precedents are combined with Gregory's moralizing purpose, Gregory's pretended interest in historical truth is shown to have been a charade:

> Die Aushöhlung des Geschichtlichen wird selten so deutlich fassbar, wie gerade in der eben erwähnten Erzählung, deren Vorlagen heute noch zu kontrollieren sind und deren paränetische Abzweckung Gregor übrigens selbste zugibt. ... Die Wirklichkeit des Vorgangs ist für Gregor selber keine Wirklichkeit mehr. Was er erzählt, ist für ihn blosser Rahmen für den lehrhaften Kern.[79]

De Vogüé and Petersen are both more moderate in their judgments, but they too maintain that a comparison of this chapter of the *Dialogues* with its literary predecessors presents strong evidence for direct literary borrowing, even though Gregory refers to a whole city of witnesses who could verify his

---

[75] *Ibid.* 5.5.39, PL 73:885-886.

[76] Cassian states right at the outset: "Regi autem inmundos spiritus a nequioribus potestatibus eisque esse subiectos praeter illa scripturarum testimonia ... etiam perspicuae visiones et experimenta sanctorum multa nos edocent."

[77] The monk who relates the story says at the end: "Hoc ego cum audissem, et vidissem, dixi intra meipsum: Valde magnus est ordo monachorum."

[78] *Dial.* 3.7.1, SC 260:278; 3.7.9, Zimmerman 122-123, SC 260:284.

[79] Hallinger, "Papst Gregor der Grosse," pp. 244-245.

story.[80] De Vogüé offers two possible explanations for the apparent contra-
diction. (1) The story did come from the people of Fondi, who had
appropriated the legend of Cassian's monk or of the anonymous heroes of
the *Vitae patrum*, and had substituted in their place a Jew whom they
attached to their own bishop Andrew. However, Gregory was aware of the
stories of Cassian and the stories of the *Vitae patrum*, which had been
translated into Latin in the sixth century by his papal predecessors, Pelagius
I and John III, and he had recourse to these sources when he wrote the story
for the *Dialogues*.[81] (2) The appeal to the citizens of Fondi is to be
understood as applying only to the transformation of the temple of Apollo
into a chapel in honour of St Andrew. For the rest of the story Gregory drew
on Cassian and the *Vitae patrum*. Gregory leads us to believe that the whole
story is supported by the people of Fondi. But if he misleads us on this
account, his conduct could be justified by the spiritual purpose the story
serves: "Le caractère édifiant de la narration, les services qu'elle rendra à une
cause sacrée—celle de la sainteté de vie du clergé—justifieraient d'ailleurs le
jeu verbal auquel Grégoire se livre en laissant entendre que l'histoire
entière—et pas seulement certains de ses éléments—lui vient des habitants du
lieu."[82]

---

[80] De Vogüé, *Introduction*, pp. 132-134; Petersen, *The Dialogues*, pp. 172-174. Whereas
de Vogüé seems most suspicious of Gregory's dependence on Cassian, Petersen maintains that
he was probably more influenced by the stories in the *Vitae patrum*. Like both Version A and
Version B, Gregory's story takes place in a pagan temple. Moreover, the element of
conversion, which Petersen regards as central to Gregory's story, functions as another factor
linking his account with the *Vitae patrum*, for the conversion of the young boy seems implicit
in Version A. Petersen also argues, however, that Gregory may have had in mind a story which
Rufinus inserted in his translation of the *Historia ecclesiastica*. It concerns Gregory Thaumaturgus, who once, in the course of a journey, took refuge for a night in a pagan temple. By
his simple presence Gregory expelled the demon who inhabited the place, so that he could
no longer respond to the invocations of the pagan priest. The latter was so impressed by the
humbling of his god that he was ultimately converted and baptized. See Eusebius, *Historia
ecclesiastica* 7.28.2, ed. E. Schwartz, with Latin trans. of Rufinus ed. T. Mommsen, 2 vols.
(Leipzig, 1903-1908), 2:954-955.

On the city of witnesses, see *Dial.* 3.7.1, SC 260:278: "Nec res est dubia, quam narro, quia
paene tanti in ea testes sunt, quanti et eius loci habitatores existunt." De Vogüé, *Introduction*,
p. 134n, points out that, because of hostilities with the Lombards, the city of Fondi was
deserted at the time. The bishop had been transferred to Terracina. However, he continues:
"il faut tenir compte du fait que les habitants, comme leur évêque, ont dû se réfugier quelque
part et peuvent encore 'témoigner', quoique plus malaisément."

[81] Pelagius I (556-561) was responsible for book 5 of the *Vitae patrum* (PL 73:851-992),
John III (561-574) for book 6 (PL 73:991-1024).

[82] De Vogüé, *Introduction*, pp. 133-134.

Of the two, the second suggestion seems particularly implausible, unless we are to accuse Gregory of blatant misrepresentation. If the people of Fondi contributed only the portion of the story that deals with the consecration of the ancient temple of Apollo, then they contributed virtually nothing. Petersen suggests that the portion of the story for which they were responsible was the part relating to Bishop Andrew and the woman. She argues that, despite the provisions of Canon III of the Council of Nicaea, bishop Andrew had had one or more women living in his house, although ultimately he was forced to yield before the gossip to which the situation gave rise. "This," says Petersen, "would be the story to which there were as many witnesses as there were inhabitants of Fondi."[83] However, this does not get us much further. If this is all that the citizens of Fondi contributed, then virtually the whole story is a fabrication based on Cassian and/or the *Vitae patrum*, and its falsity would have become common knowledge as soon as the people of Fondi got wind of it.

De Vogüé's first suggestion is much more likely. Yet even it is based on the assumption that there is clear evidence for Gregory's direct borrowing from his literary predecessors, and there is not. That Gregory was aware of both the work of Cassian and the *Vitae patrum* goes without saying. But whether he was consciously drawing on either source here is another matter entirely.[84] There is no verbal similarity between Gregory's story and the stories in the *Vitae patrum* at all, and not much more between Gregory's story and Cassian's, even where we would most expect to find it. Hence where Gregory refers to the *malignorum spirituum turba*, Cassian speaks of the *catervae daemonum* or the *daemonum multitudo*. There is some similarity, of course, because of the similarity in subject matter. When Gregory tells us that the leader of the evil spirits inquired into the activities of his subordinates, he uses the words: *Qui coepit singulorum spirituum obsequentium sibi causas actusque discutere*. At the same juncture in his narrative Cassian writes: *qui ... uniuscuiusque actus diligenti coepit examinatione discutere*. But this kind of similarity could survive several successive retellings of the story. It is simply not enough to prove that Gregory was copying directly from Cassian's text. The possibility remains that Gregory is being perfectly honest with us. The story came from the people of Fondi. Perhaps we should say that the story as Gregory remembered it came from the people of Fondi. The

---

[83] Petersen, *The Dialogues*, p. 173.

[84] On Gregory's knowledge of Cassian, see, for example, R. Gillet, Introduction to *Grégoire le Grand, Morales sur Job, Livres 1 et 2* (Paris, 1952), pp. 89-102. De Vogüé, of course, thinks that the evidence linking Gregory to Cassian is strong: "son récit ressemble à celui de Cassien jusque dans le détail de l'expression" (*Introduction*, pp. 132-133).

parallels, especially with Cassian, exist primarily because the citizens of Fondi had appropriated for their own benefit Cassian's tale, although we cannot exclude the possibility that Gregory's indistinct memories of what he had been told and what he had read contributed to the conflation of the two accounts. However, as far as Gregory's conscious mind was concerned, he could simply have been passing on for the benefit of his readers, taking care to underline its moral significance, a story that he knew the good people of Fondi would corroborate.

However, one other category of duplication must be considered before this rather lengthy discussion can be brought to an end: the duplication of stories found in Holy Scripture. When Libertinus of Fondi revived a dead child by placing on its breast the sandal of Honoratus, Gregory remarks, he was performing a wonder similar to one of Elisha's. According to Peter, Saint Benedict was doing the same when he perceived even from a distance that a visitor to his monastery had succumbed to temptation during his journey by breaking his fast.[85] Elsewhere in the *Dialogues* we read that Benedict was similar to Elijah, for he had a raven that used to receive food from his hands and that was obedient to his commands; that the same Benedict was like Moses in being able to produce a stream of water on the rocky summit of a mountain; and that Theodore, the sacristan of the church in Palestrina, who once had a vision after which he was ill for several days, resembled Daniel.[86] In each instance, however, Gregory himself notes the Biblical exemplar, and it is a model that is not followed closely. Instead of exact correspondence, it would be more appropriate to speak of a rough similarity between the deeds of the saints and those of their Biblical predecessors.

Several miracles in which the actions of the saints resemble Biblical archetypes in striking ways are perhaps more puzzling. The story in which St Benedict miraculously retrieves an iron blade from the depths of a lake parallels quite closely the episode in which Elisha recovers an axe-head from the river Jordan; the story of Maurus running across the surface of the water to rescue the young brother, Placidus, who had fallen in and was being

---

[85] Cf. *Dial.* 1.2.5-7, sc 260:26-30, and 4 Kings 2:14, where Elisha parts the waters of the Jordan with the mantle of Elijah. Cf. *Dial.* 2.13.1-4, sc 260:176-178, and 4 Kings 5:19-27, where we read that, even though he was not present at the time, Elisha knew that Gahazi had pursued Naaman, whom Elisha had earlier dismissed, and had received gifts from him.

[86] Cf. *Dial.* 2.8.3, sc 260:162, and 3 Kings 17:6, where Elijah is fed by the ravens. Peter points out the similarity at *Dial.* 2.8.8, sc 260:164-166. Cf. *Dial.* 2.5, sc 260:152-154, and Numbers 20:11, where Moses draws water from the rock. Peter again points out the similarity at *Dial.* 2.8.8, sc 260:164-166. Cf. *Dial.* 3.24, sc 260:362-364, and Daniel 8:27. It is Gregory himself who points out that Daniel also suffered illness for several days after his quite different vision.

carried away by the current, is quite similar to the miracle of St Peter; and the story in which some Goths attempt to slay a saintly man by the name of Benedict (not to be confused with Benedict of Nursia) immediately calls to mind the story of the three youths who were cast into the fiery furnace by Nebuchadnezzar.[87]

Elsewhere it is the Saviour himself who provides the exemplar for Gregory's stories. Hence one day while the Abbot Equitius was journeying at some distance from his monastery, a nun in one of the convents under his care became ill with a high fever. Word was sent to Equitius, who pronounced her cured. Later it was discovered that she had indeed been cured when the words of healing were spoken. Equitius, Gregory notes, was here following the example Christ set in his healing of the official's son, for he too was cured at the precise moment that Christ told his father he would live. In book three of the *Dialogues* Gregory tells of a holy woman in Spoleto who entered the religious life despite the disapproval of her father, and who was promptly disinherited except for a half-interest in a small farm. One day a tenant from this farm who had come to her with a gift was suddenly possessed by an evil spirit. The holy woman drove the spirit out of the man and into a small pig feeding near by. Once again Gregory remarks on the similarity of the woman's actions and Christ's, specifically Christ's casting the evil spirits out of two demoniacs and into a herd of swine. One of the most striking examples concerns the priest Sanctulus, who, Gregory takes pains to point out, repeated Christ's miracle of the feeding of the five thousand. Sanctulus was able to feed the workmen repairing the church of St Lawrence the Martyr for ten days with one loaf of bread. Each day the bread was multiplied in the fragments that were left over from the meal.[88]

The similarities are marked enough perhaps to give rise to the suspicion that Gregory consciously modelled these stories on their Biblical archetypes,

---

[87] Cf. *Dial.* 2.6, sc 260:154-156, and 4 Kings 6:1-7. Peter points out the parallel at *Dial.* 2.8.8, sc 260:164-166. Cf. *Dial.* 2.7, sc 260:156-160, and Matthew 14:29. Both Gregory himself (*Dial.* 2.7.2, sc 260:158) and Peter (*Dial.* 2.8.8, sc 260:164-166) comment on the similarity of the two episodes. Cf. *Dial.* 3.18, sc 260:344-346, and Daniel 3. The Goths first attempted to burn Benedict to death in his hermitage, but although everything around his hut was burned to the ground, the hut itself was not damaged. The infuriated Goths then cast him into an oven, but this was no more successful. The next day he was found safe and unharmed, and not even the edges of his garments had been touched by the flames. In this case it is once again Peter who says that the story reminds him of the episode in the Old Testament. Somewhat surprisingly, Gregory himself maintains that the stories are rather different.

[88] Cf. *Dial.* 1.4.4-6, sc 260:40-42, and John 4:46-53. Cf. *Dial.* 3.21, sc 260:352-356, and Matthew 8:28-32. Cf. *Dial.* 3.37.4-8, sc 260:414-416, and Mark 6:30-44; cf. also Mark 8:1-10 and Matthew 15:29-39.

a suspicion strengthened by the fact that they are not all as well attested as we would like. To confirm the story of the Benedict who was cast into the oven by the Goths, Gregory refers only to an unnamed and apparently deceased older brother in the monastic life.[89] But two other stories depend on sources who, although deceased at Gregory's time of writing, are at least mentioned by name;[90] and for the remaining three Gregory cites sources of the highest integrity. Presumably he learned of the stories of St Benedict and Maurus from the four disciples of Benedict mentioned in the prologue to book two, one of whom, Honoratus, was still alive when the *Dialogues* were being written. It is clear, however, that his source for the story of Equitius was Fortunatus, abbot of the monastery known as Cicero's Bath, who also was evidently still alive.[91] Since in none of these cases does Gregory hide the Biblical parallel, there is no real reason to doubt that he derived the stories in question from the sources he names. His informants would have been very familiar with the miracles of the Bible, so familiar in fact that Biblical miracles could well have shaped their perception of the events of their own time. They may have attributed some of the features of the Biblical accounts to modern events without even being conscious of the fact.[92]

Unfortunately, however, the number of episodes that imitate Biblical narratives is really quite large, and Gregory does not always draw the models to our attention. Some of these cases, although by no means all, could indeed arouse suspicion.[93] One which de Vogüé finds especially disturbing has to do

[89] *Dial.* 3.18.1, SC 260:344: "Frater quidam mecum est in monasterio conversatus, in scriptura sancta studiosissimus, qui me aetate praeibat et ex multis quae nesciebam me aedificare consueverat."

[90] At *Dial.* 3.37.1, SC 260:410-412, Gregory tells us that he heard of the miracles of Sanctulus from Sanctulus himself, who had recently died, and from some priests of the area of Nursia. At *Dial.* 3.21.1, SC 260:352, he tells us that his source for the story of the holy woman of Spoleto was the saintly Eleutherius, who was present at the time of the miracle. This Eleutherius, who had been abbot of the Monastery of St Mark the Evangelist in Spoleto, had lived with Gregory for some time at his monastery in Rome, and had died there. See *Dial.* 3.33.1, SC 260:392-394.

[91] On the disciples of St Benedict, see *Dial.* 2 Prol. 2, SC 260:128. On Fortunatus, see *Dial.* 1.3.5, SC 260:36, although Gregory mentions other *viri venerabiles* as well: "Fortunati viri venerabilis, abbatis monasterii quod appellatur Balneum Ciceronis, aliorumque etiam virorum venerabilium didici relatione quod narro." Cf. *Dial.* 1.4.21, SC 260:56, where Gregory says of Fortunatus: "Ea etiam quae subiungo, praedicti venerabilis viri Fortunati, qui valde mihi aetate, opere et simplicitate placet, relatione cognovi."

[92] Cf. de Vogüé, *Introduction*, pp. 139-140.

[93] Cf. O. Rousseau, "Saint Benoît et le prophète Elisée," *RMon.* 144 (1956): 103-114; Mähler, "Evocations bibliques"; and most recently, Petersen, *The Dialogues*, pp. 25-55. Petersen's treatment of the issue is the best of the three. Its major defect is that, having recognized a Biblical parallel or something that would have the status of a *topos* in hagio-

with Bishop Fortunatus of Todi. On the evening of Holy Saturday, Marcellus, *bonae actionis vir*, who lived in Todi with his two sisters, fell ill and died. Since the place of interment was some distance removed, he could not be buried right away, and in their grief his two sisters hurried to Fortunatus and asked him to bring their brother back to life. Fortunatus was saddened to hear of the death of his friend, but sent the women back home, telling them that their brother's death had occurred by divine decree, which man cannot oppose. However, early on the morning of Easter Sunday Fortunatus went to the home of his friend, where he knelt in prayer before the corpse and quietly called out: "Brother Marcellus." At the sound of his voice Marcellus came back to life.[94]

Although Gregory does not mention the parallel, this story is remarkably similar to Christ's raising of Lazarus (John 11:1-44), even down to some of the details. Like Marcellus, Lazarus had two sisters, Mary and Martha; like the sisters of Marcellus, Mary and Martha approached the Lord on behalf of

---

graphical literature, she too quickly concludes (or at least strongly implies) that Gregory has consciously modified the narrative. She does not seem to realize that both Gregory and his informants could have *thought* in terms of *topoi*. In this respect the comments of F. Graus, *Volk, Herrscher und Heiliger im Reich der Merowinger* (Praha, 1965), p. 75, are particularly appropriate. However, Petersen shows considerably better judgment than either Rousseau or Mähler, both of whom adduce, for various episodes in the *Dialogues*, Biblical parallels that often seem rather strained. Rousseau maintains that Gregory made systematic use of the miracles of Elisha when writing the life of Saint Benedict. He claims to have found nine episodes in the fourth book of Kings which he says are paralleled by episodes in the second book of the *Dialogues*. In fact, the analogies are very loose except in the one case (*Dial.* 2.6, sc 260:154-156) where Gregory points to it himself (see Peter's comment at *Dial.* 2.8.8, sc 260:164-166). The same can be said of the many Biblical precedents discovered by Mähler, especially when he locates his precedents for the various elements of one of Benedict's miracles in several different Biblical accounts. One could prove just about anything proceeding this way. At one point, however, Mähler is slightly more convincing, arguing that three consecutive chapters of the life of Saint Benedict are modelled on the same chapter of Holy Scripture (see pp. 405-407). According to Mähler, *Dial.* 2.4, sc 260:150-152, where Benedict opens the eyes of Maurus, is modelled on 4 Kings 6:15-18, where Elisha opens the eyes of his servant and blinds the Syrians; *Dial.* 2.5, sc 260:152-154, where Benedict miraculously produces water at the summit of a mountain, is patterned on 4 Kings 6:1-2, 3:9-20, where Elisha miraculously produces water for the armies of Israel, Judah and Edom; and *Dial.* 2.6, sc 260:154-156, where Benedict retrieves the blade of a scythe from the bottom of a lake, is modelled on 4 Kings 6:1-7, where Elisha recovers the axe-head from the river Jordan. With the first example we have only a very loose analogy, as is usually the case. With the second example, however, the analogy is a little closer, and the notion that Gregory's account has been influenced by Scripture gains in plausibility, especially in view of its proximity to the third example, where Gregory himself (in the person of Peter: see *Dial.* 2.8.8, sc 260:164-166) draws the precedent of Elisha to our attention.

[94] *Dial.* 1.10.17-18, sc 260:106-110.

their brother; like Fortunatus, Christ was saddened at the death of his friend, and brought him back to life by calling his name. There are also differences, of course. The sisters of Marcellus approached Fortunatus together, whereas in the Gospel account Martha first went out to meet the Lord, while Mary remained in the house. The sisters of Marcellus asked Fortunatus to bring their brother back to life, which was quite different from the conduct of Lazarus' sisters. Mary and Martha initially sent word to Christ before their brother died, for they were concerned about his illness; and when they later approached him after Lazarus' death, they did not ask Christ to revive him, something they thought scarcely possible, but rather stated simply that he would not have died had Christ been present. Furthermore, Marcellus was revived the day after his death and before his burial, whereas Lazarus had been dead for four days, and was called out of the tomb; and whereas Christ had known of the death of Lazarus without anyone having to tell him, the sisters of Marcellus had to inform Fortunatus of the fate of his friend. To de Vogüé, however, the similarities justify the conclusion that Gregory consciously copied the Biblical miracle in his account of the revival of Marcellus: "Tout suggère une imitation de l'Evangile, et celle-ci est d'autant plus suspecte qu'elle reste tacite. Si Grégoire ne souffle mot du modèle évangélique, n'est-ce pas parce qu'il a conscience de la démarquer?"[95]

De Vogüé's suspicions are not entirely unjustified, and indeed are strengthened by Gregory's inability to corroborate the truth of this story except by reference to some poor old man from the city of Todi whom he had recently met.[96] Perhaps all this establishes, however, is that Gregory was not always as discriminating as he might have been in his use of sources. This is an issue to which we shall return later, in chapter seven. In itself, the miracle performed by Fortunatus of Todi is no more remarkable than one performed by Nonnosus. In the seventh chapter of the first book of the *Dialogues* Gregory tells us that Nonnosus once miraculously increased his monastery's oil supply, a miracle strikingly similar to the one Elisha performed for a poor widow.[97] Indeed, the whole chapter is interesting for our purposes, for it contains several miracles performed by Nonnosus, and in each case Gregory expressly compares the miracle with some earlier wonder. Hence after

---

[95] De Vogüé, *Introduction*, pp. 137-138. Cf. Petersen, *The Dialogues*, pp. 34-35. In Petersen's judgment, the differences between Gregory's narrative and the Biblical account are to be explained in terms of "his practice of relying upon his memory in creating a narrative based on a biblical type."

[96] *Dial.* 1.10.11, 17, SC 260:102, 106.

[97] Cf. *Dial.* 1.7.4-6, SC 260:68-70, and 4 Kings 4:1-7; Gregory himself points to the similarity.

recording that Nonnosus miraculously moved a large rock to make a space for the monastery's garden, and that he miraculously restored one of the glass lamps of the monastery that had shattered when he dropped it on the floor, Gregory explicitly compares these wonders to miracles performed by Gregory Thaumaturgus and Donatus, Bishop of Arezzo.[98]

The miracles of Nonnosus seem a patch-work drawn from the lives of other saints. But Gregory does nothing to disguise the fact. Moreover, despite their derivative nature, they are particularly well attested. At the beginning of the chapter Gregory mentions two sources, both of them still living. One of them is an elderly monk named Laurio, presumably of Gregory's own monastery of St Andrew, for Peter is said to know him quite well. This Laurio received his early training under the saintly Anastasius in the monastery of Subpentoma near Nepi; Anastasius in turn had been a friend of Nonnosus', who had been prior of the neighbouring monastery on Mount Soracte. The other source is none other than Bishop Maximian of Syracuse, who had previously been abbot of Gregory's own monastery in Rome, and had accompanied Gregory to Constantinople. It is extremely unlikely that Gregory would attribute stories of his own invention to identifiable sources that could still be checked. But the matter is put beyond dispute by the evidence that survives in his register, for in July 593 Gregory wrote to Maximian asking him for precisely the kind of information that appears here.[99]

It is a matter of some concern that Maximian and Laurio apparently told Gregory stories of miracles that were thinly disguised repetitions of earlier wonders, but Gregory evidently saw nothing surprising in the fact. To his mind, one should expect at least some of the miracles of the saints to replicate one another, for they shared the same set of virtues and drew them from the same divine source. One should especially be prepared to acknowledge, and even to emphasize, that the miracles of the saints replicate Biblical prototypes. As de Vogüé observes: "Plus il apparaîtra que les thaumaturges italiens du vi᷃ siècle ont ressemblé, par leurs miracles et leurs vertus, aux saints de l'un et l'autre Testament, plus le lecteur sera convaincu de la présence et de l'action permanentes de Dieu parmi ses fidèles aujourd'hui encore."[100]

---

[98] *Dial.* 1.7.2-3, sc 260:66-68.

[99] See *Dial.* 1.7.1, sc 260:64-66, and *Ep.* 3.50, ccl 140:195-196.

[100] De Vogüé, *Introduction*, pp. 136-137. Hence, immediately after the story of Nonnosus miraculously increasing the oil supply, which Gregory himself says is similar to a miracle of Elisha, Peter proclaims: "Probamus cotidie impleri verba veritatis, quae ait: 'Pater meus usque modo operatur, et ego operor'" (*Dial.* 1.7.6, sc 260:70).

In these circumstances, should twentieth-century readers of Gregory be concerned that his sources are sometimes not of the highest authority, or should they rather be impressed by the fact that they often are? Should they be struck by the fact that sometimes the Biblical parallel is not mentioned, or rather by the fact that it often is, and not only mentioned but emphasized? These questions can be considered with particular reference to the resurrection of Marcellus by Fortunatus of Todi, the miracle that so troubles de Vogüé. Should this particular episode be seen as a case of invention on Gregory's part because of his rather questionable source, and because the Biblical parallel is not brought out? Or should we rather see it as an instance in which Gregory was too willing to accept what a garrulous old man thought would please him, and simply repeated it without bothering to point to a Biblical parallel that would have been obvious to even the dullest reader?

It was mentioned earlier that Moricca rejects Gregory's miracle stories outright. De Vogüé thinks this attitude simplistic, for if miracles are sometimes the product of legend, they are sometimes genuine. He argues that, in the end, it is probable that a number of the miracle stories Gregory tells have a basis in fact.[101] But he also maintains that the same cannot be said for all of them, for an examination of their literary precedents demonstrates that in some cases Gregory has drawn directly on the work of his predecessors and attributed the miracles found there to the heroes of his own account:

> Si parfois des miracles de saints étrangers ont pu être attribués par la voix publique à des héroes italiens avant d'être recueillis de bonne foi par Grégoire, il n'est guère douteux que celui-ci, dans d'autres cas, a lui-même opéré le transfert des textes à la réalité, des narrations d'écrivains antécédents à l'existence de personnages vivant en Italie au viᵉ siècle.[102]

In other words, despite all his protestations of truthfulness, in some cases Gregory has been less than honest.

According to de Vogüé, the key to sorting out fact from fiction, or at least what was believed to be true from what was invented, lies in Gregory's appeal to witnesses. On the assumption that Gregory would cover his tracks and hence not include his own fabrications among the stories that are particularly

---

[101] De Vogüé, *Introduction*, pp. 138-140. Cf. C. Lambot, "La vie et les miracles de saint Benoît racontés par saint Grégoire-le-Grand," *RMon.* 144 (1956): 97-102 at 102. Boesch Gajano, "'Narratio' e 'expositio'," p. 9, would agree to this extent, that whether or not the miracles really occurred, Gregory at least believed that they really occurred. Decisive for her are the many references in the *Dialogues* to witnesses who are still alive, and to events which are said to have transpired under the very noses of the people to whom Gregory addresses himself.

[102] De Vogüé, *Introduction*, p. 135.

well attested, doubtful passages should be approached with a number of questions in mind. Does Gregory appeal to an amorphous group of people, or to specific individuals? Are the individuals identified by name, or do they remain anonymous? Are they cited in support of one particular story, or a group of stories in which their specific responsibility might not easily be identified? Were they still alive at the time of Gregory's writing? Depending on how these questions are answered in any given case, Gregory could have given himself more or less latitude to introduce stories of his own invention.[103]

When this test is applied, however, the results are inconclusive. Some of the doubtful stories turn out to rest on doubtful authority as well: the story of the resurrection of Marcellus by Fortunatus of Todi, for example, which we have just considered. But in a surprisingly large number of cases—the story of Andrew of Fondi and the Jew, for example, or the episode shared by St Benedict and Isaac of Spoleto—the stories that seem most doubtful on literary grounds are among those that are the very best attested. If Gregory did consciously borrow from the work of his predecessors or from Scripture, this has not yet been clearly established. It would be unjustifiable to state categorically that he did not, for the proof may lie concealed in some episode not considered here. But this much can be said: that all the episodes that have been examined in this rather lengthy chapter fall short of providing convincing proof of literary invention on Gregory's part. In each case the possibility remains that Gregory was only passing on with his comments what he had received in good faith from his informants.[104]

---

[103] *Ibid.*, p. 139. Cf. Petersen, *The Dialogues*, pp. 5-9. Petersen too raises the possibility of a distinction between stories attributed to identifiable individuals and stories attributed to anonymous sources, the idea being that in the latter cases Gregory could have had more scope to indulge in mere *topoi*, or in stories that have other literary affiliations. Ultimately she quietly abandons the idea because of her conviction that literary borrowing can be detected in both classes of stories. She does concede, however, that Gregory's appeal to witnesses was not just a sham. Despite the literary borrowings, "he was working from genuine material supplied through personal enquiry and was not producing a series of names in order to give an appearance of verisimilitude to his work" (pp. 8-9).

[104] It would easily have been possible to extend our enquiry at some length, by considering, for example, some of the additional literary parallels to which de Vogüé points in his *Vie de Saint Benoît*. However, little would have been added to the results already obtained. More recently, J.M. Petersen, "The Garden of Felix: The Literary Connection between Gregory the Great and Paulinus of Nola," *SMon.* 26 (1984): 215-230, has argued that in some of the episodes of the *Dialogues* Gregory borrowed directly and consciously from the writings of Paulinus of Nola. Petersen herself acknowledges, however, that the case she constructs falls short of conclusive proof. Her case is stronger when she draws attention to the similarity between the story of Constantius, *mansionarius* of the church of St Stephen the Martyr in

Ancona (*Dial.* 1.5.1-3, sc 260:58-60), and a story Eusebius tells of Bishop Narcissus of Jerusalem (Eusebius, trans. Rufinus, *Historia ecclesiastica* 6.9, Schwartz and Mommsen 2:539). Cf. *The Dialogues*, pp. 5-6, 41-43. Petersen argues that, although Eusebius seems to have been Gregory's primary source, Gregory's story may also have been influenced by the miracle at Cana in John 2:1-11. A strong case is also made by M.P. Ciccarese, "*Vita Martini* 7: tra miracolo e visione dell'aldilà," *Augustinianum* 24 (1984): 227-233. Ciccarese points to the similarity between *Vita S. Martini* 7.1-7, sc 133:266-268, and the miracle which Gregory attributes to the priest Severus in *Dial.* 1.12.1-3, sc 260:112-114; and she argues that the influence of the same passage of *The Life of St Martin* is discernible in *Dial.* 4.37, especially (I would think) *Dial.* 4.37.3-4, sc 265:126-128. She even detects a modest amount of verbal similarity. Ciccarese's argument has particular force, enough to confirm the original Sulpician inspiration for Gregory's account. But conscious borrowing on Gregory's part is another matter. In the final analysis, neither Petersen nor Ciccarese can point to parallels any more compelling than the others we have considered.

Stancliffe, *St. Martin*, pp. 196-202, comes to a similar conclusion with regard to the alleged borrowing of Sulpicius Severus. Hence she goes on to argue for the essential historicity of Sulpicius's portrait of St Martin (pp. 341-359). Cf. J. Fontaine, "Alle fonti della agiografia europea. Storia e leggenda nella vita di San Martino di Tours," *RSLR* 2 (1966): 187-206; *Sulpice Sévère. Vie de Saint Martin*, vol. 1 (Paris, 1967), pp. 171-210. This represents a fundamental revision of the earlier assessment of E.-C. Babut, *Saint Martin de Tours* (Paris, [1912]), pp. 54-111. In Babut's judgment, "Le fond de la *Vie de s. Martin* et des *Dialogues* est ce que nous appelons une imposture. ... La *Vie de saint Martin* est une véritable anthologie de faits merveilleux de provenances diverses, que Sulpice a mis arbitrairement au compte de son personnage" (pp. 107-108).

6

Miracles and Truth

Although each of the cases considered in the preceding chapter falls short of proving conclusively that Gregory engaged in literary invention, it might be argued that they are not without their cumulative effect. If suspicions had been raised by only one or two episodes, in themselves inconclusive, the dictates of charity would probably require that we doubt literary invention on Gregory's part. But given that twenty-three different episodes were considered in detail in chapter five, perhaps we should be inclined to judge otherwise. Although Gregory's direct dependence on a literary predecessor cannot be clearly established in any given case, the sheer volume of doubtful cases increases the probability that in one or more of them suspicion is well founded. Furthermore, the likelihood of pious invention on Gregory's part is enhanced when the *Dialogues* are placed in their larger context. Protestations of complete truthfulness are not infrequent in ancient and medieval hagiography. It is much better to say nothing than to utter falsehoods, says one noted hagiographer, for we all know that we shall have to render an account for our words.[1] However, in many cases one suspects that such assurances are no more than pious rhetoric.[2] As a class, medieval hagiogra-

[1] Paulinus of Milan, *Vita Ambrosii* 2.1, ed. A.A.R. Bastiaensen, *Vite dei Santi* 3, p. 56. Cf. Sulpicius Severus, *Vita S. Martini* 1.9, SC 133:252-254; Anon., *Vita S. Cuthberti* 1.2, ed. B. Colgrave (Cambridge, 1940), pp. 62-64. See also Athanasius, *Vita S. Antonii*, Prooemium, PG 26:839; Palladius, *Historia Lausiaca*, chap 17, ed. E.C. Butler (Cambridge, 1898-1904), 2:43; Sulpicius Severus, *Vita S. Martini* 27.7, SC 133:316; *Dial.* 1.15, CSEL 1:167; 3.5, CSEL 1:203; Bede, *Vita S. Cuthberti*, Prol., ed. B. Colgrave (Cambridge, 1940), pp. 143-144.

[2] See, for example, Sulpicius Severus, *Dial.* 2.13, CSEL 1:196, where Gallus proclaims: "incredibiliora forte dicturus sum, sed Christo teste non mentior." This is an almost exact equivalent of "Incredibile est, quod dico, sed verum", an expression that, according to Quintilian, *Institutio oratoria* 9.3.87, ed. H.E. Butler (Cambridge, Mass. and London, 1920-1922), 3:496, was widely regarded as a mere figure of speech. However, on the general truthfulness of Sulpicius's account, see below, n. 53.

phers are infamous for their less than strict adherence to the canons of factual veracity. Even the most casual reader could not have failed to note a marked tendency to compromise truth in order to provide idealized portraits of their saintly heroes.

From our point of view a eulogizer who exaggerates without measure is simply dishonest, for his portrait distorts reality. Judging from their attacks on the heathen tradition of panegyric, many early Christian authors do not seem to have thought differently. But as Schreiner points out, their polemic did not prevent them from appropriating the devices of pagan rhetoric relatively early on for *encomia* of the martyrs. Although there is little evidence on the attitudes of early Christian hagiographers, Schreiner maintains with some plausibility that otherwise questionable literary techniques acquired a new legitimacy in the service of the faith. Inspiring words were necessary if the figures of the martyrs were to move the hearts of listeners and readers. Given the moralizing purpose of their legends, early medieval hagiographers possibly thought that hyperbole was not entirely dishonourable, not if the goal was to use purely literary means to evoke the same response that the martyr had once himself elicited in his own person. Whatever the explanation, the hyperbole of ancient rhetoric came to be regarded as a legitimate literary technique by medieval authors, including hagiographers; and if it was licit for them, we might think it licit for Gregory as well to stretch the literal truth somewhat in order to make the point more forcefully. From the modern scholar's point of view, however, the medieval hagiographers' use of *superiectio* or *superlatio* must be numbered among the least of their faults. More distressing is the fact that they seem to have had few qualms about indulging in wholesale literary invention, whether by drawing on their own imaginative resources, or more likely, by borrowing liberally from the work of their predecessors. Unacceptable though it may be, hyperbole at least rests upon a certain *fundamentum in re*; invention does not suffer such limits.[3]

---

[3] See K. Schreiner, "Zum Wahrheitsverständnis im Heiligen- und Reliquienwesen des Mittelalters," *Saeculum* 17 (1966): 131-169, esp. 161; cf. L. Arbusow, *Colores rhetorici*, 2nd. ed. (Göttingen, 1963), pp. 89-91. On wholesale literary invention in medieval hagiography, cf. R. Aigrain, *L'hagiographie. Ses sources, ses méthodes, son histoire* (Paris, 1953), pp. 168-169; H. Delehaye, *The Legends of the Saints* (New York, 1962), pp. 75-77; B. de Gaiffier, *Etudes critiques d'hagiographie et d'iconologie* (Brussels, 1967), pp. 458-460; "Les 'doublets' en hagiographie latine," *ABoll.* 96 (1978): 261-269; J. Leclercq, *The Love of Learning and the Desire for God*, 2nd. ed. (New York, 1977), p. 202. However, Aigrain also argues that, since the hagiographers were the beneficiaries of an educational system based on rote and the repeated reading of a small number of texts, the literary borrowings detected in their work do not always jeopardize their basic veracity: cf. Aigrain, *L'hagiographie*, pp. 168-169, 203-205, 243-244; de Gaiffier, *Etudes critiques*, esp. p. 486.

Although they have every appearance of literary fraud, in some cases these tactics may very well have been counsels of desperation. The hagiographer who was a contemporary or near contemporary of the saint whose life he was recording usually had access to at least some genuine information. But the hagiographer separated from his subject by decades or centuries often had neither the reports of contemporaries nor an earlier life. Confronted with the task of writing the life of a saint of whom little more than the name was known, borrowing from other saints' lives, or resorting to creative invention, could hardly have been avoided.[4] However, simple necessity alone cannot provide an adequate explanation of the liberties hagiographers were often willing to take. Although written a little late for our purpose, the example of Reginald of Canterbury's life of St Malchus is still instructive. Reginald's excesses were clearly not due only to a paucity of material. Although he had Jerome's early version of Malchus's life to guide him, he quite candidly warns the reader who might expect a factual account that much of what he says is deliberately fictitious, and that he has not taken the trouble to indicate where truth ends and fiction begins. Those who are concerned about the facts are counselled to compare his version with Jerome's, and to believe the earlier author whenever there is disagreement: "He has run on the royal road, and has not deviated from the channel of history. We, running like a stream, have sometimes held to the banks. But at other times we have watered the fields by publishing certain things, not for the sake of history, but rather for the sake of art." Reginald confesses that, following the custom of versifiers, he has invented a good deal; but he claims that, rather than being offended, others should show the same indulgence toward his fictions that they would have him show toward theirs.[5] The truthfulness of his account was simply not an important consideration for Reginald, nor, it would seem, for many other hagiographers either. He at least was honest about the matter; many others, without sharing Reginald's candour, would demonstrate an equally casual regard for the truth.

It is difficult for the modern reader to comprehend the attitude of those who would deliberately falsify in their zeal to celebrate the virtues of the saints. The demands of piety should require strict veracity. However, there is a good deal of evidence that suggests the existence, throughout the Middle Ages, of a theological tradition according to which lying could be justified in certain situations.[6] The single most important opinion on this issue was

---

[4] Cf. F. Graus, *Volk, Herrscher und Heiliger im Reich der Merowinger* (Praha, 1965), p. 133; de Gaiffier, "Les 'doublets'," esp. p. 268.

[5] Reginald of Canterbury, *Vita S. Malchi*, ed. Levi Robert Lind (Urbana, 1942), pp. 40-41.

[6] Cf. H. Fuhrmann, "Die Fälschungen im Mittelalter. Überlegungen zum mittelalterlichen Wahrheitsbegriff," *HZ* 197 (1963): 529-554 at 537-538; Schreiner, "Zum Wahrheitsver-

undoubtedly that of Augustine, and in both his *De mendacio* (ca. 395), and more clearly in his *Contra mendacium* (420), Augustine rejected lying in all circumstances, whether out of noble or ignoble motives, whether for good or evil purposes. Augustine defined a lie as a false statement made with an intention to deceive,[7] and maintained that it is always sinful, and ought not to be indulged for any reason.[8] In Augustine's judgment, lying is especially reprehensible in the teaching of religion, where it is to be particularly avoided. It cannot be defended even if the purpose is to bring someone to a knowledge of the true faith, and it matters not whether one is dealing with eternal matters directly, or simply with temporal matters pertaining to the establishment of religion and piety. Once a regard for truth has been weakened even slightly, says Augustine, all things are thrown into doubt.[9] But, despite Augustine's preeminent authority, other early Christian think-ers—including Clement of Alexandria, Origen, Chrysostom and Jerome—had defended a substantially different view,[10] and their opinions on the matter were not without influence.

The attitude of these theologians, ultimately a product of the ethos of the ancient world, may have been shaped by the Platonic tradition, according to which lying could be justified in cases of necessity and utility, and when it

---

ständnis," pp. 166-168; W. Speyer, *Die literarische Fälschung im heidnischen und christlichen Altertum* (München, 1971), pp. 94-96; Stancliffe, *St. Martin,* esp. pp. 183-186. The most extensive discussion is to be found in G. Müller, *Die Wahrhaftigkeitspflicht und die Proble-matik der Lüge* (Freiburg, 1962), esp. pp. 27-93.

[7] *De mendacio* 4.5, CSEL 41:419. Cf. *Ibid.* 3.3, CSEL 41:414-416; *Enar. in Psalmos* 5.7, CCL 38:22.

[8] *Contra mendacium* 7.18, CSEL 41:489; 15.31, CSEL 41:511: "Nihil autem iudicandus est dicere, qui dicit aliqua iusta esse mendacia, nisi aliqua iusta esse peccata ac per hoc aliqua iusta esse, quae iniusta sunt: quo quid absurdius dici potest?" Cf. *De doctrina christiana* 1.36.40, CCL 32:29.

[9] *De mendacio* 10.17, CSEL 41:436; 14.25, CSEL 41:444. Of course, Augustine himself has been accused of having committed pious fraud in the account he gives of his own spiritual development in the *Confessions.* However, see P. Courcelle, *Recherches sur les Confessions de Saint Augustin* (Paris, 1950). Courcelle concedes (pp. 188-202) that Augustine's account of his conversion, the garden scene, has been enriched by literary devices that give outward expression to an essentially inward process. But his general assessment (see esp. pp. 247-258) is that the charge of literary fraud is unjustifiable. Augustine's account is not merely a biography, and was designed to have a larger, paradigmatic significance; but it was also intended to be historically accurate: cf. P. Grant, "Redeeming the Time: The *Confessions* of St. Augustine," in *By Things Seen: Reference and Recognition in Medieval Thought* (Ottawa, 1979), pp. 21-32, esp. p. 23.

[10] See, for example, *Comment. in Epistolam ad Galatas* 1.2.7-14, PL 26:360-367, where Jerome argues that Saints Peter and Paul both practised dissimulation, but that they did so for genuinely good purposes.

was good in intention. But it was also a view that could be defended with several examples from Scripture itself that appeared to justify lying if it fulfilled a divinely established purpose. The extensive discussion in the seventeenth book of John Cassian's *Collations* provides one of the clearest endorsements of the idea. Cassian stresses that lying can be justified to avoid pressing danger. Its nature is akin to that of hellebore, which can be salutary when administered to a body threatened by serious disease, but is fatal when consumed by someone in good health. Although it is a grave offense, lying can be practised with good conscience when it is necessary to avoid some great harm, and when the good that may result from telling the truth cannot compensate for the evils unleashed.[11] However, Cassian also maintains that lying can be justified to attain some very great good; and along with most of his like-minded predecessors, he defends his view by recourse to Scripture:

> Who is able adequately to enumerate nearly all the patriarchs and countless holy men who, as I have said, assumed the protection of a lie: some for the defence of life, some out of the desire for a blessing, some for the sake of mercy, some for the concealment of some mystery, some for the zeal of God, some out of a consideration of truth itself (*pro examine veritatis*)?[12]

The example of Jacob is offered as a case in point. Ostensibly he was guilty of deceitful conduct, not only towards his brother, but towards his father as well; and yet, rather than condemnation, he received the rich reward of his father's blessing. The explanation is to be found in Jacob's noble purpose: "He coveted the blessing intended for the first-born, not out of greed of immediate gain, but out of faith in a perpetual sanctification."[13]

Augustine, of course, would have had none of this. In his view, any Scriptural example of lying is to be interpreted in one of two ways: either it is clearly not offered for our imitation, or it is to be understood figuratively, and in reality is not a lie at all.[14] What Jacob did at his mother's bidding in apparently deceiving his father fell into the second category: "non est mendacium, sed mysterium." Of course, Jacob *seems* to have acted deceptively, for he covered his limbs with goat skins, and at first blush we might be tempted to think that he did this in order to pass himself off as his brother.

---

[11] *Coll.* 17.17, CSEL 13:475-476; 17.20, CSEL 13:481.

[12] *Coll.* 17.25, CSEL 13:488. Cf. *Coll.* 17.14, CSEL 13:474, where the general principle involved is expressed as follows: "quidquid enim pro caritate dei et pietatis amore perficitur, quae promissionem habet vitae quae nunc est et futurae, tametsi duris atque adversis videatur principiis inchoari, non solum nulla reprehensione, sed etiam laude dignissimum est."

[13] *Coll.* 17.12, CSEL 13:472. Cf. *Coll.* 17.17, CSEL 13:476-477.

[14] *De mendacio* 5.9, CSEL 41:425; *Contra mendacium* 12.26, CSEL 41:504-505: "in figuris autem quod velut mendacium dicitur, bene intellectum verum invenitur."

But the real reason for his action, says Augustine, is to be found in its deeper signification; when that is unveiled, it turns out to be, not a case of deception at all, but rather a prefiguration of the profound truth of our redemption in Christ. The goat skins signify sins. In covering himself with these skins, therefore, Jacob signifies the One who bore, not his own sins on the cross, but those of others. As Augustine confidently concludes, "a true signification cannot in any way be rightly called a lie."

Of course, this is not the whole story. When his father asked him who he was, Jacob replied: "I am Esau, thy firstborn"— an apparently clear example of lying on his part. But, once again, Augustine would say that Jacob's statement has to be referred to the hidden signification for the sake of which it was uttered. When that is done, we can see it as a prefiguration of the words of Christ, who, when speaking of the membership of the Kingdom of Heaven, said that some who are last will be first, and some who are first will be last. As Augustine concludes: "since things so true are so truthfully signified, why should there be any suspicion here of lying in deed or in word?"[15] But to less subtle minds this story could indicate that, if Jacob was justified in tricking his blind father into bestowing on him the blessing of the first-born, lying should not be regarded as irreconcilable with Christian piety, especially if it is governed by a good purpose, or takes place *per inspirationem Dei*. According to Schreiner, the doctrine of the justifiable lie remained a significant current in theological opinion through to the 12th and early 13th centuries, and even then the issue was not completely resolved. The potential such a doctrine held for the hagiographer is illustrated by Cassian. At one point he observes that, in order to protect their humility, even the *seniores* themselves indulged in lying.[16]

Together with the doctrine of the justifiable lie, we also need to consider the possibility that the medieval hagiographer adhered to a fundamentally different conception of truth than our own. Medieval ideas of truth have received considerable attention of late, mainly in connection with the problem presented by the prevalence of forgeries and false relics throughout the medieval period. Debate on the issue was opened by Silvestre, whose attitude is largely one of disapprobation. He acknowledges that sometimes recourse was had to forgeries to establish legitimate rights (rights to property, for example) that otherwise would have been forfeited in the unsettled circumstances of the early Middle Ages. But for the most part, he maintains, forgeries were the product of less noble motives, even though they were

---

[15] *Contra mendacium* 10.24, CSEL 41:499, 501-502; trans. H.B. Jaffee (Washington, 1952), p. 155 (slightly revised). Cf. *De civitate Dei* 16.37, CCL 48:541-542.

[16] Schreiner, "Zum Wahrheitsverständnis," p. 168; Cassian, *Coll.* 17.24, CSEL 13:487-488.

produced by clerics from whom one would expect a higher standard of conduct. In the course of his discussion Silvestre suggests that medieval conceptions of truth may have been governed by some of the characteristics of the primitive mentality described by Fraser, according to which lying is particularly reprehensible only when it is discovered. But the main thrust of his analysis is that the prevalence of forgery is to be explained by the lack of sanctions against it. Among clerics who forged documents there was a tacit agreement that prevented them from exposing one another, for the moment the authenticity of one text was questioned, the genuineness of countless others would have become suspect as well.[17]

Writing a few years later, Fuhrmann examined the issue in terms of early medieval conceptions of law. Modern law is positive law, and is based on statute; a law can be made or unmade by whoever possesses the proper legislative authority. Early medieval law, by contrast, could not be based on statute, nor could it be made or unmade, for it consisted of sempeternal principles of justice that lay beyond human reach. Since a statute, or indeed any legal document, was simply an external manifestation of the fundamental moral law, it was not so much the authenticity of the document itself that was important as the idea of which it was supposed to be a representation. In these circumstances the medieval forger could have had a fundamentally different self-conception: "mag das Bewusstsein stark gewesen sein, nichts von sich aus zu versuchen und nicht rational begründetes Menschenwerk zu schaffen, sondern etwas von Gottes Heilsordnung zu finden."[18]

Although the issue remains contentious,[19] Fuhrmann's suggestions are of particular interest for the immediate problem that concerns us: the idea of truth underlying medieval hagiography. Conceivably the truth that mattered, and that was generally understood to matter, was not mere factual veracity but truth of a higher order. According to Leclercq, "medieval men took more interest in permanent and universal ideas than in specific events which are

---

[17] H. Silvestre, "Le problème des faux au Moyen Age (A propos d'un livre récent de M. Saxer)," *MA* 66 (1960): 351-370.

[18] Fuhrmann, "Die Fälschungen," p. 543. Cf. C. Brühl, "Der ehrbare Fälscher. Zu den Fälschungen des Klosters S. Pietro in Ciel d'Oro zu Pavia," *DAEM* 35 (1979): 209-218; P. Dinzelbacher, *Vision und Visionsliteratur im Mittelalter* (Stuttgart, 1981), pp. 57-64.

[19] See the "Diskussionsbeiträge" appended to Fuhrmann's article at pp. 555-601. Patze rejects the notion that the Middle Ages had a fundamentally different conception of truth, for forgery was systematically rejected in medieval codes of law and treated as a punishable offence. Bosl, however, is sympathetic to the notion that the medieval idea of truth was not the same as ours, and he criticizes Silvestre in particular for failing to appreciate the fact. For a recent view, see G. Constable, "Forgery and Plagiarism in the Middle Ages," *ADip.* 29 (1983): 1-41.

transitory in nature," and so "to understand them, one must adopt their point of view. Once this is done, legend becomes, in a sense they themselves would have approved, truer than history. It brings to us another aspect of indivisible truth, one which belongs to the realm of the ideal rather than to its passing materializations." In their emphasis on the faithful representation of a truth higher than factual veracity, Delehaye suggests, medieval hagiographers can be likened to poets: "The saints show forth every virtue in superhuman fashion—gentleness, mercy, forgiveness of wrongs, self-discipline, renunciation of one's own will: they make virtue attractive and ever invite Christians to seek it. Their life is indeed the concrete manifestation of the spirit of the Gospel; and in that it makes this sublime ideal a reality for us, legend, like all poetry, can claim a higher degree of truth than history."[20] Perhaps the analogy could be changed slightly to liken the work of the hagiographer to that of the artist. We consider it no fault if the artist rearranges the features of the landscape being painted, or even if some of them are invented. The "truth" of a painting does not inhere in any photographic likeness of its details, but in the extent to which the whole captures the essence of the subject. In a similar way, perhaps, the truth of medieval hagiography should not be sought in factual, historical detail, but in the essential character of the saint portrayed.

Although scholars have long maintained that there is a fundamental distinction between the hagiographer and the historian,[21] in the medieval context this can be accepted only with qualification. In the monasteries of medieval Europe, history and hagiography served the same general purpose, were addressed to the same audience, and were customarily written by the same authors, who frequently owed their basic intellectual formation to their training as historians.[22] Bede, for example, does not seem to have thought that his historical and his hagiographical writings belonged to distinctly different categories. In the list appended to his *Historia ecclesiastica*, his lives of Saints Felix, Anastasius and Cuthbert are explicitly referred to as "histories

---

[20] Leclercq, *The Love of Learning*, p. 206; Delehaye, *The Legends of the Saints*, p. 181 (cf. p. xviii: "it is poets that the common run of hagiographers must be called"). Cf. Aigrain, *L'hagiographie*, pp. 235-244; E. Dorn, *Der sündige Heilige in der Legende des Mittelalters* (München, 1967), pp. 152-155; G. Strunk, *Kunst und Glaube in der lateinischen Heiligenlegende* (München, 1970), p. 39; J.-C. Poulin, *L'idéal de sainteté dans l'Aquitaine carolingienne d'après les sources hagiographiques (750-950)* (Québec, 1975), pp. 13-15. More generally, see A.J. Gurevich, *Categories of Medieval Culture* (London, 1985), p. 178.

[21] See, for example, A. Marignan, *Etudes sur la civilisation française* 2: *Le culte des saints sous les Mérovingiens* (Paris, 1899), p. 93; and W. von den Steinen, "Heilige als Hagiographen," *HZ* 143 (1931): 229-256 at 236ff.

[22] B. Guenée, *Histoire et culture historique dans l'Occident médiéval* (Paris, 1980), p. 54.

of the saints," and are cited alongside his "history" of the abbots of Wearmouth-Jarrow and his ecclesiastical "history" of the English people.[23] But even if the hagiographers did conceive of themselves as historians, they may still have been governed by a conception of truth significantly different from the one that underlies modern historical scholarship. On balance, it would seem, the medieval historian possessed a sense of his duties that likened him much more to his classical predecessors than to his modern successors.

In the ancient world history was customarily regarded as a branch of rhetoric. Hence, with few exceptions, classical historians were concerned primarily with the literary effectiveness of their works. If they were inspired by any larger purpose, it was much more likely to have been a moral one than a concern for simple factual veracity. In large measure, it is said, medieval historians were heirs to this literary tradition. Rather than being purely scientific or intellectual, their purpose was to edify their readers with appropriate examples from the past. As Ray puts it, "the basic materials of history were not our facts but *digna memoriae*, things made worthy of memory by their pertinence to a Christian conduct of life. ... The medieval *veritas historiae* mainly bound the chronicler to use a biblically warranted standard in making good deeds look good and bad deeds bad, with, of course, little standing in the way of causing the good to seem better and the bad worse."[24]

[23] Bede, *Historia ecclesiastica* 5.24, ed. and trans. B. Colgrave and R.A.B. Mynors (Oxford, 1969), pp. 568-570. Cf. P. Meyvaert, "Bede the Scholar," in *Famulus Christi: Essays in Commemoration of the Thirteenth Centenary of the Birth of the Venerable Bede* (London, 1976), pp. 40-69 at 53. On Sulpicius Severus, see B.R. Voss, "Berührungen von Hagiographie und Historiographie in der Spätantike," *Frühmittelalterliche Studien* 4 (1970): 53-69, who argues that Sulpicius was greatly influenced by the classical historiographical tradition, especially historical biography, and indeed that he perceived himself as an historian in his life of St Martin. On Gregory of Tours, see E.H. Walter, "Hagiographisches in Gregors Frankengeschichte," *AKG* 48 (1966): 291-310 at 291-294; and F. Thürlemann, *Der historische Diskurs bei Gregor von Tours* (Bern, 1974), pp. 23-24, 28-30. Although Gregory seems to have been conscious of a difference between his hagiographical and his historical works, the distinction was not very pronounced. See also P.-A. Sigal, "Histoire et hagiographie: les Miracula aux XIe et XIIe siècles," *ABPO* 87 (1980): 237-257; and M. Heinzelmann, "Une source de base de la littérature hagiographique latine: le recueil de miracles," in *Hagiographie, cultures et sociétés, IVe-XIIe siècles* (Paris, 1981), pp. 235-257. Sigal and Heinzelmann concentrate on the authors of the *Miracula*, the collections of miracles performed at the shrines of the saints, arguing that, in their attitudes and in their methods, these hagiographers are difficult to distinguish from the historians of their age.

[24] R.D. Ray, "Medieval Historiography through the Twelfth Century: Problems and Progress of Research," *Viator* 5 (1974): 33-59 at 47. Cf. B. Smalley, *Historians in the Middle Ages* (London, 1974), pp. 15-16.

No less an authority than Bede could again be cited as an example. "Should history tell of good men and their good estate," he proclaims, "the thoughtful listener is spurred on to imitate the good; should it record the evil ends of wicked men, no less effectually the devout and earnest listener or reader is kindled to eschew what is harmful and perverse, and himself with greater care pursue those things which he had learned to be good and pleasing in the sight of God."[25] We are not surprised, therefore, when we encounter the suggestion that, for Bede, factual veracity is not of the highest importance. Bede himself states that, in keeping with the *vera lex historiae*, he will repeat for the reader's edification stories received from common report, although he cannot personally attest to their accuracy. The truth that matters, it would seem, is truth of a higher order than mere facts. Bede's *Ecclesiastical History*, Jones argues, was written, not as a factual account of events as they actually transpired, but rather as "a temporal representation of the state of souls in God's eternity—pulling that eternity down within the reach of the earnest, but none-too-imaginative listener."[26]

As a description of the fundamental thrust of medieval historical writing, this brief treatment leaves much out. A more adequate account would require balancing the tendencies noted above with the commitment to factual veracity that is also present in many medieval historical works. But the general contours of the relationship between medieval hagiography and medieval historiography would seem clear nonetheless. Rather than an absolute distinction between the two genres, perhaps we should speak of a continuum on which pure hagiography and pure historiography, if there be such things,

---

[25] Bede, *Historia ecclesiastica*, Praef., Colgrave and Mynors 2-3. Cf. G. Schoebe, "Was gilt im frühen Mittelalter als Geschichtliche Wirklichkeit?" in *Festschrift Hermann Aubin* (Wiesbaden, 1965), 2:625-651 at 635, 650; P. Hunter Blair, "The Historical Writings of Bede," in *La storiografia altomedievale* (Spoleto, 1970), 1:197-221 at 201.

[26] C.W. Jones, *Saints' Lives and Chronicles in Early England* (1947; repr. Archon Books, 1968), p. 92; Bede, *Historia ecclesiastica*, Praef., Colgrave and Mynors 6. After referring to the fact that his account is based either on written sources or on the testimony of trustworthy and reliable witnesses, Bede says: "Lectoremque suppliciter obsecro ut, si qua in his quae scripsimus aliter quam se veritas habet posita reppererit, non hoc nobis inputet, qui, quod vera lex historiae est, simpliciter ea quae fama vulgante collegimus ad instructionem posteritatis litteris mandare studuimus." According to Jones, Bede's true law of history "is to express the common view—to use accepted symbols as tools for attaining the ideal end, though the words may not be factually true" (p. 88). Cf. Hunter Blair, "The Historical Writings of Bede," p. 202; R.D. Ray, "Bede, the Exegete, as Historian," in *Famulus Christi*, pp. 125-140. However, for a fundamentally different point of view, one emphasizing Bede's commitment to factually accurate history, cf. G. Musca, *Il Venerabile Beda, storico dell'Alto Medioevo* (Bari, 1973), pp. 126-127, 251-256, 262-263; R.D. Ray, "Bede's *vera lex historiae*," *Speculum* 55 (1980): 1-21.

would occupy opposite ends. On this model of their relationship, the tendency to subordinate factual accuracy to the ends of some higher truth would be discernible in both genres. But it would be most pronounced in distinctively hagiographical works, whose authors had a special calling to edify their readers. Hence it would be characteristic of the hagiographers to display a marked disinterest in the specifics of character, place and time, and to offer in their stead highly idealized portraits in celebration of the virtues of their saintly heroes.[27]

The branch of ancient literature to which medieval hagiography seems to have been most closely related was that of biography, a genre in which the use of what we would regard as fiction in order to convey essential truth was standard practice. From a very early date, it would seem, Christian hagiographers adopted the same conception of the kind of truth to which they were committed.[28] To increase its effectiveness, they seem to have believed that their narrative should possess verisimilitude. Hence individual episodes are presented as if they were factual occurrences. But ultimately, or so it is argued, the truth as they conceived it did not lie in these details. What was important was not that the saint performed this or that particular miracle, but rather that the portrait as a whole was a faithful representation of a life lived in the presence of God and transformed by his influence. If this assessment of the hagiographers' attitude is correct, then the lives of the saints would approach the category of allegorical fiction, a recognized literary form in the Middle Ages. Although there were moral zealots who identified such fiction with lying and conscious fraud, generally it was regarded as a legitimate form of expression, precisely because it could be the instrument of a higher truth.[29]

Augustine's position on the issue was of considerable importance, for his formulation was adopted by Aquinas and was used quite widely in the later Middle Ages to justify poetic discourse. Augustine maintains that an invented story is not a lie, provided that it conveys some higher significance; and he illustrates his point with examples from both Sacred Scripture and secular literature.[30] Either the context or the form of the stories he defends clearly

[27] Cf. Guenée, *Histoire et culture historique*, pp. 53-54; E. Patlagean, "Ancient Byzantine Hagiography and Social History," in *Saints and their Cults: Studies in Religious Sociology, Folklore and History* (Cambridge, 1983), pp. 101-121.

[28] Cf. P. Cox, *Biography in Late Antiquity: A Quest for the Holy Man* (Berkeley and Los Angeles, 1983), esp. pp. 5, 8, 15, and p. 101, where she remarks: "Eusebius' task [in his *Life of Origen*] was not a quest for the historical Origen. Like that of other biographers, his goal was to create a convincing portrait of a magnificent man by capturing in prose the ideals which that man represented."

[29] Schreiner, "Zum Wahrheitsverständnis," pp. 162-163.

[30] See *Quaest. Evan.* 2.51, PL 35:1362, where Augustine discusses the story of the Prodigal Son: "Ficta sunt ergo ista ad rem quamdam significandam, tam longe lateque majorem, et tam

identifies them as fictitious. Hence there is nothing to suggest that Augustine would have included the lives of the saints in this category; saints' lives are not usually presented as simple collections of parables or fables. But if the higher significance of its fiction allowed poetry its truth, conceivably the truthfulness of the lives of the saints could be defended in much the same way. As Schreiner puts it:

> Wenn man schon der Dichtung ein solches Mass an natürlicher, geschichtlicher und spiritueller '*veritas*' eingeräumt hat, welchen Grad an Sinnfülle und Wahrheit dürfen dann erst die Berichte vom Leben und Wirken der grossen Gottesmänner beanspruchen? Wenn in diesen, selbst unter Verwendung poetischer Lizenzen, die Relation eines Heiligenlebens zu seinem göttlichen Grunde deutlich gemacht wird, so ist damit auch immer seine Wahrheit ausgesagt.[31]

Whether these observations faithfully reflect the mentality of the medieval hagiographer, or whether instead they are only the product of modern scholarly ingenuity, is perhaps difficult to determine. However, the example of the earliest biography of Gregory himself, the eighth-century life written by the anonymous monk of Whitby, suggests that they have at least some basis in fact. No one should take offence if he deviates from the chronological order of events, the author declares, for the Gospels themselves provide good precedent for his practice. The episode of the cleansing of the temple, for example, which appears at the end of the Gospel of St Matthew, is placed at the beginning in the Gospel of St John. The Gospels also display certain variations in the words attributed to Christ as well, although these minor differences do not affect the sense. In St Matthew's version of the parable, the sheep is lost in the mountains; in St Luke's version it is lost in the wilderness; yet in both Gospels Christ the Shepherd finds the lost sheep and carries it back to the flock on his shoulders. Details of time and place, then, are not particularly important. Although he must write perforce at second hand, and may have made mistakes of this kind, the anonymous monk is confident that the substance of his account is nevertheless true.[32]

---

incomparabiliter differentem, ut per illum fictum hominem Deus verus intelligatur." See also *Sermo* 89.6, PL 38:558, where he discusses the parable of the sower; and *Contra mendacium* 13.28, CSEL 41:508-509, where he once again mentions the story of the Prodigal Son, and then goes on to refer to secular literature. In the latter realm we can find examples where "humana etiam dicta vel facta inrationalibus animantibus et rebus sensu carentibus homines addiderunt, ut eius modi fictis narrationibus, sed veracibus significationibus quod vellent commendatius intimarent."

[31] Schreiner, "Zum Wahrheitsverständnis," p. 163.

[32] *Vita S. Gregorii*, ch. 30, ed. B. Colgrave (Lawrence, Kan., 1968), pp. 130-132. Compare Matt. 21:12-13 with John 2:13-17; and Matt. 18:12-14 with Luke 15:3-7.

More important, however, he goes on to say that he is confident of the substantial truth of his account even if some of the miracles attributed to Gregory are really the miracles of other saints. Leclercq remarks that "Nobody lends except to the rich," and in the early Middle Ages "it was even more reasonable to extend credit to the saints."[33] The few authentic miracles known could justify imagining others, and in their reconstruction the clearly established patterns in other *vitae* would obviously have been inviting. In the circumstances in which many hagiographers had to work, such a procedure would not have been reprehensible, and it could readily have been accompanied by a presumption of factual accuracy in the miracles actually attributed to any given saint. With the anonymous monk of Whitby, however, the situation seems fundamentally different. He abandons completely any such presumption, and he provides us with a clear justification of his practice, firmly basing it on an appeal to Sacred Scripture itself.

According to the doctrine of the Apostle Paul, we are all members in the one body of the church. This applies particularly to the saints, who, through the love of Christ, possess everything in common. Being all members of the same body of Christ, the benefits of the specific tasks they perform are not appropriated individually, but shared mutually. Hence, the Whitby monk maintains, if a miracle of some other saint has been attributed to Gregory, it should not be a matter of great concern. We can be confident, he says, that what was true of the other saints was equally true of Gregory as well.[34] The implicit but fundamental premise of the argument seems to be the essential identity of all the saints, an identity of purpose, vocation and character. The saints may be individuals, each with an immortal soul. But fundamentally they are all the same, for their lives have been thoroughly transformed by the spirit of Christ. Since in each case the specific details of their lives illustrate their essential saintly character, and since in any given case it is precisely this sanctity that the hagiographer wants to capture, the details of various *vitae* can be interchanged without compromising the overall purpose. If the resulting account is true nonetheless, the truth at issue must be of a higher kind than mere factual veracity. It must be the truth manifested by a portrait that, however inaccurate in detail, successfully conveys the essence of its subject.

Since the Whitby monk seems quite sincere in his convictions, presumably others had similar views. By virtue of the doctrine of the communion of the saints, one can expand the life of any one saint by drawing on the miracles

---

[33] Leclercq, *The Love of Learning*, p. 201. Cf. de Gaiffier, "Les 'doublets'," p. 262.
[34] *Vita S. Gregorii*, ch. 30, Colgrave 130-132. Cf. 1 Cor. 12:12ff.

of another; and one can do so in full confidence that the canons of truth—essential, not literal truth—will not be violated. Perhaps this was the conception of truth shared by most medieval hagiographers. If it was, its roots might be traced back to the Old Testament, or conceivably to even the more distant past.[35] One could speculate in this manner at some length. What we know for certain is relatively little. For the most part, medieval hagiographers were not very forthcoming about the theoretical principles underlying their task: they simply got on with the job. However, if at least some medieval hagiographers thought their invention or plagiarism justified, either by the doctrine of the justifiable lie or by the higher, ideal truth to which they felt bound, there were several others who did not share this view. The remarkable example of the tenth-century monk, Letaldus of Micy, is perhaps the most instructive.

Letaldus had been commissioned by Bishop Avesgaudus of Le Mans to rewrite the *acta* of the founder of the diocese, Bishop Julian. But in his dedicatory epistle the author confesses to having encountered difficulties. He begins by saying that a work such as this demands the highest standards of truthfulness lest, rather than pleasing God, it provoke his wrath. When we attribute a miracle to one of the saints, we are really attributing it to God himself. Unfortunately, however, some hagiographers offend against the truth in their zeal to celebrate the virtues of their saintly heroes, as if mendacity could increase the glory of saints who would never have reached the pinacle of sanctity if they had been mendacious themselves. Letaldus claims that, in themselves, the wonders credited to Julian provide no reason to doubt his merits. However, many of them are attributed to other saints as well, and in

---

[35] On the Old Testament background, see T. Boman, *Hebrew Thought compared with Greek* (London, 1960), pp. 201-202. Boman contrasts the objective conception of truth typical of the Greeks with the subjective conception of the Hebrews. For the ancient Hebrews, the true is what is "subjectively certain," or "faithful in the existential sense." Hence "it is not what is in agreement with impersonal objective being that interests them, but what is in agreement with the facts that are meaningful for them." On the more remote background, see Mircea Eliade, *The Myth of the Eternal Return* (Princeton, N.J., 1965). Eliade describes a primitive conception of reality, shared by traditional societies, according to which "all the important acts of life were revealed *ab origine* by gods or heroes. Men only repeat these exemplary and paradigmatic gestures *ad infinitum*" (p. 32). In such a state of affairs "an object or an act becomes real only insofar as it imitates or repeats an archetype. ... Everything which lacks an exemplary model is 'meaningless', i.e. it lacks reality." If this has Platonic overtones, it is because "Plato could be regarded as the outstanding philosopher of 'primitive mentality', that is, as the thinker who succeeded in giving philosophic currency and validity to the modes of life and behaviour of archaic humanity" (p. 34). However, if reality consists of what is archetypal and paradigmatic, truth, by extension, would be a function of the universal rather than the concrete and particular.

almost precisely the same language. He sees no way to solve the difficulty and to determine whom to believe, unless the authority of some distinguished doctor were to rescue him from error and, like an anchor, stabilize his wavering mind.[36] The position of Letaldus is unambiguous; his criterion of truth is strict factual veracity, not something that could be compromised either by the doctrine of the justifiable lie or by a higher, ideal conception of truth.

There were others whose position seems to have been much the same, and although the evidence is not as conclusive as we would like, on balance I am inclined to number Gregory the Great among them.[37] Certainly on the doctrine of the justifiable lie Gregory's position was virtually identical to Augustine's. Had Gregory not pronounced explicitly against mendacity in all its forms, he might indeed have appealed to the idea of the lie justified by good intentions. If he engaged in literary invention, he did so from the highest motives: his purpose was not to advance his own interests, but those of others, providing them with stories that would demonstrate some of the central truths of Christian doctrine and practice. If he misled his readers by claiming that events he had fabricated really took place, or that other people had really told him about them, it was only to enhance their verisimilitude and effectiveness. But all this is purely academic. Throughout his more strictly theological works Gregory consistently maintains that mendacity is hateful to the saints and always sinful. He admits that some forms of lying are worse than others: although all lying is to be avoided, premeditated lies are worse than lies on a sudden impulse, and lying for personal gain is worse than lying for the benefit of others. Indeed, if the intention really is to come to the aid of others, then the sin is a relatively minor one for being performed out of charitable motives. But, lest this be interpreted as a sign of wavering on his part, Gregory insists that the just will strenuously avoid even this kind of falsehood along with its baser variants.[38]

Gregory also maintains, with Augustine, that there is no Scriptural justification for lying. He concedes that in Old Testament times the demands of truthfulness were less strict than they are now, for the truth was then perceived under a veil. Now it has been revealed in all its brilliance. But even under the old dispensation lying in all its forms, even for the benefit of others, was still a sin, and so there are few examples of saints indulging in it.[39] Lying

---

[36] Letaldus of Micy, *Vita S. Juliani*, Epistola dedicatoria 2, PL 137:782-783.

[37] See, for example, Ennodius of Pavia, *Vita B. Epiphani*, CSEL 6:331-332, where the tendencies to exaggeration and invention displayed by some authors are roundly condemned.

[38] *Mor.* 15.62.73, CCL 143A:798; 18.3.5, CCL 143A:888-889.

[39] *Mor.* 18.3.7, CCL 143A: 889. Cf. Augustine, *De diversis quaestionibus octoginta tribus*, quaest. 53, CCL 44A:85-91, esp. 53.4, CCL 44A:91.

cannot be justified by pointing to the episode of Jacob and Esau, for example. Rather than acting fraudulently and with apparent divine approval, Jacob simply claimed what was his by right: "he did not steal the blessing of the first-born through deception, but he received it as his due, which, with his brother assenting, he had bought for the price of lentils given."[40] Nor can lying be justified on the example of the Hebrew midwives, although Gregory declares that some would seize on it as a particularly clear instance of lying that was divinely sanctioned. The midwives were ordered by Pharaoh to kill the male children of the Hebrews. But they disobeyed his command because they feared God more than man, and subsequently excused themselves by telling Pharaoh that the vigorously healthy Hebrew women managed to deliver their children on their own.[41] On the surface, it would seem that the midwives' conduct was approved by God, because it was rewarded. But, like Augustine, Gregory maintains that no divine approval for their lying can be read into the story. Indeed, he outdistances his great predecessor and is even more uncompromising in his attitude.

In his *Contra mendacium* Augustine explains that God did not reward the Hebrew midwives because they had lied, but rather because they had been merciful: "it was not their deception that was rewarded, but their benevolence; the benignity of their intention, not the iniquity of their invention." Their lying was worthy of no more than a pardon, although it was indeed worthy of that much, and so was forgiven by God. Just as God can pardon an earlier evil deed because of a good deed performed later, so he can pardon an evil deed because of a good deed performed at the same time. According to Augustine, the Hebrew midwives fall into the second category: they performed both a good deed of mercy in sparing the children and an evil deed of deception in lying about it. The good deed was judged worthy of reward, and God therefore pardoned the evil one. Moreover, the lie, although reprehensible, was itself a work of mercy, and this was a further mitigating factor. If sins committed for the lusts of the flesh can be forgiven because of works of mercy, why should works of mercy not be sufficient to

---

[40] *Hom. in Ezech.* 1.6.2, CCL 142:67-68. Gregory does not confront directly the less than edifying details of Jacob's behaviour, but chooses instead, as Augustine had done, to interpret them allegorically. Although he discusses the episode at some length, the essential part of his treatment can be found in *Hom. in Ezech.* 1.6.3, CCL 142:68-69. The allegorical significance Gregory unravels is somewhat different than the meaning discovered by Augustine, but it serves equally to put Jacob in a good light. Jacob is to be understood as a representation of the Gentiles, who would turn to Christ, whereas Esau signifies the Hebrews in all their blindness and obduracy.

[41] Exodus 1:15-21.

secure the forgiveness of sins that are themselves committed for mercy's sake?[42]

The weakness of Augustine's analysis lies in the notion that the lying of the midwives was a merciful and selfless act, an idea that Gregory rejects. Although he would agree that they initially acted for the benefit of the children in sparing them, he argues that they were not concerned about the lives of the children when they subsequently chose to lie about what they had done, but rather about their own. Hence, rather than being a blessing from God, the divine favour they received simply illustrates how, as a result of their fault, the eternal prize they might have won was replaced by rewards of a temporal and transitory nature.[43] His treatment of this episode is character- istic of his larger attitude. For Gregory, lying is not sanctioned by either Testament, and must always be regarded as more or less sinful, even in its least harmful forms.

Gregory softens his doctrine somewhat by admitting that complete candor is not always required. Indeed, on certain occasions it is to be avoided, because of the harmful consequences it can produce. Hence in his *Pastoral Care* he states that, although the sincere are to be commended for resolving never to utter falsehoods, they should be admonished to have the prudence to withhold the truth on occasion.[44] At times even misleading others by withholding the truth may be justified. An example is provided by 1 Kings (1 Samuel) 16, where we read that the Lord told Samuel to seek out the new king for the children of Israel among the sons of Jesse the Bethlehemite. Because Samuel was afraid that his life would be in jeopardy if Saul heard about his mission, the Lord told him to take a heifer with him, and, if challenged, to say that he had come to offer a sacrifice. As Gregory observes, Samuel was divinely counseled to mislead his enemies, and what was licit for Samuel can be licit for others as well: "What is shown by these words if not that the cunning and ferocity of tyrants sometimes ought to be deceived by means of pious fraud?"

---

[42] *Contra mendacium* 15.32, Jaffee 165, CSEL 41:513. Cf. *Enar. in Psalmos* 5.7, CCL 38:22.

[43] *Mor.* 18.3.6, CCL 143A:889. Augustine's analysis of the reward of the midwives is somewhat different in its emphasis. In *Contra mendacium* 15.33, CSEL 41:514, Augustine argues that, although it was simply a temporal reward that they received, it did foreshadow an eternal one. Further on, however, he acknowledges that, in itself, their reward was of little consequence. See *Contra mendacium* 16.33, CSEL 41:515: "obstetrices autem illae quamvis Hebraeae si secundum carnem tantummodo sapuerunt, quid aut quantum est quod eis profuit remuneratio temporalis, quia fecerunt sibi domos, nisi proficiendo pertinuerunt ad eam domum, de qua deo cantatur: *beati, qui habitant in domo tua; in saecula saeculorum laudabunt te?*"

[44] *Past.* 3.11, PL 77:64.

However, Gregory goes on immediately to explain that, misleading as the prescribed behaviour might have been, it did not involve telling a falsehood, for Samuel did indeed perform a sacrifice to the Lord. His behaviour would have been misleading only because he was advised to withhold part of the truth. Hence Gregory's position on the essential evil of lying remains uncompromised. If circumstances warrant, he is prepared to countenance behaviour that misleads others passively, by not telling them the whole truth, but not the kind of active deception that involves telling others something that is untrue.[45] Presumably, therefore, Gregory would have had considerable difficulty defending his own practice if he did resort to untruths, literary inventions, when writing the *Dialogues*. He certainly could not have justified his conduct by arguing that his falsehoods were in the service of a greater good. His consistent theological position simply precludes the possibility.

It is of course conceivable that what from our point of view appears to be falsehood is not falsehood at all; that the truth Gregory claims to offer is not to be sought in the details of the narrative but in their larger significance. In other words, if he had been challenged, Gregory might have attempted to reconcile his literary inventions with his protestations of truthfulness by claiming that the truthfulness he had in mind, and the truthfulness his audience would have known he had in mind, was not factual veracity but rather the higher kind of truth discussed earlier. There is some plausibility in this view. Although Gregory does not provide the kind of theoretical justification advanced by the Whitby monk,[46] his narrative does offer a higher truth that, in the final analysis, is of much greater import than the details of any of the miracle stories. His stories are told not for their own sake, but for the pedagogical purpose they serve. They are carefully chosen examples that demonstrate with particular effectiveness fundamental Christian truths, and Gregory takes pains to emphasize their value. Very few episodes pass without significant comment, clarification and explanation.

---

[45] *In 1 Reg.* 6.71, CCL 144:591. Cf. Augustine, *Enar. in Psalmos* 5.7, CCL 38:22-23; *Contra Faustum* 22.34, CSEL 25.1:628; 22.36, CSEL 25.1:630-631.

[46] Cf. *Mor.* 28.10.22, CCL 143B:1413-1414, where, like the Whitby monk, Gregory too commits himself to the doctrine of the communion of the saints. However, Gregory's point is essentially a moral one. The fact that the gifts of individual members of the faithful are given to all and for all reinforces the doctrine that the church is the one body of Christ. In hearts bound by charity there is no place for the envy that divides. Cf. L. Weber, *Hauptfragen der Moraltheologie Gregors des Grossen* (Freiburg, 1947), pp. 152-153; P. Catry, "L'amour du prochain chez saint Grégoire le Grand," *SMon.* 20 (1978): 287-344 at 329-330. Cf. also Augustine, *In Iohannis Evangelium* 32.8, CCL 36:304-305; *Enar. in Psalmos* 130.6, CCL 40:1901-1902.

However, to accept the hypothesis that truth resides exclusively on this higher level, one must also believe that the point would have been clear to Gregory's audience; that the people for whom he was writing would have realized that the only kind of truth he had in mind was the higher truth that the miracles demonstrate, and not factual veracity as well; that none but the simple-minded would have believed that the miracles themselves actually took place; and this is not easily done. The only clearly fictitious element in the *Dialogues* is the dialogue form itself. Although Peter was a genuine historical character,[47] and although some discussion with Peter on the saints of his own time may well have taken place, the *Dialogues* cannot be conceived as the literal transcription of an actual conversation. If Gregory initially presents it that way, very shortly thereafter he speaks of his *readers*. Although he is not as explicit as Sulpicius Severus, medieval readers should still have been able to grasp that the dialogue form was only a literary device.[48] The evidence that remains, however, suggests that they took it very seriously.[49] In these circumstances, what are we to think of their reaction to the miracle stories themselves? Far from suggesting that they are simple allegories, Gregory offers them as statements of fact, and he stresses their factual nature by systematically providing witnesses who can vouch for them.

The appeal to reliable witnesses, and even the claim to have been an eyewitness, were standard features of the medieval hagiographical tradition, features firmly established in its earliest exemplars. Undoubtedly such assurances were often simple *topoi* without any foundation in fact.[50] It is

[47] Cf. A. de Vogüé, *Grégoire le Grand, Dialogues 1: Introduction, bibliographie et cartes* (Paris, 1978), p. 44.

[48] Cf. *Dial.* 1 Prol. 7, sc 260:14, where, after a short introduction establishing the circumstances in which Gregory and Peter came to talk about the miracles of the saints, Gregory says: "Sed iam quae prolata sunt melius insinuo, si ea quae per inquisitionem ac responsionem dicta sunt sola nominum praenotatione distinguo"; and *Dial.* 1 Prol. 10, sc 260:16, where Gregory says to Peter: "ut dubitationis occasionem *legentibus* subtraham, per singula quae describo, quibus mihi haec auctoribus sint conperta manifesto." Sulpicius Severus provides a more straight-forward statement: "dialogi speciem, quo ad levandum fastidium lectio variaretur, adsumpsimus" (*Dial.* 3.5, csel 1:203). Cf. B.R. Voss, *Der Dialog in der Frühchristlichen Literatur* (München, 1970), pp. 308-310. On the reasons why Gregory may have chosen the dialogue form, see, most recently, G. Penco, "Sulla struttura dialogica dei Dialoghi di S. Gregorio," *Benedictina* 33 (1986): 329-335.

[49] See, for example, Paul the Deacon, *Historia Langobardorum* 4.5, mgh, srl, p. 117; Bede, *Historia ecclesiastica* 2.1, Colgrave and Mynors 124.

[50] See, for example, Athanasius, *Vita S. Antonii*, Prooemium, pg 26:839; Palladius, *Historia Lausiaca*, Prooemium, Butler 2:4-5; Sulpicius Severus, *Dial.* 1.15, csel 1:167; 3.5, csel 1:203; Bede, *Vita S. Cuthberti*, Prol., Colgrave 143-144. Cf. H. Delehaye, "Les recueils antiques de Miracles des Saints," *ABoll.* 43 (1925): 5-85, 305-325, at 66; A.-J. Festugière, "Lieux communs littéraires et thèmes de folklore dans l'Hagiographie primitive," *WS* 73

difficult to be certain, but it is at least possible that the intended audience was not misled by such tactics. Generally, late antique and early medieval readers had difficulty in recognizing the category of historical fiction. Hence works like the apocryphal New Testament were read as history, and were either accepted at face value or rejected as unauthentic or false.[51] But it is at least conceivable that the hagiographers' audience would have recognized in the many references to the witnesses who could guarantee the truth of their accounts only a means of enhancing verisimilitude.

In Gregory's case, however, this hypothesis is especially problematic. First, it is doubtful that Gregory's appeal to witnesses was simply a literary device. The evidence of his register strongly suggests that he did appeal to the sources he mentions.[52] Second, even if his appeal was merely the product of literary convention, it is unlikely that it would have been recognized as such by Gregory's readers. These suspicions cannot be fully substantiated, of course, but the weight of the evidence is in their favour. The sources to whom Gregory appeals are given a much more prominent and convincing role than was usually the case. More often than not, as we have seen, they are identified by name, and frequently they are among the most distinguished ecclesiastics of his time, men, he tells us, whose honesty is unimpeachable. All of this seems designed to convince Gregory's readers that he did draw his information from the sources he mentions, and that, to the best of his knowledge, the events of which they informed him did take place.[53]

(1960): 123-152 at 134-135; Speyer, *Die literarische Fälschung*, pp. 50-56. B. Colgrave, "Bede's Miracle Stories," in *Bede: His Life, Times and Writings* (Oxford, 1935), pp. 201-229 at p. 225, refers to the striking example of Jonas of Orleans, who claimed to be an eyewitness of the events recorded in his life of St Hubert. St Hubert died in 727, whereas Jonas himself survived until 843.

[51] Speyer, *Die literarische Fälschung*, pp. 210-218, esp. p. 215.

[52] See *Ep.* 3.50, CCL 140:195-196, where Gregory asks Bishop Maximian of Syracuse for information about Nonnosus. The miracles of Nonnosus are reported in *Dial.* 1.7, SC 260:64-70, and there Gregory names Maximian and an old monk named Laurio as his sources.

[53] The conclusion applies to the miracle stories in the *Homilies on the Gospels* as well. They too are usually, although not always, supported by explicit appeals to witnesses. See, for example, *Hom. in Evan.* 2.39.10, PL 76:1300: "charitati vestrae indicare studeo quod is qui praesto est filius meus Epiphanius diaconus, Isauria provincia exortus, in vicina factum terra Lycaoniae solet narrare miraculum"; and *Hom. in Evan.* 2.40.11, PL 76:1310: "Rem, fratres, refero, quam bene is qui praesto est frater et compresbyter meus Speciosus novit." The second example is especially interesting because it introduces the story of Romula and Redempta, a story in which Gregory draws on his own knowledge in a particularly realistic fashion: "Huic (i.e. Redemptae) duae in eodem habitu discipulae adhaerebant: una nomine Romula, et altera, quae nunc adhuc superest, quam quidem facie scio, sed nomine nescio."

Stancliffe, *St. Martin*, pp. 324-327, is similarly impressed by the appeal to witnesses in

If, as seems likely, this was Gregory's design, he must himself have believed that the events he reports actually happened. If he did not, he was guilty of the kind of falsehood his own theology will not allow. Had he simply told his stories with as much realistic detail as possible without repeatedly insisting that they had actually occurred and that witnesses had reported them to him, then he could have invented these stories without violating his own principles. But having committed himself to the truthfulness of his account, and having named witnesses, his conduct was dishonourable by his own standards if his stories were fabrications. That his purpose was honourable matters not at all, for his consistent position is that the uttering of falsehoods is never acceptable, even for a work as pious in its purpose as the *Dialogues*. Not only is it unacceptable; it is unnecessary. Heretics may require falsehood to prop up their errors, but the truth of the faith does not need that kind of support in order to prevail.[54]

In the preceding chapter it was argued that, although Gregory may have been guilty of literary invention by borrowing from the work of his predecessors and attaching to his own heroes the miracles reported of others, this has not been established conclusively in any particular case. He may indeed have been doing precisely that, and the probability that he was is increased by the large number of suspect passages; but in each of the questionable cases the possibility remains that he was simply passing on with his comments what had been provided to him by his informants. Here we have argued that, if Gregory did engage in literary invention, the work of the hagiographer would have been difficult to reconcile with the work of the theologian. His own theology eliminates the possibility of pious fraud, and the manner in which he appeals to witnesses to authenticate his stories makes it unlikely that his claims to factual veracity are not meant to be taken seriously. If our reading of the evidence is correct, and if we are charitable enough to reject the possibility of Gregory doing something that would have been dishonourable in his own eyes, there is one preferred conclusion: Gregory believes the miracle stories he tells, and is anxious that his readers believe them as well.

Sulpicius's work, particularly in the last of his *Dialogues*. According to E.-C. Babut, *Saint Martin de Tours* (Paris, [1912]), pp. 54-111, "on ne peut jamais compter sur la bonne foi de Sulpice. Ses serments de véracité n'ont aucune valeur" (p. 108). However, Stancliffe's assessment is fundamentally different: "It is one thing to claim eyewitness testimony in general terms; but it is quite another to name witnesses who would have been well known at the time, and to invite people to question them" (pp. 325-326).

[54] *Mor.* 11.26.37, CCL 143A:607: "Deus mendacio non eget quia veritas fulciri non quaerit auxilio falsitatis. Haeretici autem quia ea quae prave de Deo intellegunt ex veritate tueri non possunt, quasi ad probandum radium luminis umbram falsitatis requirunt."

7

Miracles and Belief

A memorable miracle story recorded in the fourth chapter of the first book of the *Dialogues* tells of the misfortune that once befell a nun. One day she entered the garden of her convent and, seeing some lettuce that appealed to her, began to eat it greedily, forgetting to say the customary blessing. The Devil immediately possessed her, and threw her to the ground in such agony that the other nuns quickly summoned the abbot, Equitius. As soon as the saintly man appeared, the Devil, crying out in the woman's voice, began to protest his innocence. "'I haven't done anything!' he kept shouting. 'I haven't done anything! I was sitting here on the lettuce when she came and ate me!'" However, Equitius was unmoved by his appeal. He commanded the Devil to depart the handmaiden of the Lord, which he did immediately, and thereafter he no longer had any power over her.[1]

Stories of this sort, not unusual in the *Dialogues*, have not failed to make their impression on modern scholars; and rather than being charmed by their innocence, they have often been repelled by their simple-mindedness. Dudden, for example, refers to "the strange combination of shrewdness and superstition which characterized the mind of Gregory. It is certainly astonishing," he says, "that the clear-headed man who managed the Papal estates and governed the Church with such admirable skill, should have contributed to the propagation of these wild tales of demons and wizards and haunted houses, of souls made visible, of rivers obedient to written orders, of corpses that scream and walk. And yet such was the fact. The landlord of the Papal patrimonies and the author of the *Dialogues* are one and the same person. And in him we have, perhaps, the first genuine Italian example of the medieval intellect." Dudden distinguishes between Gregory the pope and Gregory the hagiographer. If, in his former capacity, he appears to us as "the practical man with a knowledge of finance and a talent for the management

---

[1] *Dial.* 1.4.7, Zimmerman 18, SC 260:44.

of estates, a man whom neither dishonest agents nor plausible tenants can take in or deceive," in his latter capacity he takes on a fundamentally different guise: that of "the superstitious monk, the collector of relics, the devout compiler of the legends of the Italian saints, the firm believer in miracles and portents and diabolic apparitions."[2]

Dudden's views have been echoed by many other historians. Moricca argues that the legends of the *Dialogues* must appear "puerile and ingenuous" to the cultivated reader of the twentieth century. To Howorth, they provide "an excellent example of the extreme credulity of the times." Like Dudden, Howorth also was impressed by the startling inconsistency in Gregory's character, "the extraordinary superstition which (in the case of the Pope) was consistent with so many high qualities." He too maintains that "in many of the legendary tales which Gregory tells us in the *Dialogues*, about which he seems to have no doubts, there is a naive childishness which seems incredible in one so endowed with practical wisdom." More recently, Auerbach has pointed out that a belief in miracles is by no means unusual in a Christian thinker, but that in Gregory's case openness to miracles is taken to absurd lengths: "What is striking is the scope and character of this belief in miracles in a man of Gregory's stamp. The *Dialogues* disclose an almost childlike, fairy-tale world."[3]

It has sometimes been suggested that in late antiquity and the early Middle Ages there was an important connection between credulous belief in miracles and a relatively low level of cultural attainment.[4] Hence Gregory's attitude toward contemporary miracles might have been less disconcerting had he been an avowed opponent of secular culture, or a simple fideist in his

[2] F.H. Dudden, *Gregory the Great: His Place in History and Thought*, 2 vols. (1905; repr. New York, 1967), 1:356, 295.

[3] Moricca, p. xiv; H.H. Howorth, *Saint Gregory the Great* (London, 1912), pp. 62, 225, 231; E. Auerbach, *Literary Language and its Public in Late Latin Antiquity and in the Middle Ages* (London, 1965), p. 96. Cf. C. Lambot, "La vie et les miracles de saint Benoît racontés par saint Grégoire-le-Grand," *RMon.* 143 (1956): 49-61 at 50; H. de Lubac, *Exégèse médiévale. Les quatre sens de l'Ecriture*, part 1, vol. 2 (Paris, 1959), p. 472; G. Cremascoli, '*Novissima hominis' nei 'Dialogi' di Gregorio Magno* (Bologna, 1979), p. 14.

[4] See, for example, A.-J. Festugière, *Les moines d'Orient* 1: *Culture ou sainteté* (Paris, 1961), esp. pp. 75-91; F. Prinz, "Zur geistigen Kultur des Mönchtums im spätantiken Gallien und im Merowingerreich," *ZBLG* 26 (1963): 29-102, esp. 40-44; *Frühes Mönchtum im Frankenreich* (München and Wien, 1965), esp. pp. 458-461. Festugière draws a parallel between the credulity demonstrated by the fathers of the desert and the stream of anti-intellectualism also evident in their thought. Conversely, Prinz discusses the reserve toward the miraculous demonstrated by individuals shaped by the monastic culture of Lerins, a reserve he attributes to their high social standing and especially to their high level of cultural attainment.

approach to the central issues of Christian faith and doctrine. Neither was
the case, however. Gregory of Tours says that his own contemporaries
considered Gregory second to none in his command of grammar, rhetoric
and logic. The authenticity of this claim may be open to dispute, but the
accuracy of the judgment it contains is not. It has been confirmed by some
of the best modern research on the issue.[5]

Although Gregory's ignorance of Greek may seem surprising in view of
the time he spent at the Byzantine court, it is possible that his own
disclaimers were no more than *confessiones humilitatis,* and that he had at
least a modest knowledge of the language. Given the extent to which he was
dependent on Latin authors for etymologies and the explanation of Greek
terms, in all likelihood Gregory's command of the language was not enough
to enable him to handle Greek texts in the original. But this does not mean
that he was completely cut off from sources of Greek culture and spirituality
and had to rely only on the western, Latin tradition, as has sometimes been
thought. Gregory's formidable intellectual and theological learning is hardly
diminished by an imperfect or suspect knowledge of Greek. Much of the
learning of eastern Christendom would have been available to him, either
orally through his Greek-speaking acquaintances, or in the many Latin
translations prepared by Rufinus and others.[6]

---

[5] Gregory of Tours, *Historia Francorum* 10.1, MGH, SRM 1, p. 478: "Litteris grammaticis
dialecticisque ac rethoricis ita est institutus, ut nulli in Urbe ipsa putaretur esse secundus." Cf.
Paul the Deacon, *Vita S. Gregorii* 2, PL 75:42: "Disciplinis vero liberalibus, hoc est grammatica, rhetorica, dialectica, ita a puero est institutus, ut quamvis eo tempore florerent adhuc
Romae studia litterarum, tamen nulli in urbe ipsa secundus esse putaretur." Gregory of Tours
tells us a little later (p. 481) that he owed his information to one of his own deacons who
had been sent to Rome in the year 590. Cf. *Liber in gloria martyrum,* chap. 82, MGH, SRM 1.2,
p. 94.

O. Chadwick, "Gregory of Tours and Gregory the Great," *JTS* 50 (1949): 38-49, argues
that the first chapter in the tenth book of the *Historia Francorum* was likely an eighth-century
interpolation. However, the quality of Gregory's education has been stressed by P. Riché,
Education and Culture in the Barbarian West: Sixth through Eighth Centuries (Columbia, S.C.,
1976), pp. 145-152; cf. his *Les écoles et l'enseignement dans l'Occident chrétien de la fin du
Ve siècle au milieu du XIe siècle* (Paris, 1979), pp. 17-18.

[6] Gregory's own statements imply almost complete ignorance of Greek. See, for example,
Ep. 7.29, CCL 140:487-489 at 487; and *Ep.* 11.55, CCL 140A:959-960 at 960: "Nam nos nec
Graece novimus nec aliquod opus aliquando Graece conscripsimus." Cf. *Ep.* 1.28, CCL
140:36; *Ep.* 3.63, CCL 140:213-214 at 214; *Ep.* 10.21, CCL 140A:852-856 at 855. However,
C. Dagens, "Grégoire le Grand et le monde oriental," *RSLR* 17 (1981): 243-252, esp.
244-245, argues that "son ignorance semble plus politique que réelle: elle lui permet de
s'affirmer comme un latin, face à des Orientaux dont il ne goûte pas les subtilités, et comme
un Romain qui s'étonne que la langue de sa patrie ne soit plus universelle" (p. 245).

For a more thorough discussion of the issue, see J.M. Petersen, "Did Gregory the Great

Of course, his own level of cultural attainment notwithstanding, Gregory still could have developed a marked aversion to the cultural tradition from which he benefited. This seems to have been the prevailing view in scholarship some fifty years ago. It has tended to yield to a more moderate assessment in recent research, although the earlier harsh judgment can still be found.[7] Cracco, for instance, maintains that the representation of early medieval life we encounter in the *Dialogues* shows virtually no evidence of a higher, literary culture, and although he overstates his case somewhat, he is essentially correct. The references to men of learning are few and far between. Perhaps the most prominent example is Paschasius, the former deacon of the Roman church who supported Lawrence over Pope Symmachus in the papal schism. Although Gregory is more impressed by his personal sanctity than anything else (the context of the story demands it), he

---

Know Greek?" in *The Orthodox Churches and the West*, ed. D. Baker (Oxford, 1976), pp. 121-134. Petersen offers a revised assessment in *The Dialogues of Gregory the Great in their Late Antique Cultural Background* (Toronto, 1984), esp. pp. 151-152, 190. See also her recent articles: "The Influence of Origen upon Gregory the Great's Exegesis of the Song of Songs," *SPatr.* 18.1 (1985): 343-347; "Greek Influences upon Gregory the Great's Exegesis of Luke 15, 1-10 in *Homelia in Evang.* II, 34," in *Grégoire le Grand*, Chantilly, 15-19 septembre 1982 (Paris, 1986), pp. 521-528; "'Homo omnino Latinus?' The Theological and Cultural Background of Pope Gregory the Great," *Speculum* 62 (1987): 529-551.

[7] For the earlier view, see, for example, A. Sepulcri, "Gregorio Magno e la scienza profana," *AAST* 39 (1904): 962-976; and Howorth, *Saint Gregory the Great*, p. 322, who maintains that "the barren darkness of the next four centuries in culture and in learning can be largely traced to Gregory's vehement campaign against both, and to his substitution in the Western lands, of obscurantism for art and literature and science and philosophy." However, cf. J. Spörl, "Gregor der Grosse und die Antike," in *Christliche Verwirklichung* (Rothenfels, 1935), pp. 198-211. For examples of recent scholarship, see C. Dagens, "Grégoire le Grand et la culture: de la '*sapientia huius mundi*' à la '*docta ignorantia*'," *REAug.* 14 (1968): 17-26; and his *Saint Grégoire le Grand. Culture et expérience chrétiennes* (Paris, 1977), pp. 31-54; cf. J. Fontaine, "L'expérience spirituelle chez Grégoire le Grand," *RHSp.* 52 (1976): 141-154. An overview is provided by V. Paronetto, "Gregorio Magno e la cultura classica," *Studium* 74 (1978): 665-680.

The older view persists in N. Scivoletto, "I limiti dell''ars grammatica' in Gregorio Magno," *GIF* 17 (1964): 210-238; C. Leonardi, "I commenti altomedievali ai classici pagani: da Severino Boezio a Remigio d'Auxerre," in *La cultura antica nell'occidente latino dal VII all'XI secolo* (Spoleto, 1975), 1:459-504 at 471-475; G. Cracco, "Uomini di Dio e uomini di chiesa nell'alto medioevo (per una reinterpretazione dei 'Dialogi' di Gregorio Magno)," *RSSR* n.s. 12 (1977): 163-202, esp. 199-200; "Ascesa e ruolo dei 'Viri Dei' nell'Italia di Gregorio Magno," in *Hagiographie, cultures et sociétés, IVe-XIIe siècles* (Paris, 1981), pp. 283-296, esp. 289-290. See also P. Boglioni, "Miracle et nature chez Grégoire le Grand," in *Cahiers d'études médiévales* 1: *Epopées, légendes et miracles* (Montreal and Paris, 1974), pp. 11-102, esp. p. 22, where Boglioni refers to "le jugement assez négatif qu'exprime Grégoire sur la culture profane."

does inform us that Paschasius was a man of great learning. But the learning for which he was renowned was theological learning. To the best of my knowledge there are only two passages in which Gregory draws secular learning to our attention. One of them has to do with Paulinus of Nola, who is described as *vir eloquentissimus atque adprime exterioribus quoque studiis eruditus*; the other concerns the two brothers, Speciosus and Gregory, *nobiles ... atque exterioribus studiis eruditi*, whom Benedict agreed to receive as monks in his monastery at Terracina. Clearly, Gregory did not regard intellectual accomplishment of any kind as a constitutive element of sanctity. For that, one must await the later Middle Ages.[8] However, this does not mean, as Cracco suggests, that Gregory was hostile to literary culture and its representatives, that the *Dialogues* must be regarded as "un'opera che volutamente prescinde da cultura e scuola e anzi esalta l'"ignoranza'."[9] Indeed, such a view can be advanced only at the cost of considerable distortion of Gregory's text. If Gregory was indeed an opponent of secular learning, he successfully managed to suppress his convictions while writing his book of miracles.

It might be argued, not unconvincingly, that nothing less than a strong aversion to secular learning seems to be implied by the portrait of Saint Benedict at the beginning of the second book of the *Dialogues*. Benedict was born to a distinguished family in the district of Nursia, Gregory says, and was sent to Rome for a liberal education, but he soon dissociated himself from the culture of the schools:

> When he saw many of his fellow students falling headlong into vice, he stepped back from the threshold of the world in which he had just set foot. For he was afraid that if he acquired any of its learning he, too, would later plunge, body and soul, into the dread abyss. In his desire to please God alone, he turned his back on further studies, gave up home and inheritance, and resolved to embrace the religious life. *Recessit igitur scienter nescius et sapienter indoctus.*

Benedict does not simply abandon the lesser good of secular learning to devote himself completely to the greater good represented by the knowledge of God, as Dagens suggests. Such a view hardly does justice to the vehemence of his reaction: secular learning is not merely given up for something more praiseworthy; it is rejected absolutely, out of the conviction that it poses grave dangers to moral and spiritual welfare. Gregory, of course, is content to

---

[8] Cf. *Dial.* 4.42.1, sc 265:150-152; 3.1.2, sc 260:258; 4.9.1, sc 265:42. On the later Middle Ages, see A. Vauchez, *La sainteté en Occident aux derniers siècles du Moyen Age* (Rome, 1981), pp. 460-472.

[9] Cracco, "Ascesa e ruolo dei 'Viri Dei'," pp. 289-290, esp. 290.

report Benedict's reaction rather than give his own. Yet he does so with apparent approval, suggesting that his own view would not have been very different. Although learning itself is not characterized as morally damnable, the environment in which it is pursued is clearly shown to place the Christian soul in grave jeopardy.[10]

We should, however, be wary of attaching too much significance to this atypical episode. The *Dialogues* describe several saints who were simple, uninstructed men. But nowhere else do they even faintly suggest that secular learning is incompatible with Christian sanctity. Gregory is concerned only to stress that learning is not essential, for the true abode of sanctity is the heart, not the intellect. It is available to all, even the most humble, who allow their lives to be governed by the precepts of charity. As Dagens argues:

> Faire de lui un adversaire de la culture profane serait donc un non-sens. Ce serait méconnaitre le fait qu'il aborde presque toujours ce sujet en auteur spirituel. Comme Pascal, il met l'ordre de la charité bien au-dessus de l'ordre de l'intelligence; c'est pourquoi le moindre moine qui a pratiqué, durant toute sa vie, l'amour de Dieu et du prochain, mérite à ses yeux d'être glorifié plus que tous les sages du monde.[11]

Gregory's portrait of Benedict is indeed paralleled by other texts scattered throughout his works. In a famous letter to Leander of Seville, he seems to be contemptuous of even the most basic rules of Latin grammar. In another, perhaps equally famous, letter to Desiderius of Vienne, he chastises the bishop for offering instruction in grammar, a task not suitable even for a religious layman.[12] However, studies by scholars like Fontaine and de Lubac have clearly shown that Gregory's primary intent in the letter to Leander was to register his disapproval of a misguided exegetical technique, one that would reduce Sacred Scripture to the level of profane texts by interpreting it exclusively from the grammatical point of view. At issue, therefore, is only an excessive regard for grammar at the expense of other considerations, a one-dimensional approach that with pedantic exactitude would require God's Word to conform to the norms of human discourse. As Gregory himself suggests, this is a commonplace of traditional medieval theology; similar

[10] *Dial.* 2 Prol. 1, Zimmerman 55-56, SC 260:126. Cf. Cracco, "Uomini di Dio," p. 199, who calls the portrait of Benedict "un'aspra condanna contro gli *studia litterarum liberalia*"; Dagens, *Saint Grégoire le Grand*, pp. 48-49; and Scivoletto, "I limiti," p. 227n: "qui le arti sono un baratro!"

[11] Dagens, "Grégoire le Grand et la culture," p. 26; cf. *Saint Grégoire le Grand*, p. 50. The portraits of Sanctulus (*Dial.* 3.37.19-20, SC 260:424-426) and Servulus (*Dial.* 4.15.2-5, SC 265:60-62) provide examples of simple, uneducated saints.

[12] See *Ep. ad Leandrum*, CCL 143:1-7 at 7; and *Ep.* 11.34, CCL 140A:922-923 at 922.

ideas can be found in virtually all the fathers of the church, including Augustine.[13] Gregory's further claim, that he has neglected to observe the rules of Donatus in his own prose as well, most modern scholars agree, should be understood *cum grano salis*.[14] Gregory adduces the letter to Leander as evidence, but the letter itself tells us something different. The barbarisms and solecisms he claims to embrace so willingly are not to be found in it, or indeed anywhere else in Gregory's writings. If anything, they reveal a meticulous care, rather than negligence, about the literary quality of his work.

The letter to Desiderius presents more formidable difficulties: here Gregory insists that grammar is not to be taught by anyone with serious religious convictions. De Lubac argues that the reason for Gregory's fears can be appreciated properly only when the nature of their object is fully understood. Grammar involved more than studying the rules of correct discourse. That first stage of instruction was followed by the systematic study of the poets. De Lubac claims that for Gregory the poets constituted the greatest danger. It was the poets Gregory had in mind when he referred in the letter to *nugae et seculares litterae*, or when he questioned the appropriateness of trying to combine the praises of Christ *cum Iovis laudibus*. Gregory expressed no condemnation of the historians or the orators, but the poets were a different matter, for "la littérature païenne n'était pas encore dévitalisée; elle n'était pas devenue chose purement 'littéraire'." For Gregory, and others like him, classical poetry was not a civilizing, humanizing influence, but rather the voice of an ancient paganism that had not yet been defeated. De Lubac argues that Gregory's anti-paganism must be distinguished from his alleged anti-hellenism. We must avoid seeing his justifiable concern over a recrudescence of pagan superstition as a condemnation of all secular literary culture.[15] Dagens' conclusions are much the same:

[13] See J. Fontaine, *Isidore de Séville et la culture classique dans l'Espagne wisigothique* (Paris, 1959), pp. 35-36; de Lubac, *Exégèse médiévale*, part 2, vol. 1 (Paris, 1961), pp. 59-60; Riché, *Education and Culture*, p. 153.

On the excessive attention to grammar in Biblical exegesis, see Augustine, *In Iohannis Evangelium* 2.14, CCL 36:18; *Enar. in Psalmos* 50.19, CCL 38:613. The commonplace is charted by de Lubac, *Exégèse médiévale* 2.1, pp. 77-98; cf. G.R. Evans, *The Language and Logic of the Bible: The Earlier Middle Ages* (Cambridge, 1984), pp. 34-35.

[14] Fontaine, *Isidore de Séville*, p. 36; cf. Scivoletto, "I limiti," p. 229n; Paronetto, "Gregorio Magno," p. 670.

[15] De Lubac, *Exégèse médiévale* 2.1, pp. 68-77, esp. 73. Cf. *ibid.*, part 1, vol. 1 (Paris, 1959), pp. 66-74, where, without dealing explicitly with Gregory, de Lubac discusses the medieval attitude to secular literature: "Même de bons auteurs prennent aujourd'hui trop facilement pour un manque de sympathie envers la culture profane, voire pour un mépris de toute culture, ce qui n'était que mise en garde, toujours renouvelée parce que toujours

les lettres à Léandre et à Didier sont l'oeuvre non d'un ennemi des lettres classiques, mais d'un auteur spirituel, qui proteste contre les prétensions excessives de l'art grammatical et contre l'immoralité de la mythologie païenne, parce qu'il entend préserver la suprématie de la science sacrée.[16]

Unfortunately, this argument cannot allay all doubts. The main question is whether Gregory was able to sustain de Lubac's distinction. The letter to Desiderius suggests there were at least some occasions when he found it difficult. True, Gregory's concerns in this letter are moral, and arise from his fear of the contaminating influence of ancient paganism. But that very fear apparently leads him to advocate extreme solutions. Precisely because of the moral dangers attendant upon it, grammar is not a proper occupation for any Christian, Gregory claims. He does not argue for a selective reading of the poets, preserving what is compatible with a Christian view of life and discarding the rest; instead, he seems here to favour, if not complete rejection, at least systematic overhaul of the ancient model of grammatical instruction.

Gregory's statements need not imply a condemnation of elementary instruction in the fundamental principles of the Latin language. Indeed, it is not even likely that he would have disapproved of bishops involving themselves in the dispensing of such instruction, for he undoubtedly knew that that was the established pattern in many of the episcopal schools of the time.[17] However, on this occasion at least he seems to have been prepared to reject the more advanced instruction that included the reading and explication of the poets. If this was indeed the case, he was advocating a strict separation of two branches of grammar that hitherto had been inseparable, with the consequent impoverishment of literary education that it would have entailed. As Scivoletto points out, in place of an education that included solid grounding in the literature of antiquity, he was advocating a course of study that would have been purely technical in nature.[18]

---

nécessaire, en face du paganisme dans lequel avaient été nourris les poètes et 'les philosophes de ce siècle'. Les plus vigilants à cet égard sont souvent eux-mêmes les plus cultivés" (p. 74). For similar observations on the early medieval monastic critics of literary culture, cf. Prinz, "Zur geistigen Kultur," p. 61; *Frühes Mönchtum*, p. 477.

[16] Dagens, *Saint Grégoire le Grand*, p. 34; cf. R. Gillet, "Grégoire le Grand," *DSp.* 6:872-910 at 876.

[17] Cf. A. Guillou, "L'école dans l'Italie Byzantine," in *La scuola nell'occidente latino dell'alto medioevo* (Spoleto, 1972), 1:291-311 at 301-302.

[18] Scivoletto, "I limiti," pp. 228-231. Cf. his "Saeculum Gregorianum," *GIF* 18 (1965): 41-70, where Scivoletto argues that, with the exception of Visigothic Spain, Gregory's attitude would dominate western Europe up to the Carolingian Renaissance. It would provide the foundation for a cultural programme to which the most representative thinkers of the seventh

Perhaps equally disconcerting is a passage found in the *Moralia*. It deserves to be quoted at length:

> It is the wisdom of this world to conceal the heart with machinations, to veil understanding with words, to declare that things which are false are true, to demonstrate that things which are true are false. To be sure, this sagacity is known by young men through experience; it is learned by boys for a price. Those who know it take pride in looking down on the rest; those who do not know it, submissive and timid, marvel at it in others, because it is this same iniquitous duplicity (*duplicitas iniquitatis*), its true name concealed, that captures their esteem as long as perversity of mind is called sophistication (*dum mentis perversitas urbanitas vocatur*). It teaches those who yield to it to seek the highest peaks of honours; to delight in the attained vanity of temporal glory; to pay back in spades the evils inflicted by others. It teaches them to yield to no resistance when they have the upper hand (*cum vires suppetunt nullis resistentibus cedere*); and when they do not, to indulge their weakness through malice, and to give this the appearance of peace-loving kindness (*cum virtutis possibilitas deest, quicquid explere per malitiam non valet, hoc in pacifica bonitate simulare*). But, on the other hand, it is the wisdom of the just to feign nothing through display, to lay bare understanding through words, to esteem true things as they are, to avoid falsehoods, to offer good things without recompense, to endure evils more willingly than to do them, to seek no revenge for injury, to consider reproach suffered for the sake of truth as gain. But this simplicity of the just is derided, because the virtue of purity is believed to be foolishness by the wise of this world. Indeed, everything that is done innocently is without doubt thought by them to be foolish; and whatever truth approves in deed sounds fatuous to worldly wisdom.[19]

A thoroughly conventional contrast underlies these words: the wisdom of this world should be rejected, the wisdom of the just emulated. But the passage is remarkable for the way it associates the wisdom of the world with the educational tradition of the schools (*mentis perversitas urbanitas vocatur*). So close is the association that the rejection of the one seems to imply the rejection of the other.

Gregory was quite capable, of course, of distinguishing between a literary education and the sinful impulses that it might generate. After all, in the passage that follows immediately upon the one just quoted he distinguishes the possession of property from the vice of cupidity with which it is often associated, and argues that only cupidity is evil in itself. Since some people

---

and early eighth centuries would subscribe. In the Carolingian period, however, through the agency of scholars like Paul the Deacon and Peter of Pisa, the importance of the classical authors would once again gain recognition.

[19] *Mor.* 10.29.48, CCL 143:570-571.

can use their wealth to achieve works of virtue rather than their own debasement, presumably the same could be said about those who have had a secular education. Indeed, Gregory could have used himself (no doubt immodestly) as an example, for he was much more familiar with the ancient literary tradition than was once thought.[20] In fact, however, these mitigating claims are not made. They are not made in his portrait of St Benedict either, where the worldliness associated with secular education is again at issue; nor in his letter to Desiderius of Vienne, where, if de Lubac is correct, it is the paganism associated with secular literature that gives rise to his severe views. On each of these occasions Gregory's Christian conscience is so outraged that any positive value in secular culture is effectively denied.

However, these passages have to be kept in proper perspective. As Dufner points out, we must beware of overestimating the significance of isolated statements in a corpus of work as extensive as Gregory's. Even if he sometimes railed against the *artes liberales*, Gregory would have spoken out much more frequently had it been one of his major preoccupations.[21] We also need to be attentive to the concerns that were uppermost in his mind on those few occasions of outburst: the concerns of a Christian moralist temporarily overwhelmed by the worldliness or paganism that seemed inextricably bound up with the secular literary tradition.

In the final analysis, when it is taken as a whole, the work of Gregory the Great does indeed reveal a certain detachment from the culture of classical antiquity. The point is well illustrated by the fundamental differences that separate the *Moralia on Job* from the *Consolation of Philosophy*. As Dagens observes, "Ses *Moralia in Job*, qui sont pourtant une méditation sur les souffrances d'un juste, ne ressemblent en rien, ni par le fond, ni par la forme, au *De consolatione philosophiae* de Boèce. C'est la Parole de Dieu, et non la philosophie païenne, qui peut éclairer l'homme en proie à l'infortune." However, Dagens immediately continues, "on aurait tort de soupçonner Grégoire d'une hostilité calculée à l'égard de la tradition classique."[22] Although his duties as a Christian moralist sometimes obtruded on his assessment of the classical literary tradition, Gregory was far from being an avowed opponent of that tradition, intent on exalting ignorance over learning.

[20] See, in particular, P. Courcelle, "Grégoire le Grand à l'école de Juvénal," *SMSR* 38 (1967): 170-174; "'Habitare secum' selon Perse et selon S. Grégoire le Grand," *REAnc.* 69 (1967): 266-279; *Connais-toi toi-même, de Socrate à Saint Bernard*, 2 vols. (Paris, 1974-1975), 1:217-229.

[21] G. Dufner, *Die Dialoge Gregors des Grossen im Wandel der Zeiten und Sprachen* (Padua, 1968), pp. 21-22.

[22] Dagens, *Saint Grégoire le Grand*, p. 436.

If characterizing Gregory as an enemy of secular culture distorts his true attitude, viewing him as a simple fideist in matters of faith and doctrine is equally misleading, although an inattentive reading of some of his statements could easily leave a mistaken impression. On more than one occasion Gregory declares that the works of the Creator are beyond our grasp, and simple veneration is a more appropriate response than feeble and inadequate attempts to comprehend them. The desire to uncover mysteries is a mark of sinful pride, and can issue only in vain labour. Penetrating the divine secrets is utterly beyond our ability. Such remarks have generally prompted scholars to minimize the role of reason in Gregory's thought. Hence Dudden, for example, maintains that "his dislike of theological and philosophical specula-tion, combined with a profound consciousness of the limitations of his own knowledge, inclined him to depreciate the function of reason, and to lay all the stress on faith and authority."[23] Dudden's assessment is an exaggeration, although it does indeed contain some truth. Gregory's approach to theologi-cal issues is not to be compared with that of Aquinas. What needs to be noted, however, is that comments of the sort recorded above are usually designed to have limited application. Generally Gregory has quite specific theological issues in mind.

The doctrine of predestination, the Incarnation, the workings of Provi-dence, and God's judgment are ultimately inscrutable. Mysteries all, they exceed the limits of our finite minds. Before them we can only bow obediently, in silence and grateful admiration; to seek to know them fully is but empty pride.[24] But this does not mean that there is no role for reason in elucidating matters of the faith. To be sure, reason must not be allowed to supplant faith. Hence the error of rationalism, which consists of the refusal to believe whatever cannot be grasped by human comprehension, is stren-uously to be avoided.[25] But in Gregory's judgment there are many Christian doctrines that can profit from rational investigation, not the least of which are the very existence of God himself and the doctrine of the resurrection.

---

[23] See, for example, *Hom. in Ezech.* 2.8.10, CCL 142:344; and *Mor.* 9.15.22, CCL 143:472; and see also Dudden, *Gregory the Great,* 2:296. Although more recent assessments are generally more balanced, they still tend to depreciate the role attributed to human reason in Gregory's thought. See, for example, L. Weber, *Hauptfragen der Moraltheologie Gregors des Grossen* (Freiburg, 1947), pp. 38-40; Boglioni, "Miracle et nature," pp. 24-28; Dagens, *Saint Grégoire le Grand,* pp. 101-103. Perhaps the most optimistic assessment is provided by M. Frickel, *Deus totus ubique simul. Untersuchungen zur allgemeinen Gottgegenwart im Rahmen der Gotteslehre Gregors des Grossen* (Freiburg, 1956), esp. pp. 132-133.

[24] On predestination, for example, cf. *Mor.* 9.15.22, CCL 143:472; *In 1 Reg.* 1.102, CCL 144:115; *Dial.* 4.27.9-14, SC 265:92-94. On the mysteries of the Incarnation, see *Mor.* 23.19.36, CCL 143B:1171.

[25] *Mor.* 16.67.81, CCL 143A:846-847.

Gregory's handling of the former issue does not constitute a proper proof, although he does show that reason has a role to play in bringing us to a knowledge of God through his creatures. His treatment of the doctrine of the resurrection, by contrast, is developed at some length and should be discussed in detail. In both the *Moralia on Job* and the *Homilies on Ezechiel* he avails himself of much that Augustine had had to say on the issue, weaving together a number of arguments on different levels.[26] For those whose reasoning powers are weak, he maintains, the example of Christ should alone be sufficient to provide assurance of the truth: Christ's resurrection guarantees the resurrection that will be ours. However, for those whose reasoning powers are adequate to the task, rational enquiry can be used to advantage, not only in clarifying the doctrine of the resurrection, but also in proving it.[27]

Since sceptics unwilling to believe in the resurrection often were also Christians, Gregory tries to persuade them by arguing from basic Christian premises they should have been prepared to accept. If you are willing to believe that God created the universe, he exhorts, you should be willing to believe in the resurrection. A God who created everything out of nothing is surely capable of the lesser deed of refashioning human bodies out of dust and ashes. You may not understand how such a miracle could be possible, but there are many other miracles reported in Scripture that you are quite willing to believe, despite their being equally mysterious. How was it possible for Moses to divide the Red Sea, or produce water out of the hardness of a rock? How was it possible for a Virgin to conceive and bring forth a child? How was it possible for Lazarus, who had been dead for four days, to be revived by the word of Christ? These are mysteries beyond understanding as

---

[26] On the existence of God, cf. *Mor.* 5.29.52, CCL 143:254; 26.12.17-18, CCL 143B:1277-1279. See also Frickel, *Deus totus ubique simul,* esp. pp. 14-21. On the resurrection, cf. *Mor.* 6.15.19, CCL 143:296-297; 14.55.69-70, CCL 143A:741-743; *Hom. in Ezech.* 2.8.6-10, CCL 142:339-344. Cf. also *Hom. in Evan.* 2.26.12, PL 76:1203-1204.

Like Augustine, Gregory was much moved by the fact that some people who considered themselves Christians did not believe in the resurrection of the body: "triste nimis et valde lugubre est quod quosdam in Ecclesia stare, et de carnis resurrectione dubitare cognoscimus" (*Hom. in Ezech.* 2.8.6, CCL 142:339). Augustine frequently refers to the scepticism—indeed, the derision—with which pagans were inclined to respond to the doctrine of the resurrection. See, for example, *Enar. in Psalmos* 88.2.5, CCL 39:1237; *Sermo* 361.6.6, PL 39:1601; *Retract.* 1.17, CCL 57:52-54. No other article of the Christian faith, says Augustine, encountered quite as much opposition. What was most distressing, however, was that even some baptized Christians were sceptical; see *Enar. in Psalmos* 73.25, CCL 39:1021; 129.7, CCL 40:1894.

[27] *Mor.* 14.55.70, CCL 143A:742: "si resurrectionis fidem ex oboedientia non tenent, certe hanc tenere ex ratione debuerunt." On Christ's example, cf. Augustine, *Enar. in Psalmos* 129.7, CCL 40:1894.

well, and yet you are prepared to accept them. Why, therefore, dispute about the resurrection of the body when there are many other miracles which you are willing to believe without reservation?[28]

Strictly speaking, this line of argument is theological in nature. It is addressed to Christians who believe implicitly in most of the tenets of the faith, and it rests on premises drawn from that faith. It thus falls short of being a proof in the strictest sense of the term. However, Gregory does not limit himself to theological premises, but also argues from human experience in general, maintaining that the basic pattern of death and resurrection is evident in nature:

> The very elements, the very forms of things, proclaim to us the image of the resurrection. Indeed, to our eyes the sun dies on a daily basis, and daily it rises again. To us the stars set in the morning hours, and rise again in the evening. We see the groves filled in summertime with leaves, flowers and fruits, groves which in wintertime are bare of leaves, flowers and fruits, and remain as though they were withered. But with the sun returning in spring, when the moisture has risen up from the root, again they are clothed in their beauty. Why, therefore, is what is seen to happen in trees distrusted as far as men are concerned?[29]

Again, he says, you may be troubled because you do not understand how a body that has decomposed into the dust of death could possibly be refashioned in all its complexity. Indeed, this *is* something that we cannot comprehend. Yet belief in the resurrection is rational nonetheless. We see the precise analogue occur regularly in the natural realm, when the complexity of a mature tree develops out of the simplicity of a single seed:

> Where in that tiny smallness of the seed was hidden so immense a tree which sprang forth from it: where the wood, where the bark, where the greenness of leaves, where the abundance of fruits? Was anything at all to be seen in such a seed when it was cast on the ground? And yet, with the secret maker of all things wondrously arranging everything, even in the softness of the seed the hardness of bark lay hidden; even in its tenderness the mightiness of the trunk (*fortitudo roboris*) was concealed; even in its dryness the bounty of bearing fruit. What wonder, therefore, is there if, when he wishes, he who restores immense

---

[28] *Hom. in Ezech.* 2.8.7-10, CCL 142:341-343. Augustine too frequently argues that, if God is capable of creating men who once were nothing at all, he is certainly capable of restoring deceased human bodies to their former condition. See, for example, *Enar. in Psalmos* 62.6, CCL 39:797; 96.17, CCL 39:1368; *De catechizandis rudibus* 27.54, CCL 46:176-177; *Sermo* 127.10.14-11.15, PL 38:713; *Sermo* 242.1.1, PL 38:1139; *Sermo* 361.12.12, PL 39:1605. Cf. *De Genesi ad litteram* 8.5, CSEL 28:239; *In Iohannis Evangelium* 49.1, CCL 36:419-420.

[29] *Hom. in Ezech.* 2.8.7, CCL 142:341; cf. *Mor.* 14.55.70, CCL 143A:742. Cf. also Augustine, *Sermo* 361.10.10, PL 39:1604; Gregory of Tours, *De cursu stellarum*, chap. 11, MGH, SRM 1.2, p. 410.

groves from the tiniest seeds also refashions the finest dust, even that which has been reduced to invisible elements (*a nostris oculis in elementis redactum*), into a man again?

We may not understand how the miracle will be effected, but this is not a rational basis for withholding belief. We do not understand how the tree develops either. Indeed, there are a great many purely natural processes we would have to reject if that were our criterion of belief. Reason cannot explain *how* the resurrection will occur, but it can demonstrate convincingly *that* it will occur, and it can do so without arguing from characteristically Christian premises.[30] In fact, as Gregory goes on to show, it can even demonstrate what the nature of our resurrection-body must be.

At one point in the *Moralia* Gregory outlines for us his dispute with Eutychius of Constantinople, who had denied a physical resurrection and maintained that we would rise with a kind of spiritualized body. Gregory's position was that our resurrected bodies would be the physical bodies we have now, although they would somehow or other be transformed; and he supported his claim with characteristically theological arguments, by pointing, for instance, to the example of Christ. Our resurrected bodies must be physical, palpable bodies, for when Christ showed himself to the disciples after his resurrection, he said: "See my hands and my feet, that it is I myself; handle me, and see; for a spirit has not flesh and bones as you see that I have." However, he also maintained that the nature of the resurrection-body could be proven in a strictly logical fashion:

I hear of the resurrection, and yet I seek the result of this same resurrection. For I believe that I shall be resurrected, but I wish to hear how. Indeed, I should like to determine whether I shall rise again in some other, subtle or etheral body perhaps, or in the one in which I shall die. But if I am to arise in an etheral

---

[30] *Mor.* 14.55.70, CCL 143A:742. Gregory presents essentially the same argument in *Mor.* 6.15.19, CCL 143:297; *Hom. in Ezech.* 2.8.7, CCL 142:341-342; and *Hom. in Evan.* 2.26.12, PL 76:1204. In the first of these passages he emphasizes its status as an analogy that can elicit belief. We cannot understand how the resurrection will take place; if we could, it would no longer be a miracle. But, for the mind that is troubled, an analogy from the natural realm pointing to similar events that we cannot understand can still be helpful. Cf. Augustine, *Epist.* 102.1.5, CSEL 34.2:549; *Sermo* 247.2, PL 38:1157-1158. See also *Hom. in Ezech.* 2.8.8-9, CCL 142:342-343, where Gregory lists a number of processes we do not understand, and yet do not for that reason reject as unworthy of belief. These range from the creation of the universe out of nothing, to the functioning of our own selves (in which spirit and matter somehow work together in harmony), to the mysteries of our own birth: "Cur autem ratione vis comprehendere quomodo redeas, qui ignoras quomodo venisti?" Cf. Augustine, *De catechizandis rudibus* 25.46, CCL 46:169-170; and especially *De civitate Dei* 21.5, CCL 48:764-766.

body, then it will not be I myself who rises again. For how can it be a true resurrection if the flesh is not real? Therefore, clear reason suggests that, if the flesh is not real, undoubtedly the resurrection cannot be real either. For one cannot rightly speak of a resurrection when that which has fallen does not rise again.[31]

Once the truth of the resurrection has been established, the nature of the resurrection-body follows as a matter of course.

Gregory's use of reason in defence of the faith can be found, not only in his more serious theological works, but in the *Dialogues* as well. There, however, the issue is not the resurrection of the body but rather the immortality of the soul. At the end of book three Peter points out that there are many within the bosom of the church itself who doubt the existence of the soul after death. For the benefit of these sceptics, he asks Gregory to prove the doctrine if he can, either by means of rational argument, or by providing examples of souls that have continued in existence after this life.[32]

Gregory takes up the matter at the beginning of the fourth book, and initially at least it seems that, rather than attempting to prove it, he will content himself with showing that the immortality of the soul is a reasonable tenet of the faith: "It is evident from reason—I mean reason joined to faith—that the soul lives on after the death of the body."[33] There *is* something resembling a rational, philosophical argument in the fifth chapter of book four. But in the final analysis it falls short of being a strict proof. The argument might be reconstructed as follows. Given a belief in a God, unbounded and invisible, it is reasonable to believe that he has invisible servants: the angels and the souls of the just. If we can be assured of the soul's existence in this life from the movements of the body it governs, we can assume its continued existence after death from the unending existence of the Lord it serves. Peter replies that, be that as it may, it is difficult to believe in a soul that cannot be seen. But Gregory in turn answers that, were it not for the invisible power of the mind that governs the senses, the corporeal eye would see nothing at all: "in this visible world ... nothing can be achieved except through invisible forces."[34]

This does not amount to a strict demonstration, and it is unlikely that Gregory so intended it. It rests on too many challengeable premises. At best,

---

[31] *Mor.* 14.55-56.71-72, CCL 143A:743; cf. Luke 24:39. Augustine's position on the nature of the resurrection-body was fundamentally the same. See, for example, *Epist.* 147.22.51, CSEL 44:326; *Sermo* 242.8.11, PL 38:1142. Cf. *Retract.* 1.17, CCL 57:52-54; 2.3, CCL 57:91-92, where he corrects some of his earlier and possibly misleading statements.

[32] *Dial.* 3.38.5, SC 260:432.

[33] *Dial.* 4.2.3, Zimmerman 191, SC 265:22.

[34] *Dial.* 4.5.4-8, SC 265:34-38, esp. 4.5.8, Zimmerman 199, SC 265:38.

it represents some rational buttressing for faith. However, the next chapter contains an argument that Gregory does seem to regard as a proof, although it too is far from being irrefutable. Says Gregory:

> You acknowledge that the life of the soul in the body is recognized from the physical movements of the body. Now consider those who laid down their lives willingly because of their faith in a life hereafter, and see how renowned they have become through their miracles. The sick approach the lifeless remains of these martyrs and are healed; perjurers come and find themselves tormented by Satan; the possessed come and are delivered from the power of the Devil; lepers approach and are cleansed; the dead are brought and are restored to life. Consider what a fullness of life they must enjoy where they now live, if even their dead bodies here on earth are alive with such miraculous powers. So, if you accept the presence of a soul in the body because of the body's physical activities, why do you not also recognize the continued life of the soul after death from the miracles performed through its lifeless body.[35]

Peter flatters Gregory by declaring this an argument of compelling force, a judgment that seems to correspond to Gregory's own.[36] Modern readers probably view it quite differently. For our immediate purposes, however, the validity of the argument, or of the argument for the resurrection of the body for that matter, is of minor significance compared to Gregory's attitude in his treatment of these issues. If the miracle stories of the *Dialogues* strike us as being such as to appeal to a rather simple-minded, childlike faith, Gregory himself was no simple-minded and credulous fideist. He was, as we have seen, a man of considerable intellectual breadth, not fundamentally hostile to the culture of classical antiquity, and sympathetic to the use of rational analysis in treating some of the central truths of Christian doctrine.

Despite his cultured outlook, however, Gregory was also disposed to a belief in the miraculous, a disposition that becomes clear when the methodology of the *Dialogues* is examined in detail. As we noted in an earlier chapter, there is relatively little in the *Dialogues* that rests on Gregory's own first-hand

---

[35] *Dial.* 4.6.1-2, Zimmerman 199-200, sc 265:40. Cf. *Hom. in Evan.* 2.32.6, PL 76:1237. Cf. also *De civitate Dei* 22.9, CCL 48:827-828, where Augustine appeals to the miracles taking place at the shrines of the martyrs. However, Augustine's purpose is to argue, not for the immortality of the soul, but for the doctrine of the resurrection.

[36] See *Dial.* 4.6.3, sc 265:40, where Peter says: "Nulla, ut opinor, huic allegationi ratio obsistit, in qua et ex rebus visibilibus cogimur credere quod non videmus." Gregory does not disagree. However, he immediately proclaims his intention to buttress his argument with some specific examples to clear away the disturbing doubts that reason alone might be insufficient to handle: "Unde mihi nunc necesse est vel qualiter egredientes animae visae sint, vel quanta ipsae, dum egrederentur, viderint enarrare, quatenus fluctuanti animo, quod plene ratio non valet, exempla suadeant" (*Dial.* 4.7, sc 265:40-42).

experience. He draws on the experience of others to testify to the wonder-working power of the saints, and because he feels it important that he do whatever he can to enhance the credibility of his account, his customary practice is to identify his sources by name and to insist that they are worthy of our confidence. However, Gregory is not always discriminating, leading some readers to suspect that he was willing to believe absolutely anything he was told.[37] Perhaps the best example occurs in the tenth chapter of the first book, where he admits that a couple of his stories about Bishop Fortunatus of Todi were obtained from some anonymous old man whom he did not even know. The description almost seems casual:

> There is another miracle I should mention. It was related to me about twelve days ago by a rather poor old man who had been directed to me. Since I always delight in conversing with old men, I asked him where he was from. He informed me that he came from the city of Todi. "Tell me, then, my dear man," I said, "did you know Bishop Fortunatus?"
> "I knew him well," he replied.
> "Do you know of any miracles he performed?" I continued. "What kind of man was he? I would be very happy to know."

The old man tells a long story about marauding Goths, two kidnapped boys, Fortunatus's miraculous healing of a broken rib, and the boys' restoration, and is about to continue with another miracle story when, pressed for an audience, Gregory leaves. However, the very next day, says the pope, "the old man told me about another miracle of Fortunatus even more remarkable than the previous one."[38] This second story concerns the miraculous resurrection of Marcellus, which was discussed in detail in chapter five.

Dudden maintains that in the great majority of cases the authorities cited by Gregory spoke in good faith: "It is quite incredible that distinguished bishops, abbots, clergy, and monks should have all conspired to invent fables to deceive the credulous pope." In this particular instance, however, he suspects that we have an example of deliberate falsehood: "We cannot here help suspecting that the unnamed poor old man, finding the great Bishop so eager to listen to his recital, thought it no harm to draw a little on his imagination," and so we are not at all surprised to find that on the second day "he had a yet more marvellous tale to pour into the ears of his interested patron."[39] Dudden may well be right. One can readily imagine the talkative old man seeking to accommodate the pope and telling him what he clearly

---

[37] See, for example, Moricca, p. xxxii.

[38] *Dial.* 1.10.11, Zimmerman 45-46, sc 260:102; 1.10.17, Zimmerman 48, sc 260:106.

[39] Dudden, *Gregory the Great*, 1:339.

wanted to hear. What cannot be imagined quite so readily is Gregory's willingness to accept his testimony at face value. Petersen has recently reminded us that "oral testimony is not necessarily unreliable, particularly among illiterate and semi-literate country people, who are accustomed to rely on their memories."[40] But even so, in this particular case, as Gregory himself admits, the man was a complete stranger; neither his personal integrity nor his reliability as a witness could be ascertained. Although Gregory elsewhere acknowledged the principle that we ought not to believe indiscriminately those who are unknown to us,[41] in this instance he clearly seems to have contravened it.

However, rather than treat this as an example of Gregory's usual practice, we would be better advised to acknowledge the isolated character of the episode, and to suppose that Gregory was willing to accept the old man's testimony only because the saintly pattern had already been established in Fortunatus's case, and on much better authority. At the beginning of the chapter Gregory declares that his principal source for the miracles of Fortunatus was Julian. A former *defensor* of the Roman church who had died some time in the recent past in Rome, Julian had been an intimate friend of Fortunatus and had witnessed many of his deeds at first hand.[42] In particular, he attested to Fortunatus's ability to cast out demons and to cure the blind. If he could cure the blind, why could he not heal a broken rib? And if he could achieve both of these wonders, why could he not raise a man from the dead? Since Gregory already knew on the authority of Julian that Fortunatus was a saintly man endowed with miraculous powers, he probably saw no harm in registering what the old man from Todi had to say. Had Gregory known nothing about Fortunatus at all, presumably he would have rejected the man's tales, or else accepted them only after careful examination. His customary practice is to insist that he has passed on only what he has learned from the most trustworthy of sources.

Gregory's concept of the trustworthy source, however, is something that itself merits attention. In his assessment of the relative merits of different kinds of witnesses, Gregory was obviously impressed by those who were strategically placed to give a well-substantiated account. He often claims his sources were eyewitnesses to the miracles they reported, or at least part of the intimate circle of the saint who performed them. But he was even more impressed by moral qualities. Hence he constantly emphasizes the good character of the witnesses he has chosen to follow. With some authors such

[40] Petersen, *The Dialogues*, p. 15.
[41] *Ep.* 9.27, CCL 140A:588-589 at 588.
[42] *Dial.* 1.10.1, SC 260:92-94.

assurances were no more than a familiar *topos*, part and parcel of the hagiographical tradition.[43] However, Gregory is particularly insistent. One source is described as having lived the religious life with uncommon zeal. Another is described as a man known for his honesty; another as a man renowned for his uprightness; and yet another as a man of both high rank and honest character.[44] Elsewhere in the *Dialogues* his sources are variously characterized as devout and truthful men, men of simplicity and genuine honesty, serious-minded and trustworthy people, or men who are both trustworthy and devout.[45] His informants, Gregory never tires of telling us, are well known for their personal piety; their lives are such as to confirm our faith in their words.[46]

To some extent at least, Gregory's very great confidence in the testimony of honest and upright witnesses stems from his conviction that such people were in the best position to attest to the facts. The deeds of good men, he says, usually become known most quickly to those of similar character.[47] Probably more important is the fact that he really had little choice. Only rarely would there have been any evidence, physical or documentary, to support the claim that a miracle had taken place. In such circumstances, as Moricca points out, the basic veracity and integrity of his sources would have been his best guarantee.[48] However, this falls short of a complete explanation. In view of the very great emphasis Gregory places on moral qualities, often to the exclusion of all others, it would seem that, to his mind, the unimpeachable character of his source was in itself sufficient to guarantee the truth of what he had to say. Gregory says of the miracles of Paulinus, for example, that they were widely known, and were reported to him by people of such

[43] Cf. A.-J. Festugière, "Lieux communs littéraires et thèmes de folklore dans l'Hagiographie primitive," *WS* 73 (1960): 123-152 esp. 133-134.

[44] *Dial.* 1.5.1, sc 260:58: "vitam non mediocriter religiosam duxit"; 3.10.1, sc 260:288: "vir veracissimus"; 4.32.1, sc 265:106: "quidam honestus senex"; 4.55.1, sc 265:180: "vir nobilissimus atque veracissimus."

[45] *Dial.* 3.8.1, sc 260:286: "religiosi veracesque viri"; 3.37.1, sc 260:412: "iam tamen sine formidine virtutes narro, quas a vicinis eius sacerdotibus, mira veritate et simplicitate praeditis, agnovi"; 4.14.1, sc 265:54: "Interea neque hoc silendum arbitror, quod mihi personarum gravium atque fidelium est relatione conpertum"; 4.59.1, sc 265:196: "fideles ... ac religiosi viri." Cf. *Dial.* 4.23.1, sc 265:78: "Quibusdam religiosis quoque viris adtestantibus. ..."

[46] *Dial.* 3.14.1, sc 260:302: "... et eius verbis vita fidem praebebat."

[47] See, for example, *Dial.* 3 Prol., sc 260:256: "Sicut enim bonorum facta innotescere citius similibus solent, senioribus nostris per iustorum exempla gradientibus praedicti venerabilis viri [i.e. Paulini] celebre nomen innotuit, eiusque opus admirabile ad eorum se instruenda studia tetendit. Quorum me necesse fuit grandaevitati tam certo credere, ac si ea, quae dicerent, meis oculis vidissem." Cf. *Dial.* 3.37.1, sc 260:412.

[48] Moricca, p. xxxiv.

great sanctity that it was impossible for him to have any doubts about them. In Dudden's judgment, passages like this imply that "Gregory was satisfied if he was assured of the good character of his informant. He looked, not to mental, but to moral qualities as the guarantee of truth. If the witness was honest, Gregory was content to believe him as trustworthy." Gregory may not have accepted absolutely everything he was told. But if his information came from people whose basic honesty and integrity could not be questioned, he seems to have believed, as Howorth suggests, that "the credibility of the story followed as a matter of course."[49]

Gregory's attitude on this matter would make a great deal more sense to the modern reader if what his sources were required to certify was simply the kind of moral truth suggested by Jones. Jones maintains that what the hagiographer wrote was simply "the book of manners for the age." Hence in a hagiographical work like Gregory's *Dialogues*, as in any book of manners, "no one wanted evidence whether the story was true or false in fact, but whether the witness would testify that the implications of it were in the saintly pattern."[50] The idea here is that the ultimate criterion of significance was a moral one. That a similar moral criterion seems to have obtained in questions of Scriptural exegesis adds to its authority and credibility.

It comes as no surprise to discover that Gregory was prepared to tolerate different and rival interpretations of Scripture. In understanding sacred Scripture, he says, we ought not to reject whatever is consistent with a sound faith. Like Augustine before him, Gregory was not in the habit of offering his own allegorical expositions as infallible and final, but was open to other possible interpretations as well. In a manner perfectly consistent with a proper sense of humility, he acknowledges that, in the final analysis, the specific meaning attached to some Scriptural passage is not particularly important, provided only that the interpretation is compatible with the basic principles of the faith.[51] Much more dubious is the suggestion that an interpretation of Scripture that manifestly differs from the intent of its human author can be endorsed, provided only that it serve the twin precepts of charity, the love of God and the love of neighbour. And yet this would seem

---

[49] *Dial.* 3.1.10, sc 260:266: "... quae [i.e. miracula] et multis iam nota sunt, et ego tam religiosorum virorum relatione didici, ut de his omnimodo ambigere non possim." Cf. *Dial.* 3.15.1, sc 260:314: "... de cuius verbis ipse non dubitas, quia eius vitam fidemque minime ignoras." See Dudden, *Gregory the Great*, 1:340; Howorth, *Saint Gregory the Great*, p. 238.

[50] C.W. Jones, *Saints' Lives and Chronicles in Early England* (Ithaca, 1947), pp. 75-76.

[51] *Ep.* 3.62, ccl 140:211-213 at 212. Cf. Augustine, *Enar. in Psalmos* 36.1.2, ccl 38:338; *Epist.* 102.6.37, csel 34.2:577. See de Lubac, *Exégèse médiévale* 1.1, pp. 127-128; part 2, vol. 2 (Paris, 1964), pp. 89-90.

to have been Gregory's position. Unless these principles are compromised, to Gregory's mind one interpretation is apparently as good as another.[52] In a similar way, perhaps, the specific events attributed to the lives of the saints are not particularly important either, provided only that their implications conform to the Christian pattern.

It is precisely to these implications, Jones argues, that Gregory's witnesses are called to attest. In Jones's view, Gregory's position is indistinguishable from that of Bede, who was equally impressed by the moral qualities of his informants. Jones notes that Bede does not cite witnesses when relating political or military events, but is content to follow written sources like Orosius, Vegetius or records from his native England. Witnesses are cited only for miracle stories. To most scholars this would probably suggest that, in view of their extraordinary nature, miracle stories needed special corroboration.[53] Jones, however, concludes that, if witnesses are cited only for miracle stories, witnesses whose moral qualifications are their most striking feature, then clearly their purpose is not to corroborate factual statements, but rather to attest to moral truth. As Ward puts it, "the witnesses are 'true and religious men', those ... who can be relied upon to judge events rightly and see what is significant about them." Their value does not inhere in their being "the most accurate observers of facts." Their function is not to confirm what actually happened, for their moral qualifications are inadequate for such a purpose: personal integrity cannot be confused with reliability in reporting factual matters. Their function is to confirm that, whatever happened, the lives of the saints to whose deeds they attest conformed to the pattern of Christian sanctity, and hence can be offered for our enlightenment and edification.[54]

---

[52] *Hom. in Ezech.* 1.10.14, ccl 142:150: "quisquis expositor in explanatione sacri eloquii, ut fortasse auditoribus placeat, aliquid mentiendo componit, sua et non Domini verba loquitur, si tamen placendi vel seducendi studio mentiatur. Nam si in verbis Dominicis virtutem requirens, ipse aliter quam is per quem prolata sunt senserit, etiamsi sub intellectu alio aedificationem caritatis requirat, Domini sunt verba quae narrat, quia ad hoc solum Deus per totam nobis sacram Scripturam loquitur, ut nos ad suum et proximi amorem trahat." Again, similar remarks can be found in Augustine, although Augustine places more emphasis on the necessity of genuine effort to determine the thought of the author: cf. *Conf.* 12.18.27, ccl 27:229-230; *De doctrina christiana* 1.36.40-41, ccl 32:29-30.

[53] See, for example, G. Musca, *Il Venerabile Beda, storico dell'Alto Medioevo* (Bari, 1973), pp. 166-167, 207-208. This is also the conclusion Thürlemann draws from a similar use of witnesses by Gregory of Tours: see F. Thürlemann, *Der historische Diskurs bei Gregor von Tours* (Bern, 1974), pp. 23, 28-30.

[54] Jones, *Saints' Lives*, pp. 75-76; B. Ward, "Miracles and History: A Reconsideration of the Miracle Stories used by Bede," in *Famulus Christi: Essays in Commemoration of the Thirteenth Centenary of the Birth of the Venerable Bede* (London, 1976), pp. 70-76 at 72.

The main problem with this interpretation, however, is that it completely undermines Gregory's commitment to factual veracity, which, as we have seen, was one of his highest priorities. Of course, Gregory's sources would have been well qualified to pass the kind of moral judgment that Jones has in mind. But they were required to do more than that. They were called on to substantiate the claim that the miracles attributed to the saintly heroes of the *Dialogues* were actually performed, and to Gregory's mind their personal integrity alone was apparently sufficient for the purpose. To us it is obvious that integrity and accuracy are not the same thing. But some of Gregory's remarks seem to indicate that he was not fully aware of the distinction. In a very interesting letter of February 591 to Anastasius, Patriarch of Antioch, Gregory is troubled that Anastasius' assessment of him does not correspond to his own modest assessment of himself:

> You have stated that I am the mouth and lantern of the Lord [says Gregory]. You have maintained that I profit many and am able to provide light for them by speaking. But I confess that you have brought my own estimate of myself into the greatest doubt, for I am mindful of what I am, and I detect in myself no sign of this good. But I am also mindful of what you are, and do not think you could lie. When, therefore, I would believe what you say, I am contradicted by my infirmity, and when I would dispute what you say in my praise, I am contradicted by your sanctity. I beg you, let us come to some agreement in this contest of ours, so that, although things are not as you say, they may be so because of your statements.[55]

This passage seems stylized and artificial; its faults could easily have been eliminated if only Gregory could have brought himself to admit openly that a holy man might make an honest mistake.

It should be noted that Gregory's apparent weakness in assessing personal testimony cannot be seen as a personal fault. Augustine also was disposed to accept what he had learned from the testimony of honest and trustworthy witnesses, and the same confidence was characteristic, not only of medieval hagiographers, but of medieval historians as well.[56] It was capable of

---

[55] *Ep.* 1.25, CCL 140:33-34 at 33.

[56] See Augustine, *De civitate Dei* 15.23, CCL 48:489; 18.18, CCL 48:609; *De cura pro mortuis gerenda* 17.21, CSEL 41:655-656; and *De Genesi ad litteram* 12.2, CSEL 28:381, where, after telling a story about a man who had a vision, he states: "verum tamen simpliciter fidelis [erat], ut eum sic audirem, ac si illud, quod se vidisse narrabat, ipse vidissem." According to F. van der Meer, *Augustine the Bishop* (London and New York, 1961), p. 553, Augustine displays "a credulity which to us today seems incredible."

See also Gregory of Tours, *Liber in gloria confessorum*, Praef., MGH, SRM 1.2, p. 297; Bede, *Historia ecclesiastica* 3.15, 3.19, 4.3, ed. B. Colgrave and R.A.B. Mynors (Oxford, 1969), pp. 260, 274, 344; Orderic Vitalis, *Historia ecclesiastica* 8.19, ed. M. Chibnall, *The Ecclesiastical*

coexisting alongside scrupulous efforts to reach the truth. Partner argues that as late as the twelfth century "the concepts of 'trustworthiness' and 'accuracy' were not sufficiently distinguished, just as the difference between 'possibility' and 'probability'... was less marked than it is now." She gives the example of the twelfth-century historian William of Newburgh, who was capable of adopting a sceptical attitude towards his sources, but only when he suspected them of conscious deception; otherwise he was inclined to accept at face value what individuals known for their trustworthiness had to tell him.[57]

Furthermore, moral criteria were not only central to the medieval historian's assessment of his sources, but were also instrumental in shaping his criteria of probability. The medieval historian was often inclined to believe that what ought to have happened must indeed have been the case, and that what ought not to have happened could not possibly have taken place. Since the word *augustus* is derived from *augere* ("to increase"), the emperor's obligation was to expand rather than diminish the empire, and so a deed of alienation like the Donation of Constantine could not possibly have occurred. Throughout the Middle Ages this was one of the principal reasons why the partisans of the empire refused to accept the authenticity of what was probably the most celebrated fraud of the time. After the twelfth century there is increasing evidence of more rational criticism; but in many cases it fell somewhat short of the mark, and the moral criteria of probability continued to be significant for some time. As late as the fifteenth century, in the debate over the merits of Lorenzo Valla's *Historiarum Ferdinandi Regis Aragoniae Libri III*, Bartolommeo Facio could criticize Valla for reporting as fact events that could not have happened, because they were incompatible with the *dignitas* of his royal subject.[58] If Gregory, therefore, was inclined to accept the reports that came his way because they were consistent with the dignity of his saintly heroes and were attested to by witnesses of unimpeachable character, he was in good company: he was only using standard critical precepts that would not be superseded for centuries.

History of Orderic Vitalis, vol. 4 (Oxford, 1973), p. 260; Peter the Venerable, *De miraculis* 1.10, PL 189:873; Caesarius of Heisterbach, *Dialogus miraculorum* 9.31, 11.5, ed. J. Strange, 2 vols. (Cologne, 1851), 2:188, 274. Cf. A.J. Gurevich, *Categories of Medieval Culture* (London, 1985), p. 161, who argues that in medieval thought as a whole legal and moral qualities tended to be confounded, as did moral, aesthetic and intellectual qualities.

[57] N.F. Partner, *Serious Entertainments: The Writing of History in Twelfth-Century England* (Chicago and London, 1977), pp. 191-192.

[58] Cf. B. Guenée, *Histoire et culture historique dans l'Occident médiéval* (Paris, 1980), p. 131; H. Fuhrmann, "Die Fälschungen im Mittelalter. Überlegungen zum mittelalterlichen Wahrheitsbegriff," *HZ* 197 (1963): 529-554 at 545; and L.G. Janik, "Lorenzo Valla: The Primacy of Rhetoric and the De-Moralization of History," *HTh* 12 (1973): 389-404, esp. 396-397.

In point of fact, however, on occasion at least Gregory was capable of more rigorous standards of criticism. A letter of October 594 to John, Archbishop of Ravenna, provides an interesting example. John had evidently been distressed over the pope's prohibition of his use of the pallium during litanies, and had therefore employed the good offices of the patrician, the prefect and other distinguished citizens of the city of Ravenna to make representations to Gregory on his behalf.[59] In his letter of October 594 Gregory reports back to John that, on receipt of these representations, he undertook to inform himself further about the practices of the church of Ravenna. He made enquiries of Adeodatus, a former deacon of that church, and learned from him that it had never been the custom of John's predecessors to use the pallium during litanies. The only exceptions were at the solemnities of the blessed John the Baptist, the blessed Apostle Peter, and the blessed martyr Apollinaris. Gregory rules, therefore, that the general prohibition must remain in force, but that John can be allowed the use of the pallium on these three special occasions, and, as an extra concession, on the anniversary of his own ordination as well.

As the tenor of the ruling suggests, Gregory had evidently allowed himself to be governed by the testimony of Adeodatus. However, he makes it clear that it was not because he was convinced of the accuracy of Adeodatus's report, but rather was only because he wished to do what he could to acknowledge John's petition and to relieve his distress. Many of Gregory's own representatives had told him that they had never witnessed the use of the pallium in Ravenna on the occasions Adeodatus had mentioned. Gregory was inclined to accept their word because, in his view, the testimony of many outweighs the testimony of a single individual, especially one attesting to something on behalf of his own church.[60] Gregory knew as well as any of us that the word of any individual has to be discounted if it is about a matter in which he has a personal interest. Even where there could be no question of deliberate misrepresentation, Gregory would have realized that, ideally, personal testimony should not simply be accepted without further ado. He was quite conscious of the mind's capacity for deceiving itself, even about its own inner states;[61] if it can do that, it can certainly deceive itself about external matters of fact too. Gregory did place great confidence in the testimony of honest and reliable witnesses. But in another part of his mind

---

[59] For the background to the dispute, see R.A. Markus, "Ravenna and Rome, 554-604," *Byzantion* 51 (1981): 566-578.

[60] *Ep.* 5.11, CCL 140:277.

[61] *Past.* 1.9, PL 77:22: "Nam saepe sibi de se mens ipsa mentitur, et fingit se de bono opere amare quod non amat, de mundi autem gloria non amare quod amat."

he realized, although he may not have done so consistently, that personal
evidence, even the evidence of unimpeachable sources, can be problematic.
It would be a mistake, therefore, to maintain that he always believed blindly
whatever miracle stories such sources told him.

Gregory's attitude toward contemporary miracles was quite different from
his attitude toward the miracles of Scripture. With modern miracles doubt is
possible; with Biblical miracles it is out of the question. Although he made
extensive use of allegorical interpretation, and maintained that the literal
sense of Scripture could not always be accepted as historical truth, Gregory
had no doubts about what Scripture clearly reported as historical fact.[62] If he
tended to treat the literal sense cursorily, it was only because he thought its
meaning obvious. Why spend time with the *aperta historiae verba* when the
much more challenging matters of the spiritual sense cry out for attention?[63]
Hence in his many discussions of the miracles of Christ, Gregory very rarely
dwells on the miracle itself, for that is simply to be taken for granted. His
treatment of Christ's healing of the official's son provides one of the very few
occasions on which he has anything of significance to say about the literal
sense, and even here he claims that the story stands on its own and needs

[62] See *Ep. ad Leandrum*, CCL 143:1-7 at 4-6, where Gregory explains that, on some
occasions, treating the literal sense of Scripture as historical truth could lead to serious error.
However, this should not be taken to imply a lack of faith in the literal sense; it means only
that one must not understand literally statements intended to be taken only metaphorically.
Like the other Latin Fathers, Gregory may on occasion have been too quick to give up on
the literal sense, but only, Hofmann suggests, because of a very narrow conception of
Scripture's literal meaning that excluded figurative language. Like Augustine, Gregory believed
that the truth of the literal sense was to be taken for granted, and that it served as the necessary
foundation for the work of allegorical exegesis. Cf. Weber, *Hauptfragen*, pp. 58-59; D.
Hofmann, *Die geistige Auslegung der Schrift bei Gregor dem Grossen* (Münsterschwarzach,
1968), pp. 22-31, 73-74; H.-I Marrou, *Saint Augustin et la fin de la culture antique*, 2 vols.
(Paris, 1938-1949), pp. 492-494. De Lubac, *Exégèse médiévale* 1.2, pp. 429-466, discusses
this same issue within the context of medieval theology as a whole, and argues similarly that
the medieval exegete's preoccupation with allegorical interpretation did not imply any
devaluation of the literal sense as historical record. See also *Exégèse médiévale* 1.2, pp.
384-396, 513-522, and 2.2, pp. 125-149, where de Lubac contrasts Christian allegory, which
preserves the truth of the literal sense, with pagan allegory, which explains it away.

[63] *Ep. ad Leandrum*, CCL 143:1-7 at 4: "Aliquando vero exponere aperta historiae verba
neglegimus, ne tardius ad obscura veniamus." Cf. Weber, *Hauptfragen*, pp. 59-60. De Lubac,
Exégèse médiévale 1.2, pp. 472-478, points out that, in general, the medieval view on this
matter was the same. In view of the straight-forward nature of the literal sense, "c'était cette
allégorie que le commentateur devait s'appliquer à mettre en lumière. C'était sur elle qu'il
devait concentrer son effort" (p. 478). Cf. Augustine, *In Iohannis Evangelium* 44.1, CCL
36:381; 44.7, CCL 36:385.

little exposition, except to clarify why this man, who had come to Christ seeking healing for his son, was rebuked with the words: "Unless you see signs and wonders you will not believe." Having settled that minor difficulty (the man's faith was less than perfect), Gregory proceeds immediately to the spiritual sense, without any further consideration of the miracle itself.[64]

In his treatment of the appearance of the risen Christ to the apostles, Gregory does comment on the astonishing nature of his resurrection-body. Human reason, he says, cannot conceive how a true body could pass through closed doors, nor can it comprehend how the same body could be both incorruptible and palpable at the same time. But rather than pursue the matter, he quickly announces that there is no real merit in believing what can be deciphered by the human intellect, and then passes on to the mystical sense.[65] When he turns his attention to Christ's appearance by the Sea of Tiberias, Gregory does not speak of the miraculous nature of his risen body at all, even though it seems to demand comment. He discourses at some length on the meal Christ shared with his followers, for it illustrates a complex lesson in Christology. However, he shows no interest at all in the puzzling fact that Christ's risen body, capable of passing through doors, was apparently also capable of consuming food.[66]

This is typical of Gregory's treatment of the miracles of Christ and of Biblical miracles in general. They are relatively straight-forward, and should simply be accepted as reported; our efforts should rather be directed at clarifying the spiritual significance they contain.[67] What puzzles us does not seem to puzzle Gregory. Contemporary miracles, however, cannot be accepted with the same easy faith. With modern miracle stories doubt is possible. Hence there is some evidence that, even when dealing with sources

---

[64] John 4:46-53; *Hom. in Evan.* 2.28.1, PL 76:1211.

[65] John 20:19-31; *Hom. in Evan.* 2.26.1, PL 76:1197-1198.

[66] John 21:1-14; *Hom. in Evan.* 2.24.5, PL 76:1186-1187.

[67] See *Mor.* 6.15.19, CCL 143:296-297; *Hom. in Evan.* 1.2.1, PL 76:1082: "miracula Domini et Salvatoris nostri sic accipienda sunt, fratres charissimi, ut et in veritate credantur facta, et tamen per significationem nobis aliquid innuant." Cf. Hofmann, *Die geistige Ausle-gung*, pp. 22-23. Cf. also Augustine, *De diversis quaestionibus octoginta tribus* 65, CCL 44A:147; *Epist.* 102.6.33, CSEL 34.2:572-573; *Sermo* 77.5.7, PL 38:486.

For additional passages illustrating Gregory's attitude toward New Testament miracles, see *Hom. in Ezech.* 1.6.7, CCL 142:70 (the miracle at Cana); and *Hom. in Evan.* 2.30.1, 4-6, PL 76:1220, 1222-1224 (the miracle at Pentecost). His attitude to Old Testament miracles is much the same. See, for example, *Hom. in Ezech.* 1.7.10, CCL 142:88-89 (Moses and the burning bush); *In 1 Reg.* 5.118, CCL 144:492-493 (the earthquake reported in 1 Sam. 14:15); *In 1 Reg.* 4.46, CCL 144:318 (Elijah and the flaming chariot); *Mor.* 9.40.63, CCL 143:502 (Elisha and the son of the Shunammite woman); *Mor.* 22.5.9, CCL 143A:1098-1099 (Elisha and the axe-head in the river Jordan).

of known good character, Gregory attempted to verify their reports. Since the *Dialogues* as we have them represent the final result of Gregory's investigations, and thus include only those stories he had good reason to believe were true, they cast only a dim light on this aspect of his methodology. But at least a few episodes do show traces of his efforts, although they also indicate that he tended to be satisfied by standards of proof that to the modern reader are simply inadequate.

Gregory narrates several miracle stories that he had heard from the saintly Eleutherius, a man, he says, whose life was such as to strengthen faith in his words.[68] Eleutherius had been abbot of the monastery of St Mark the Evangelist in Spoleto. He had also lived with Gregory for some time in Gregory's own monastery in Rome, and in fact had died there. Gregory knew him personally, and was inclined to accept his testimony, because he was a man whose integrity could not be questioned. In addition to being a witness of miracles performed by others, Eleutherius informed Gregory of a miracle he had performed himself. He was a man of such simplicity and compunction of heart, says Gregory, that through his tears he was able to obtain many favours from almighty God. Hence on one occasion, as Eleutherius himself confessed, by the power of prayer alone he and his monks were able to cure a young boy who had been possessed by the Devil.[69] In this particular case, however, Gregory did not have to rely exclusively on Eleutherius's own word, but was able to confirm what the holy man had told him through personal experience.

Once, while he was still living in his monastery, says Gregory, he was so seriously ill with pains in his intestines that he thought death would soon overtake him. But once Eleutherius had prayed for him, relief followed instantaneously, and he was able to observe the fast on Holy Saturday. For Gregory, this experience of Eleutherius's power was sufficient to put what Eleutherius himself had told him beyond doubt,[70] and that seems reasonable enough. A saintly man who could relieve the pains of an intestinal disorder by his power of prayer would probably have been capable of relieving the affliction of demonic possession as well. Surprisingly, however, Gregory does not limit himself to such a modest conclusion, but strongly implies that the miracle performed for his own benefit could assure him that, although he had

[68] See, for example, *Dial.* 3.14.1, sc 260:302: "Multa autem de eodem viro, narrante venerabili patre Eleutherio, agnovi, qui et hunc familiariter noverat, et eius verbis vita fidem praebebat."

[69] *Dial.* 3.33.1-6, sc 260:392-396.

[70] *Dial.* 3.33.7, sc 260:396: "Huius viri oratio quantae virtutis esset, in memetipso expertus sum."

not been present to witness them, all the other miracles attributed to Eleutherius were true as well, even though at least one of them was a miracle of much greater import. Apparently the not extraordinary miracle Gregory himself experienced was sufficient to confirm the truth of what the disciples of Eleutherius had told him: that the efficacy of Eleutherius's prayer was great enough once to have raised a dead person to life.[71]

In an even more striking example a few chapters later, Gregory says that he had learned from Bishop Floridus, a man known for his truthfulness and personal sanctity, that one of his priests had the power of miraculously curing the sick by laying his hands on them. The priest, Amantius, was also reputed to have the power of killing serpents by making the sign of the cross. The poor creatures could not escape even by crawling into their holes: Amantius could kill them simply by placing the sign of the cross over the entrances to their hiding places. Gregory tells us that he wished to meet a man endowed with such remarkable powers. Hence, after Amantius was brought to him, he had him spend a few days in a hospital, so that any grace of healing he might possess could be verified there. Even though the virtues of Amantius had been attested to by a witness of unimpeachable character, Gregory took the opportunity to verify the claims that were made on his behalf.[72] Equally significant, however, is the ease with which Gregory was satisfied.

One night, a deranged patient in the hospital began shouting at the top of his voice, making it impossible for the others to get any rest. But after Amantius had led him away to a chapel where he could pray for him undisturbed, the man returned to his bed completely cured. Dudden is summary in his dismissal: "if an English clergyman with such a reputation for miraculous powers were placed for some days in a London hospital, and in that time succeeded only in quieting one lunatic, his pretensions, to say the least, would be somewhat discredited." But Gregory maintains that this one miracle was enough to justify his belief in everything that he had heard about the man, even though it was not a miracle he had witnessed himself. Gregory had given the order that Amantius be taken to the hospital to test his powers of healing, but he had not stayed there to conduct the experiment. His knowledge of the event was strictly second-hand; his sources were Bishop Floridus, who had remained with Amantius at the hospital, and the young man who had been in charge of the patients that night.[73]

---

[71] Cf. *Dial.* 3.33.1, sc 260:394, where we learn of the resurrection, and *Dial.* 3.33.9, sc 260:398: "Sicque factum est, ut in me probarem ea etiam de illo vera esse, quibus ipse minime interfuissem."

[72] *Dial.* 3.35.1-5, sc 260:404-406.

[73] *Dial.* 3.35.4-5, sc 260:406 (note especially Gregory's claim: "Ex quo eius uno facto didicimus, ut de eo illa omnia audita crederemus"). See also Dudden, *Gregory the Great*,

Gregory has been criticized because, as Dudden maintains, he "was often content to accept the evidence of persons whom he thought he could trust, without taking pains to verify and confirm their assertions." To a large extent at least, this misses the point. In most cases Gregory would not have had much choice but to accept such evidence; it was the only kind of evidence available, and it was not easily tested. Moreover, even Dudden admits that "Gregory ... did not rashly accept every miraculous tale he heard, but made some attempt to sift and investigate." Judging from the two episodes just examined, it would seem that, when possible, Gregory tried to test what his sources told him, even if their personal integrity was beyond question. But the fact remains that "what satisfied Gregory does not by any means satisfy us," for Gregory was inclined to regard any manifestation of extraordinary power as sufficient to justify belief in even the most astonishing miracles.[74]

Dudden argues that "Gregory had no capacity either for weighing and testing evidence brought forward by others, or for drawing correct inferences from what fell within his personal observation"[75]—as if the answer were to be found in some intellectual inability on Gregory's part. But since in his work as governor of the church and administrator of the papal estates Gregory demonstrated critical powers that would meet even the most rigorous standards, the answer to this puzzle is to be sought elsewhere—primarily in a willingness to believe few of us can share. This is an issue we shall have to confront directly in our next chapter. Here only a couple of preliminary observations are possible. However, the contrast between Gregory's late antique perspective and our modern one should be clear. It is not easy to be convinced that a miracle has taken place merely because some temporary relief for a painful intestinal disorder has permitted religious observances that otherwise would have been impossible. But Gregory could be convinced that his relief was more than coincidence, because he expected miracles and was watching for them. He saw them where we would not, and he was inclined to regard the few miracles he did see as conclusive evidence for the occurrence of others. Equally important, however, was his conviction that miracles were the work of God. The distinctions between them that may

---

1:343. S. Boesch Gajano, "Demoni e miracoli nei 'Dialogi' di Gregorio Magno," in *Hagiographie, cultures et sociétés*, pp. 263-280 at 268, points out that what we have here seems to be a case of "malattia riconosciuta come tale." However, she continues: "Se l'insonnia e l'agitazione notturna sono sintomi propri della frenesia nei testi medici, le urla ricordano quelle dei posseduti e i modi della guarigione quelli usati da altri santi nei confronti degli indemoniati: un rapporto a due, anche prolungato, spesso sottratto alla vista degli altri."

[74] Dudden, *Gregory the Great*, 1:342, 338, 340.

[75] *Ibid.*, p. 343.

otherwise obtain become insignificant when their derivation from the same divine source is stressed. Few in the twentieth century would regard the ability to relieve a stomach ailment as proof of an ability to raise the dead. But, again, Gregory could so regard it, because to his mind the one implied the other. Miracles were performed by saints acting, not on their own resources, but in virtue of the same divine power. Provided that the moral criteria for sanctity had been met, even a minor miracle was enough to establish the saintly pattern for the individual in question.

8

Miracles and Nature

Both scepticism and credulity about miracles have been constants in human history. We are sometimes inclined to regard credulity as a characteristic of earlier benighted centuries, and to flatter ourselves into thinking disbelief a particularly modern phenomenon; but this distorts reality, past and present. The roots of scepticism can be traced back at least to classical Greece, and "credulity about miracles, especially healing, is as modern as television evangelists."[1] Perhaps because of these prejudices, however, it has sometimes been claimed that Gregory's openness to miracle is to be explained simply in terms of his being a child of his time. The people of the sixth century, we are told, were a credulous lot. "The wonder to the men of this time," says Dudden, "was not that a saint should work miracles, but that he should not do so. Any miraculous account, therefore, was accepted almost without question as perfectly credible, probable, and even ordinary."[2] Even if such generalizations were accurate, their explanatory force would be minimal. The alleged credulity of the sixth century would itself still require explanation. In fact, however, they cannot be accepted without many reservations, as more than one recent commentator has pointed out.[3]

It seems incongruous that a society noted for its widespread credulity should have had within it a significant number who found it difficult to accept some fundamental truths of the faith. Yet that, apparently, was the case. At the end of the third book of the *Dialogues* Peter confesses that there are many within the bosom of the church who doubt the existence of the soul after

---

[1] H.C. Kee, *Miracles in the Early Christian World* (New Haven and London, 1983), p. 2.

[2] F.H. Dudden, *Gregory the Great: His Place in History and Thought* (1905; repr. New York, 1967), 1:339. Cf. Moricca, p. xvii.

[3] See, for example, F. Graus, *Volk, Herrscher und Heiliger im Reich der Merowinger* (Praha, 1965), pp. 46-47, 451-455; P. Brown, "Relics and Social Status in the Age of Gregory of Tours," in *Society and the Holy in Late Antiquity* (Berkeley and Los Angeles, 1982), pp. 222-250.

death, and he urges Gregory to offer rational proof of the doctrine, and to illustrate it with whatever examples from the lives of the saints come to mind. Gregory honours the request by devoting virtually the entirety of book four to the issue.[4] The doctrine of the resurrection was another source of difficulty, as Gregory points out in both his *Homilies on Ezechiel* and his *Moralia on Job.* "It is very sad and quite grievous for us to know," he says, "that there are some who stand within the church and yet have doubts about the resurrection of the body." Although the fathers of the Old Testament believed in the resurrection without the support of any specific example, there are modern Christians who are sceptical even though they have the assurance provided by the resurrection of Christ himself. They have the proof at hand, and yet they refuse to believe: "Pignus tenent, et fidem non habent."[5]

Possibly, says Gregory, these sceptics think that the example of Christ does not apply to our circumstances. Conceivably, they believe that the death he suffered as a function of his humanity was conquered only through his divinity. If so, it should be sufficient to point out that at the time of Christ's resurrection the bodies of many saints also rose from the grave. If the resurrection of the Saviour does not suffice to settle the matter, the example of ordinary humans being raised from the dead should be enough to put it beyond dispute. Unfortunately, however, it would seem that the problem ran deeper, and that some simply refused to acknowledge the possibility of the resurrection. Says Gregory:

> Truly there are some who, considering that the spirit is released from the flesh, that the flesh is turned to rottenness, that the rottenness is reduced to dust, that the dust is so dissolved into its elements that it may not be seen at all by human eyes, despair that the resurrection could happen; and when they look on dry bones, they distrust that these could be clothed in flesh and once again be restored to life (*ad vitam viridescere*).[6]

Equally significant as the doubt itself was the basis on which it apparently rested—a crude materialism that refused to acknowledge any dimension to human existence beyond the physical.

In view of the other pastoral difficulties he encountered, it should scarcely surprise us that Gregory anticipates a sceptical response to contemporary miracles as well, among some readers at least. Of course, it was customary

---

[4] *Dial.* 3.38.5, SC 260:432; cf. *Hom. in Evan.* 2.32.6, PL 76:1237. See M. Van Uytfanghe, "Scepticisme doctrinal au seuil du Moyen Age? Les objections du diacre Pierre dans les *Dialogues* de Grégoire le Grand," in *Grégoire le Grand,* Chantilly, 15-19 septembre 1982 (Paris, 1986), pp. 315-324.

[5] *Hom. in Ezech.* 2.8.6, CCL 142:339, 340; cf. 2.8.7, CCL 142:341.

[6] *Mor.* 14.55.69-70, CCL 143A:741-742.

among hagiographers to allude to the possibility that one or more of their miracle stories might meet with open disbelief.[7] Such statements seem to have been a standard feature of proper hagiographical style, and they often function merely as rhetorical devices designed to emphasize the extraordinary nature of the miracles described. "What I am about to say may be incredible, but Christ is my witness that I do not lie," Sulpicius Severus loudly proclaims.[8] Frequently, however, we would do well to take the hagiographers seriously. When Jerome refers to the scepticism that had greeted his life of St Paul the Hermit, implying that some had accused him of invention, he is not simply indulging in a literary conceit. Nor is Sulpicius Severus when he reports in his *Dialogues* that some readers had accused him of outright lying in his earlier account of the miracles of St Martin.[9] There had been widespread disbelief, and even some of the members of Martin's own monastery of Marmoutier had proved sceptical. Sulpicius therefore resolves to enhance the credibility of the stories in the *Dialogues* by referring to living witnesses who can attest to their truth.[10] Gregory of Tours reports that he too had met people openly incredulous about the miracles of St Martin. Indeed, he confesses to his own initial scepticism, not about the saint's merits, but about the wonder-working powers of the relics of the true cross at Poitiers: "On account of the stupidity of a stubborn mind," he says, "never was I moved to believing these things." Ultimately, however, he witnesses their virtue with his own eyes, and is convinced.[11]

In some cases the scepticism reported by the hagiographers has to do, not with specific miracles, but with claims made on behalf of some particular saint. The hostile disbelief the Gallic bishops and monks directed at Sulpicius Severus, for example, in all likelihood was not engendered by miracles as such, but by whether Martin was the kind of sainted individual who could have performed them.[12] However, as Gregory the Great clearly observes,

---

[7] See, for example, Athanasius, *Vita S. Antonii*, chap. 83, PG 26:959; Jerome, *Vita S. Pauli*, chap. 8, PL 23:24; Palladius, *Historia Lausiaca*, chap. 17, ed. E.C. Butler (Cambridge, 1898-1904), 2:43; Rufinus, *Historia monachorum*, chap. 15, PL 21:435; Sulpicius Severus, *Vita S. Martini* 24.8, SC 133:308; *Dial.* 3.2, CSEL 1:200.

[8] *Dial.* 2.13, CSEL 1:196. Cf. *Dial.* 1.15, CSEL 1:167: "Ne cui autem hoc incredibile forte videatur, maiora memorabo."

[9] Jerome, *Vita Hilarionis* 1.6, ed. A.A.R. Bastiaensen, *Vite dei santi* 4, p. 74; Sulpicius Severus, *Dial.* 1.26, CSEL 1:178-179.

[10] *Dial.* 2.13, CSEL 1:196; 3.5, CSEL 1:203.

[11] *De virtutibus S. Martini* 2.32, MGH, SRM 1.2, p. 170 (cf. *Liber in gloria confessorum*, chap. 6, MGH, SRM 1.2, p. 302); *Liber in gloria martyrum*, chap. 5, MGH, SRM 1.2, p. 40. See Graus, *Volk, Herrscher und Heiliger*, pp. 451-455, for additional examples.

[12] See C. Stancliffe, *St. Martin and His Hagiographer* (Oxford, 1983), pp. 311-312. For later examples of the same phenomenon, see P.-A. Sigal, *L'homme et le miracle dans la France*

scepticism about contemporary miracles in general was also possible. In the first chapter we alluded to the problematic nature of miracle both in the New Testament and in the late antique and early medieval church. In the first several centuries of the Christian era more than one theologian had argued that the age of miracles was over, that the kind of wonders performed by Christ and the apostles no longer occurred with anything resembling the same frequency; and the reservations of the theologians had been accompanied, although perhaps not for precisely the same reasons, by recurring scepticism in popular piety. By the sixth century, it would seem, the balance had shifted firmly in favour of the miraculous. As Van Uytfanghe remarks, "l'hagiographie du VIe siècle, surtout en Gaule, est largement dominée par les grands recueils de miracles dont l'ampleur dépasse de loin des *libelli* précédents." But a current of scepticism or even hostility towards the miraculous remained and would continue throughout the Middle Ages, and Gregory was quite aware of its existence.[13]

The miracle stories Gregory relates show the saints of his time as the equal of the apostles. They can expel evil spirits, heal the sick, and even raise the dead to life once again. However, in his *Homilies on the Gospels* he tells us that there were many people who were tempted to think that God had withdrawn his grace precisely because they had never witnessed miracles of this sort. At the beginning of the *Dialogues* we learn that they had not been witnessed by Peter either, and so the suggestion seems well-founded that in the astonishment he expresses throughout the treatise Peter is doing no more than reflecting the doubts of many at the time.[14] Gregory recognized that his

---

médiévale (XIe-XIIe siècle) (Paris, 1985), pp. 213-214; and A. Vauchez, *La sainteté en Occident aux derniers siècles du Moyen Age* (Rome, 1981), pp. 561-581, esp. p. 576.

[13] Theological reservations about miracles are discussed by H. Delehaye, "Saint Martin et Sulpice Sévère," *ABoll.* 38 (1920): 5-136, esp. 73-79; A. Fridrichsen, *The Problem of Miracle in Primitive Christianity* (Minneapolis, 1972); M. Van Uytfanghe, "La controverse biblique et patristique autour du miracle, et ses répercussions sur l'hagiographie dans l'Antiquité tardive et le haut Moyen Age latin," in *Hagiographie, cultures et sociétés, IVe-XIIe siècles* (Paris, 1981), pp. 205-231 (the quotation is from p. 217); and H. Silvestre, "Le 'plus grand miracle' de Jésus," *ABoll.* 100 (1982): 1-15. On hostility toward miracles, see E. Demm, "Zur Rolle des Wunders in der Heiligkeitskonzeption des Mittelalters," *AKG* 57 (1975): 300-344.

[14] *Hom. in Evan.* 27.18.36, PL 76:420; *Dial.* 1 Prol. 7, SC 260:14. Cf. *Dial.* 1.3.5, SC 260:36, where Peter confesses that he had obviously been mistaken: "Nunc usque, ut invenio, incassum ego non fuisse patres in Italia qui signa facerent aestimabam."

On Peter's reaction to miracles, see Moricca, p. lv; Dudden, *Gregory the Great* 1:324; F. Tateo, "La struttura dei dialoghi di Gregorio Magno," *VetC* 2 (1965): 101-127 at 107-108. Cf. A. Vitale-Brovarone, "Forma narrativa dei *Dialoghi* di Gregorio Magno: prospettive di struttura," *AAST.M* 109 (1975): 117-185 at 148-149: "L'impegno che Gregorio pone nella successiva confutazione dei dubbi di Pietro fa fascere il giustificato sospetto che Gregorio stia

readers were easily prey to disbelief. Indeed, he tells us that it was precisely because of such a possibility that, like Sulpicius Severus, he chose to reinforce the factual credibility of his miracle stories by carefully indicating his sources.[15]

However, if the blind credulity of the sixth century cannot be accepted without reservation, it also needs to be acknowledged that, in all likelihood, the genuine sceptics constituted a small minority. In view of the plethora of miracle literature that came to light in the sixth century, for the most part Christians of the time undoubtedly were more predisposed toward belief in miracles than most of their modern counterparts. They possessed an openness to miracle that was a product, not only of their Biblical culture, but of the traditions of the ancient world as well.[16] It would be absurd to suggest that they were prepared to accept the miracles of modern saints with the same easy acquiescence accorded to ordinary events. Colin Brown puts it well: "If miracles were as commonplace in antiquity as we popularly assume, they would hardly have counted as miracles at all. ... The miraculous was still miraculous for ancient man."[17] This is confirmed by the very logic of Gregory's *Dialogues*. The miracles there recorded are intended to capture the attention of his readers, so that important moral and doctrinal lessons might be brought home to them. In order to have served their purpose, they must have struck contemporary readers as being stories of extraordinary events which well exceeded the bounds of normal everyday experience. That is

---

combattendo non tanto i dubbi dell'*average ecclesiastic of the period*, come supponeva il Dudden, ma i suoi propri dubbi, con la sistematicità di chi vuol credere nonostante tutto."

[15] *Dial.*, 1 Prol. 10, sc 260:16-18. Cf. Gregory of Tours, *Liber vitae patrum* 13.3, 17 Praef., MGH, SRM 1.2, pp. 267, 277.

[16] On the credulity of the Romans, who by and large did not possess the critical attitudes of the Greeks, see R. Bloch, *Les prodiges dans l'antiquité classique* (Paris, 1963), esp. p. 114. On the superstitions shared by Christians and pagans alike in late classical society, see R. MacMullen, "Constantine and the Miraculous," *GRBS* 9 (1968): 81-96. R.M. Grant, *Miracle and Natural Law in Graeco-Roman and Early Christian Thought* (Amsterdam, 1952), p. 120, maintains that "at least in some respects Christians were far less credulous than their contemporaries, at least in the period before Augustine. While we have found many writers of the second, third, and fourth centuries accepting the most absurd stories of mythology and miracle, the Christian attitude as expressed by theologians is much more reserved." This is in accordance with what has been said above about the problematic nature of miracles in early Christian thought.

[17] Colin Brown, *Miracles and the Critical Mind* (Grand Rapids and Exeter, 1984), p. 281; cf. p. 283: "The very idea of a miracle presupposes both a uniformity of events and the occurrence of something so unexpected and unusual that it defies explanation in terms of nature taking its normal course." Cf. C.S. Lewis, *Miracles: A Preliminary Study* (New York, 1947), pp. 56-58.

certainly the way they struck Peter. But as the mere existence of works like the *Dialogues* is sufficient to attest, the sixth century still showed a greater willingness to believe in such events than the modern age.

For many scholars, the key to this disposition lies in the medieval attitude toward the natural realm. Hence it is to a critical examination of this suggestion that the remainder of this chapter will be devoted. Whereas in the modern age nature is seen as a closed, self-sustaining system that has little room for the possibility of miracle, in the early Middle Ages, it is argued, the world was seen as subject at every instant to the direct intervention of the Creator.[18] Only in the twelfth century did thinkers like William of Conches and Adelard of Bath focus their attention on secondary causes and develop a conception of nature as an autonomous domain governed by its own chains of necessity. Until then, it is claimed, the prevailing view was dominated by the conviction that the omnipotence of God is revealed "as plainly by the buds of spring as by the flowering of Aaron's rod, as much by the squeezing of wine from grapes as by the miracle at Cana, as much by the daily birth of infants as by the raising of a dead man to life."[19] It seems to have been a view of the natural realm that owed much more to the ancient Hebrews than it did to the Greeks.[20] Although he was considerably more cultured than the majority of his contemporaries, it was a view of nature, scholars argue, that Gregory the Great shared as well.

* * *

[18] Moricca, p. xvii: "la fede in una causa prima ha come cancellata l'idea delle cause secondarie, così che nulla sembra più naturale del soprannaturale, più ordinario dello straordinario." Cf. A. de Vogüé, "Le procès des moines d'autrefois," *Christus* 12 (1965): 113-128 at 122; B. de Gaiffier, "Miracles bibliques et vies de saints," in *Etudes critiques d'hagiographie et d'iconologie* (Brussels, 1967), pp. 50-61 at p. 55; J. Sumption, *Pilgrimage: An Image of Medieval Religion* (Totowa, N.J., 1975), pp. 13-14, 66-67. Cf. also P. Rousset, "La croyance en la justice immanente à l'époque féodal," *MA* 54 (1948): 225-248.

[19] M.-D. Chenu, "Nature and Man: The Renaissance of the Twelfth Century," in *Nature, Man and Society in the Twelfth Century* (Chicago and London, 1968), pp. 1-48 at 41-42. Cf. Tullio Gregory, "L'idea di natura nella filosofia medievale prima dell'ingresso della fisica di Aristotele," in *La filosofia della natura nel medioevo* (Milan, 1966), pp. 27-65; "La nouvelle idée de nature et de savoir scientifique au XIIe siècle," in *The Cultural Context of Medieval Learning* (Dordrecht and Boston, 1975), pp. 193-212 (with discussion on pp. 212-218), esp. pp. 193-195 and 212-213; R.C. Dales, "A Twelfth-Century Concept of the Natural Order," *Viator* 9 (1978): 178-192; C.M. Radding, *A World Made by Men: Cognition and Society, 400-1200* (Chapel Hill, 1985), pp. 213-220.

[20] Cf. L. Köhler, *Hebrew Man* (London, 1956), esp. pp. 128-134; J.P. Ross, "Some Notes on Miracle in the Old Testament," in *Miracles: Cambridge Studies in their Philosophy and History* (London, 1965), pp. 43-60; L. Sabourin, "Les miracles de l'Ancien Testament," *BTB* 1 (1971): 235-270, esp. 237.

Although Gregory was a theologian and no scientist, he was certainly not uninterested in the natural realm. His concern with strictly scientific matters was indeed limited, as was Augustine's before him; and again like Augustine, his knowledge was largely restricted to what could be found in compendia like the *Naturalis historia* of Pliny the Elder or the *Collectanea rerum memorabilium* of Solinus, the closest approximations to science available in the world of late antiquity. But judged by the standards of their time, both Augustine and Gregory were reasonably well informed on such matters. One searches in vain in the corpus of Gregory's work for lengthy discourses about the workings of nature. He was quite capable, however, of drawing on his knowledge of the physical universe when the need arose, and when he did so he treated it with some sensitivity.[21]

Augustine sometimes appears to deprecate scientific enquiry as mere *vana curiositas* that has nothing to do with essential Christian vocation, and one might expect to find echoes of a similarly negative attitude in Gregory. But early Christian thought was not endemically hostile to the investigation of nature, and so we should be careful not to misunderstand Augustine.[22] What distressed him was not so much scientific enquiry *per se* as the pride to which it could give occasion.[23] To be sure, Augustine could not acknowledge an

[21] On Augustine, see H.-I. Marrou, *Saint Augustin et la fin de la culture antique*, 2 vols. (Paris, 1938-1949), pp. 137-138, 233-235. On Pliny, see W.H. Stahl, *Roman Science: Origins, Development and Influence to the later Middle Ages* (Madison, 1962), esp. pp. 101-119. Although he considers Pliny's *Natural History* "the key work in any comprehensive study of what constituted Roman science" (p. 102), Stahl's assessment of Pliny himself is not flattering: "It is not really science but the curious phenomena of natural science that absorb him" (p. 103).

For contrasting appraisals of the extent of Gregory's scientific knowledge, cf. P. Boglioni, "Miracle et nature chez Grégoire le Grand," in *Cahiers d'études médiévales* 1: *Epopées, légendes et miracles* (Montreal and Paris, 1974), pp. 11-102, esp. pp. 18-20, with P. Riché, *Education and Culture in the Barbarian West* (Columbia, S.C., 1976), esp. pp. 149-150. Whereas Boglioni is inclined to discount the scientific knowledge displayed in Gregory's works, Riché gives a more positive assessment: "though superficial, [it] is nonetheless there" (p. 150).

[22] See D.C. Lindberg, "Science and the Early Christian Church," *Isis* 74 (1983): 509-530. Augustine refers to a "vana et curiosa cupiditas nomine cognitionis et scientiae palliata" at *Conf.* 10.35.54-55, CCL 27:184-185; cf. *Enchiridion* 3.9, CCL 46:52-53; 5.16, CCL 46:56-57.

[23] See, for example, *Conf.* 5.3.4-5, CCL 27:58-59, where Augustine acknowledges the legitimacy of the kind of enquiry undertaken by the classical astronomers, but laments that it has become an occasion for pride. Hence in *De doctrina christiana* 2.41.62, CCL 32:75-76, his explanation of the kinds of secular knowledge useful for interpreting Scripture is followed by an exhortation to humility: "Sed hoc modo instructus divinarum scripturarum studiosus, cum ad eas perscrutandas accedere coeperit, illud apostolicum cogitare non cesset: *Scientia inflat, caritas aedificat*" (p. 75).

inherent, independent value to knowledge of the physical universe. For Augustine, not even knowledge of Scripture can be defended in those terms. Knowledge of any kind is valuable only in so far as it promotes charity.[24] Hence a study of nature should be undertaken, not in the spirit of idle curiosity, but to deepen our grasp of eternal verities.[25] Within these limits, however, it does have a legitimate purpose: "on all sides everything cries out to you of its Author; nay the very forms of created things are as it were the voices with which they praise their Creator."[26]

Gregory's position was much the same. At the Fall, he says, our original parents were deprived of the spiritual insight with which they had originally been endowed. Ever since then human knowledge has been limited to the physical realm experienced through the senses.[27] But although our capacity for a knowledge of the divine has been impaired, it has not been completely destroyed. As the Apostle points out (Rom. 1:20), God reveals himself to us through nature. Our love for sensible things was the occasion for our downfall. But the same physical universe that drew us away from God can serve to call us back to him again: "Indeed, when reflected upon, the works of creation are roads to the Creator. When we see what has been done, we marvel at the power of the doer."[28] Hence Gregory's theology was one that recognized the value of a knowledge of the physical universe, and frequently used such knowledge to illustrate matters doctrinal or moral.[29]

However, despite his obvious interest in such knowledge, Boglioni has recently argued that Gregory had no real sense of nature as a whole: "le

---

[24] *Epist.* 55.21.39, CSEL 34.2:213. Cf. Marrou, *Saint Augustin*, pp. 278-280, 345.

[25] *De vera religione* 29.52, CCL 32:221. Cf. *Conf.* 13.21.31, CCL 27:259.

[26] *Enar. in Psalmos* 26.2.12, CCL 38:161; trans. S. Hebgin and F. Corrigan (Westminster, Maryland; and London, 1960), p. 272. Indeed, Augustine maintains that scientific knowledge is essential for those engaged in the work of Scriptural exegesis: see *De doctrina christiana*, 2.16.24, CCL 32:49: "Rerum autem ignorantia facit obscuras figuratas locutiones, cum ignoramus vel animantium vel lapidum vel herbarum naturas aliarumve rerum, quae plerumque in scripturis similitudinis alicuius gratia ponuntur."

[27] *Mor.* 5.34.61, CCL 143:261. Cf. *Dial.* 4.1.1-5, SC 265:18-22.

[28] *Mor.* 26.12.17-18, CCL 143B:1278; cf. 5.29.52, CCL 143:254, and see M. Frickel, *Deus totus ubique simul. Untersuchungen zur allgemeinen Gottgegenwart im Rahmen der Gotteslehre Gregors des Grossen* (Freiburg, 1956), pp. 14-21.

[29] See, for example, *Hom. in Ezech.* 2.5.10, CCL 142:282-283, where Gregory employs an analogy from the natural realm to illustrate the simplicity of the divine nature; or *Mor.* 11.6.8, CCL 143A:589-590, where he uses another analogy from the natural order to illustrate the operation of Providence. In *Past.* 3.22, PL 77:90, Gregory underlines the evil of discord by pointing out that it is avoided even by irrational creatures like birds, which maintain the unity of their flocks, or brute beasts, which feed together in herds: "si solerter aspicimus, concordando sibi irrationalis natura indicat, quantum malum per discordiam rationalis natura committat, quando haec a rationis intentione perdidit, quod illa motu naturali custodit."

monde de la nature physique est étranger à sa culture. ... Il n'est touché ni
par la complexité de cet immense spectacle, ni par son autonomie, ni par la
rigueur de ses lois." Gregory could not have been completely oblivious to the
regularity of nature, of course, for some awareness of its processes is an
integral part of all human experience; only of the most primitive humanity
could one venture the suggestion that such an awareness was lacking. But any
conception of a *lex naturae*, says Boglioni, was no more than embryonic in
Gregory's thought. He had no real appreciation of nature as an independent
system with its own rhythms and laws, but tended instead to dwell on
nature's symbolic significance.[30] Hence, although he was fascinated by
medical matters and managed to accumulate considerable knowledge of
common ailments and their treatments, for the most part this knowledge was
pressed into the service of allegory. Although he was not unaware of the
operation of secondary causes, they failed to impress him, and he preferred
instead to perceive everything, even purely natural events, in terms of the
direct causality of God. Boglioni puts it thus:

> il ne s'agit de nier que Grégoire reconnaît les causes secondes et leur rôle, mais
> seulement de relever ... qu'elles sont comme oblitérées en faveur de la cause
> première; que le mécanisme intrinsèque d'un événement naturel ou social ne
> retient en rien son attention, toute concentrée sur la signification même de
> l'événement; que, en somme, une vision neutre et scientifique de la nature est
> psychologiquement évacuée en faveur d'une lecture anthropocentrique, reli-
> gieuse et morale.[31]

As a result, argues Boglioni, Gregory was so disposed to the miraculous that
he regarded it as an evident part of experience. Indeed, miracles were so
obvious to him that he did not trouble himself over a definition. Instead of
elucidating the ontology of miracles, Gregory was inclined to focus on their
function:

> On dirait que, pour lui, la finalité d'un événement en définit la nature: d'où la
> tendance à insérer parmi les *miracula patrum* de nombreux épisodes qui,
> surtout dans le domaine des visions et guérisons, pourraient faire l'objet d'une
> interprétation purement naturelle, même en s'en tenant au texte de Grégoire.
> S'ils possèdent une particulière fonction pédagogique ou morale d'avertisse-
> ment, de prémonition, de consolation, de condamnation, pourquoi dès lors ne

---

[30] Boglioni, "Miracle et nature," pp. 20, 31, 32. Gregory's mind, says Boglioni, was
governed by "une perception surtout pédagogico-morale des événements naturels" (p. 37). On
primitive humanity, see G. Mensching, *Das Wunder im Glauben und Aberglauben der Völker*
(Leiden, 1957), pp. 8-9, 81. However, see also E. Ehnmark, *Anthropomorphism and Miracle*
(Uppsala, 1939), pp. 199-207.

[31] Boglioni, "Miracle et nature," p. 37.

pas leur attribuer une particulière origine divine et donc un caractère miraculeux?[32]

If Gregory did possess the strictly theocentric conception of the universe
Boglioni attributes to him, he may have been inspired by Augustine. The
Bishop of Hippo frequently observes that even the most familiar processes
of nature are divinely produced miracles. The daily alternation of light and
darkness, the annual progression of the four seasons, the cycle of sowing and
harvest, all of these are as miraculous as the most striking wonders recorded
in the Gospels. But we dismiss them lightly, not because they are easily
understood, but because they are constants of our experience. Indeed, the
greatest of all miracles, although we fail to appreciate it, is the unique wonder
that is the world itself. Assertions such as these might well create the
impression that, for Augustine, the distinction between nature and miracle
is at best tenuous, and that ultimately everything is a miracle dependent on
the direct causality of God.[33]

This interpretation would be a disservice to Augustine, however. In the
sixteenth book of *The City of God* he offers a definition of miracle that
presupposes a clear distinction between miraculous and natural occurrences.
Miracles are divinely produced events that are contrary to the ordinary course
of nature. If Augustine also argues that the regular processes of nature are
miracles in some sense, it is not to blur the distinction, but rather to
emphasize the radical contingency of the entire created order, and the
overarching sovereignty of God.[34]

---

[32] *Ibid.*, pp. 75, 71. For endorsements of Boglioni's view, see, for example, G. Cremascoli,
'*Novissima hominis*' *nei* '*Dialogi*' *di Gregorio Magno* (Bologna, 1979), p. 12; and S. Boesch
Gajano, "La proposta agiografica dei 'Dialogi' di Gregorio Magno," *SM* 3rd. ser. 21 (1980):
623-664 at 645-646. Boesch Gajano, however, adds a proviso: "l'origine divina del miracolo,
anzi lo stesso carattere miracoloso di un fatto non si evince, come vuole il Boglioni, dalla
funzione pedagogica e morale per l'individuo e la comunità, ma al contrario è l'autorità del
pontefice con la sua scelta e la sua spiegazione che ne sanzione l'origine divina" (p. 645).
Apparently an event becomes a miracle by papal fiat.

[33] See, for example, *De civitate Dei* 10.12, CCL 47:286-287; *De utilitate credendi* 16.34,
CSEL 25.1:43-44; *Enar. in Psalmos* 110.4, CCL 40:1623; *Epist.* 102.1.5, CSEL 34.2:549;
137.3.10, CSEL 44:109; *In Iohannis Evangelium* 9.1, CCL 36:90-91; 24.1, CCL 36:244; *Sermo*
126.3.4, PL 38:699-700; 247.2, PL 38:1157-1158. In particular, note *De civitate Dei* 21.9, CCL
48:775: "Ipse est enim Deus, qui omnia in hoc mundo magna et parva miracula ... fecit,
eademque ipso mundo uno atque omnium maximo miraculo inclusit." Cf. *De civitate Dei*
10.12, CCL 47:286-287; *De trinitate* 4.19.25, CCL 50:194. See also R.A. Markus, "Augustine:
God and Nature," in *The Cambridge History of Later Greek and Early Medieval Philosophy*
(Cambridge, 1967), pp. 395-405.

[34] See *De civitate Dei* 16.5, CCL 48:506, where he comments on Genesis 11:5: "And the
Lord came down to see the city and the tower, which the sons of men had built." Says

Initially it may be somewhat surprising to find that, in the *City of God*, Augustine apparently considers whole categories of natural phenomena to be miracles in some sense or another. While he acknowledges that unusual occurrences like earthquakes and extraordinary births are purely natural events which conceivably someday we might be able to explain,[35] paradoxically he also lists a number of other wonders that apparently allow of no natural explanation whatever. He refers to the salt of Agrigentum which, in a manner precisely opposite to ordinary salt, melts when put in fire and crackles when put in water. He cites the spring of the Garamantes which, in defiance of normal patterns, is so cold by day that it is undrinkable and so hot by night that it is untouchable. Because of their strikingly unusual properties, even lime and the loadstone are regarded as miracles. The fire lime seems to carry within itself is kindled rather than quenched by water, although oil, which is well known as a fuel, does not produce the same effect. It is only because we experience its wondrous properties on a regular basis, says Augustine, that we are not properly impressed: "If we had either read or heard about this miracle with regard to some stone from India, without it being able to form part of our own experience, we should certainly have considered it a falsehood, or at least have been greatly astonished."[36] The science of Augustine's day would have sought to explain the behaviour of such marvelous objects in terms of their specific natures. But Augustine is contemptuous of all such attempts, and appeals instead to the direct causality of God.[37]

It is inherently unlikely, however, that Augustine considered all these marvels miracles in the strict sense of the term. The salt of Agrigentum and the spring of the Garamantes may have been so considered, for in each instance Augustine apparently thought that he was dealing with a genuinely unique object. However, lime and the loadstone clearly fall into a different category. Augustine would have acknowledged that, remarkable though it may be, lime has a specific nature in accordance with which it always behaves

---

Augustine: "non loco movetur Deus, qui semper est ubique totus, sed descendere dicitur, cum aliquid facit in terra, quod praeter usitatum naturae cursum mirabiliter factum praesentiam quodam modo eius ostendat." Cf. *De cura pro mortuis gerenda* 16.19, CSEL 41:652-653; *De trinitate* 3.6.11, CCL 50:138. See also *De Genesi ad litteram* 4.12, CSEL 28:108-110; *De trinitate* 3.4.9, CCL 50:136.

[35] *De civitate Dei* 10.16, CCL 47:290; *De trinitate* 3.2.7, CCL 50:132-133; 3.8.19-3.9.19, CCL 50:145-146. However, cf. *De civitate Dei* 16.8, CCL 48:508-509.

[36] *De civitate Dei* 21.4, CCL 48:763; trans. H. Bettenson (Harmondsworth, 1972), p. 970 (significantly revised). Cf. *ibid* 21.5, CCL 48:764-765 (Agrigentum and the Garamantes); 21.7, CCL 48:769 (lime and the loadstone).

[37] *Ibid.* 21.7, CCL 48:768-769.

in the same way. It is not different in kind from other natural objects, all of which behave the way they do because of the specific natures they possess. If he is scornful of attempts to explain the behaviour of lime in terms of its nature, it is not because it does not possess one. It is rather because, in the final analysis, appeals to its nature are not very enlightening.

In Augustine's view, the properties of lime are unparalleled; they cannot be related to any broader patterns of experience. To appeal to its nature, therefore, is simply to label the problem, not to solve it. The only viable explanation is in terms of God's ability to produce creatures and objects of even the most astonishing kind. However, this does not mean that nature is miraculous in the strict sense, as if purely natural processes required God's active intervention. Augustine's point is simply that much of nature is mysterious. Unbelievers demand rational proof when Christians proclaim the miracles of God, and refuse to believe if it cannot be provided. In Augustine's view, this is not a reasonable standard of belief. There are a great many purely natural phenomena that similarly defy all attempted explanation, although their existence cannot be denied.[38]

Although he was aware that there is an important difference between natural and supernatural births, and that in normal circumstances human birth occurs *usitata lege naturae*,[39] we may be troubled to read on more than one occasion in *The City of God* that all instances of human conception and parturition are divinely produced events. Augustine often applies the same perspective to all living things: their existence is to be attributed to the action of Providence rather than natural causes. Hence we cannot consider farmers creators or producers of their crops, for as the Apostle says: "neither he who plants nor he who waters is anything, but only God who gives the growth."[40]

Augustine's intent, however, was to underline the significance of God as the first cause on which everything else depends. It was not to deny that God has embedded in the natural realm a definite causal order in accordance with which events normally unfold. Augustine was as confident of the order of nature as the Greek fathers before him. In the very act of Creation itself, he says, God infused the created realm with the *rationes seminales*, fundamental

[38] *Ibid.* 21.5, CCL 48:764.

[39] *Ibid.* 15.3, CCL 48:456; 15.12, CCL 48:470. Cf. *ibid.* 12.28, CCL 48:384, where he distinguishes between the way God operated in creating Adam and Eve and the way he operates now: "Haec opera Dei propterea sunt utique inusitate, quia prima. Qui autem ista non credunt, nulla facta prodigia debent credere; neque enim et ipsa, si usitato naturae curriculo gignerentur, prodigia dicerentur."

[40] On human births, see *ibid.* 12.24, CCL 48:381; 12.26, CCL 48:382-383; 22.24, CCL 48:847-848. On farmers and their crops, see *ibid.* 12.26, CCL 48:382; cf. 1 Cor. 3:7.

principles that would ensure, not only that night would follow day according to the fixed patterns of the heavenly bodies, but that each creature would develop in a manner appropriate to its kind. It is because of the virtue embedded in these structural and developmental principles that a bean is not produced from a grain of wheat, or a beast from a man.[41]

Because God was responsible for infusing this order into nature, and because the entire system would dissolve into nothingness were it not for the sustaining hand of Providence, one can speak of God as still at work in the governance of the world.[42] But God's active involvement in the processes of nature is not required to explain why, under the guidance of the *rationes seminales*, one plant develops in a certain way and another differently, or why one time of life is fertile while another not. The seminal reasons have been infused by God into the basic structure of nature itself—"non tantum in deo sunt, sed ab illo etiam rebus creatis inditae atque concretae"—and the causal efficacy they possess is a purely natural force.[43]

Hence Augustine would acknowledge that it is really nature that is responsible for natural processes, although nature in turn is subject to the overall design of Providence. When he maintains that God is the creator of the farmer's crops, what he means is that God is the creator of the seminal reasons.[44] He does not intend to rob nature of its consistency and transform its processes into miracles directly dependent on the divine will. Despite his frequent statements to the effect that the natural realm displays miracles as striking as those recorded in Holy Scripture—evidence of a profoundly religious sense of the world that has its modern parallels[45]—Augustine adhered to a clear distinction between the natural and the miraculous. Indeed, if he was tempted to compromise the distinction at all, it was not by resolving nature into miracle, but rather the other way around.

We have already noted that Augustine defines a miracle as a divinely produced event that takes place contrary to the ordinary course of nature. In

---

[41] *De Genesi ad litteram* 9.17, CSEL 28:292. Cf. D.S. Wallace-Hadrill, *The Greek Patristic View of Nature* (New York and Manchester, 1968), esp. pp. 107-108.

[42] Cf. *De Genesi ad litteram* 6.10, CSEL 28:182-183.

[43] *Ibid.* 9.17, CSEL 28:292. See *ibid.* 8.9, CSEL 28:244, where he describes the role of the seminal reasons as a *naturalis operatio providentiae*.

[44] *Ibid.* 9.15, CSEL 28:287-288: "natura id agit interiore motu nobisque occultissimo. cui tamen si deus subtrahat operationem intimam, qua eam substituit et facit, continuo tamquam extincta nulla remanebit." On the farmer and his crops, see *ibid.* 9.16, CSEL 28:289-290; cf. *De trinitate* 3.7.13, CCL 50:140-141.

[45] Cf. F. Heiler, "Vom Naturwunder zum Geisteswunder. Der Wandel des primitiven Wunderglaubens in der hohen Religion," in *Festschrift Walter Baetke* (Weimar, 1966), pp. 151-166 at pp. 160-163.

one of his early works, however, he seems to suggest that no such distinction between miracles and natural events is possible at the ontological level. In the *De utilitate credendi* he defines miracles only in psychological terms, as events that produce wonder in those privileged to witness them.[46] Moreover, in several other places he maintains that, strictly speaking, miracles are not contrary to nature at all, but to our knowledge of nature. Such passages have led more than one scholar to suggest that Augustine sees no fundamental difference between miracles and natural events. Striking and astonishing though they may be, miracles are simply natural events for which we have no explanation.[47]

Conceivably, the nature to which miracles are not contrary is not nature in the ordinary sense of the term but the divine nature itself. This seems to be Augustine's point in *The City of God.* Immediately after noting that miracles take place, "not contrary to nature, but contrary to what is known of nature" (*non contra naturam, sed contra quam est nota natura*), he refers to miracles clearly conceived in more conventional terms:

> What is so firmly disposed by the Author of the nature of the sky and the earth as the most orderly course of the stars? What is established by laws so firm and fixed? And yet, when it so pleased him who rules his own creation with supreme dominion and power, the star renowned beyond all others for size and

---

[46] *De utilitate credendi* 16.34, CSEL 25.1:43: "miraculum voco quicquid arduum aut insolitum supra spem vel facultatem mirantis adparet."

[47] *Contra Faustum* 26.3, CSEL 25.1:731; 29.2, CSEL 25.1:745; *De civitate Dei* 21.8, CCL 48:771; *De Genesi ad litteram* 6.13, CSEL 28:188. Cf. *Epist.* 120.5, CSEL 34.2:708; and *Epist.* 162.7, CSEL 44:517-518: "habent itaque omnia causas suas atque rationes rectas et inculpabiles, quae deus vel usitata vel inusitata operatur. sed hae causae atque rationes cum latent, miramur, quae fiunt, cum autem patent, consequenter ea vel convenienter fieri dicimus nec mirandum esse, quia facta sunt, quae ratio exigebat ut fierent, aut, si miramur, non inopinata stupendo sed excellentia laudando miramur."

See, for example, Grant, *Miracle and Natural Law,* p. 219: "Both classes of events are natural, and both have their origin in God." For a similar emphasis, see J. Grange, *Le miracle d'après saint Augustin* (Brignais, 1912); T.A. Lacey, *Nature, Miracle and Sin: A Study of St. Augustine's Conception of the Natural Order* (New York, 1916); F.M. Brazzale, *La dottrina del miracolo in S. Agostino* (Rome, 1964). Cf. C. Bologna, "Natura, miracolo, magia nel pensiero cristiano dell'Alto Medioevo," in *Magia. Studi di storia delle religioni in memoria di Raffaela Garosi* (Rome, 1976), pp. 253-272. For interpretations that strive to maintain an objective distinction between the natural and the miraculous in Augustine's thought, see D.P. de Vooght, "La notion philosophique du miracle chez saint Augustin. Dans le 'De Trinitate' et le 'De Genesi ad litteram'," *RTAM* 10 (1938): 317-343; J.A. Hardon, "The Concept of Miracle from St. Augustine to Modern Apologetics," *TS* 15 (1954): 229-257; C. Boyer, "La notion de nature chez Saint Augustin," *DCom.* 8 (1955): 65-76. Cf. A. Van Hove, *La doctrine du miracle chez Saint Thomas* (Paris, 1927), esp. pp. 26-33.

splendour altered its colour, its size, its shape and, still more wonderful, the decreed order of its course.[48]

Rather than perceiving miracles as ultimately reducible to the laws of nature, here Augustine clearly conceives them as violations of those same laws. When he maintains, therefore, that it is only nature as it is known to us to which they are contrary and not nature itself, the nature he has in mind is God's nature. Augustine's point, and it is one he develops over a couple of pages, is that God is at perfect liberty to effect changes in the natural realm he has ordained. Just as he established the natures of all creatures according to his will, so can he change those natures in any way that he chooses. His point in the *Contra Faustum* is much the same. The nature to which miracles are not contrary is not the nature whose designs all men, the godly and ungodly, can experience with the senses. It is rather what Augustine calls the supreme law of nature, the equivalent of the plan of Providence, of which miracles are an essential part.[49]

At best, however, this represents only a partial explanation. When Augustine maintains that miracles are not contrary to nature, "nature" often does have its usual meaning. Miracles are contrary to this nature as we know it, but not as it is in itself, because they are governed by the same principles that direct purely natural processes. Just as the *rationes seminales* provide for the ordinary course of nature, so they provide for the occurrence of miracles: "they were created to exercise their causality in either one way or the other: by providing for the ordinary development of creatures in time, or by providing for rare and miraculous occurrences, in accordance with what God might will as proper for the occasion."[50]

There is an important difference between the two categories of events, however. When nature follows its regular course, the *rationes seminales* actively produce the effects in question, with only the general concurrence of Providence. In miracles, the seminal reasons simply allow for the possibility of God's special intervention. That an acorn should develop into an oak tree

---

[48] *De civitate Dei* 21.8, Bettenson 980 (revised), CCL 48:771.

[49] *Ibid.*, CCL 48:772-773. Cf. *Contra Faustum* 26.3, CSEL 25.1:731: "deus autem creator et conditor omnium naturarum nihil contra naturam facit; id enim erit cuique rei naturale, quod ille fecerit, a quo est omnis modus, numerus, ordo naturae. ... contra naturam non incongrue dicimus aliquid deum facere, quod facit contra id, quod novimus in natura. hanc enim etiam appellamus naturam, cognitum nobis cursum solitumque naturae, contra quem deus cum aliquid facit, magnalia vel mirabilia nominantur. contra illam vero summam naturae legem a notitia remotam sive inpiorum sive adhuc infirmorum tam deus nullo modo facit quam contra se ipsum non facit."

[50] *De Genesi ad litteram* 6.14, CSEL 28:189; trans. J.H. Taylor (New York, 1982), 1:196 (revised).

and not a maple is due to the productive capacity God infused in nature itself. That a dry stick should suddenly blossom is also due to a capacity implanted in nature, but only because it is inconceivable that such events should take place without nature being open to God's intervention. Whereas the first event occurs because of natural forces, the second does not, but rather only because nature has been designed to be subject to the will of its Creator.[51] Ultimately, therefore, the ontological distinction between nature and miracle retains its force. Natural events arise from causes embedded in nature; the causes of miracles are hidden in the depths of the Godhead alongside the mysteries of grace, where they are a function of the divine will:

> God has within himself the hidden causes of certain things, causes which he has not placed in creatures; and he makes them operative, not in that work of Providence by which he sustains things in being, but in that by which he administers according to his will the things that he has willed to create. In this sphere of God's action is the grace by which sinners are saved. ... The apostle has said that the mystery of this grace was hidden, not in the world, in which the causal reasons of all things destined to come forth in the processes of nature have been hidden, ... but in God, who created all. Therefore, all things that have been made, not in the natural development of things, but in a miraculous way to signify this grace, have had their causes hidden in God as well.[52]

* * *

Gregory the Great does not discuss the nature of miracle with anything resembling the thoroughness of Augustine. Indeed, it is a frequently made point in recent studies that Gregory was not interested in dealing with the problem of miracle on the conceptual level at all. Although miracles are prominent not only in the *Dialogues* but in his other works as well, Gregory, we are told, never attempts to offer a definition.[53] But the same reluctance

---

[51] *Ibid.* 9.17, CSEL 28:291-292: "alius ergo est rerum modus, quod illa herba sic germinat, illa sic, illa aetas parit, illa non parit, homo loqui potest, pecus non potest. horum et talium modorum rationes non tantum in deo sunt, sed ab illo etiam rebus creatis inditae atque concretae. ut autem lignum de terra excisum, aridum, perpolitum, sine radice ulla, sine terra et aqua repente floreat et fructum gignat, ut per iuventam sterilis femina in senecta pariat, ut asina loquatur et si quid eius modi est, dedit quidem naturis, quas creavit, ut ex his et haec fieri possent—neque enim ex eis vel ipse faceret, quod ex eis fieri non posse ipse praefigeret, quoniam se ipso non est nec ipse potentior—verum tamen alio modo dedit, ut *non haec haberent in motu naturali, sed in eo, quo ita creata essent, ut eorum natura voluntati potentiori amplius subiaceret.*" The emphasis has been added.

[52] *Ibid.* 9.18, Taylor 2:93-94 (revised), CSEL 28:292-293. Cf. *Epist.* 137.2.8, CSEL 44:107: "in talibus rebus tota ratio facti est potentia facientis."

[53] See Boglioni, "Miracle et nature," pp. 72-73; Boesch Gajano, "La proposta agiografica," pp. 645-646. A. de Vogüé, *Grégoire le Grand, Dialogues* 1: *Introduction, bibliographie et cartes*

to discuss conceptual problems explicitly was also characteristic of other early medieval thinkers, and should not be taken to imply a lack of carefully formulated ideas. Gregory does not provide us with a proper definition of sin either, although he manages to advance a quite coherent doctrine on the topic.[54] When he is read carefully, the general outlines of his concept of miracle become relatively clear, and it turns out to be precisely the same as that of his great mentor.

It was noted earlier that Gregory posits an important connection between miracles and sanctity: miracles are performed by saints. However, rather than crediting the saints with any inherent power of their own, Gregory endorses the view customary among the hagiographers and maintains that, ultimately, miracles are produced by God alone. As Delehaye says, "Attribuer aux saints une puissance indépendante de celle de Dieu, c'est une pensée qui ne pourrait venir qu'à un chrétien ignorant les principles les plus élémentaires de sa religion."[55] At one point in the *Dialogues* Gregory distinguishes between the miracles saints accomplish by virtue of their own power and the miracles made possible by means of prayer, thus suggesting that the saints possess at least some intrinsic miraculous virtue. This was not an entirely unfamiliar

---

(Paris, 1978), pp. 94-95, comments on the surprising lack of any definition of miracle in the *Dialogues*. Cf. L. Cracco Ruggini, "Il miracolo nella cultura del tardo impero: concetto e funzione," in *Hagiographie, cultures et sociétés*, pp. 161-202 at 164.

[54] B. Ward, *Miracles and the Medieval Mind* (Philadelphia, 1982), p. 1, refers to the lack of theoretical discussion of the nature of miracle from the time of Augustine right up to that of Aquinas: "No treatise *De miraculis* survives in which the concept of the miraculous is discussed and related to other kinds of reality." On Gregory's concept of sin, see F. Gastaldelli, "Prospettive sul peccato in San Gregorio Magno," *Salesianum* 28 (1966): 65-94 at 65.

[55] H. Delehaye, *Sanctus: Essai sur le culte des saints dans l'antiquité* (Brussels, 1927), p. 260. See, for example, *Vitae patrum* 6.2.8, PL 73:1001-1002; Athanasius, *Vita S. Antonii*, chap. 38, PG 26:898-899; chap. 56, PG 26:926; chap. 80, PG 26:954-955; chap. 84, PG 26:962; John Cassian, *Coll.* 15.6, CSEL 13:431; 15.9, CSEL 13:434-435; Gregory of Tours, *De virtutibus S. Martini*, 1 Praef., MGH, SRM 1.2, p. 135; *Liber vitae patrum* 6.7, 8.12, MGH, SRM 1.2, pp. 236, 252. Cf. Ward, *Miracles and the Medieval Mind*, p. 170. On Gregory of Tours specifically, see E. Delaruelle, "La spiritualité des pèlerinages à Saint-Martin de Tours du Ve au Xe siècle," in *Pellegrinaggi e culto dei santi in Europa fino alla Ia crociata* (Todi, 1963), pp. 199-243, esp. pp. 215-220; and L.J. van der Lof, "De san Agustín a san Gregorio de Tours. Sobre la intervención de los mártires," *Augustinus* 19 (1974): 35-43. Delaruelle detects in Gregory's treatment of St Martin "une théologie de l'incarnation du Christ se perpétuant ici-bas dans les reliques, pour rendre présent le saint qui habite déjà le ciel" (p. 218). However, see also Van Uytfanghe, "La controverse biblique," pp. 217-218, who points out that "il y a dans l'oeuvre de Grégoire d'autres passages où il semble admettre l'existence d'une *virtus* propre au saint lui-même ou incluse dans ses reliques en tant qu'objets matériels."

view in the hagiographical tradition.[56] Elsewhere in the *Dialogues*, however, Gregory makes it clear that the distinction has only relative value. Strictly speaking, the saints possess no miraculous power whatever, but are only agents through whom the power of God is made manifest.[57] Indeed, the saints themselves uniformly ascribe the miracles they perform to God, as Saint Peter did in Acts 3:1-6, when he miraculously cured the man who had been lame from birth.[58]

One can, of course, distinguish between the miracles God produces himself and those he produces only indirectly. When God provided manna to the children of Israel in the desert, he performed the miracle himself; when he divided the Red Sea to allow the children of Israel to pass through, he ordered Moses to touch the waters with his rod, and so accomplished the

---

[56] *Dial.* 2.30.2-4, SC 260:220-222. See, for example, Palladius, *Historia Lausiaca*, chap. 22, Butler 2:73-74, where we have an episode in the life of Paul the Simple. Although it is probably implicit in most of the stories that Palladius tells that it is divine power that is responsible for whatever miracles are produced, in this particular episode the point is not clearly perceived. The *Life of Saint Martin* provides an even better example. In the *Dialogues* there are some indications that Sulpicius Severus would have acknowledged the abstract principle that it was God who worked the miracles of St Martin, rather than Martin himself. See, for example, *Dial.* 1.22, CSEL 1:175; and *Dial.* 1.10, CSEL 1:162: "opus illud non suae fidei, sed divinae fuisse virtutis." However, the point is not made anywhere in the *Life of St Martin*, or anywhere else for that matter where Martin is being discussed. Indeed, at times it seems to be denied, at least implicitly. See, for example, *Vita S. Martini* 18.4, SC 133:292, where we learn of the miraculous power inherent in threads removed from Martin's clothing or hair shirt; and *Vita S. Martini* 19.1-2, SC 133:292, where we are told how the daughter of Arborius was cured of a fever simply by having one of Martin's letters placed on her chest. Arborius evidently gave the credit directly to Martin himself: "Quae res apud Arborium in tantum valuit, ut statim puellam Deo voverit et perpetuae virginitati dicarit. Profectusque ad Martinum, puellam ei, praesens virtutum eius testimonium, quae per absentem licet curata esset, obtulit." In *Dial.* 3.3, CSEL 1:201, we find that miracles, even trivial ones, were worked by others in Martin's name. The net effect of these examples is to make Martin himself the locus of miraculous power. Cf. Stancliffe, *St. Martin*, pp. 230-232, 246-248.

[57] See, for example, *Dial.* 3.37.18, SC 260:424, where, after telling us how the priest Sanctulus of Nursia was delivered from death when the arm of his Lombard executioner miraculously stiffened and prevented him from delivering the blow, Gregory says: "Nihil in hac re in Sanctulo mireris, sed pensa, si potes, quis ille spiritus fuerit, qui eius tam simplicem mentem tenuit, atque in tanto virtutis culmine erexit." In *Dial.* 2.8.9, SC 260:166, Gregory informs us that the saints have never been able to pass their miraculous virtues on to others. He had evidently never heard of St Eugendus, who delegated his wonder-working power to his co-workers in his monastery: see *Vita patrum Jurensium* 3.148, SC 142:396-398. In Gregory's judgment, Christ alone had that prerogative, undoubtedly because the power to perform miracles is really a divine power.

[58] Cf. *Mor.* 30.2.6-7, CCL 143B:1495; *Hom in Ezech.* 1.5.14-15, CCL 142:64-65.

miracle through the agency of the prophet.[59] In no case, however, can any independent miraculous power be attributed to human agency. All power is vested in God himself, and we are but his instruments. This explains why, in the final analysis, miracles must completely transcend human reason. Miracles defy comprehension because their causes transcend the created realm and are hidden in the depths of the Godhead itself.[60]

Although Gregory does not develop the idea, these comments seem to presuppose the kind of ontological distinction between miracle and natural event noted in Augustine. Natural events, which are produced by a causality inherent in the universe, are in principle intelligible; supernatural events, miracles, which are produced by a divine causality transcending the universe, are necessarily beyond human comprehension. This conception of miracle also seems to have been characteristic of early medieval hagiography in general. It rests on the assumption that there is a normal course of events that is to be explained in naturalistic terms, but it also acknowledges that the natural order may be suspended through the direct intervention of God.[61]

There are, of course, Gregorian texts that might suggest a rather different view of miracle, but the evidence is finally not very persuasive. In his commentary on the first book of Kings Gregory observes that most men regard as miracles only the unusual events that astonish them, and fail to be impressed with the wonders that God performs regularly. Unlike such simple rustics, the saints are conscious of the hand of God everywhere, and in everything that is done, and never fail in their astonishment. In an even more

---

[59] *In 1 Reg.* 5.118, CCL 144:492.

[60] *Hom. in Ezech.* 2.8.10, CCL 142:344: "quidquid ratione hominis comprehendi potest mirum esse iam non potest, sed sola est in miraculis ratio potentia facientis." Cf. *Mor.* 6.15.19, CCL 143:296-297; *Hom. in Evan.* 2.26.1, PL 76:1197.

[61] Hagiographers customarily limit themselves to relating the miracles of the saints, devoting little effort to theoretical considerations. Generally, their concept of miracle is no more than implicit in their thought. However, scattered observations would seem to indicate that they conceived of miracles as divinely produced events that transcend the usual course of nature. Indeed, Demm, "Zur Rolle des Wunders," p. 311, describes this as the usual medieval view, which in the thirteenth century was systematically defined by Aquinas. See, for example, John Cassian, *Coll.* 19.8, CSEL 13:542: "non enim a parte minima, id est de consideratione paucorum, sed ex his quae multorum, immo omnium subiacent facultati, universalis est regula proponenda. si qua vero rarissime atque a paucissimis obtinentur ac possibilitatem communis virtutis excedunt, velut supra condicionem humanae fragilitatis naturamque concessa a praeceptis sunt generalibus sequestranda nec tam pro exemplo quam pro miraculo proferenda." On the views of the early medieval hagiographers in general, see Graus, *Volk, Herrscher und Heiliger,* p. 48. On Gregory of Tours specifically, see G. de Nie, "Roses in January: A Neglected Dimension in Gregory of Tours' *Historiae*," *JMH* 5 (1979): 259-289 at 263 and 279.

interesting passage of the *Moralia* Gregory mentions a number of Biblical miracles, and points out that they all have their parallels in nature. But because familiarity breeds contempt, we marvel only at the former, and remain unmoved by the latter. We wonder that Christ could change water into wine at the marriage feast in Cana, and not that this happens daily when the moisture of the earth is transformed into the fruit of the vine. We are astonished that Christ could feed a multitude of five thousand by multiplying five simple loaves, and yet not that this happens regularly when a few scarce seeds are multiplied in the richness of the harvest. The wonders of nature are as marvelous as the miracles of Scripture, and yet we fail to be impressed by them because we simply take them for granted.[62]

Prima facie, this is a line of reasoning that might be understood as depriving nature of any consistency of her own. It might be taken to imply that both natural processes and miracles in the strict sense are to be attributed directly to God. In fact, however, the ideas Gregory expresses here have a number of almost direct parallels in the thought of St Augustine;[63] and there, of course, they have no such implication. Augustine was very much aware of the important difference between the wonders God performs every day and the more striking manifestations of his power: "those which occur on a daily basis are accomplished as it were in the course of nature; but the others appear exhibited to the eyes of men by the efficacy of a power, as it were, immediately present."[64] Given the Augustinian inspiration of his thought, it is unlikely that the distinction was unknown to Gregory. Like Augustine, Gregory knew that God is sovereign over all and therefore the ultimate cause on which everything else depends. In the final analysis the divine causality underlies both the natural process by which wine is produced and the miraculous transformation of water into wine at Cana. It is not so clear, however, that Gregory understood divine causality to operate in the same way in these two cases. Indeed, in all likelihood he did not. In the second God's direct causality is clear; in the first it is his indirect causality that is at issue, his operating through the processes he has infused into nature.

---

[62] *In 1 Reg.* 5.115, CCL 144:491; *Mor.* 6.15.18, CCL 143:295-296. Cf. C.S. Lewis, *Undeceptions: Essays on Theology and Ethics* (London, 1971), p. 9, where the idea is given modern expression: "The miracles [of Christ] in fact are a retelling in small letters of the very same story which is written across the whole world in letters too large for some of us to see." See also his *Miracles*, p. 162.

[63] Cf. *De trinitate* 3.5.11, CCL 50:137-138; *In Iohannis Evangelium* 8.1, CCL 36:81-82; 9.1, CCL 36:90-91; 24.1, CCL 36:244; *Enar. in Psalmos* 90.2.6, CCL 39:1272; *Sermo* 126.3.4, PL 38:699-700; *Sermo* 130.1, PL 38:725.

[64] *In Iohannis Evangelium* 9.1, CCL 36:91.

In the last chapter we saw that Gregory tried to persuade sceptics of the truth of the resurrection by arguing that there are many things in our common everyday experience equally incomprehensible, such as the growth of a tree from a seed. Gregory argues this way in a number of passages, some of which might be taken to imply that the development of the seed and the resurrection of the body are dependent on divine causality in the same way. Indeed, in the *Homilies on the Gospels* Gregory calls the development of the seed, not merely a wonder, but a miracle whose familiarity blinds us to its true nature.[65]

However, as Gregory himself clearly explains in the very same passage from the *Homilies*, the features of the mature tree are latent in the seed and unfold in a natural, predictable sequence governed by secondary causes. Although these causes are of course dependent on God, divine causality is not directly responsible. The distinction between natural processes and miracles in the strict sense remains unshakeable. Unlike the miracle of the resurrection, the development of the tree does not issue from God's direct intervention in nature. The logic of the comparison does not lie in the fact that both are dependent on divine causality in the same sense, but in the fact that both ultimately are mysteries. The conclusion, therefore, seems clear. Gregory's openness to miracles cannot be explained in terms of the conviction that, in all its normal operations, nature is directly and immediately subject to the rule of Providence. He was aware of the existence of secondary causes governed by fundamental principles of order embedded in the bosom of nature itself.

Of course, Gregory's conception of the kind of order that God has established in the natural realm was quite different from the one that has prevailed since the scientific revolution. Until very recently at least, modern science has tended to concentrate its search for the order of nature in mathematical laws that describe general causal processes, and that govern the behaviour of objects of the most diverse kinds. Medieval science explained the behaviour of an individual object, not in terms of such general laws, but in terms of its own specific character. According to this view, Empedoclean in origin but Aristotelian in authority, each of the four elements is governed by an inherent tendency that impels it to its proper place: earth and water tend to fall toward the centre of the universe, air and fire to rise away from the centre. In turn, all physical objects, which are constituted by these elements, behave in an analogous way, each according to its kind. The growth

---

[65] *Hom. in Evan.* 2.26.12, PL 76:1203-1204. Cf. *Mor.* 6.15.19, CCL 143:297: "Quid ergo est difficile, ut pulvis in membra redeat, dum conditoris potentiam cotidie cernimus, qui et ex grano ligna mirabiliter et adhuc mirabilius fructus ex lignis creat?"

of an acorn into an oak does not depend on general principles but on the specific nature with which it is endowed, which dictates this particular course of development and no other.

The main weakness of this approach was its particularism. In the final analysis there were as many principles of order in the universe as there were discrete kinds of entities. Marrou suggests that the preoccupation with *mirabilia* so evident in the science of the late antique period may have been a direct consequence.[66] Interest in the unique for its own sake could well have gained ground precisely because of the lack of genuine explanatory force in the prevailing scientific view. Augustine was well aware of its weaknesses as well, and so, as we have already seen, he heaps scorn upon a scientific procedure that often simply labelled mysteries rather than really explaining them.[67] However, Augustine and his contemporaries really had no alternative. Hence, all its weaknesses notwithstanding, the conviction that order is to be sought in the specific natures of discrete kinds of things was shared by Augustine himself. Either directly or indirectly, it was passed on to his early medieval successors, including Isidore of Seville and Gregory the Great; and it then became the established medieval view. In the thirteenth century it found one of its most articulate expositors in Thomas Aquinas. It was never seriously challenged until the fourteenth century at the earliest.[68] The kind of

[66] Marrou, *Saint Augustin*, pp. 150-155.

[67] *De civitate Dei* 21.7, CCL 48:768-769.

[68] See, for example, *De Genesi ad litteram* 2.1-2.3, CSEL 28:33-36, where Augustine discusses the classical theory of the natural places of the four elements. In accordance with this theory, Augustine states (*ibid.* 4.18, CSEL 28:117) that each body has its own natural place to which it is drawn by the specific weight, a kind of innate instinct, that it possesses. Cf. *Conf.* 13.9.10, CCL 27:246; *De civitate Dei* 11.28, CCL 48:348; *Enar. in Psalmos* 29.2.10, CCL 38:181-182; *Epist.* 55.10.18, CSEL 34.2:189. On Isidore, whose etymological method reinforced the same view of nature, see J. Fontaine, *Isidore de Séville et la culture classique dans l'Espagne wisigothique* (Paris, 1959), p. 814. On Aquinas, see Van Hove, *La doctrine du miracle*, pp. 67-72. On the early medieval view of nature in general, see W.J. Brandt, *The Shape of Medieval History: Studies in Modes of Perception* (New Haven and London, 1966), pp. 1-42.

A.J. Gurevich, *Categories of Medieval Culture* (London, 1985), pp. 42-91, speaks of the inability of medieval men to distinguish clearly between themselves and their natural environment: "medieval man's relationship with nature was not that of subject to object. Rather, it was a discovery of himself in the external world, combined with à perception of cosmos as subject" (p. 56). This may well be related to the medieval inclination to perceive nature in terms of discrete kinds of objects behaving in accordance with certain inherent tendencies or desires. By the later Middle Ages, however, there is some evidence that the qualitative physics of the earlier period was being challenged by a quantitative, mathematical approach much closer to a modern perspective. See, for example, A.C. Crombie, "The Significance of Medieval Discussions of Scientific Method for the Scientific Revolution," in *Critical Problems*

order, therefore, that Gregory and other early medieval hagiographers
posited in the natural realm—and the kind of order that they believed miracles
suspended—was significantly different from its modern equivalent.[69] However, this does not indicate a lack of sensitivity to the regularity of nature. It
simply implies a concept of nature's regularity somewhat different from our
own.

There is, however, one other passage that has sometimes been singled out
for its special significance. Gregory here is commenting on Job 23:13, where
it is said of God: "Indeed, he himself alone is, and no one can avert his
judgment." The passage deserves to be quoted at length:

> Are there not angels and men, heaven and earth, air and seas, all things that
> fly or walk on four feet and creep? And surely it is written: "He created so that
> all things might be." Since, therefore, there are so many things in nature, why
> is it now said in the voice of the blessed man: "Indeed, he himself alone is?"
> But it is one thing to be, another thing to be principally; one thing to be
> changeably, and another to be unchangeably. Indeed, all these things exist, but
> they do not exist principally, because they by no means subsist in themselves,
> and unless they are sustained by the hand of a governor, they are not able to
> exist at all. For all things subsist in him by whom they were created. Living
> things do not give life to themselves, nor are those things that are moved and
> do not live led to motion by their own wills; but he it is who moves all things
> who gives certain things life, and ruling wondrously preserves other non-living
> things in their ultimate essence (*in extremam essentiam*). Truly all things were
> made from nothing, and their essence would tend back to nothingness unless
> the Author of all things restrained it with his guiding hand. Hence all created
> things have power neither to subsist nor to be moved through themselves, but

---

in the History of Science (Madison, Wisconsin, 1962), pp. 79-101; "The Relevance of the
Middle Ages to the Scientific Movement," in *Perspectives in Medieval History* (Chicago,
1963), pp. 35-57; E.A. Moody, "Galileo and his Precursors," in *Studies in Medieval
Philosophy, Science and Logic: Collected Papers 1933-1969* (Los Angeles, 1975), pp.
393-408.

[69] Of course, these are subjects on which the hagiographers do not normally discourse at
length, and very frequently we are left to draw our own conclusions. But some of the episodes
they relate are quite revealing nonetheless. See, for example, *Dial.* 1.5.2, sc 260:58-60; 3.15.4,
sc 260:316-318; 3.16.10, sc 260:334-336; 3.18.3, sc 260:346; 3.19.1-4, sc 260:346-348.
In the first of these passages Gregory tells us that Constantius, sacristan of the church of St
Stephen the Martyr near Ancona, was once able to make the lamps of his church burn on
water when the oil supply had been exhausted. Says Gregory: "Perpende igitur, Petre, cuius
meriti iste vir fuerit, qui, necessitate conpulsus, *elementi naturam mutavit*" (emphasis added).
Cf. Sulpicius Severus, *Dial.* 1.19, cSEL 1:171-172; Gregory of Tours, *De virtutibus S. Martini*
1.2, MGH, SRM 1.2, p. 139. Cf. also Augustine, *De Genesi ad litteram* 2.1, cSEL 28:33; *De
civitate Dei* 21.8, ccL 48:773: "Sicut ergo non fuit inpossibile Deo, quas voluit instituere, sic
ei non est inpossibile, in quidquid voluerit, quas instituit, mutare naturas."

they subsist only in so far as they have accepted the right to existence (*ut esse debeant*), and they are moved only in so far as they are disposed by a hidden impulse. For behold the sinner who is to be scourged for his human faults (*de rebus humanis*): the earth dries up in his labours; the sea is agitated in his shipwrecks; the air burns in his toils; the sky grows dark with floods against him; men are stirred up (*inardescunt*) in his oppression, and angelic virtues are excited in his adversity. Are these things of which we have spoken, whether animate or inanimate, driven by their own instincts and not rather by divine impulses? Hence, whatever it is that rages externally, through this adversity it is he who arranges it internally who is to be contemplated. In every situation, therefore, he alone is to be feared who exists principally, even he who says to Moses: "I am who I am. So you may tell the sons of Israel: He who is has sent me to you." Accordingly, when we are scourged by those things which we see, we ought to fear anxiously him whom we do not see. Hence, let the holy man [i.e. Job] despise whatever terrifies externally, whatever would tend toward nothingness unless guided through its essence; and with his mind's eye, everything else having been suppressed, let him consider the one in comparison with whose essence our being is non-being; and let him say: "Indeed, he himself alone is."[70]

Gregory maintains that God is not only the creator of the universe but its sustainer as well. Unless it were supported by the hand of Providence, all created being would cease to exist.[71] But this is a conventional notion that has always been regarded as an important tenet of the Christian faith; its import is not to deny the consistency of the natural realm but to point to its radical contingency. Gregory also maintains that whatever lives receives its life from God, and that whatever moves is put in motion by him. But, again, the point is not to deny naturally-produced motion so much as to underline that it is not self-explanatory, that the principles of motion do not arise from the objects themselves but have been placed in them by the Creator.

Perhaps more important, Gregory observes that God is the only cause worth contemplating (or fearing), as if the entire realm of secondary causation were simply being dismissed. Says Boglioni: "On remarquera ensuite comment essence et mouvement des êtres naturels sont vus sur le même plan, dans leur dépendance radicale de Dieu, en sorte que la considération du dynamisme des causes secondes est comme escamotée pour remonter directement aux intentions de la cause première."[72] It is important to notice, however, that God alone is worthy of attention, not because he is

---

[70] *Mor.* 16.37.45, CCL 143A:825-826.

[71] Cf. *Mor.* 24.20.46, CCL 143B:1222; Frickel, *Deus totus ubique simul*, pp. 95-96.

[72] Boglioni, "Miracle et nature," p. 37. Cf. Frickel, *Deus totus ubique simul*, pp. 59, 126, 131.

the only cause, but because he is the principal cause: "In omni igitur causa solus ipse metuendus est, qui *principaliter* est." The language implies two levels of causation, parallel to the levels of mutable and immutable being mentioned at the beginning.

Gregory does maintain that the natural realm can serve the divine purpose by rising up against us, moving not on blind instinct but through divine direction.[73] We can be smitten by a blazing sun, which brings sweat to our brows, by an arid land, which dries up under our labours, by the heavens, which darken and loosen against us torrential downpours, by the sea, which rages against us and threatens shipwreck. But these remarks refer to theologically significant situations, in which the sinner feels more than the operation of impersonal natural forces in the misfortunes that befall him, for behind them lies the weight of divine judgment. These notions may appear quaint to some, but they are an integral part of a Christian perspective, and Gregory shares them with even twentieth-century Christians.

Modern believers who argue similarly are not seeking to deprive the natural realm of its consistency and make it radically and directly dependent on the will of God. They wish only to claim that the significance of events is not always exhausted by a natural explanation. The same event can be viewed both scientifically and theologically: scientifically, because of the operation of natural forces; theologically, because these same forces, dependent on God for both their existence and whatever consistency they possess, can be perceived as part of his purpose. These are more, I think, than the rationalizations of twentieth-century Christians who want earnestly to show that there is no conflict between their Christian faith and the tenets of a modern scientific world-view. Every indication is that Gregory's view on these matters was substantially the same.

Perhaps because of his own chronically poor health, Gregory mentions most frequently the chastising power of illness, which he believes is a scourge sent from God to bring us to repentance. This perspective dominates several epistles in his register. Hence in a letter of January 599 to Andrew the *scholasticus*, of whose illness he had heard, Gregory quotes the apostle in Hebrews 12:6: "the Lord disciplines him whom he loves, and chastises every son whom he receives"; he also cites the words of the Saviour himself in John 15:1-2: "I am the true vine, and my Father is the vinedresser. Every branch of mine that bears no fruit, he takes away, and every branch that does bear fruit he prunes that it may bear more fruit." Just as ears of corn are beaten on the threshing-floor to strip them of their chaff, just as olives are crushed in the press to yield the fatness of the oil, and just as grapes are pounded

---

[73] Cf. *Mor.* 6.12.14, CCL 143:293.

under foot so that the wine may flow forth, so the sinner is disciplined with the scourge of illness to be brought to more abundant grace. Illness is an occasion for rejoicing. It is evidence that those who suffer it are loved by the eternal judge.[74] The *Pastoral Care* also contains similar remarks. Although illness is an affliction, it makes us mindful of our sins. The more we suffer outwardly, the more we are brought to grieve inwardly for all our misdeeds. Hence the sick should be admonished to realize that their very misfortunes mark them as the children of God. They are to be encouraged to consider how great a gift has been bestowed upon them, for the wounds of penitence inflicted by their bodily illness can cleanse their souls of sin.[75]

However, Gregory was also aware that illness has natural causes, and that to combat it natural remedies might be sought.[76] In a letter of February 601 to Marinianus, Bishop of Ravenna, Gregory expresses the sorrow he felt on hearing that Marinianus had taken ill and begun to vomit blood. On the advice of physicians available at Rome, all of whom have prescribed rest before all else, he instructs him to make provision for the interim government of the church of Ravenna and to come to Rome, where Gregory himself will see that he obtains the rest he needs. He encourages him to make the trip before the summer season, which the physicians maintain is particularly dangerous for his kind of illness. At the very least, however, Marinianus is to take care not to overextend himself. He is to refrain from vigils, and he is to leave the particularly taxing spiritual responsibilities of the church of Ravenna to someone else. Above all he is not to fast, unless some very great solemnity demands it, and no more than five times during the year, for the advice of the Roman physicians is that fasting would be particularly harmful given the disorder he suffers.[77]

One of the most interesting things about this letter is the very positive attitude it betrays toward the medical profession.[78] Of even greater signifi-

---

[74] *Ep.* 9.102, CCL 140A:654. Cf. *Ep.* 9.228, CCL 140A:802-805 at 804; *Ep.* 11.18, CCL 140A:887-888; *Ep.* 11.20, CCL 140A:889-890.

[75] *Past.* 3.12, PL 77:67-69. Cf. *Dial.* 4.16.3, SC 265:64, where the point is illustrated in the person of Romula.

[76] There are many references to the remedies of contemporary medical science in the *Pastoral Care*, where Gregory likes to draw parallels between the physical healing performed by the physician and the spiritual healing that is the responsibility of the pastor: see, for example, *Past.* 3.13, PL 77:71; 3.37, PL 77:122-123; cf. also *Ep.* 4.35, CCL 140:255-256.

[77] *Ep.* 11.21, CCL 140A:891-892. See also the letter of March 603 to Marinianus: *Ep.* 13.28, CCL 140A:1029-1030. Gregory repeats his injunction that Marinianus avoid fasting, although he is prepared to permit it once or twice a week if his correspondent's condition has improved.

[78] S. Boesch Gajano, "Demoni e miracoli nei 'Dialogi' di Gregorio Magno," in *Hagiographie, cultures et sociétés*, pp. 263-280 at pp. 270-271, maintains that Gregory's opinion of

cance, however, is the light it casts on Gregory's attitude toward illness, especially in view of his customary insistence that it be regarded as a scourge sent by God to induce a state of repentance. Clearly, illness can be perceived from a naturalistic perspective as well. Although it can be seen as a product of Providence, it can also be seen as the effect of purely natural causes. Presumably the providential perspective would have prevailed when the moral character of the afflicted warranted it, or when Gregory's primary concern was to elicit spiritual significance from questions of sickness and health. Gregory was a moral theologian above all else, and we should not be surprised that this latter perspective tends to dominate his work. In other circumstances, however, the naturalistic perspective would have suggested itself. This is precisely what occurs in the letter to Marinianus. Not only is the providential intepretation avoided, but the bishop is encouraged to abstain from precisely those practices (fasts and vigils) that would have been of most value if the point of his illness had been to prompt him to call his sins to mind and to repent them.

A parallel to these twin perspectives can be found in Gregory's treatment of human temptation and sin, which he discusses from both natural or human

---

the medical profession was not consistently favourable. In the *Dialogues*, she says, physicians are presented in very negative terms: "il medico e i suoi rimedi sono o rifiutati o addirittura visti come strumento del demonio, in una netta contrapposizione con la scelta religiosa e la *virtus* guaritrice dei santi" (p. 271). However, this overstates the case considerably. For the most part, the physicians who appear in the *Dialogues* are simple spectators of the principal events. See, for example, *Dial.* 4.13, sc 265:52-54, where Gregory tells us that, toward the end of his life, Bishop Probus of Rieti became severely ill, and his father, Maximus, summoned doctors to attend to him. After taking the sick man's pulse, the physicians pronounce that death is imminent, and they are quite correct. But from this point on they are pushed to the margins of the story, and they have nothing to do but confirm the death of the bishop at the end. In particular, they do not witness the miracle that takes place. However, they do not suffer any reproaches either. The fact that Probus dies an extraordinary death, being ushered to heaven by saints Juvenal and Eleutherius, implies no attack on the doctors or on their profession.

Doctors make an appearance in the story of the widow Galla as well, where once again they provide an accurate diagnosis. See *Dial.* 4.14, sc 265:54-58. They inform Galla that, because of her passionate nature, she will grow a beard if she does not remarry, and that is precisely what happens. However, the saintly woman was unconcerned about the physical blemish: "sancta mulier nil exterius deformitatis timuit, quae interioris sponsi speciem amavit, nec verita est si hoc in illa foedaretur, quod a caelesti sponso in ea non amaretur" (sc 265:56). Rather than being singled out for opprobrium, once again the physicians are simply shown to be irrelevant. There is one doctor who does indeed appear in a very poor light in the *Dialogues*: Gregory's personal physician, the monk Justus. See *Dial.* 4.57.8-17, sc 265:188-194. However, the sin of which Justus was guilty was strictly a personal failing on his part, and essentially had nothing to do with his being a physician.

and supernatural or demonic points of view. That mankind's tendency to sinfulness can be perceived in distinctly human terms is clear. Without once mentioning the influence of Satan, Gregory devotes an entire chapter of the *Moralia* to a discussion of the way in which the various vices give rise to one another in a perfectly natural manner.[79] The principal vice is pride, from which arise the seven deadly sins; each of these, in turn, produces a host of other offences. The root of all this evil is an innate instability or infirmity that Gregory believes is a product of the Fall.[80] Although he is somewhat ambivalent in identifying more precisely the foundation of human sinfulness, oscillating between a view that would locate the weakness in the human spirit, and one that would place it in the flesh, for the most part it is the latter view that tends to prevail: temptation arises naturally from the weakness of the flesh, just as a moth arises naturally from the very garment it consumes.[81] Elsewhere, however, Gregory adopts a very different point of view. Rather than speaking of the inherent weaknesses of the flesh, he endorses the tradition particularly strong among the desert fathers, and assigns responsibility for the temptations that assault us to Satan and his minions.

It is at least conceivable that not all the statements of the heroes of the desert and the stories that accompany them are to be taken in a straightforward and literal fashion. The *Historia monachorum* informs us that the monk Pityrion, who spoke with particular authority on the discernment of spirits, taught that the demons disposing us to evil follow the human passions. The key to driving off evil spirits, therefore, is to master the passions: in overcoming any particular passion one also overcomes the corresponding demon. Rufinus fudges the issue somewhat in his Latin translation. But Pityron is more properly to be judged by the Greek original; and on that basis one could argue with some plausibility that, for Pityron, demons were not much more than hypostatized human vices.[82]

A similar impression could be derived from a story Rufinus added to his Greek original. St Macarius of Alexandria once witnessed a group of demons besieging the brethren who had assembled to celebrate vigils. During the reading of the Psalm the demons scurried among the brethren, placing their

---

[79] *Mor.* 31.45.87-91, CCL 143B:1610-1613.

[80] *Mor.* 8.6.8, CCL 143:386.

[81] *Mor.* 5.38.68, CCL 143:268-269; 11.48.64, CCL 143A:622. See F. Gastaldelli, "Il meccanismo psicologico del peccato nei *Moralia in Job* di San Gregorio Magno," *Salesianum* 27 (1965): 563-605 at 573-574.

[82] Cf. *Historia monachorum in Aegypto* 15.2-3, ed. A.-J. Festugière (Brussels, 1971), p. 111; and Rufinus, *Historia monachorum*, chap. 13, PL 21:432-433. Cf. also Athanasius, *Vita S. Antonii*, chap. 42, PG 26:906.

fingers over the eyes of some to put them to sleep, or forcing their fingers into the mouths of others to make them yawn. When the Psalm was finished, the demons transformed themselves into enticing visions to distract the brethren from their prayers. Although some of the monks were able to repel the illusions, corresponding distractions entered into the minds of others.[83] Festugière laments the fact that stories of this sort totally obliterate the distinction between temptations that are genuinely demonic and those that arise naturally from our fallen human nature. Everything is attributed to demons! But he maintains that they were intended to be taken quite seriously. They were an expression of the primitive folk belief that had always lain in the subsoil of the ancient world, hidden from view by the more sophisticated literary products of that culture. With equal plausibility, however, one might argue that, if demons are responsible for everything, then there is no real distinction between action that is demonic and action that is human. Conceivably, the demons of the desert fathers were simply personified human failings, a set of enabling abstractions in their psychology of the spiritual life.[84]

Occasional passages in the *Dialogues* suggest a similar interpretation. In book two, in a story to which we have referred before, Benedict puts to flight a demon who used to draw a restless monk out of the chapel at time of prayer. The demon, a small black boy who tugged at the hem of the monk's habit, could be little more than an artistic representation of the monk's inherent obstinacy. That the image of the black boy was a familiar *topos*, and that the remedy applied was a summary thrashing, suggest as much. Throughout the second book of the *Dialogues* the depictions of Satan are conventional literary *topoi*. Quite conceivably they are to be understood, not as depictions of an objective reality, but as symbolic representations of human spiritual states.[85] The *Moralia*, where the psychology of temptation and fall is discussed in more detail, could be used in support of this view. Like Pityrion before him, Gregory declares that there are as many demons as there are individual human vices, and that Satan adapts temptations to the

---

[83] *Historia monachorum*, chap. 29, PL 21:454.

[84] A.-J. Festugière, *Les moines d'Orient* 1: *Culture ou sainteté* (Paris, 1961), pp. 23-39. Cf. P. Brown, *The Making of Late Antiquity* (Cambridge, Mass., 1978), pp. 89-91; A. Grün, *Der Umgang mit dem Bösen. Der Dämonenkampf im alten Mönchtum* (Münsterschwarzach, 1980), pp. 29-30; L. Leloir, "Le diable chez les pères du désert et dans les écrits du moyen âge," in *Typus, Symbol, Allegorie bei den östlichen Vätern* (Regensburg, 1982), pp. 218-237 at pp. 228-229, 235n.

[85] *Dial.* 2.4, SC 260:150-152. See also M. Puzicha, " *Vita iusti* (Dial. 2,2). Grundstrukturen altkirchlicher Hagiographie bei Gregor dem Grossen," in *Pietas. Festschrift für Bernard Kötting* (Münster Westfalen, 1980), pp. 284-312, esp. p. 298.

characters of his targets, enticing them with the sins to which they are predisposed.[86]

However, even if he would have acknowledged that, in some sense, demons are extensions of the personality, there can be little doubt that the demons in the air were as objectively real to Gregory as they had been to St Antony before him.[87] Not mere metaphors, Satan and his host were personal agents of evil intent on corrupting the entire human race. Of course, says Gregory, Satan enjoys only the sphere of influence he has received by divine licence, and God has ordained that we will not be tempted beyond our means. But his temptations are severe nonetheless. Initially they can be combatted with relative ease, but once we succumb, subsequent temptations become much stronger. The just are to be particularly on guard, since Satan can be expected to make special efforts to undermine their spiritual security. The dangers tend to increase as the end of life approaches, when Satan redoubles his efforts to ensure that the departing soul will not elude his grasp.[88] It would seem, therefore, that, in addition to the inherent human instability that is a product of man's original fall from grace, Satan and his demonic accomplices represent an external cause for temptation that needs to be combatted vigourously. But if this is the case, how do we sort out the natural and supernatural sources of temptation in Gregory's thought? The simple answer is that they cannot really be sorted out at all, anymore than they can in the thought of Cassian. In his *Collations* Cassian is content to list side by side the evil thoughts implanted by the Devil and those that arise *naturaliter*, without offering any principle to distinguish them.[89]

---

[86] *Mor.* 15.27.33, CCL 143A:768-769 (cf. John Cassian, *Coll.* 7.17, CSEL 13:195-196); *Mor.* 14.13.15, CCL 143A:706-707; 29.22.45, CCL 143B:1464-1465. At *Mor.* 33.24.44, CCL 143B:1712, Gregory explains that Satan adopts different tactics to deceive religious and worldly people: "Leviathan iste aliter religiosas hominum mentes, aliter vero huic mundo deditas temptat; nam pravis mala quae desiderant aperte obicit, bonis autem latenter insidians, sub specie sanctitatis illudit." Cf. *Mor.* 34.15.28, CCL 143B:1754.

[87] Cf. N.H. Baynes, "St. Antony and the Demons," *JEA* 40 (1954): 7-10; J. Daniélou, "Les démons de l'air dans la 'Vie d'Antoine'," in *Antonius Magnus eremita, 356-1956* (Rome, 1956), pp. 136-147; M. Jourjon, "Qui allait-il voir au désert? Simple question posée au moine sur son démon," *Lumière et vie* 78 (1966): 3-15; W. Schneemelcher, "Das Kreuz Christi und die Dämonen. Bemerkungen zur Vita Antonii des Athanasius," in *Pietas. Festschrift für Bernhard Kötting,* pp. 381-392. More generally, see P.B. Steidle, "Der 'schwarze kleine Knabe' in der alten Mönchserzählung," *BenM* 34 (1958): 339-350.

[88] See *Mor.* 29.22.44, 46, CCL 143B:1464, 1465; 32.19.33-34, CCL 143B:1654-1655. The emphasis on Satan's efforts to ensnare the souls of those departing this life was a major theme in Gregory's work. Cf. A.C. Rush, "An Echo of Christian Antiquity in St. Gregory the Great: Death a Struggle with the Devil," *Traditio* 3 (1945): 369-378; J. Ntedika, *L'évocation de l'au-delà dans la prière pour les morts* (Louvain and Paris, 1971), esp. pp. 59-60.

[89] *Coll.* 1.19, CSEL 13:27-29.

At one point in the *Moralia* Gregory refers to four stages by which sin is committed, attributing only the first of them to Satan:

> Indeed, sin is committed in the heart in four ways, and in four ways is consummated in deed. For in the heart it is committed by suggestion, by delight, by consent and by boldness of defense. Indeed, suggestion comes through the Enemy, delight through the flesh, consent through the spirit, boldness of defense through pride.[90]

This needs to be combined with what he says elsewhere about Satan adapting his strategems to the character of each individual.[91] It would seem, therefore, that Satan takes the initiative, although he tailors the temptations he presents to individual minds according to the specific kinds of sinful conduct to which their weakened human nature has left them exposed. It would also seem that the role of Satan is limited to planting the initial sinful thought. The other stages, which consist of taking delight in the sinful suggestion, yielding consent to it, and then stubbornly and pridefully defending the sinful choice, are apparently human responsibilities. Although the role of Satan remains a significant one, the result is a doctrine that seems to emphasize the human dimension of temptation and sin, a perspective further enhanced by Gregory's insistence that sin necessarily involves our free will.[92] Unfortunately, however, in the very same passage quoted above Gregory also manages to attribute all four stages of sin to Satan; and elsewhere he maintains that, whereas temptation arises from our natural condition and is unavoidable, it takes on a demonic quality precisely when it is accompanied by our consent.[93] In the end it would appear that, rather than having natural and

---

[90] *Mor.* 4.27.49, CCL 143:193.

[91] *Mor.* 29.22.45, CCL 143B:1464. Cf. *Mor.* 14.13.15, CCL 143A:706-707.

[92] *Mor.* 13.16.19, CCL 143A:680. Cf. Augustine, *Enar. in Psalmos* 7.19, CCL 38:48; Cassian, *Coll.* 7.8, CSEL 13:189-190. See also Gastaldelli, "Il meccanismo psicologico," pp. 584-585.

[93] See *Mor.* 4.27.49, CCL 143:193, where he goes on to discuss the fall of Adam: "Unde et illam primi hominis rectitudinem antiquus hostis *his quattuor ictibus* fregit" (emphasis added). Elsewhere he talks of three stages, but to the same effect. Cf. *Mor.* 32.19.33, CCL 143B:1654-1655: "Quia enim peccatum tribus modis admittitur, cum videlicet serpentis suggestione, carnis delectatione, spiritus consensione perpetratur, Behemoth iste, prius illicita suggerens, linguam exserit; post ad delectationem pertrahens, dentem figit; ad extremum vero, per consensionem possidens, caudam stringit. Hinc est enim quod nonnulli peccata longo usu perpetrata in semetipsis ipsi reprehendunt; atque haec ex iudicio fugiunt, sed vitare opere nec decertantes possunt; quia dum Behemoth istius caput non conterunt, plerumque cauda et nolentes ligantur."

See also *Mor.* 21.3.7, CCL 143A:1069: "Et nimirum mentem nequaquam cogitatio immunda inquinat cum pulsat, sed cum hanc sibi per delectationem subiugat. Hinc etenim praedicator egregius dicit: *Temptatio vos non apprehendat, nisi humana.* Humana quippe temptatio est, qua

supernatural dimensions that can be clearly distinguished, the entire process of temptation and fall can be viewed from two different and mutually enriching points of view.

It is not beyond possibility that the coexistence of natural and supernatural perspectives in Gregory's thought might have direct application to his doctrine of miracle. If temptation can be regarded as both natural and demonic, or if illness can be regarded at one and the same time as both a product of purely natural causes and a product of Providence, conceivably some of the miracles that Gregory reports can be interpreted in the same way. It has been claimed of the Venerable Bede that he was "on the whole a rational historian" who "obviously regarded rational causation as compatible with divine intervention."[94] Much the same might be said of Gregory the Great. As has frequently been pointed out, several of Gregory's miracle stories are such as to allow of purely natural explanations.[95] In several cases, however, it seems evident that the natural explanation would have been obvious even to Gregory himself.

In the first book of the *Dialogues* Gregory speaks of a fire that broke out one day in Ancona. Despite vigorous efforts to extinguish it, it spread and threatened to destroy the entire city. However, Bishop Marcellinus, who was accustomed to being carried from place to place because gout made walking difficult, was conveyed to the scene of the conflagration. As soon as he was set down in the path of the fire, "the flames doubled back over themselves as if thereby to indicate that they could not pass over the bishop. Once the fire was checked at this point, it advanced no farther, but gradually died away without causing further destruction." Gregory certainly considered this change of fortune a miracle, for he invites both Peter and his readers to "consider what great sanctity was required for a sick man to sit there and by prayers subdue the flames." But presumably Gregory himself would have realized that a fortuitous change in the direction of the prevailing wind would have been sufficient to produce the same effect.[96]

Several other places in the *Dialogues* yield stories of similar miracles. In each case, however, the natural explanation is avoided. It is always the

---

plerumque in cogitatione tangimur etiam nolentes, quia ut nonnunquam et illicita ad animum veniant, hoc utique in nobismetipsis ex humanitatis corruptibilis pondere habemus. Iam vero daemoniaca est et non humana temptatio, cum ad hoc quod carnis corruptibilitas suggerit per consensum se animus astringit."

[94] A. Gransden, *Historical Writing in England* 1: *c. 550 to c. 1307* (Ithaca, N.Y., 1974), p. 21.

[95] See, for example, Dudden, *Gregory the Great*, 1:325; Boglioni, "Miracle et nature," p. 75.

[96] *Dial.* 1.6.2, Zimmerman 27-28 at 28, SC 260:64.

transcendent character of the event that is emphasized.[97] The same is true of comparable tales told by both Sulpicius Severus and Gregory of Tours, although, significantly, their stories are frequently accompanied by the insistence that chance would not have been a sufficient explanation of the wonders that occurred.[98] Clearly, both Sulpicius and Gregory of Tours at least considered the possibility: the miracles in question *could have been* regarded as mere happy coincidences. But that was not the interpretation they preferred. In adopting a providential view—in judging the events in question as miracles in some sense or other—their assessment was not unlike that of the mother in a story told by R.F. Holland.

In slightly revised form, the story concerns a young child who one day was out riding on his tricycle. Being particularly venturesome, he managed to stray onto some railway tracks where he became firmly stuck. The mother, of course, went out in search of the child, and eventually managed to spot him. But at that very moment a large freight train was bearing down upon the child at full throttle. The mother had no hope of reaching him in time, and her frantic shouts and gesticulations made no impression on the distracted youngster. At the last possible moment, however, disaster was averted, not because the driver of the train had noticed the child, but because he had suddenly taken ill. When his hand fell from the throttle, the brakes were automatically applied, and the train came screeching to a halt. By-standers might have regarded the child's deliverance simply as a coincidence—a happy coincidence indeed—but little more than the simultaneous occurrence of unrelated events. But this is not how the mother interpreted it. Judging the event only in those terms would have failed utterly to do justice

---

[97] See, for example, *Dial.* 2.21.1-2, sc 260:198; 3.11.4-6, sc 260:294-296; 3.16.6, sc 260:330-332; 3.37.2-3, sc 260:412-414. The second last of these stories concerns a young boy who fell off the steep pathway leading up the side of the mountain towards the cave of the saintly hermit Martin. Although there were huge groves of trees growing in the valley below, apparently everyone was certain that his body would have been shattered by the sharp rocks jutting out from the cliff. The fact that he was found unharmed, says Gregory, is decisive evidence that he had been protected by Martin's prayers: "Tunc *cunctis patenter innotuit,* quod ideo laedi non potuit, quia hunc in casu suo Martini oratio portavit" (sc 260:332; emphasis added).

[98] See, for example, Sulpicius Severus, *Dial.* 3.3, csel 1:201; 3.7, csel 1:204-205; Gregory of Tours, *Historia Francorum* 4.48, mgh, srm 1, pp. 184-185; *De passione et virtutibus S. Iuliani,* chap. 27, mgh, srm 1.2, pp. 125-126. The last of these stories concerns a bolt of lightening that struck the church at Brioude, but exited through the window above the tomb of the martyr without harming any of the assembled faithful. Comments Gregory: "Quod si haec fortuitu quis putat, admiretur magis et stupeat incliti potentiam martyris, quod praeteriens ignis per medium populi neminem nocuit, sed ibi tantum explevit vota, ubi se cognovit habere licentiam" (p. 126).

to its significance for both herself and her child. It must have been an act of Providence.[99]

In order to accommodate the mother's not unreasonable reaction, Holland distinguishes between two categories of miracles: those that fall under the violation concept, since they seem to involve a violation or suspension of the laws of nature, and those that fall under the contingency concept. The miracle involving the child is to be assigned to the second category: none of the laws of nature was suspended; they simply happened to intersect in a particularly fortuitous manner. A similar distinction may well have been adopted by Gregory the Great, Sulpicius Severus and Gregory of Tours. Many of their miracle stories might be thought simple happy coincidences, as they themselves frequently seem to realize. But this is not the interpretation they adopted. In each of these stories a man of renowned sanctity (or his relics) had central importance, and this they judged sufficient to transform them into events of a higher order. Not simple chance occurrences, they became events invested with meaning; all naturalistic explanations notwithstanding, they possessed a transcendent, revelatory dimension. To those who insist on interpreting them only in naturalistic terms, they would probably reply that, at best, such an explanation is incomplete, for it fails to do justice to their significance. A natural explanation does not rule out a providential one, although the point fails to impress those who insist on reducing every aspect of reality to physical terms.

Much of this is simply conjecture, of course, and if it casts light on some of Gregory's miracle stories, it does not help with others. In some cases reported in the *Dialogues* the natural and the miraculous are coterminous, but usually the miracle involves the suspension of the normal operations of nature and God's direct intervention in the natural realm. Gregory was obviously much more ready to accept this possibility than most of us are, but not because of a failure to appreciate the autonomy and regularity of nature. The explanation is more probably to be found in the fact that, like Augustine, he was more profoundly impressed than we are by how imperfectly he understood it.

We have already referred to Augustine's critique of the prevailing scientific orthodoxy of his day. Despite its pretensions, it possessed remarkably little explanatory force; vast stretches of nature remained immune to its categories, veiled behind a shroud of mystery. Gregory's sense of mystery was equally as great. It will be remembered that when Gregory discusses the doctrine of the resurrection, he invites us to consider the development of a tree out of

[99] See R.F. Holland, "The Miraculous," in *Religion and Understanding*, ed. D.Z. Phillips (Oxford, 1967), pp. 155-170.

a single seed, a perfectly natural process, and one with which we are all well acquainted, but in the final analysis a complete mystery. Indeed, he goes on to mention other natural processes of which we are similarly ignorant, among them the mysteries of our own birth, and he argues from them in the same manner. The argument does not rest on any denial of nature's autonomy and regularity, but rather on our ignorance of the way nature functions.

Twentieth-century readers do not always find the argument compelling. But Gregory thought it appropriate, and it was probably effective at the time. Gregory lived in a world he understood much less completely than we do ours. We are so well informed about nature's causal processes (or at least know of people whom we believe to be so well informed) that we are often tempted to explain everything in terms of them, and to doubt that they have ever been suspended. But Gregory suffered no such temptation, and experienced no such doubt. He had to accept a good deal more mystery in his life than we do, and hence was much more willing to accept that some of these mysteries have only God for an explanation.

Epilogue

The Structure of Miracle

One of the recurring themes in the recent scholarly literature on the *Dialogues* of Gregory the Great is that, in both their manner of life and their miracles, Gregory's saints rival the heroes of Sacred Scripture itself. Like the saints in other examples of early medieval hagiography—like St Martin of Tours, for example, whom Sulpicius Severus could acclaim as the virtual equal, not only of the prophets and apostles, but of Christ himself[1]—the saints of the *Dialogues* perform miracles that often are strongly reminiscent of Biblical prototypes. We have already discussed many of these in chapter five. Suffice it here to say that Gregory usually makes a point of emphasizing the Biblical parallel for us, so that the stature of his modern saints will be quite apparent.[2]

---

[1] See *Dial.* 2.5, CSEL 1:186; and especially *Dial.* 3.10, CSEL 1:208, where Sulpicius (in the words of Gallus) describes Martin as "vere Christi iste discipulus, gestarum a Salvatore virtutum, quas in exemplum sanctis suis edidit, aemulator." Cf. E. Delaruelle, "La spiritualité des pèlerinages à Saint-Martin de Tours du Ve au Xe siècle," in *Pellegrinaggi e culto dei santi in Europa fina alla Ia crociata* (Todi, 1963), pp. 199-243 at 207.

[2] Cf. O. Rousseau, "Saint Benoît et le prophète Elisée," *RMon.* 144 (1956): 103-114; M. Mähler, "Evocations bibliques et hagiographiques dans la Vie de Saint Benoît par Saint Grégoire," *RBén.* 83 (1973): 398-429; G. Cracco, "Uomini di Dio e uomini di chiesa nell'alto medioevo (per una reinterpretazione dei 'Dialogi' di Gregorio Magno," *RSSR* n.s. 12 (1977): 163-202 at 187, 195-196; A. de Vogüé, *Grégoire le Grand, Dialogues 1: Introduction, bibliographie et cartes* (Paris, 1978), pp. 135-138; M. Puzicha, "*Vita iusti* (Dial. 2,2). Grundstrukturen altkirchlicher Hagiographie bei Gregor dem Grossen," in *Pietas. Festschrift für Bernhard Kötting* (Münster-en-Westfalen, 1980), pp. 284-312, esp. pp. 304, 307-308; J.M. Petersen, *The Dialogues of Gregory the Great in their Late Antique Cultural Background* (Toronto, 1984), pp. 25-55.

The tendency to model the miracles of the saints on Biblical archetypes characterizes medieval hagiography as a whole: see B. Ward, *Miracles and the Medieval Mind* (Philadelphia, 1982), pp. 167-171. On the Merovingian period specifically, see A. Marignan, *Etudes sur la civilisation française 2: Le culte des saints sous les Mérovingiens* (Paris, 1899), esp. pp. 99-100; F. Graus, *Volk, Herrscher und Heiliger im Reich der Merowinger* (Praha, 1965), esp. pp. 49, 79-80, 84; J. Fontaine, "Bible et hagiographie dans le royaume Franc mérovingien

It is possible that Gregory favoured such miracles because of their greater credibility. In book two, for example, Peter expresses some doubt when told that Benedict once appeared in a dream to the abbot and prior of the monks of Terracina, and instructed them where to locate the various monastic buildings. However, his anxiety is quickly abated when Gregory confirms the tale by pointing to a Biblical parallel.[3] Gregory also could have been drawn to miracles with Biblical precedents in order to illustrate God's continuing concern for his people. Indeed, it has frequently been suggested that this was an important purpose the miracles of the *Dialogues* in general were designed to serve.[4] They function to mitigate the impact of death, illness, want and natural disaster, and effectively demonstate that, despite the troubled circumstances of sixth-century Italy, God has not abandoned the Christian people. Peter himself acknowledges the consoling effect that miracles could have in the society of his time. Even though we are in great distress, he says, these amazing miracles testify that we are not forsaken by our Creator.[5]

(600-750)," *ABoll.* 97 (1979): 387-396. Of course, the Bible exerted a profound influence, not simply on their presentation of miracles, but on the work of the medieval hagiographers in general: cf. J. Leclercq, "L'Ecriture sainte dans l'hagiographie monastique du haut moyen âge," in *La Bibbia nell'alto medioevo* (Spoleto, 1963), pp. 103-128; B. Smalley, "L'exégèse biblique dans la littérature latin," in *La Bibbia nell'alto medioevo*, pp. 631-655, esp. pp. 640-653; E. Dorn, *Der sündige Heilige in der Legende des Mittelalters* (München, 1967), pp. 131-141; G. Penco, "Le figure bibliche del 'vir Dei' nell'agiografia monastica," *Benedictina* 15 (1968): 1-13; M. Van Uytfanghe, "La Bible dans les vies de saints mérovingiennes. Quelques pistes de recherche," *RHEF* 62 (1976): 103-111; "Modèles bibliques dans l'hagiographie," in *Le Moyen Age et la Bible* (Paris, 1984), pp. 449-488; "L'empreinte biblique sur la plus ancienne hagiographie occidentale," in *Le monde latin antique et la Bible* (Paris, 1985), pp. 565-611.

[3] *Dial.* 2.22.4-5, SC 260:204. Peter says: "Manus tuae locutionis tersit a me, fateor, dubietatem mentis." The Venerable Bede would also choose to emphasize the Biblical precedents for some of the wonders attributed to Saint Cuthbert, and for essentially the same reason: cf. *Vita S. Cuthberti*, chaps. 1 and 2, ed. and trans. B. Colgrave, *Two Lives of Saint Cuthbert* (Cambridge, 1940), pp. 156-160.

[4] In particular, see B. de Gaiffier, "Miracles bibliques et vies de saints," in his *Etudes critiques d'hagiographie et d'iconologie* (Brussels, 1967), pp. 50-61, esp. pp. 54-56; de Vogüé, *Introduction*, pp. 136-137. The general thesis is expounded, for example, by Moricca, p. xviii; P. Batiffol, *Saint Gregory the Great* (London, 1929), p. 181; E. Auerbach, *Literary Language and its Public in Late Latin Antiquity and in the Middle Ages* (London, 1965), p. 102; de Gaiffier, "Miracles bibliques," p. 56; Cracco, "Uomini di Dio," esp. pp. 176-177; de Vogüé, *Introduction*, p. 47. Cf. G. Cracco, "Ascesa e ruolo dei 'Viri Dei' nell'Italia di Gregorio Magno," in *Hagiographie, cultures et sociétés, IVe-XIIe siècles* (Paris, 1981), pp. 283-296, esp. p. 290; Petersen, *The Dialogues*, pp. 56-57.

[5] *Dial.* 3.30.7, SC 260:382. Cf. S. Boesch Gajano, "'Narratio' e 'expositio' nei Dialoghi di Gregorio Magno," *BISIAM* 88 (1979): 1-33 at 10-19, where she develops a typology of miracle in the *Dialogues*.

Miracles of all kinds could have been effective in this regard, but those alluding to Biblical exemplars would have been particularly appropriate. In the final analysis, however, the significance of these miracles reaches beyond any conscious purpose Gregory may have had in mind in employing them. As de Gaiffier points out, they are evidence of a "mentalité biblique" that profoundly shaped Gregory's thought,[6] as it did the thought of most other early medieval authors.

Over the years, much has been made of the fact that the Middle Ages lacked a proper sense of the past. More specifically, it is claimed, they lacked the sense of anachronism, the awareness of qualitative differences between the past and the present. As Denys Hay puts it: "'Autre temps, autres moeurs' was a concept which had little real meaning in antiquity and none in the Middle Ages." This broad generalization can probably be accepted only with reservations, but it is not without relevance to Gregory the Great.[7] For modern Christians, a virtually unbridgeable chasm often seems to separate the sacred time of the Old and New Testaments from the secular time in which their own lives are lived. But, like the Venerable Bede, Gregory was aware of no such hiatus in the course of human history.[8] He was, of course, capable of comparing his own period with that of the apostles, and of noting that time had passed and circumstances had changed. In his *Homilies on the Gospels* he admits that the miracles necessary when the church was in its infancy no longer occur with the same frequency now that much of the world has been brought to a knowledge of the true faith.[9] But Gregory saw no radical discontinuity between his own historical period and that of the New Testament, and so was inclined to perceive contemporary events as a direct continuation of the sacred history of the apostolic church. Like the medieval historian as described by Smalley, Gregory lived in an expanding Bible. In relating the miracles of his sainted contemporaries, Gregory felt that he was simply adding one more page to the Gospel story.[10]

---

[6] De Gaiffier, "Miracles bibliques," p. 60.

[7] D. Hay, *Annalists and Historians: Western Historiography from the Eighth to the Eighteenth Centuries* (London, 1977), p. 91; cf. P. Rousset, "La conception de l'histoire à l'époque féodale," in *Mélanges d'histoire du moyen âge dédiés à la mémoire de Louis Halphen* (Paris, 1951), pp. 623-633 at 630; P. Burke, *The Renaissance Sense of the Past* (London, 1969), p. 1. See the qualifications introduced by B. Guenée, *Histoire et culture historique dans l'Occident médiéval* (Paris, 1980), pp. 240-241, 346-350.

[8] Cf. G. Schoebe, "Was gilt im frühen Mittelalter als Geschichtliche Wirklichkeit? Ein Versuch zur 'Kirchengeschichte' des Baeda Venerabilis," in *Festschrift Hermann Aubin zum 80. Geburtstag* (Wiesbaden, 1965), 2:625-651, esp. 642.

[9] *Hom. in Evan.* 1.4.3, PL 76:1090-1091; 2.29.4, PL 76:1215-1216. See above, Chapter 1.

[10] B. Smalley, *Historians in the Middle Ages* (London, 1974), p. 63. Cf. P. Brown, *The Cult of the Saints* (Chicago, 1981), p. 81, who comments on the Biblical quality of the lives of the

This last point has immediate bearing on Gregory's openness to miracles. To a large extent Gregory believed in the miracles of contemporary saints for theological reasons. He believed in modern miracles because he believed in the miracles of the Bible, and he saw no reason to think that God had ceased to intervene directly in human affairs for the benefit of his church. However, equally significant was the fact that the same theological, or more precisely, exegetical principles would govern his interpretation of both Biblical miracles and their modern counterparts. Gregory the theologian believed that underneath the literal surface of the miracles of Scripture there was an allegorical or a spiritual sense it was the duty of the exegete to clarify; Gregory the hagiographer believed that a similar spiritual sense could be found behind the miracles of modern saints. Rather than residing simply in the words of the sacred text, the allegory of the Bible was embedded in the realities themselves which the words served only to describe,[11] and was not, therefore, necessarily limited to the canon of Scripture. Hence, in Gregory's view, modern miracles possessed an allegorical depth comparable to that of their Biblical archetypes, and could serve to illustrate important lessons about Christian life and doctrine. The Gregory of the *Dialogues* is identical to the Gregory of the *Moralia*; he is only working with different material. As de Vogüé puts it, "Au lieu d'interpréter le texte sacré, le pape explique ici l'histoire qu'il raconte."[12]

In his *Homilies on the Gospels* Gregory often observes that Christ's teaching is not limited to exhortation: "Our Lord and Saviour, dearest brethren, admonishes us sometimes by words, but sometimes by deeds. Indeed, these very deeds of his are precepts, because, while doing something in silence, he makes known to us what we ought to do." Such claims are not intended to suggest only that Christ practised what he preached, that his example illustrated *in concreto* the fundamental precepts of the Christian life. They also imply that even minor details in the life of the Saviour are not without significance.[13] In Luke 10:1 we read that, after Christ appointed the seventy-two disciples, he sent them out ahead of him, two by two, to every place and city he planned to visit. Although it may not seem important,

---

saints, maintaining that "the *passio* abolished time. The deeds of the martyr or of the confessor had brought the mighty deeds of God in the Old Testament and the Gospels into his or her own time. The reading of the saint's deeds breached yet again the paper-thin wall between the past and the present."

[11] H. de Lubac, *Exégèse médiévale. Les quatre sens de l'Ecriture*, part 1, vol. 2 (Paris, 1959), pp. 493-498. Cf. H.-I. Marrou, *Saint Augustin et la fin de la culture antique*, 2 vols. (Paris, 1938-1949), p. 650.

[12] De Vogüé, *Introduction*, p. 49.

[13] *Hom in Evan.* 1.17.1, PL 76:1139; cf. 2.31.1, PL 76:1228. See also de Lubac, *Exégèse médiévale*, part 2, vol. 2 (Paris, 1964), pp. 106-123.

Gregory says that the sending out of the disciples in twos has a profound meaning. They were sent out this way because there are two precepts of charity, the love of God and the love of neighbour, and because the exercise of charity requires at least two persons. No one can properly be said to have charity towards himself: by its very definition, charity reaches out to others. Behind the apparently insignificant details of this episode, therefore, there is an important spiritual lesson. In the very act of commissioning the disciples, Christ tacitly admonishes us that those who are not charitable to others should not be entrusted with the office of preaching.[14]

In his more theoretical pronouncements on the issue, Gregory maintains that the process of Scriptural interpretation has three stages, passing from the historical sense, which follows the letter of the text, to the allegorical sense, which applies to Christ or the church, and finally to the moral sense, which clarifies important principles of the Christian life. In practice, however, the author of the *Moralia* is often content to treat two senses rather than three; he frequently limits himself to searching out the inner or spiritual significance of the letter. As the example just given indicates, this spiritual significance is revealed by identifying the appropriate analogy: "Debemus ex rebus exterioribus introrsus aliquam similitudinem trahere."[15] Just as there are two fundamental precepts of charity, so were the disciples sent out in twos. The text of Scripture is able to bear as much meaning as it does because of analogical relationships between orders of reality—on the one hand the

[14] *Hom. in Evan.* 1.17.1, PL 76:1139. Here Gregory seems to have followed the lead of Augustine: see, for example, *In Iohannis Evangelium* 17.6, CCL 36:173: "Binario ergo isto numero cum aliquid boni significatur maxime bipertita caritas commendatur." Cf. D. Hofmann, *Die geistige Auslegung der Schrift bei Gregor dem Grossen* (Münsterschwarzach, 1968), p. 57; P. Catry, "L'amour du prochain chez saint Grégoire le Grand," *SMon.* 20 (1978): 287-344 at 291-293. De Lubac, *Exégèse médiévale* 2.2, pp. 13-15, maintains that the number two generally had negative connotations: "Deux, cela signifie duel, conflit insoluble; c'est brisure, scission, opposition, scandale; c'est le résultat de la fissure qui détruit l'unité" (p. 14). However, this does not seem to have been a view that found much favour with Gregory.

[15] *Hom. in Evan.* 2.39.3, PL 76:1295. On Gregory's threefold model of Scriptural interpretation, see de Lubac, *Exégèse médiévale*, part 1, vol. 1 (Paris, 1959), pp. 187-189; Hofmann, *Die geistige Auslegung*, pp. 7-12. On its influence in later centuries, see R. Wasselynck, "L'influence de l'exégèse de S. Grégoire le Grand sur les commentaires bibliques médiévaux (VIIe - XIIe s.)," *RTAM* 32 (1965): 157-204. On Gregory's exegetical practice, see C. Dagens, *Saint Grégoire le Grand. Culture et expérience chrétiennes* (Paris, 1977), p. 242; cf. Hofmann, *Die geistige Auslegung*, pp. 12-15, 50-53, 72-73; P. Catry, "Lire l'écriture selon Saint Grégoire le Grand," *CCist.* 34 (1972): 177-201 at 185-186. De Lubac, *Exégèse médiévale* 1.2, pp. 405-406, points out that an original and fundamental distinction between two senses was widespread, and that it was not in conflict with the three-fold or four-fold schemes of interpretation.

physical, on the other the moral or spiritual—that modern readers usually prefer to keep distinct.

The basic exegetical rule here described applies, of course, to Christ's miracles as well as to his other deeds. Augustine had maintained that the miracles recorded in Scripture are facts, but facts invested with a certain significance.[16] The miracles of the Saviour are like visible words, he says, the terms of a divine discourse whose meaning is carefully to be determined. Alternatively, they are like the script in a book: to limit oneself to their external features would be tantamount to admiring only the elegance of the hand or the beauty of the characters. Gregory's attitude was very similar. Christ's miracles possess a deeper meaning that must be clarified by analogical reasoning.[17]

Gregory's interpretation of Christ's healing of the woman who had been bent over for eighteen years (Luke 13:11-13) is governed by an analogy between physical and moral deformity. Like the woman, human nature is so bent on earthly things that it is deformed, unable to lift its spiritual eyes to things celestial. This condition, too, can be seen to have lasted for eighteen years. Numerologically, eighteen is the product of six and three: six, representing the sixth and final day of Creation, when man was fashioned from the dust of the earth; and three, representing the three great periods of sacred history—the period before the law, the period under the law, and the period of grace—in which man has existed since the fall from an original state of justice.[18]

When Gregory discusses the miraculous draught of fishes produced by the risen Christ (John 21:1-14), it is an analogy between the harvesting of fish and the winning of souls (probably suggested by Mark 1:17) that enables him to identify the hidden spiritual significance, which has to do with the nature of the church.[19] It is once again a set of analogies that reveals the complex

---

[16] *De div. quaest. octoginta tribus* 65, CCL 44A:147; *Epist.* 102.6.33, CSEL 34.2:572-573; cf. *In Iohannis Evangelium* 9.1, CCL 36:91; *Sermo* 124.1.1, PL 38:687.

[17] Miracles like visible words: see *In Iohannis Evangelium* 25.2, CCL 36:248; 25.5, CCL 36:250; *Sermo* 77.5.7, PL 38:486; *Sermo* 95.3, PL 38:581-582; *Sermo* 130.1, PL 38:725; cf. *Epist.* 102.6.33, CSEL 34.2:573. Miracles like script: see *In Iohannis Evangelium* 24.2, CCL 36:244-245; *Sermo* 98.3.3, PL 38:592. For Gregory's view, cf. *Hom. in Evan.* 1.2.1, PL 76:1082: "miracula Domini et Salvatoris nostri sic accipienda sunt, fratres charissimi, ut et in veritate credantur facta, et tamen per significationem nobis aliquid innuant. Opera quippe ejus et per potentiam aliud ostendunt, et per mysterium aliud loquuntur."

[18] *Hom. in Evan.* 2.31.6, PL 76:1230. Cf. Augustine, *Enar. in Psalmos* 37.10, CCL 38:389; *Sermo* 110.1.1, PL 38:638; 110.2.2, PL 38:639.

[19] *Hom. in Evan.* 2.24.3, PL 76:1185. Cf. Augustine, *De div. quaest. octoginta tribus* 57.2, CCL 44A:101; *In Iohannis Evangelium* 122.7, CCL 36:671-672.

lesson in Christology concealed in Christ's subsequent sharing of a meal with the disciples (John 21:9-14). Gregory notes that in the Gospels it is twice remarked that Christ ate broiled fish after his resurrection: at the occasion described in the text under consideration, and at Luke 24:36-43; and what is mentioned twice, he confidently asserts, must be important: "Non enim vacat a mysterio quod iteratur in facto."[20]

In John 21 we read that Christ ate fish and bread; in Luke 24 that he ate fish and honeycomb. The fish in each case, says Gregory, is a representation of Christ's humanity; more specifically, it represents his passion. Like the fish which, before its capture, lives concealed in the waters of the deep, Christ took it upon himself to conceal his divinity in the waters of human nature, before he was ultimately taken and sacrified on our behalf.[21] The bread and the honeycomb represent Christ's divine nature, as suggested by the bread that came down from heaven of John 6:41; or his nature both human and divine, the honey in the wax suggesting divinity in human form. These episodes, therefore, are allegories of the nature and work of the Redeemer. The eating of fish and bread signifies that, whereas his passion was a function of his humanity, the redemption he purchased for us was a function of his divinity.[22]

More than one scholar has suggested that similarly concealed layers of meaning can be found in Gregory's *Dialogues*, as if they too constituted a kind of sixth-century Bible requiring its own exegete. Vitale-Brovarone, for example, maintains that Gregory's stories possess an allusive quality in their language or their texture that, once deciphered, could clarify many other aspects of the *Dialogues* and possibly alter their interpretation. He refers to the episode in book two in which the monks of Vicovaro attempt to murder St Benedict by offering him a poisoned cup. Since later on in the *Dialogues* we are informed that the cup of Matthew 20:22-23 is a sign of the Passion, Vitale-Brovarone suggests that the story of the attempted poisoning may have

---

[20] *Hom. in Evan.* 2.24.5, PL 76:1186-1187. Cf. Augustine, *In Iohannis Evangelium* 123.2, CCL 36:676.

[21] Gregory's language is actually more graphic, distastefully so by modern standards: "Ipse enim latere dignatus est in aquis generis humani, capi voluit, laqueo mortis nostrae, et quasi tribulatione assatus est tempore passionis suae."

[22] Gregory goes on to say that there is an important moral lesson in these passages as well, particularly, it would seem, in the passage from Luke. Christ partook of both fish and honeycomb to signify that heavenly rest will be the portion of those who, while suffering persecution on the Lord's behalf, do not draw back from the love of his consoling sweetness. Alternatively, his actions demonstrate that those who in this life suffer persecution on his behalf will be rewarded with the sweetness of the delights of heaven in the world to come.

been designed to establish a connection between the life of the saint and the life of Christ.[23]

When the incident is analyzed in its larger context, however, this reading turns out to be not very plausible. After the death of their abbot, Gregory reports, the rather unruly monks of Vicovaro came to Benedict to insist that he become their superior. Benedict tried to discourage them by warning them of the strict discipline he would impose, but finally gave in. Ultimately, however, his worst fears were realized. The monks resented Benedict's rule, reproached themselves for having chosen him, and finally tried to do away with him by poisoning his wine. When, however, the pitcher containing the poison was presented to Benedict for his blessing, it shattered as he made the sign of the cross over it: because of the deadly drink it contained, says Gregory, it could not bear the sign of life.

In all of this Gregory makes no allusion to the life of the Saviour whatever, not even when underlining the lesson of the incident: that the life of the just is a burden to the wicked. Moreover, even if there is an extended parallel between Benedict's life and the life of Christ, the occurrence of this particular episode early in Benedict's ministry makes it inherently unlikely that it is the analogue of the Passion that Vitale-Brovarone suggests. His argument rests primarily on the allusive nature of Gregory's language; but it is certainly not obvious that Gregory intends an allusion to the cup (*calix*) of Matthew 20 when he describes the poisoned vessel offered to Benedict as a glass pitcher (*vas vitreum, in quo ille pestifer potus habebatur*).

Vitale-Brovarone also refers to the episode in book two in which the Devil causes a wall to collapse on a young monk, breaking his bones and apparently killing him. The significance of the story, he suggests, is enhanced when it is read with Gregory's commentary on Job 10:11, where bones are regarded as a representation of virtue. Reading it as a story of the monk's loss of virtue, he maintains, makes it easier to understand why it is the Devil who is responsible for the collapse of the wall, and why Benedict is as fearful of his attacks as he appears to be.[24]

However, this interpretation overlooks the fact that it was Benedict against whom Satan was plotting, not the young monk. The incident is one of several showing the Devil's open if unavailing warfare against Benedict: "the Devil fought against the man of God with renewed violence. But, contrary to his plans, all these attacks only supplied the saint with further opportunities for

---

[23] A. Vitale-Brovarone, "Forma narrativa dei *Dialoghi* di Gregorio Magno: prospettive di struttura," *AAST.M* 109 (1975): 117-185 at 120n. See *Dial.* 2.3.1-5, sc 260:140-142; and 3.26.8, sc 260:370-372.

[24] *Dial.* 2.11, sc 260:172-174.

victory." Hence Gregory concludes the tale by proclaiming: "in spite of the Devil's attempt to mock the man of God by causing this tragic death, the young monk was able to rejoin his brethren and help them finish the wall."[25] Vitale-Brovarone might reply that an assault on the moral integrity of one of his disciples would have been a more effective way of attacking Benedict and undermining his authority than an attack on the young monk's physical well being would have been. But that is not what Gregory says; and given that he supplies no hint that there is additional meaning hidden beneath the surface of his story, it seems perilous to argue that that is what he really meant.

In fairness it should be pointed out that Vitale-Brovarone offers these episodes only as possibilities. More thorough-going attempts to decipher the hidden meaning in the *Dialogues* have been advanced by Wansbrough and Cusack. Cusack discusses the episode of the awkward Goth in the second book of the *Dialogues*. Gregory's story is strikingly similar to a Biblical story of Elisha, he maintains, and so its deeper meaning can be unravelled with the help of the exegesis of the Biblical analogue that Gregory himself provides in the *Moralia*. Although it too rests on the assumption that Gregory dealt in hidden meanings without giving his readers the slightest hint as to how they may be unveiled, his interpretation is not entirely implausible.[26] Wansbrough's argument, however, is somewhat more problematic.

Wansbrough maintains that Gregory gives characters in the *Dialogues* names indicative of the function he chooses them to perform, or of the moral he wishes them to illustrate. Scholastica and Benedict are two obvious examples. Scholastica's name means "contemplation", Benedict's "the bles-sed one". Apparently Wansbrough does not wish to imply that these characters are mere inventions; the question of Scholastica's historicity remains open, and there can be no doubt about the historical existence of her brother. Yet he maintains that Benedict bears his particular name because he represents *the* ideal of a holy man. Whereas in the other books of the *Dialogues* Gregory offers us individual aspects of sanctity, in the second book he presents us with a full portrait of his ideal saint.

Unfortunately, there is a disabling ambiguity in this argument. Does Wansbrough mean that Gregory changed the names of Scholastica and Benedict in the interests of his allegory, or does he mean only that Gregory

---

[25] *Dial.* 2.8.13, Zimmerman 75, sc 260:170; 2.11.2, Zimmerman 76-77, sc 260:174. Cf. *Dial.* 2.8.10, sc 260:166: "Sanctus vir, ad alia demigrans, locum, non hostem mutavit. Nam tanto post graviora praelia pertulit, quanto contra se aperte pugnantem ipsum magistrum malitiae invenit."

[26] P.A. Cusack, "The Story of the Awkward Goth in the Second Dialogue of St Gregory i," *SPatr.* 17 (1982): 472-476. See *Dial.* 2.6, sc 260:154-156.

benefited from the allegorical potential that their names already possessed? His language implies the former alternative; his comments about the historical existence, unequivocal or possible, of these characters imply the latter. Wansbrough never resolves the question, perhaps because he considers it unimportant. In both the *Moralia* and the *Dialogues*, says Wansbrough, Gregory "writes as a moralist, not as a historian; his concern ... is not to conduct historical research but to instruct."[27] Just as Gregory's Scriptural commentaries place their greatest emphasis on the hidden spiritual significance of the text, so must we expect to find a deeper significance in the text of the *Dialogues* as well. Indeed, says Wansbrough, the Scriptural commentaries themselves can provide the clues.

The result of these assumptions is that an episode like Gregory's encounter with Scholastica is shown to possess deeper meaning than anyone had formerly suspected. Says Wansbrough:

> If our first conclusion was correct, that Gregory sees Scholastica as playing in the story of Benedict the role of the very personification of the virtue of Contemplation, then we may learn yet more about the incident from his exposition of the first chapter of Job. When the sons of Job make a feast, each in turn in his own house, it is the seven virtues who in turn provide a banquet, inviting their fellows to partake of their riches. ... When Benedict, therefore, goes to sup with Scholastica, he goes to refresh himself with contemplation, with a day of recollection, as we should say nowadays.[28]

Other incidents in the life of Benedict assume greater significance as well. Wansbrough maintains that the lesson of the miracle in which Benedict produces water from the rock is made explicit later in the *Dialogues* when the saintly hermit Martin performs a similar wonder: it is an indication of God's especial love. But he goes on to claim that the story possesses "a deeper meaning" that needs to be decoded as well, for in the *Moralia* Gregory tells us that water has allegorical significance. In Wansbrough's judgment, therefore, the real meaning of the story is that "Benedict brings forth knowledge of divine things in the hearts of his disciples."[29]

Impressive as all this appears, Wansbrough's evidence is rather weak. If he wants to maintain that Gregory invented the names of Scholastica and Benedict to facilitate his allegory, the point is certainly not an obvious one. Names denoting some virtue or other have always been in common use, as

[27] J.H. Wansbrough, "St. Gregory's Intention in the Stories of St. Scholastica and St. Benedict," *RBén.* 75 (1965): 145-151 at 147.

[28] *Ibid.* See *Dial.* 2.33, SC 260:230-234.

[29] Wansbrough, "St. Gregory's Intention," p. 150. Cf. *Dial.* 2.5, SC 260:152-154, with *Dial.* 3.16.1-2, SC 260:326-328, and *Mor.* 19.6.9, CCL 143A:961.

both these names were in the sixth century.[30] Gregory may indeed have seized upon the allegorical possibilities of the names for his own purpose. But, other than a couple of references to the etymology of "Benedict",[31] there is not much evidence that he actually did so. In itself, the meaning Wansbrough sees in the meeting between Scholastica and Benedict is not implausible. Indeed, Gregory himself tells us that they passed the whole day "singing God's praises and conversing about the spiritual life."[32] But the suggestion that Gregory sought to emphasize the point through the symbolism of Scholastica's name is another matter. If Gregory had been tempted to capitalize on the allegorical potential of her name, the idea of contemplation, as de Vogüé suggests, would not likely have been the first thing to occur to him.[33] Moreover, the only evidence that he was thinking in allegorical terms (the connection between this episode and the *Moralia*) is tenuous in the extreme.

Wansbrough's analysis of the episode of Benedict and the rock is even less plausible, for it is very different from what Gregory himself says his story means. This particular miracle, he declares, was occasioned by complaints from the brethren of three of Benedict's monasteries, who wanted to have their retreats moved from the mountainous terrain in which they were located. Descending the steep mountain slope every day to obtain water, they complained, was a dangerous hardship. Benedict solved their problem by producing a stream at the rocky summit itself, one, Gregory tells us, that was still flowing at his time of writing. The incident reminds Peter of the miracle performed by Moses, and those that follow immediately after in the *Dialogues* suggest other Biblical exemplars.[34] It would seem, therefore, that the main purpose of the story is to demonstrate that, like the saints of the Old and New Testaments, Benedict had been singled out for special favour by God.

The miracle performed by Martin, the hermit, has a similar significance. As soon as he took up residence in the cave that was to serve as his cell, water started to trickle from the rock, and in precisely sufficient quantity—never too

[30] Cf. P.A. Cusack, "St. Scholastica: Myth or Real Person?" *DR* (July 1974), 145-159 at 147; A. de Vogüé, "La rencontre de Benoît et de Scholastique. Essai d'interprétation," *RHSp.* 48 (1972): 257-273 at 261-264.

[31] *Dial.* 2 Prol. 1, SC 260:126: "gratia Benedictus et nomine"; *Dial.* 2.8.12, SC 260:170: "Maledicte, non Benedicte."

[32] *Dial.* 2.33.2, Zimmerman 102, SC 260:230. Cf. *Dial.* 2.33.4, SC 260:232, where, after telling us that Scholastica forced Benedict to spend the night by causing a thunderstorm to erupt, Gregory adds: "factum est ut totam noctem pervigilem ducerent, atque per sacra spiritalis vitae conloquia sese vicaria relatione satiarent."

[33] De Vogüé, "La rencontre," pp. 261-264.

[34] See *Dial.* 2.8.8, SC 260:164-166.

much and never too little—to meet his daily needs. Says Gregory: "Through this miracle almighty God showed how carefully He watched over His saint, for in imitation of the ancient miracle He provided him in the wilderness of his retreat with cool water from a hard rock."[35] There is nothing in any of this to suggest that the production of water signifies the dispensing of sacred knowledge. As Wansbrough notes, Gregory does speak of this significance in the *Moralia*, when he considers the hidden meanings water can possess in Sacred Scripture. However, he mentions several other possibilities as well. As Augustine points out, the figures used in Scripture do not always bear the same meaning. Much depends on the context in which they are employed.[36]

Wansbrough contends that the allegories he has uncovered are clear enough in the text of the *Dialogues*. But the deeper meaning he detects in the episode of Benedict and the rock is far from self-evident, and Gregory himself does nothing to ensure that his reader will grasp it. This is hardly what one would expect, given Gregory's great concern with the religious credibility of his miracle stories. Why would he explain only the more obvious meaning, leaving the deeper significance of the story to go unremarked? Why would an author who took such pains in uncovering the hidden, spiritual sense of the events in Scripture neglect hidden levels of meaning in the events recorded in his own *Dialogues*? Surely this would only have meant that the majority of his readers would have been spiritually impoverished, especially if, as Wansbrough also contends, "the Dialogues are addressed to simple people, to an audience far less sophisticated than the readers of [Gregory's] 'Expositiones'."[37]

This does not mean that the miracles of the *Dialogues* are uniformly different from the miracles of Holy Scripture, that Gregory's stories bear their meaning on the surface as it were, and only Biblical narrative has a deeper, allegorical significance. However, it does suggest that in these matters we should be guided by what Gregory himself says. As Catry reminds us, "Grégoire est un virtuose de l'allégorie, c'est entendu. Mais quand il allégorise, il sait le dire explicitement."[38] If this principle of interpretation is followed, many of the stories in the *Dialogues* do turn out to be perfectly straightforward: the story about Boniface of Ferentis and the minstrel, for example. When this man of God was angered, the consequences were

---

[35] *Dial.* 3.16.2, Zimmerman 141, sc 260:328.

[36] *Mor.* 19.6.9, CCL 143A:961: "Aquae in scriptura sacra aliquando sanctum Spiritum, aliquando scientiam sacram, aliquando scientiam pravam, aliquando tribulationem, aliquando defluentes populos, aliquando mentes fidem sequentium designare solent." Cf. Augustine, *De doctrina christiana* 3.25.35, CCL 32:97-98; *Enar. in Psalmos* 8.13, CCL 38:57.

[37] Wansbrough, "St. Gregory's Intention," p. 150.

[38] Catry, "L'amour du prochain," p. 304n.

dreadful. Men of God, therefore, are to be revered as the temples of God, and should not be provoked to wrath.[39] In several other cases, however, the miracle story not only makes a point but demonstrates it symbolically, so that the significance of the miracle is reinforced by the structure or language of the narrative itself.

One interesting example occurs in the story of the meeting of Benedict and Scholastica we have just been considering. As was his custom on her yearly visits, Benedict went to meet his sister at a house that belonged to the monastery, where they spent the whole day in prayer and conversation about the spiritual life. When darkness was about to set in, Scholastica asked her brother to stay until morning, so that they could continue their talk. Benedict refused, because of his responsibilities back at the monastery. But Scholastica had her way; she folded her hands on the table, rested her head upon them, and produced, through the force of prayer alone, such a downpour that Benedict had to relent. The sky had been cloudless, but "the thunderstorm was already resounding as she raised her head from the table. The very instant she ended her prayer the rain poured down." Gregory uses this story to illustrate both the efficacy of prayer and the fact that the holy do not always obtain what they desire. Because of her very great love, Scholastica's influence with God was greater on this occasion. What is of special note, however, is that the point is underlined by a curious parallelism between the tears of Scholastica and the downpour she produced: "*By shedding a flood of tears* while she prayed," says Gregory, "this holy nun had darkened the cloudless sky with a heavy rain."[40]

---

[39] *Dial.* 1.9.8-9, SC 260:82-84.

[40] *Dial.* 2.33.3, Zimmerman 103 (emphasis added), SC 260:232. Note especially: "Sanctimonialis quippe femina, caput in manibus declinans, lacrimarum fluvios in mensam fuderat, per quos serenitatem aeris ad pluviam traxit." J. Laporte, "Saint Benoît et les survivances du paganisme," in *Etudes Ligériennes d'histoire et d'archéologie médiévales* (Auxerre, 1975), pp. 233-246, at pp. 243-244, maintains that Benedict and his companions originally perceived this wonder as an example of sympathetic magic, which is what explains Benedict's astonished reaction: "Parcat tibi omnipotens Deus, soror. Quid est quod fecisti?" Benedict's fear was that the shedding of tears, presumably accompanied by some sort of magical incantation, had itself produced the rain. Only subsequently did the miracle come to be seen in characteristically Christian terms as a product of prayer. Laporte's thesis needs to be taken seriously. De Vogüé, "La rencontre," esp. pp. 258-259, argues that Benedict would have clearly understood the Christian nature of the prodigy from the outset. He reacted as he did, says de Vogüé, not because he feared that the rain had been produced by magic, but rather because it meant that he would not be able to return to the monastery, and therefore would be in violation of the rule. This is certainly how Gregory himself would have us understand the episode. However, I'm not sure that it is easily reconcilable with the moral portrait of Benedict Gregory himself provides throughout the second book of the *Dialogues*. As Laporte observes: "Voilà un homme qui est témoin, si l'on suit l'interprétation traditionnelle de l'anecdote, d'un miracle

Book three of the *Dialogues* seems particularly rich in other examples. Thus the archdeacon who was impatient to replace Sabinus, the saintly Bishop of Canossa, conspired with one of the servants to poison him, but the plan backfired. When Sabinus made the sign of the cross over the cup offered him, and consumed its poisoned contents, it was the archdeacon who died. "Though he was in a different place," says Gregory, "it seemed as if the poison had passed from the bishop's lips into the archdeacon's body. The actual poison had no power to kill the one, while the other, by a sentence of the eternal Judge, *perished by the poison of his own malice*." In another, especially effective, example, the analogy is reversed. Cerbonius, Bishop of Populonia, whom Totila, the Gothic king, had condemned to death, was to be devoured by a wild bear specially chosen for the occasion. But instead of showing its innate ferocity, the beast humbled itself before the bishop and licked his feet. "The hearts of men had been brutal toward the bishop," says Gregory, "while the brute beast acted with a heart almost human."[41]

In a third example from this same book Gregory tells of the wonders that occurred when an Arian church was consecrated to the Catholic faith. A large crowd had gathered, and some of those who were outside the sanctuary were disturbed by a pig scurrying around at their feet. Although they could not see it, they could feel it, and as it made its way out through the door its significance became clear: "In this way," says Gregory, "God helped us to realize that the unclean spirit had departed from the building." Among other remarkable occurrences, Gregory observes, "the unlit lamps hanging in the

---

éclatant, qu'il sait accordé par Dieu aux prières de sa soeur; et ce paragon d'humilité va faire la moue, et reprocher en somme au Seigneur d'avoir négligé ses sacrosaints règlements monastiques et ses idées sur la régularité! Quelle inconscience et quel orgueil!" I'm not sure that it does justice to the vehemence of Benedict's reaction either. "May God forgive you," he says to his sister. "What have you done?" Why would God's forgiveness be required for a miracle that God himself had sanctioned? It is impossible to be certain here, but beneath the surface of Gregory's story, and despite Gregory's own understanding of its meaning, there may indeed be discernible vestiges of a primitive magical tradition. If that is the case, it is perhaps noteworthy that, as Fraser points out, sympathetic or imitative magic is premised on the notion that like produces like. The gestures of the magician imitate the effect he desires to produce; the one is an analogue of the other. See J.G. Frazer, *The Golden Bough: A Study in Magic and Religion*, 3rd. ed., part 1: *The Magic Art and the Evolution of Kings*, 2 vols. (London, 1911), esp. 1:174. In Gregory's finished version of this particular story, the analogical relationship between the tears and the rain on which the magic was originally premised has been retained. But in the process of Christianization its character has changed. Gregory does not draw on it to explain a causal relationship—the tears do not actually *produce* the rain—but rather to provide the texture for a symbolic one.

[41] *Dial.* 3.5.4, Zimmerman 119 (emphasis added), sc 260:276; 3.11.2, Zimmerman 126, sc 260:292.

church were lighted by a fire sent from heaven." A few days later the same miracle was repeated: "The sacristan had put out the lamps after Mass and had left the church. In a little while he re-entered, to find them burning. Thinking he had forgotten to extinguish them, he took special care this time that not a single lamp should be left burning. Then he went out and locked the door. When he came back again after three hours, he once more found them burning. *It was now clear to him that this place had passed from darkness to light.*"[42]

Of all the examples that might be cited, the story of the saintly priest Sanctulus is particularly revealing. Worried about how in a time of famine he would provide bread for the large number of labourers he had hired to rebuild the church of St Lawrence, he one day came upon an oven, and to his surprise found it contained a large, unusually white loaf of bread that none of the neighbourhood women claimed as hers. When the bread was offered to the workmen and they had taken their fill, the fragments left over amounted to more than the original loaf. Multiplying itself many times, this one loaf was enough to feed the workmen for ten days. Each time it was served they were left with more fragments of bread than they had had when they began. At the end of the story Peter comments on the similarity between this miracle and the one of our Lord. But it is Gregory who finishes the thought: "In this case, Peter, it was through His servant that Christ fed a large crowd with one loaf of bread. He himself had personally satisfied five thousand men with five loaves. He continues even today to multiply a few kernels of grain into a bountiful harvest. And He who makes the seed spring up from the ground is the same One who created everything out of nothing." The Biblical parallel is more than obvious. The important point is that the story teaches that God provides for those who put their trust in him, and its lesson is made more compelling by the symbolism.[43]

Comparable miracle stories can be found in the works of other early medieval authors as well. After describing how Cuthbert once imitated a miracle of Bishop Marcellinus of Ancona by turning back the flames that were threatening to engulf an entire town, Bede declares that the power such men demonstrate over the strength of fire is scarcely to be wondered at: "By daily practice of virtue they learned both to overcome the lusts of the flesh and '*to quench all the fiery darts of the wicked one*'." Gregory of Tours tells us that Quirinus, Bishop of Siscia, suffered martyrdom during the persecution of Diocletian. A millstone was fastened around his neck and he was thrown

---

[42] *Dial.* 3.30.3, 6, Zimmerman 164-165 (emphasis added), SC 260:380, 382.
[43] *Dial.* 3.37.8, Zimmerman 180-181, SC 260:416.

into a river, but miraculously Quirinus floated on the surface. In virtue of his blameless life, says Gregory, there was no weight of sin to drag him down.[44]

The force of such examples is that miracles in contemporary history can have a resonance similar to those in sacred history. Not only do they possess spiritual significance, but on occasion at least they reveal it in their very structure, or in the language with which they must be described. The relationship between a miracle event, which pertains to the natural order, and its significance, which pertains to the spiritual order, is often mediated by analogies between the two realms. This has interesting implications: it seems to presuppose that reality is structured in such a way that the moral or spiritual order is reflected in the physical order, that the one is an analogue of the other; it seems to imply a holistic view of reality in which the most basic connections are not causal but analogical.

This view was not unique to Gregory and a few other early medieval thinkers, but typical of the entire Middle Ages. Its roots reach back into antiquity, and it is still discernible in the literature of the Renaissance. It seems to have been particularly prominent in the twelfth century, in a period often thought to have witnessed the rekindling of scientific interest in the processes of nature after several centuries of eclipse.[45] An especially striking example is provided by the Anglo-Saxon *Handboc* of Byrhtferth, written half a century before the Norman Conquest. Among other things, Byrhtferth discusses numbers:

> The number four is a perfect number, and it is adorned with four virtues—righteousness, temperance, fortitude, and prudence. The number is also crowned with the four seasons of the year, whose names are: spring, summer, autumn and winter. It is also adorned with the doctrines of the four Evangelists, who are said to be the four animals in the Book of Ezechiel, the famous prophet. The number four is reverently upheld by the four letters in the name

---

[44] Bede, *Vita S. Cuthberti*, chap. 14, Colgrave 202-203 (emphasis added). The analogy was suggested by Eph. 6:16. Gregory of Tours, *Historia Francorum* 1.35, MGH, SRM 1, p. 26: "Igitur cum cecidisset in gurgite, diu super aquas divina virtute ferebatur, nec sorbebant aquae, quem pondus criminis non praemebat." Cf. *Historia Francorum* 2.3, 2.34, MGH, SRM 1, pp. 42-43, 83. See also G. de Nie, "The Spring, the Seed and the Tree: Gregory of Tours on the Wonders of Nature," *JMH* 11 (1985): 89-135.

[45] See A.J. Gurevich, *Categories of Medieval Culture* (London, 1985), pp. 292-294. On the ancient world, see R. Bloch, *Les prodiges dans l'antiquité classique* (Paris, 1963), pp. 4-6, 19. On the early Christian tradition, see D.S. Wallace-Hadrill, *The Greek Patristic View of Nature* (New York and Manchester, 1968), esp. p. 122ff; and more recently, M.J. Curley, "'Physiologus', *physiologia* and the Rise of Christian Nature Symbolism," *Viator* 11 (1980): 1-10. See also M.D. Chenu, *Nature, Man and Society in the Twelfth Century* (Chicago and London, 1968), pp. 99-145; and J.M. Steadman, *Nature into Myth: Medieval and Renaissance Moral Symbols* (Pittsburgh, 1979).

of God, that is to say, D, E, U, S, and likewise by the name of the first created man, namely, ADAM. Fittingly it has an attraction which I do not think ought to be passed over in silence—I mean the fact that there are two equinoxes and two solstices. There are indeed four principal winds, whose names are these: the east, west, north and south winds. There are four elements: air, fire, water, and earth. There are four regions of the world, viz. east, west, north and south. If these parts are carefully studied, they will be found in the name of ADAM, according to Greek numeration. For the Greeks term the east *Anatole*, and the west *Dysis*, and the north *Arktos*, and the south *Mesembrion*.[46]

In Byrhtferth's hands, analogical thinking becomes a powerful tool, powerful enough to enable him to transcend what to most modern minds are clearly distinct and separate orders of reality, and to consider phenomena as disparate as the four elements, the four Gospels, and the four cardinal virtues as if they all existed on the same plane. Analogues one of another, they call one another to mind, with the result that the universe becomes a vast allegory in which physical reality constantly summons us to the transcendent. However, Byrhtferth is only a representative of a much wider trend. Late medieval examples also could be cited. *The Quest of the Holy Grail*, and perhaps even more clearly, Dante's *Paradiso*, where the hierarchy of the heavenly spheres is paralleled by the hierarchy of the virtues, and where physical ascent becomes an allegory of moral ascent through the various stages of the Christian life, come to mind. To medieval theologians the realm of nature is like a book, and the various creatures it contains like so many words or letters bearing the meaning inscribed in them by God. Augustine invests the commonplace with eloquent meaning: "May the sacred page be your book, so that you may hear. ... May the sphere of the earth be a book for you, so that you may see. ... Only those with a knowledge of letters read those books of Scripture. But even the uneducated may read in the book of the whole world."[47]

---

[46] Quoted in Charles Singer, "The Dark Age of Science," in L.P. Williams and H.J. Steffens, *The History of Science in Western Civilization* 1: *Antiquity and Middle Ages* (Washington, 1977), pp. 239-250 at 244-245. Not all of this was simply a product of Byrhtferth's fertile imagination. On the significance of the name of Adam, cf. Augustine, *In Iohannis Evangelium* 9.14, CCL 36:98.

[47] *Enar. in Psalmos* 45.7, CCL 38:522: "Liber tibi sit pagina divina, ut haec audias; liber tibi sit orbis terrarum, ut haec videas. In istis codicibus non ea legunt, nisi qui litteras noverunt; in toto mundo legat et idiota." Cf. de Lubac, *Exégèse médiévale* 1.1, p. 124; 2.2, pp. 173-181; T. Gregory, "L'idea di natura nella filosofia medievale prima dell'ingresso della fisica di Aristotele," in *La filosofia della natura nel medioevo* (Milan, 1966), pp. 27-65, esp. 27-28; C. Bologna, "Natura, miracolo, magia nel pensiero cristiano dell'alto medioevo," in *Magia. Studi di storia delle religioni in memoria di Raffaela Garosi* (Rome, 1976), pp. 253-272, esp. p. 254.

It is sometimes said, with particular reference to the early Middle Ages, that people who thought in this way were incapable of perceiving the world in causal terms. But a few examples should be sufficient to show that this was clearly not the case.[48] Although he was inclined to read nature allegorically, the Venerable Bede also believed in nature's regularity, and subjected the natural realm to careful empirical observation. Although Isidore of Seville was primarily attracted by the allegorical significance of the heavens, the very treatise in which his allegorizing tendencies are particularly prevalent, the *De natura rerum*, is also very much in the tradition of ancient astronomy. Isidore's interest in the allegorical potential of heavenly phenomena did not preclude a desire to explain these same phenomena for their own sake. The same capacity for viewing the natural realm both allegorically and scientifically was equally evident in the twelfth century. As Chenu remarks, even for William of Conches, "the philosopher of Chartres most interested in nature, the universe, however fully explained it might come to be, remained a sacramental projection of the divine thought."[49]

The point is confirmed by the example of Gregory the Great himself. Because Gregory sees the world as a sacramental allegory, the parts of which are related by analogical thinking, his mind is drawn in the first instance to contemplate the divinely established significance of things rather than their place in the causal order. This explains his tendency to see even natural phenomena as produced by God; their causal relationships notwithstanding, God alone provides them with meaning. But in Gregory's thought the analogical perspective supplements the causal, rather than replacing it. Just as allegorical exposition of Scripture is not incompatible with its literal interpretation, so an allegorical treatment of nature does not necessarily exclude the possibility of viewing it scientifically.[50] Unlike us moderns, however, Gregory could never have been convinced of the self-sufficiency of

---

[48] The point is not as widely recognized as it should be. But see R. Grégoire, "Il contributo dell'agiografia alla conoscenza della realtà rurale," in *Medioevo rurale* (Bologna, 1980), pp. 343-360, esp. 359; G.C. Garfagnini, "La cosmologia altomedievale," in *La cultura in Italia fra tardo antico e alto medioevo* (Rome, 1981), 2:745-753, esp. 751; and especially A.M. Torchio, "L'osservazione della natura nell'alto medioevo. Il contributo dei benedettini," *SCat.* 110 (1982): 254-271.

[49] Chenu, *Nature, Man and Society*, p. 129. On Bede, see, for example, T.R. Eckenrode, "Venerable Bede's Theory of Ocean Tides," *ABR* 25 (1974): 56-74. On Isidore, see J. Fontaine, *Isidore de Séville et la culture classique dans l'Espagne wisigothique* (Paris, 1959), pp. 585, 597. Fontaine also points out (pp. 587, 813-814) that it is only in the *De natura rerum* that the allegorical treatment of the heavens is prevalent. In the encyclopedia Isidore considers the heavenly bodies from a more strictly scientific point of view.

[50] Cf. de Lubac, *Exégèse médiévale* 1.2, pp. 662-667, esp. p. 662.

science, for he perceived the world scripturally.[51] He thought of it as another book of the Bible, and believed his basic exegetical principles could be extended to the realm of nature as well. To Gregory's mind, the world is not, or not simply, a machine functioning on its own; it is a realm in which God converses with us by means of the very structure he has posited in things, and it is open at any moment to his direct intervention.

[51] On the centrality of the Bible to Gregory's whole perspective, cf. R. Manselli, "Gregorio Magno e la Bibbia," in *La Bibbia nell'alto medioevo* (Spoleto, 1963), pp. 67-101; *Gregorio Magno* (Torino, 1967), pp. 115-137; B. Calati, "S. Gregorio Magno e la Bibbia," in *Bibbia e spiritualità* (Rome, 1967), pp. 121-178. Even on purely administrative matters Gregory's point of view was dominated by Sacred Scripture: see V. Recchia, *Gregorio Magno e la società agricola* (Rome, 1978), esp. pp. 115-137.

Appendix A
The Sources of the *Dialogues*: An Alphabetical Register

Individuals who are not named as sources, but can reasonably be assumed to be such from the context, are marked with an asterisk.

*Albinus, bishop of Rieti	*Dial.* 1.4.9-19, sc 260:46-56
Ammonius, a monk of St Andrew's	*Dial.* 4.27.9-14, sc 265:92-94
Aptonius, *vir inlustris*, a layman	*Dial.* 2.26, sc 260:214
Athanasius, identified as a priest from Isauria, but a monk as well	*Dial.* 4.40.10-12, sc 265:144-146
Boniface, a monk of St Andrew's	*Dial.* 3.29.1-4, sc 260:376-378
*Castorius, probably a monk	*Dial.* 1.4.8, sc 260:44
Constantine, abbot of Monte Cassino	Cf. *Dial.* 2. Prol. 2, sc 260:128
*Copiosus, a physician and layman	*Dial.* 4.57.8-17, sc 265:188-194
Deusdedit, *honestus senex*, probably a layman. He is said to be a friend of the nobility.	*Dial.* 4.32.1-5, sc 265:106-108
Eleutherius, abbot of St Mark's at Spoleto	*Dial.* 3.14.1-3, 4-7, 8, 9, sc 260:302-304, 304-308, 308-310, 310; *Dial.* 3.21.1-5, sc 260:352-356; *Dial.* 3.33.1-6, sc 260:392-396; *Dial.* 4.36.1-6, sc 265:116-120
Felix, bishop of Porto	*Dial.* 4.27.6-8, sc 265:90-92; *Dial.* 4.53.1-3, sc 265:178; *Dial.* 4.57.3-7, sc 265:184-188
Felix, prior of Fondi	*Dial.* 1.3.1-5, sc 260:34-36
Floridus, bishop of Città di Castello	*Dial.* 3.13.1-4, sc 260:298-302; *Dial.* 3.35.1, 2, 3-5, sc 260:404, 404, 404-406
Fortunatus, abbot of Cicero's Bath	*Dial.* 1.4.1-2, 3-6, 7, 21, sc 260:38, 38-42, 42-44, 56-58; *Dial.* 1.11, sc 260:110-112; *Dial.* 1.12.1-3, sc 260:112-114

Gaudentius, a priest

Dial. 1.9.1-5, 8-9, 10-13, 14, sc
260:76-80, 82-84, 84-88, 88

Honoratus, abbot of Subiaco

Cf. *Dial.* 2 Prol. 2, sc 260:128; *Dial.*
2.15.4, sc 260: 184

John, vice-prefect of Rome

Dial. 3.10.1-4, sc 260:288-290; *Dial.*
4.54.1-2, sc 265:178-180

John, a tribune

Dial. 3.19.1-4, sc 260:346-348

Julian, *defensor* of the church of Rome

Dial. 1.10.1-5, 6-7, 8, 9-10, sc
260:92-96, 96-100, 100, 100-102;
Dial. 4.31.1-4, sc 265:104-106

Laurio, a monk

Dial. 1.7.1-2, 3-4, 4-6, sc 260:64-68,
68, 68-70; *Dial.* 1.8.1-4, sc
260:70-72

Lawrence, *religiosus vir*, probably a
layman

Dial. 1.1.3-4, sc 260:20; *Dial.* 1.2.1-3,
4, 5-7, 8-12, sc 260:24-26, 26,
26-30, 30-34

Liberius, *vir nobilissimus*, a layman of
high rank

Dial. 4.55.1-4, sc 265:180-182

Maximian, bishop of Syracuse, former
abbot of St Andrew's

Dial. 1.7.1-2, 3-4, 4-6, sc 260:64-68,
68, 68-70; *Dial.* 3.36.1-5, sc
260:408-410; *Dial.* 4.33.1-5, sc
265:108-112

Pelagius II, pope

Dial. 3.16.1-2, 3-4, 5, 6, 7-8, 9-10, sc
260:326-328, 328-330, 330,
330-332, 332-334, 334-336

Peregrinus, a monk, Benedict's disciple

Dial. 2.27.1-2, sc 260:214-216

Peter, abbot of St Andrew's

Dial. 4.49.4-5, sc 265:170

*Pretiosus, prior of St Andrew's

Dial. 4.57.8-17, sc 265:188-194

Probus, abbot of the monastery of
Renatus in Rome

Dial. 4.13.1-4, sc 265:52-54; *Dial.*
4.18.1-4, sc 265:70-72; *Dial.*
4.20.1-4, sc 265:74-76; *Dial.*
4.40.6-9, sc 265:142-144

Quadragesimus, subdeacon of the
church at Baxentium

Dial. 3.17.1-5, sc 260:336-340

Redemptus, bishop of Ferentis

Dial. 3.38.1-5, sc 260:428-432

Sanctulus, a priest	*Dial.* 3.15.1-8, 11-12, 18-19, SC 260:314-320, 320-322, 326; *Dial.* 3.37.1-3, 4-8, 9-20, SC 260:410-414, 414-416, 416-426
Simplicius, abbot of Monte Cassino	Cf. *Dial.* 2 Prol. 2, SC 260:128
Speciosus, a priest	*Dial.* 4.16.1-7, SC 265:62-68
Stephen, an abbot	*Dial.* 4.12.1-5, SC 265:48-52
Stephen, *inlustris vir*, a layman of high rank	*Dial.* 4.37.5-6, SC 265:128
Theodore, a layman, sacristan of the church at Palestrina	*Dial.* 3.24.1-3, SC 260:362-364
Valentinian, abbot of the Benedictine monastery at the Lateran	Cf. *Dial.* 2 Prol. 2, SC 260:128
Valentio, abbot of St Andrew's, former abbot in Valeria	*Dial.* 1.4.20, SC 260:56; *Dial.* 3.22.1-4, SC 260:356-358; *Dial.* 4.22.1-2, SC 265:78
Venantius, bishop of Luni	*Dial.* 3.9.1-3, SC 260:286-288; *Dial.* 3.10.1-4, SC 260:288-290; *Dial.* 3.11.4-6, SC 260:294-296; *Dial.* 4.55.1-4, SC 265:180-182

Appendix B
The Sources of the *Dialogues*: An Analysis by Episode

BOOK ONE

Dial. 1.1.1-2, SC 260:18-20	Anonymous; elderly men who are highly respected: *Seniorum valde venerabilium didici relatione quod narro*
Dial. 1.1.3-4, SC 260:20	Lawrence, *religiosus vir,* probably a layman
Dial. 1.1.5-8, SC 260:20-22	Exposition
Dial. 1.2.1-3, SC 260:24-26	The same Lawrence mentioned above
Dial. 1.2.4, SC 260:26	The same Lawrence
Dial. 1.2.5-7, SC 260:26-30	The same Lawrence
Dial. 1.2.8-12, SC 260:30-34	The same Lawrence
Dial. 1.3.1-5, SC 260:34-36	Felix, prior of Fondi
Dial. 1.4.1-2, SC 260:38	Fortunatus, abbot of Cicero's Bath
Dial. 1.4.3-6, SC 260:38-42	The same Fortunatus
Dial. 1.4.7, SC 260:42-44	The same Fortunatus
Dial. 1.4.8, SC 260:44	Probably Castorius, a monk
Dial. 1.4.9-19, SC 260:46-56	Probably Albinus, bishop of Rieti
Dial. 1.4.20, SC 260:56	Valentio, abbot of St Andrew's
Dial. 1.4.21, SC 260:56-58	Fortunatus, abbot of Cicero's Bath
Dial. 1.5.1-2, SC 260:58-60	Anonymous; a bishop who had been a monk in the city of Ancona
Dial. 1.5.3-6, SC 260:60-62	Probably the same anonymous bishop
Dial. 1.6.1-2, SC 260:62-64	No source; but since the story centres in Ancona, possibly the same anonymous bishop
Dial. 1.7.1-2, SC 260:64-68	Maximian, bishop of Syracuse; Laurio, a monk
Dial. 1.7.3-4, SC 260:68	The same Maximian and Laurio
Dial. 1.7.5-6, SC 260:68-70	The same Maximian and Laurio
Dial. 1.8.1-4, SC 260:70-72	No source, but probably the monk Laurio
Dial. 1.8.5-7, SC 260:74-76	Exposition
Dial. 1.9.1-5, SC 260:76-80	Gaudentius, a priest
Dial. 1.9.6-7, SC 260:80-82	Exposition

Dial. 1.9.8-9, SC 260:82-84	Gaudentius, the priest
Dial. 1.9.10-13, SC 260:84-88	The same Gaudentius
Dial. 1.9.14, SC 260:88	The same Gaudentius
Dial. 1.9.15, SC 260:88	Anonymous; an elderly cleric, probably a priest
Dial. 1.9.16-17, SC 260:88-90	The same anonymous cleric
Dial. 1.9.18-19, SC 260:90-92	The same anonymous cleric
Dial. 1.10.1-5, SC 260:92-96	Julian, *defensor* of the church of Rome
Dial. 1.10.6-7, SC 260:96-100	Probably the same Julian
Dial. 1.10.8, SC 260:100	Probably the same Julian
Dial. 1.10.9-10, SC 260:100-102	Probably the same Julian
Dial. 1.10.11-16, SC 260:102-106	Anonymous; a poor, old man
Dial. 1.10.17-19, SC 260:106-110	The same old man
Dial. 1.11, SC 260:110-112	Fortunatus, abbot of Cicero's Bath
Dial. 1.12.1-3, SC 260:112-114	The same Fortunatus
Dial. 1.12.4-7, SC 260:116-118	Exposition

BOOK TWO

In the prologue (*Dial.* 2 Prol. 2, SC 260:128) Gregory mentions four sources on whom his account of Benedict is based: Constantine, abbot of Monte Cassino; Valentinian, abbot of the Benedictine monastery at the Lateran; Simplicius, Benedict's second successor as abbot of Monte Cassino; and Honoratus, abbot of Subiaco. Thereafter he does not mention specific sources except on a few occasions: *Dial.* 2.15.4, SC 260:184 (Honoratus, abbot of Subiaco); *Dial.* 2.26, SC 260:214 (Aptonius, *vir inlustris*, a layman); and *Dial.* 2.27.1-2, SC 260:214-216 (Peregrinus, Benedict's disciple).

BOOK THREE

Dial. 3.1.1-8, SC 260:256-264	Anonymous; *seniores nostri*
Dial. 3.1.9, SC 260:264	The annals of the church of Nola: *apud eius* [i.e. Paulini] *ecclesiam scriptum est.* De Vogüé, *Introduction*, p. 111, identifies this as a reference to Uranius, *Epistula de obitu Paulini.*
Dial. 3.2.1-2, SC 260:266	Anonymous; *religiosi viri*
Dial. 3.2.3, SC 260:268	Anonymous; *seniores nostri*
Dial. 3.3.1-2, SC 260:268-270	Probably the *religiosi viri* mentioned earlier
Dial. 3.4.1-4, SC 260:270-272	Probably the same *religiosi viri*
Dial. 3.5.1-2, SC 260:272-274	Anonymous; *religiosi viri Apuliae provinciae partibus cogniti*

Dial. 3.5.3-4, sc 260:274-276	The same *religiosi viri* from Apulia
Dial. 3.6.1-2, sc 260:276-278	Anonymous; *multi ... de Narniensi civitate*
Dial. 3.7.1-9, sc 260:278-284	Anonymous; the citizenry of Fondi: *nec res est dubia, ... quia paene tanti in ea testes sunt, quanti et eius loci habitatores existunt*
Dial. 3.8.1-2, sc 260:284-286	Anonymous; *religiosi veracesque viri*
Dial. 3.9.1-3, sc 260:286-288	Venantius, bishop of Luni
Dial. 3.10.1-4, sc 260:288-290	The same Venantius; John, vice-prefect of Rome
Dial. 3.11.1-3, sc 260:292-294	Anonymous, but apparently eyewitnesses who are still alive
Dial. 3.11.4-6, sc 260:294-296	Venantius, bishop of Luni
Dial. 3.12.1-4, sc 260:296-298	Anonymous; *quidam clericus senex*
Dial. 3.13.1-4, sc 260:298-302	Floridus, bishop of Città di Castello
Dial. 3.14.1-3, sc 260:302-304	Eleutherius, abbot of St Mark's at Spoleto
Dial. 3.14.4-7, sc 260:304-308	The same Eleutherius
Dial. 3.14.8, sc 260:308-310	The same Eleutherius
Dial. 3.14.9, sc 260:310	The same Eleutherius
Dial. 3.14.10-14, sc 260:310-314	Exposition
Dial. 3.15.1-8, sc 260:314-320	Sanctulus, a priest
Dial. 3.15.9-10, sc 260:320	Exposition
Dial. 3.15.11-12, sc 260:320-322	Probably Sanctulus
Dial. 3.15.13-17, sc 260:322-326	Exposition
Dial. 3.15.18-19, sc 260:326	Probably Sanctulus, although Gregory also refers to townspeople: *cives urbis illius*
Dial. 3.16.1-2, sc 260:326-328	Pope Pelagius II and other *religiosissimi viri*
Dial. 3.16.3-4, sc 260:328-330	Same as above
Dial. 3.16.5, sc 260:330	Same as above
Dial. 3.16.6, sc 260:330-332	Same as above
Dial. 3.16.7-8, sc 260:332-334	Same as above
Dial. 3.16.9-10, sc 260:334-336	Same as above
Dial. 3.17.1-5, sc 260:336-340	Quadragesimus, subdeacon of the church at Baxentium
Dial. 3.17.6-14, sc 260:340-344	Exposition
Dial. 3.18.1-3, sc 260:344-346	Anonymous; a brother in the monastic life: *frater quidam mecum ... in monasterio conversatus*
Dial. 3.19.1-4, sc 260:346-348	John, a tribune

Dial. 3.20.1-2, sc 260:350	Anonymous; *quidam qui nunc nobiscum sunt.* The story concerns a priest named Stephen, who is described as being a relative of Boniface: *nostri Bonifatii diaconi atque dispensatoris ecclesiae.* Boniface was possibly the future Boniface IV.
Dial. 3.21.1-5, sc 260:352-356	Eleutherius, abbot of St Mark's at Spoleto
Dial. 3.22.1-4, sc 260:356-358	Valentio, abbot of St Andrew's
Dial. 3.23.1-5, sc 260:358-360	Anonymous; the monks of the monastery of St Peter at Palestrina
Dial. 3.24.1-3, sc 260:362-364	Theodore, sacristan of the church in Palestrina
Dial. 3.25.1-3, sc 260:364-366	Anonymous; *nostri seniores*
Dial. 3.26.1-2, sc 260:366	Anonymous; witnesses as numerous as the people familiar with the province of Samnium
Dial. 3.26.3, sc 260:366-368	Same as above
Dial. 3.26.4-6, sc 260:368-370	Same as above
Dial. 3.26.7-9, sc 260:370-372	Exposition
Dial. 3.27, sc 260:372-374	Anonymous, but eyewitnesses
Dial. 3.28.1, sc 260:374	No source
Dial. 3.28.2-5, sc 260:374-376	Exposition
Dial. 3.29.1-4, sc 260:376-378	Boniface, a monk of St Andrew's
Dial. 3.30.1-3, sc 260:378-380	Of the four stories in this chapter, the first seems to have been based on popular account, and the others seem to have been derived from the priest and sacristans of the church of St Agatha in Rome. The episodes take place in Rome.
Dial. 3.30.4, sc 260:380-382	See above.
Dial. 3.30.5, sc 260:382	See above.
Dial. 3.30.6, sc 260:382	See above.
Dial. 3.31.1-8, sc 260:384-390	Anonymous; many people from Spain
Dial. 3.32.1-4, sc 260:390-392	Anonymous; an elderly bishop (*senior quidam episcopus*) whom Gregory met in Constantinople
Dial. 3.33.1-6, sc 260:392-396	Eleutherius, abbot of St Mark's at Spoleto
Dial. 3.33.7-9, sc 260:396-398	Gregory himself. Eleutherius relieves his intestinal disorder.

Dial. 3.34.1-6, sc 260:400-404   Exposition
Dial. 3.35.1, sc 260:404   Floridus, bishop of Città di Castello
Dial. 3.35.2, sc 260:404   The same Floridus
Dial. 3.35.3-5, sc 260:404-406   The same Floridus, and an anonymous
                                          young man in charge of the patients
                                          in the hospital

Dial. 3.36.1-5, sc 260:408-410   No source, but undoubtedly Maximian,
                                          bishop of Syracuse and former abbot
                                          of St Andrew's

Dial. 3.37.1-3, sc 260:410-414   Gregory mentions two sources for the
                                          contents of this chapter, which is
                                          devoted to the miracles of Sanctulus,
                                          the priest of Nursia: Sanctulus him-
                                          self, and some anonymous priests of
                                          his area.

Dial. 3.37.4-8, sc 260:414-416   See above.
Dial. 3.37.9-20, sc 260:416-426   See above.
Dial. 3.37.21-23, sc 260:426   Exposition
Dial. 3.38.1-4, sc 260:428-430   Redemptus, bishop of Ferentis
Dial. 3.38.5, sc 260:432   Exposition

BOOK FOUR

Dial. 4.1-7, sc 265:18-42   Exposition
Dial. 4.8, sc 265:42   The disciples of St Benedict
Dial. 4.9.1-2, sc 265:42-44   The disciples of St Benedict
Dial. 4.10, sc 265:44   Anonymous; probably a monk in Grego-
                                          ry's own monastery: *Quidam autem
                                          religiosus atque fidelissimus vir adhuc
                                          mihi in monasterio posito narravit.* ...

Dial. 4.11.1-4, sc 265:44-48   Anonymous; probably a monk: *Adhuc in
                                          monasterio meo positus, cuiusdam
                                          valde venerabilis viri relatione cog-
                                          novi.* ...

Dial. 4.12.1-5, sc 265:48-52   Stephen, an abbot
Dial. 4.13.1-4, sc 265:52-54   Probus, abbot of the monastery of Rena-
                                          tus in Rome

Dial. 4.14.1-5, sc 265:54-58   Anonymous; *personae graves atque fide-
                                          les*, probably nuns

Dial. 4.15.1-5, sc 265:58-62   Anonymous; a monk of St Andrew's
Dial. 4.16.1-7, sc 265:62-68   Speciosus, a priest
Dial. 4.17.1-3, sc 265:68-70   No source; possibly Gregory himself
Dial. 4.18.1-4, sc 265:70-72   Probus, abbot of the monastery of Rena-
                                          tus in Rome

Dial. 4.19.1-5, sc 265:72-74	No source; but the episode took place in Rome three years earlier, and Gregory does mention eyewitnesses.
Dial. 4.20.1-4, sc 265:74-76	Probus, abbot of the monastery of Renatus in Rome, and other saintly men: *alii religiosi viri*
Dial. 4.21, sc 265:78	Exposition
Dial. 4.22.1-2, sc 265:78	Valentio, abbot of St Andrew's
Dial. 4.23.1-2, sc 265:78-80	Anonymous; *quibusdam religiosis quoque viris adtestantibus ...*
Dial. 4.24.1-3, sc 265:80-82	No source
Dial. 4.25-26, sc 265:82-86	Exposition
Dial. 4.27.1-3, sc 265:86-88	No source; but the story concerns a man who had died two years earlier in Rome.
Dial. 4.27.4-5, sc 265:88-90	No source; but the story concerns an event in Gregory's own monastery ten years earlier.
Dial. 4.27.6-8, sc 265:90-92	Felix, bishop of Porto
Dial. 4.27.9-14, sc 265:92-94	Ammonius, a monk of St Andrew's
Dial. 4.28.1-5, sc 265:96-98	Anonymous; common report: *multis ... adtestantibus*
Dial. 4.29-30, sc 265:98-102	Exposition
Dial. 4.31.1-4, sc 265:104-106	Julian, *defensor* of the church of Rome
Dial. 4.32.1-5, sc 265:106-108	Deusdedit, *honestus senex*, probably a layman. He is said to have been on friendly terms with the nobility.
Dial. 4.33.1-5, sc 265:108-112	Maximian, bishop of Syracuse and former abbot of St Andrew's
Dial. 4.34.1-5, sc 265:112-116	Exposition
Dial. 4.35, sc 265:116	Anonymous; probably the monks at St Andrew's. The story seems to concern one of the monks, who died four years earlier.
Dial. 4.36.1-6, sc 265:116-120	Eleutherius, abbot of St Mark's at Spoleto
Dial. 4.36.7-12, sc 265:120-122	Anonymous; some former neighbours. However, cf. de Vogüé, *Introduction*, p. 43n. The story concerns the son of a next-door neighbour Gregory had had while still a layman.
Dial. 4.36.13-14, sc 265:122-124	Exposition
Dial. 4.37.1-4, sc 265:124-128	Anonymous; a monk of Illyria from Gregory's own monastery

Dial. 4.37.5-6, sc 265:128	Stephen, *inlustris vir*, a layman of high rank
Dial. 4.37.7-16, sc 265:128-134	No source, but conceivably the Roman soldier himself whom the story concerns. Gregory tells us that the episode took place in Rome three years earlier, and that it became known to many.
Dial. 4.38.1, sc 265:136	No source; but the story is of Roman provenance and from the recent past.
Dial. 4.38.2-6, sc 265:136-138	Exposition
Dial. 4.39, sc 265:138	Exposition
Dial. 4.40.1-5, sc 265:138-142	No source, but presumably the monks of St Andrew's. The story concerns a monk by the name of Theodore.
Dial. 4.40.6-9, sc 265:142-144	Probus, abbot of the monastery of Renatus in Rome
Dial. 4.40.10-12, sc 265:144-146	Athanasius, identified as a priest of Isauria, but a monk as well
Dial. 4.41.1-6, sc 265:146-150	Exposition
Dial. 4.42.1-5, sc 265:150-154	Anonymous; *a maioribus atque scientibus audivi ...*
Dial. 4.43-47, sc 265:154-168	Exposition
Dial. 4.48, sc 265:168	No source
Dial. 4.49.1-3, sc 265:168-170	No source, but presumably the monks of St Andrew's. The story concerns a monk by the name of Antony.
Dial. 4.49.4-5, sc 265:170	No source, but presumably the monks of St Andrew's. The story concerns a monk by the name of Merulus. It receives some confirmation from Peter, the present abbot.
Dial. 4.49.6-7, sc 265:170-172	No source, but presumably the monks of St Andrew's once again, although Gregory might be taken as implying that he heard the story directly from John, the monk whom it concerns.
Dial. 4.50-52, sc 265:172-176	Exposition
Dial. 4.53.1-3, sc 265:178	Felix, bishop of Porto
Dial. 4.54.1-2, sc 265:178-180	John, vice-prefect of Rome
Dial. 4.55.1-4, sc 265:180-182	Venantius, bishop of Luni; Liberius, *vir nobilissimus atque veracissimus*, a layman

Dial. 4.56.1-3, sc 265:182-184	Anonymous; the dyers of the city of Rome
Dial. 4.57.3-7, sc 265:184-188	Felix, bishop of Porto
Dial. 4.57.8-17, sc 265:188-194	No source, but presumably the monks of St Andrew's. The chapter concerns events that transpired there three years earlier. Gregory himself was involved in these events, and informs us of his role, but he does not seem to have witnessed their miraculous aspects himself. These he learned from others, most likely the prior, Pretiosus, and Copiosus, a lay physician and brother of the monk, Justus.
Dial. 4.58.1-2, sc 265:194-196	No source
Dial. 4.59.1, sc 265:196	No source
Dial. 4.59.2-6, sc 265:196-200	Anonymous; *fideles ... ac religiosi viri*
Dial. 4.60-62, sc 265:200-206	Exposition

Bibliography

<small>PRIMARY SOURCES</small>
Only the editions and translations that have been used are cited.

Apophthegmata patrum latinorum. See *Vitae patrum.*
Athanasius, Saint. *Vita S. Antonii.* PG 26:835-975.
Augustine, Saint. *Confessionum libri XIII.* Ed. Lucas Verheigen. CCL 27. 1981.
——. *Contra Faustum.* Ed. Joseph Zycha. CSEL 25.1:249-797. 1891.
——. *Contra litteras Petiliani libri tres.* Ed. Michael Petschenig. CSEL 52:1-227. 1909.
——. *Contra mendacium.* Ed. Joseph Zycha. CSEL 41:467-528. 1900.
——. ——. Trans. Harold B. Jaffee. The Fathers of the Church 16, pp. 111-179. Washington: Catholic University of America Press, 1952.
——. *De baptismo libri VII.* Ed. Michael Petschenig. CSEL 51:143-375. 1908.
——. *De catechizandis rudibus.* Ed. I.B. Bauer. CCL 46:115-178. 1969.
——. *De civitate Dei.* Ed. Bernard Dombart and Alphonse Kalb. CCL 47, 48. 1955.
——. ——. Trans. Henry Bettenson. Harmondsworth: Penguin Books, 1972.
——. *De consensu Evangelistarum.* PL 34:1041-1230.
——. *De cura pro mortuis gerenda.* Ed. Joseph Zycha. CSEL 41:619-660. 1900.
——. *De diversis quaestionibus ad Simplicianum.* Ed. Almut Mutzenbecher. CCL 44. 1970.
——. *De diversis quaestionibus octoginta tribus.* Ed. Almut Mutzenbecher. CCL 44A:1-249. 1975.
——. *De doctrina christiana.* Ed. Joseph Martin. CCL 32:1-167. 1962.
——. *De Genesi ad litteram.* Ed. Joseph Zycha. CSEL 28:1-456. 1894.
——. ——. Trans. J.H. Taylor. Ancient Christian Writers 41, 42. New York and Ramsey, N.J.: Newman Press, 1982.
——. *De mendacio.* Ed. Joseph Zycha. CSEL 41:411-466. 1900.
——. *De sermone Domini in monte.* Ed. Almut Mutzenbecher. CCL 35. 1967.
——. *De trinitate.* Ed. W.J. Mountain and Fr. Glorie. CCL 50, 50A. 1968.
——. *De utilitate credendi.* Ed. Joseph Zycha. CSEL 25.1:1-48. 1891.
——. *De vera religione.* Ed. K.-D. Daur. CCL 32:169-260. 1962.
——. *Enarrationes in Psalmos.* Ed. D. Eligius Dekkers and Iohannes Fraipont. CCL 38-40. 1956.
——. ——. Trans. (up to Ps. 37) S. Hebgin and F. Corrigan. Ancient Christian Writers 29, 30. Westminster, Maryland: Newman Press; London: Longmans, Green, 1960-1961.

——. *Enchiridion ad Laurentium de fide et spe et caritate.* Ed. E. Evans. CCL 46:21-114. 1969.

——. *Epistula ad catholicos de secta Donatistarum.* Ed. Michael Petschenig. CSEL 52:229-322. 1909.

——. *Epistulae.* Ed. Al. Goldbacher. CSEL 34, 44, 57, 58. 1895-1923.

——. ——. Ed. Johannes Divjak. CSEL 88. 1981.

——. *In Iohannis Evangelium tractatus CXXIV.* Ed. D.R. Willems. CCL 36. 1954.

——. *Quaestionum Evangeliorum libri duo.* PL 35:1321-1364.

——. *Retractationum libri duo.* Ed. Almut Mutzenbecher. CCL 57. 1984.

——. *Sermones.* PL 38, 39.

——. *Sermo 88: Tractatus de duobus caecis.* Pierre-Patrick Verbraken, ed. "Le sermon LXXXVIII de saint Augustin sur la guérison des deux aveugles de Jéricho." *RBén.* 94 (1984): 71-101.

Beda Venerabilis. *De rerum natura.* PL 90:187-278.

——. *Historia ecclesiastica gentis Anglorum.* Ed. and trans. Bertram Colgrave and R.A.B. Mynors. Oxford: Clarendon Press, 1969.

——. *Vita S. Cuthberti.* Ed. and trans. Bertram Colgrave. In *Two Lives of Saint Cuthbert: A Life by an Anonymous Monk of Lindisfarne and Bede's Prose Life,* pp. 141-307. Cambridge: Cambridge University Press, 1940.

Caesarius of Arles. *Sermones.* Ed. D.G. Morin. CCL 103, 104. 1953.

Caesarius of Heisterbach. *Dialogus miraculorum.* Ed. Joseph Strange. 2 vols. Cologne, Bonn and Brussels: J.M. Heberle (H. Lempertz and Co.), 1851.

Constantius of Lyons. *Vita S. Germani.* Ed. René Borius. SC 112. 1965.

Cyprian of Toulon. *Vitae Caesarii episcopi Arelatensis libri II.* Ed. Bruno Krusch. MGH, SRM 3:433-501. 1896.

Dionysius Exiguus. *Vita Pachomii.* PL 73:227-282.

Ennodius of Pavia. *Vita B. Epiphani.* Ed. Guilelmus Hartel. CSEL 6:331-383. 1882.

Eugippius. *Vita S. Severini.* Ed. Pius Knoell. CSEL 9.2. 1886.

Eusebius. *Historia ecclesiastica.* Ed. Eduard Schwartz; Latin version of Rufinus ed. Theodor Mommsen. Die griechischen christlichen Schriftsteller der ersten drei Jahrhunderte 9. 2 vols. Leipzig: J.C. Hinrichs'sche Buchhandlung, 1903-1908.

Gregory of Tours. *De cursu stellarum ratio.* Ed. Bruno Krusch. MGH, SRM 1.2:404-422. 1885.

——. *De miraculis beati Andreae apostoli.* Ed. Max Bonnet. MGH, SRM 1.2:371-396. 1885.

——. *De passione et virtutibus sancti Iuliani martyris.* Ed. Bruno Krusch. MGH, SRM 1.2:112-134. 1885

——. *De virtutibus sancti Martini episcopi.* Ed. Bruno Krusch. MGH, SRM 1.2:134-211. 1885.

——. *Historia Francorum (Historiarum libri X).* Ed. Bruno Krusch and Wilhelm Levison. MGH, SRM 1. 1937-1951.

——. *Liber in gloria confessorum.* Ed. Bruno Krusch. MGH, SRM 1.2:294-370. 1885.

——. *Liber in gloria martyrum.* Ed. Bruno Krusch. MGH, SRM 1.2:34-111. 1885.

——. *Liber vitae patrum.* Ed. Bruno Krusch. MGH, SRM 1.2:211-294. 1885.

——. *Passio sanctorum martyrum septem dormientium apud Ephesum.* Ed. Bruno Krusch. MGH, SRM 1.2:397-403. 1885.

——. ——. Ed. Bruno Krusch. MGH, SRM 7:757-769. 1920.

Gregory the Great. *Dialogorum libri quatuor de miraculis patrum italicorum.* Ed. Umberto Moricca. Fonti per la storia d'Italia pubblicate dall'Istituto storico italiano: scrittori secolo VI. Rome, 1924.

——. ——. Ed. Adalbert de Vogüé. SC 251, 260, 265. 1978-1980.

——. ——. Trans. Odo John Zimmerman. The Fathers of the Church 39. New York: Fathers of the Church Inc., 1959.

——. *Expositio in Canticum Canticorum.* Ed. P. Verbraken. CCL 144:1-46. 1963.

——. *Homiliae in Evangelia.* PL 76:1075-1312.

——. *Homiliae in Hiezechihelem prophetam.* Ed. M. Adriaen. CCL 142. 1971.

——. *In librum primum Regum expositionum libri VI.* Ed. P. Verbraken. CCL 144:47-614. 1963.

——. *Moralia in Iob.* Ed. M. Adriaen. CCL 143-143B. 1979-1985.

——. *Registrum epistularum.* Ed. D. Norberg. CCL 140, 140A. 1982.

——. *Regulae pastoralis liber.* PL 77:13-128.

Hennecke, E. *New Testament Apocrypha.* Ed. W. Schneemelcher; English translation ed. R.McL. Wilson. 2 vols. London: Lutterworth Press, 1963-1965.

Hilary of Arles. *Sermo de vita S. Honorati.* Ed. Marie-Denise Valentin. SC 235. 1977.

Historia monachorum in Aegypto. Ed. A.-J. Festugière. Subsidia hagiographica 53. Brussels: Société des Bollandistes, 1971.

——. ——. Trans. Norman Russell. Oxford: Mowbray; Kalamazoo: Cistercian Publications, 1981.

Isidore of Seville. *Sententiarum libri tres.* PL 83:537-738.

Jerome, Saint. *Commentariorum in Epistolam ad Galatas libri tres.* PL 26:331-468.

——. *Vita Hilarionis.* Ed. A.A.R. Bastiaensen. *Vite dei Santi* 4:69-142. Milan: Fondazione Lorenzo Valla, Arnoldo Mondadori Editore, 1975.

——. *Vita Malchi.* PL 23:55-62.

——. *Vita S. Pauli.* PL 23:17-30.

John Cassian. *Collationes.* Ed. Michael Petschenig. CSEL 13. 1886.

——. *De institutis coenobiorum.* Ed. Michael Petschenig. CSEL 17:1-231. 1888.

Letaldus of Micy. *Vita S. Juliani.* PL 137:781-796.

Orderic Vitalis. *Historia ecclesiastica.* Ed. Marjorie Chibnall. 5 vols. Oxford: Oxford University Press, 1969-1980.
Origen. *Contra Celsum.* Ed. Marcel Borret. SC 132, 136, 147, 150, 227. 1967-1976.

Palladius. *Historia Lausiaca.* Ed. E.C. Butler. Texts and Studies 6. 2 vols. Cambridge: Cambridge University Press, 1898-1904.
——. ——. Trans. Robert T. Meyer. Ancient Christian Writers 34. Westminster, Maryland: Newman Press; London: Longmans, Green, 1965.
Paulinus of Milan. *Vita Ambrosii.* Ed. A.A.R. Bastiaensen. *Vite dei Santi* 3:51-124. Milan: Fondazione Lorenzo Valla, Arnoldo Mondadori Editore, 1975.
Paul the Deacon. *Historia Langobardorum.* Ed. L. Bethmann and G. Waitz. MGH, SRL, pp. 12-187. 1878.
——. *Vita S. Gregorii.* PL 75:41-60.
Peter the Venerable. *De miraculis libri duo.* PL 189:851-954.
Pliny the Elder. *Naturalis historia.* Ed. L. Jahn and C. Mayhoff. 5 vols. Leipzig: B.G. Teubner, 1892-1909.
Pontius. *Vita Cypriani.* Ed. A.A.R. Bastiaensen. *Vite dei Santi* 3:1-48. Milan: Fondazione Lorenzo Valla, Arnoldo Mondadori Editore, 1975.
Possidius of Calama. *Vita Augustini.* Ed. A.A.R. Bastiaensen. *Vite dei Santi* 3:127-240. Milan: Fondazione Lorenzo Valla, Arnoldo Mondadori Editore, 1975.

Quintilian. *Institutio oratoria.* Ed. H.E. Butler. Loeb Classical Library. 4 vols. London: Heinemann; Cambridge, Mass: Harvard University Press, 1920-1922.

Reginald of Canterbury. *Vita S. Malchi.* Ed. Levi Robert Lind. Illinois Studies in Language and Literature 27.3-4. Urbana: University of Illinois Press, 1942.
Rufinus (trans.). *Historia monachorum.* PL 21:387-462.

Sulpicius Severus. *Dialogi.* Ed. C. Halm. CSEL 1:152-216. 1866.
——. *Epistulae.* Ed. Jacques Fontaine. SC 133:316-345. 1967.
——. *Vita S. Martini.* Ed. Jacques Fontaine. SC 133-135. 1967-1969.

Theodoret of Cyrrhus. *Histoire des moines de Syrie (Histoire Philothée).* Ed. Pierre Canivet and Alice Leroy-Molinghen. SC 234, 257. 1977-1979.

Valerius Maximus. *Factorum et dictorum memorabilium libri novem.* Ed. Carolus Kempf. Leipzig: B.G. Teubner, 1888.
Victricius of Rouen. *De laude sanctorum.* Ed. J. Mulders and R. Demeulenaere. CCL 64:53-93. 1985.
Vitae patrum. Book 5, trans. Pope Pelagius I, PL 73:851-992. Book 6, trans. Pope John III, PL 73:991-1024.
Vita patrum Jurensium. Ed. François Martine. SC 142. 1968.

Vita S. Cuthberti. Ed. and trans. Bertram Colgrave. In *Two Lives of Saint Cuthbert*, pp. 59-139 [*see* Beda Venerabilis].

Vita S. Gregorii. Ed. Bertram Colgrave. *The Earliest Life of Gregory the Great by an Anonymous Monk of Whitby.* Lawrence, Kansas: University of Kansas Press, 1968.

SECONDARY SOURCES

Abrahamse, Dorothy de F. "Magic and Sorcery in the Hagiography of the Middle Byzantine Period." *ByzF* 8 (1982): 3-17.

Aigrain, René. *L'hagiographie. Ses sources, ses méthodes, son histoire.* Paris: Bloud and Gay, 1953.

Altman, Charles F. "Two Types of Opposition and the Structure of Latin Saints' Lives." *MHum.* n.s. 6 (1975): 1-11.

Antonius magnus eremita, 356-1956. Studia ad antiquum monachismum spectantia. Ed. Basilius Steidle. *SAns.* 38. Rome: Pontificium institutum S. Anselmi; Herder, 1956.

Arbusow, Leonid. *Colores Rhetorici. Eine Auswahl rhetorischer Figuren und Gemeinplätze als Hilfsmittel für akademischen Übungen an mittelalterlichen Texten.* 2nd. ed. edited by Helmut Peter. Göttingen: Vandenhoeck and Ruprecht, 1963.

Ashe, Geoffrey. *Miracles.* London: Routledge and Kegal Paul, 1978.

Atti del 6° congresso internazionale di studi sull'alto medioevo. Milano, 21-25 ottobre 1978. Spoleto: Centro italiano di studi sull'alto medioevo, 1980.

Aubin, Paul. "Intériorité et extériorité dans les Moralia in Job de saint Grégoire le Grand." *RSR* 62 (1974): 117-166.

Aubrun, Michel. "Caractères et portée religieuse et sociale des 'Visiones' en Occident du VIe au XIe siècle." *CCM* 23 (1980): 109-130.

Auerbach, Erich. *Literary Language and its Public in Late Latin Antiquity and in the Middle Ages.* Trans. Ralph Manheim. London: Routledge and Kegan Paul, 1965.

Babut, Ernest-Charles. *Saint Martin de Tours.* Paris: H. Champion, [1912].

Banniard, Michel. "*Iuxta uniuscuiusque qualitatem.* L'écriture médiatrice chez Grégoire le Grand." In *Grégoire le Grand*, pp. 477-487, with discussion, pp. 487-488.

Bardy, G. "Les miracles contemporains dans l'apologétique de saint Augustin." In *La Cité de Dieu, livres XIX-XXII*, pp. 825-831. Oeuvres de Saint Augustin 37. Paris: Desclée de Brouwer, 1960.

Batiffol, Pierre. *Saint Gregory the Great.* Trans. John L. Stoddard. London: Burns, Oates and Washbourne Ltd., 1929.

Bauerreiss, Romuald. "Religionsgeschichtliches zu Gregors Dialogen." *EuA* 26 (1950): 216-222.

Baynes, Norman H. "St. Antony and the Demons." *JEA* 40 (1954): 7-10.

Bell, Rudolph M. *See* Weinstein, Donald.

Benton, John F. "Consciousness of Self and Perceptions of Individuality." In *Renaissance and Renewal in the Twelfth Century*, ed. Robert L. Benson and Giles Constable, with Carol D. Lanham, pp. 263-295. Cambridge, Mass.: Harvard University Press, 1982.

Bertolini, Ottorino. "I papi e le missioni fino alla metà del secolo VIII." In *La conversione al cristianesimo nell'Europa dell'alto medioevo*, 14-19 aprile 1966, pp. 327-363, with discussion, pp. 537-553. Settimane di studio del Centro italiano di studi sull'alto medioevo 14. Spoleto, 1967.

(*La*) *Bibbia nell'alto medioevo*. 26 aprile-1 maggio 1962. Settimane di studio del Centro italiano di studi sull'alto medioevo 10. Spoleto, 1963.

Bloch, Raymond. *Les prodiges dans l'antiquité classique (Grèce, Etrurie et Rome)*. Paris: Presses universitaires de France, 1963.

Boesch Gajano, Sofia. "Missione, cristianizzazione, conversione. In margine à un recente convegno." *RSCI* 21 (1967): 147-166.

——. ed. *Agiografia altomedioevale*. Bologna: Società editrice il Mulino, 1976.

——. "Il santo nella visione storiografica di Gregorio di Tours." In *Gregorio di Tours*, pp. 27-91.

——. "Dislivelli culturali e mediazioni ecclesiastiche nei *Dialogi* di Gregorio Magno." In *Religioni delle classi popolari*, ed. C. Ginzburg, *QS* 41 (1979): 398-415.

——. "'Narratio' e 'expositio' nei Dialoghi di Gregorio Magno." *BISIAM* 88 (1979): 1-33.

——. "La littérature hagiographique comme source de l'histoire ethnique, sociale et économique de l'Occident européen entre Antiquité et Moyen Age." In *XVe Congrès international des sciences historiques*, Bucarest, 10-17 août 1980, *Rapports II: Section chronologique*, pp. 177-181. Bucharest: Editura academiei republicii socialiste România, 1980.

——. "La proposta agiografica dei 'Dialogi' di Gregorio Magno." *SM* 3rd. ser. 21 (1980): 623-664.

——. "Demoni e miracoli nei 'Dialogi' di Gregorio Magno." In *Hagiographie, cultures et sociétés*, pp. 263-280, with discussion, pp. 280-281.

——. "Il culto dei santi: filologia, antropologia e storia." *SStor.* 23 (1982): 119-136.

——. "La tipologia dei miracoli nell'agiografia altomedievale. Qualche riflessione." *Schede medievali* 5 (1983): 303-312.

——. *See also* Desideri, Paolo.

Boglioni, Pierre. *Pour l'étude du miracle au moyen âge: Grégoire le Grand et son milieu.* Cahiers d'études des religions populaires 16. Montreal: CERP, Institut d'études médiévales, Université de Montréal, 1972.

——. "Miracle et nature chez Grégoire le Grand." In *Cahiers d'études médiévales* 1: *Epopées, légendes et miracles*, pp. 11-102. Montreal: Institut d'études médiévales; Paris: J. Vrin, 1974.

——. "Gregorio Magno, biografo di San Benedetto." In *Atti del 7° congresso internazionale di studi sull'alto medioevo*, Norcia - Subiaco - Cassino - Montecassino, 29 settembre-5 ottobre 1980, pp. 185-229. Spoleto: Centro italiano di studi sull'alto medioevo, 1982.

——. "Spoleto nelle opere di Gregorio Magno." In *Atti del 9° congresso internazionale di studi sull'alto medioevo*, Spoleto, 27 settembre-2 ottobre 1982, 1:267-318. Spoleto: Centro italiano di studi sull'alto medioevo, 1983.

Bologna, Corrado. "Natura, miracolo, magia nel pensiero cristiano dell'alto medioevo." In *Magia. Studi di storia delle religioni in memoria di Raffaella Garosi*, pp. 253-272. Rome: Bulzone editore, 1976.

Bolton, W.F. "The Supra-Historical Sense in the Dialogues of Gregory I." *Aevum* 33 (1959): 206-213.

Bonner, Gerald. "The Extinction of Paganism and the Church Historian." *JEH* 35 (1984): 339-357.

Borghini, B. "Congetture topografiche sul Libro II dei Dialoghi di S. Gregorio." *Benedictina* 19 (1972): 587-593.

Bosl, Karl. *See* Fuhrmann, Horst.

Bouyer, Louis. *La vie de S. Antoine. Essai sur la spiritualité du monachisme primitif.* Abbaye S. Wandrille: Editions de Fontenelle, 1950.

Bowman, Thorlief. *Hebrew Thought compared with Greek.* Trans. Jules L. Moreau. London: SCM Press, 1960.

Boyer, Charles. "La notion de nature chez Saint Augustin." *DCom.* 8 (1955): 65-76.

Boyer, Régis. "An Attempt to Define the Typology of Medieval Hagiography." In *Hagiography and Medieval Literature: A Symposium*, ed. Hans Bekker-Nielsen, Peter Foote *et al.*, pp. 27-36. Odense: Odense University Press, 1981.

Brandt, William J. *The Shape of Medieval History: Studies in Modes of Perception.* New Haven and London: Yale University Press, 1966.

Brazzale, Felice M. *La dottrina del miracolo in S. Agostino.* Rome: Edizioni 'Marianum,' 1964.

Bremond, Claude, Jacques Le Goff and Jean-Claude Schmitt. *L''exemplum.'* Typologie des sources du moyen âge occidental 40. Turnhout: Brepols, 1982.

Brown, Colin. *Miracles and the Critical Mind.* Grand Rapids: Eerdmans; Exeter: Paternoster Press, 1984.

Brown, Peter. *Augustine of Hippo.* London: Faber and Faber, 1967.

——. *The World of Late Antiquity: From Marcus Aurelius to Muhammad.* London: Thames and Hudson, 1971.

——. *Religion and Society in the Age of Saint Augustine.* New York: Harper and Row, 1972.

——. *The Making of Late Antiquity.* Carl Newell Jackson Lectures. Cambridge, Mass.: Harvard University Press, 1978.

——. *The Cult of the Saints: Its Rise and Function in Latin Christianity.* The Haskell Lectures On History of Religions, n.s., 2. Chicago: University of Chicago Press, 1981.

——. *Society and the Holy in Late Antiquity.* Berkeley and Los Angeles: University of California Press, 1982.

Brühl, Carlrichard. "Der ehrbare Fälscher. Zu den Fälschungen des Klosters S. Pietro in Ciel d'Oro zu Pavia." *DAEM* 35 (1979): 209-218.

Burke, Peter. *The Renaissance Sense of the Past.* London: Edward Arnold, 1969.

Bynum, Caroline Walker. "Did the Twelfth Century Discover the Individual?" *JEH* 31 (1980): 1-17.

Calati, Benedetto. "I dialoghi di S. Gregorio Magno (Tentativo di indagine di spiritualità monastica)." *VMon.* 11 (1957): 61-70, 108-116.

——. "S. Gregorio Magno e la Bibbia." In *Bibbia e Spiritualità*, pp. 121-178. Biblioteca di cultura religiosa, ser. 2, 79. Rome: Edizione Paoline, 1967.

——. "L'expérience de Dieu dans la Règle de saint Benoît avec quelques remarques sur l'hagiographie des Dialogues de saint Grégoire." In *L'expérience de Dieu dans la vie monastique*, pp. 138-150. Saint-Léger-Vauban: Les Presses monastiques; Abbaye Sainte-Marie de la Pierre-Qui-Vire, 1973.

——. "Saggio per una lettura dei Dialoghi di S. Gregorio Magno secondo la metodologia del senso spirituale della scrittura inteso dai padri medioevali." In *Lex orandi, lex credendi. Miscellanea in onore di P. Cipriano Vagaggini*, ed. Gerardo J. Békés and Giustino Farnedi, pp. 109-130. *SAns.* 79. Rome: Pontificio Ateneo S. Anselmo; Editrice Anselmiana, 1980.

——. "La 'Vita Silvestri' letta nel confronto con i Dialoghi di S. Gregorio Magno e con la Regola di S. Benedetto." In *Aspetti e problemi del monachesimo nelle Marche*, pp. 363-378. Bibliotheca Montisfani 6, 7. Fabriano: Editiones Montisfani, 1982.

Catry, Patrick. "Epreuves du juste et mystère de Dieu. Le commentaire littéral du *Livre du Job* par saint Grégoire le Grand." *REAug.* 18 (1972): 124-144.

——. "Lire l'écriture selon Saint Grégoire le Grand." *CCist.* 34 (1972): 177-201.

——. "Amour du monde et amour de Dieu chez saint Grégoire le Grand." *SMon.* 15 (1973): 253-275.

——. "Désir et amour de Dieu chez saint Grégoire le Grand." *RAug.* 10 (1975): 269-303.

——. "L'amour du prochain chez saint Grégoire le Grand." *SMon.* 20 (1978): 287-344.

Chadwick, Owen. "Gregory of Tours and Gregory the Great." *JTS* 50 (1949): 38-49.

——. *John Cassian.* 2nd. ed. Cambridge: Cambridge University Press, 1968.

Chapman, John. *Saint Benedict and the Sixth Century.* London: Sheed and Ward, 1929.

Chenu, M.-D. *Nature, Man and Society in the Twelfth Century.* Ed. and trans. J. Taylor and L.K. Little. Chicago and London: University of Chicago Press, 1968.

Christophe, Paul. *Cassien et Césaire. Prédicateurs de la morale monastique.* Gembloux: Duculot; Paris: Lethielleux, 1969.

(*The*) *Church in Town and Countryside.* Ed. Derek Baker. Studies in Church History 16. Oxford: Basil Blackwell, 1979.

Ciccarese, Maria Pia. "Alle origini della letteratura delle visioni: il contributo di Gregorio di Tours." *SSR* 2 (1981): 251-266.

——. "Le più antiche rappresentazioni del purgatorio, dalla *Passio Perpetuae* alla fine del IX sec." *Romanobarbarica* 7 (1982-1983): 33-76.

——. " *Vita Martini* 7: tra miracolo e visione dell'aldilà." *Augustinianum* 24 (1984): 227-233.

Clark, Francis. "The Authenticity of the Gregorian *Dialogues*: A Reopening of the Question?" In *Grégoire le Grand*, pp. 429-442, with discussion, pp. 442-443.

——. *The Pseudo-Gregorian Dialogues.* Studies in the History of Christian Thought 37-38. Leiden: E.J. Brill, 1987.

Clasen, Sophronius. "Das Heiligkeitsideal im Wandel der Zeiten. Ein Literatur-bericht über Heiligenleben des Altertums und Mittelalters." *WW* 23 (1970): 46-64, 132-164.

Colgrave, Bertram. "Bede's Miracle Stories." In *Bede: His Life, Times and Writings*, ed. A. Hamilton Thompson, pp. 201-229. Oxford: Clarendon Press, 1935.

Colish, Marcia L. *The Mirror of Language: A Study in the Medieval Theory of Knowledge.* rev. ed. Lincoln, Nebraska and London: University of Nebraska Press, 1983.

Consolino, Franca Ela. *Ascesi e mondanità nella Gallia tardoantica. Studi sulla figura del vescovo nei secoli IV-VI.* Koinonia: Collana di studi e testi 4. Napoli: M. D'Auria Editore; Associazione di studi tardoantichi, 1979.

Constable, Giles. "Forgery and Plagiarism in the Middle Ages." *ADip.* 29 (1983): 1-41.

Corbett, John H. "The Saint as Patron in the Work of Gregory of Tours." *JMH* 7 (1981): 1-13.

Courcelle, Pierre. *Recherches sur les Confessions de Saint Augustin.* Paris: E. de Boccard, Editeur, 1950.

——. "Les Pères de l'Église devant l'enfers vergiliens." *AHDLMA* 22 (1955): 5-74.

——. "Grégoire le Grand à l'école de Juvenal." *SMSR* 38 (1967): 170-174.

——. "'Habitare secum' selon Perse et selon Grégoire le Grand." *REAnc.* 69 (1967): 266-279.

——. "Saint Benoît, le merle et le buisson d'épines." *JS* (July-September 1967) 154-161.

——. "La vision cosmique de Saint Benoît." *REAug.* 13 (1967): 97-117.

——. *Late Latin Writers and their Greek Sources.* Trans. Harry E. Wedeck. Cambridge, Mass.: Harvard University Press, 1969.

——. *Connais-toi toi-même, de Socrate à saint Bernard.* 2 vols. Paris: Etudes Augustiniennes, 1974-1975.

Cox, Patricia. *Biography in Late Antiquity: A Quest for the Holy Man.* Transformation of the Classical Heritage 5. Berkeley and Los Angeles: University of California Press, 1983.

Cracco, Giorgio. "Uomini di Dio e uomini di chiesa nell'alto medioevo (per una reinterpretazione dei 'Dialogi' di Gregorio Magno)." *RSSR* n.s. 12 (1977): 163-202.

——. "Chiesa e cristianità rurale nell'Italia di Gregorio Magno." In *Medioevo rurale*, pp. 361-379.

——. "Gregorio Magno interprete di Benedetto." In *S. Benedetto e otto secoli (xii-xix) di vita monastica nel Padovano*, pp. 7-36. Miscellanea erudita 33. Padova: Editrice Antenore, 1980.

——. "Ascesa e ruolo dei 'Viri Dei' nell'Italia di Gregorio Magno." In *Hagiographie, cultures et sociétés*, pp. 283-296, with discussion, pp. 296-297.

——. "Gregorio e l'oltretomba." In *Grégoire le Grand*, pp. 255-265, with discussion, pp. 265-266.

Cracco Ruggini, Lellia. "The Ecclesiastical Histories and the Pagan Historiography: Providence and Miracles." *Athenaeum* n.s. 55 (1977): 107-126.

——. "Potere e carismi in età imperiale." *SStor.* 20 (1979): 585-607.

——. "Il miracolo nella cultura del tardo impero: concetto e funzione." In *Hagiographie, cultures et sociétés*, pp. 161-202, with discussion, pp. 202-204.

——. "Gregorio Magno, Agostino e i quattro Vangeli." *Augustinianum* 25 (1985): 255-263.

——. "Grégoire le Grand et le monde byzantin." In *Grégoire le Grand*, pp. 83-93, with discussion, pp. 93-94.

Cremascoli, Giuseppe. *'Novissima hominis' nei 'Dialogi' di Gregorio Magno.* Bologna: Pàtron editore, 1979.

——. "Tradizione esegetica e teologica nell'alto medioevo." In *La cultura in Italia fra tardo antico e alto medioevo*, 2:713-729.

Crombie, A.C. "The Significance of Medieval Discussions of Scientific Method for the Scientific Revolution." In *Critical Problems in the History of Science*, ed. Marshall Clagett, pp. 79-101. Madison, Wisconsin: University of Wisconsin Press, 1962.

——. "The Relevance of the Middle Ages to the Scientific Movement." In *Perspectives in Medieval History*, ed. K.F. Drew and F.S. Lear, pp. 35-57. Chicago: University of Chicago Press, 1963.

(*La*) *cultura antica nell'occidente latino dal VII all' XI secolo.* 18-24 aprile 1974. Settimane di studio del Centro italiano di studi sull'alto medioevo 22. Spoleto, 1975.

(*La*) *cultura in Italia fra tardo antico e alto medioevo.* Atti del Convegno tenuto a Roma, Consiglio Nazionale delle Richerche, dal 12 al 16 novembre 1979. Rome: Herder, 1981.

Curley, Michael J. "'Physiologus', *physiologia* and the Rise of Christian Nature Symbolism." *Viator* 11 (1980): 1-10.

Curtius, Ernst Robert. *European Literature and the Latin Middle Ages.* Trans. Willard R. Trask. 1953. Reprint New York and Evanston: Harper and Row, 1963.

Cusack, Pearse Aidan. "St Scholastica: Myth or Real Person?" *DR* 92 (1974): 145-159.

——. "Some Literary Antecedents of the Totila Encounter in the Second Dialogue of Pope Gregory I." *SPatr.* 12 (1975): 87-90.

——. "The Temptation of St. Benedict: An Essay at Interpretation through the Literary Sources." *ABR* 27 (1976): 143-163.

——. "The Story of the Awkward Goth in the Second Dialogue of St Gregory I." *SPatr.* 17 (1982): 472-476.

——. "Number Games and the Second Dialogue of St Gregory." *SPatr.* 15 (1984): 278-284.

Dagens, Claude. "Grégoire le Grand et la culture: de la '*sapientia huius mundi*' à la '*docta ignorantia.*'" *REAug.* 14 (1968): 17-26.

——. "La 'conversion' de Saint Benoît selon Saint Grégoire le Grand." *RSLR* 5 (1969): 384-391.

——. "La fin des temps et l'église selon saint Grégoire le Grand." *RSR* 58 (1970): 273-288.

——. *Saint Grégoire le Grand. Culture et expérience chrétiennes.* Paris: Etudes Augustiniennes, 1977.

——. "Grégoire le Grand et le monde oriental." *RSLR* 17 (1981): 243-252.

Dagron, Gilbert. "Le saint, le savant, l'astrologue. Etude de thèmes hagiographiques à travers quelques recueils de 'Questions et réponses' des Ve-VIIe siècles." In *Hagiographie, cultures et sociétés*, pp. 143-155, with discussion, pp. 155-156.

Dales, Richard C. "A Twelfth-Century Concept of the Natural Order." *Viator* 9 (1978): 178-192.

Daniélou, Jean. "Les démons de l'air dans la 'Vie d'Antoine.'" In *Antonius magnus eremita*, pp. 136-147.

Dekkers, Eloi. *Clavis patrum latinorum.* rev. ed. Sacris erudiri 3. Bruges: C. Beyaert, 1961.

Delaruelle, Etienne. "La spiritualité des pèlerinages à Saint-Martin de Tours du Ve au Xe siècle." In *Pellegrinaggi e culto dei santi in Europa fino alla Ia crociata*, pp. 199-243. Convegni del Centro di studi sulla spiritualità medievale 4. Todi: Presso l'Accademia Tudertina, 1963.

Delehaye, Hippolyte. "Les premiers 'libelli miraculorum.'" *ABoll.* 29 (1910): 427-434.

——. "Saint Martin et Sulpice Sévère." *ABoll.* 38 (1920): 5-136.

——. "Les recueils antiques de Miracles des Saints." *ABoll.* 43 (1925): 5-85, 305-325.

——. *Sanctus: Essai sur le culte des saints dans l'antiquité.* Subsidia Hagiographica 17. Brussels: Société des Bollandistes, 1927.

——. *The Legends of the Saints.* Trans. Donald Attwater. New York: Fordham University Press, 1962.

Delforge, Thomas. "Songe de Scipion et vision de saint Benoît." *RBén.* 69 (1959): 351-354.

Delling, Gerhard. *Studien zum Neuen Testament und zum hellenistischen Judentum. Gesammelte Aufsätze, 1950-1968.* Ed. Ferdinand Hahn, Traugott Holtz, Nikolaus Walter. Göttingen: Vandenhoeck and Ruprecht, 1970.

Demm, Eberhard. "Zur Rolle des Wunders in der Heiligkeitskonzeption des Mittelalters." *AKG* 57 (1975): 300-344.

Derouet, Jean-Louis. "Les possibilités d'interprétation sémiologique des textes hagiographiques." *RHEF* 62 (1976): 153-162.

Desideri, Paolo, *et al.* "Il culto dei santi." *QS* 19 (1984): 941-969.

Dhanis, E. "Qu'est-ce qu'un miracle?" *Gregorianum* 40 (1959): 201-241.

Dinzelbacher, Peter. *Vision und Visionsliteratur im Mittelalter.* Monographien zur Geschichte des Mittelalters 23. Stuttgart: Anton Hiersemann, 1981.

Dodds, E.R. *Pagan and Christian in an Age of Anxiety: Some Aspects of Religious Experience from Marcus Aurelius to Constantine.* Cambridge: Cambridge University Press, 1965.

Dorn, Erhard. *Der sündige Heilige in der Legende des Mittelalters.* Medium Aevum: Philologische Studien 10. München: Wilhelm Fink Verlag, 1967.

Doucet, Marc. "La tentation de Saint Benoît: Relation ou création par saint Grégoire le grand?" *CCist.* 37 (1975): 63-71.

——. "Pédagogie et théologie dans la 'Vie de saint Benoît' par saint Grégoire le Grand." *CCist.* 38 (1976): 158-173.

——. "'Vera philosophia.' L'existence selon saint Grégoire le Grand." *CCist.* 41 (1979): 227-253.

Drijvers, Han J.W. "Die Legende des heiligen Alexius und der Typus des Gottesmannes im syrischen Christentum." In *Typus, Symbol, Allegorie,* pp. 187-217.

Dudden, Frederick Homes. *Gregory the Great: His Place in History and Thought.* 2 vols. 1905. Reprint New York: Russell and Russell, 1967.

Dufner, Georg. *Die Dialoge Gregors des Grossen im Wandel der Zeiten und Sprachen.* Miscellanea erudita 19. Padua: Editrice Antenore, 1968.

Dulaey, Martine. *Le rêve dans la vie et la pensée de saint Augustin.* Paris: Etudes Augustiniennes, 1973.

Duval, Yvette. *Loca sanctorum Africae. Le culte des martyrs en Afrique du IVe au VIIe siècle.* Collection de l'École française de Rome 58. 2 vols. Rome: Ecole française, 1982.

Eckenrode, Thomas R. "Venerable Bede's Theory of Ocean Tides." *ABR* 25 (1974): 56-74.

Ehnmark, Erland. *Anthropomorphism and Miracle.* Uppsala Universitets Arsskrift 1939:12. Uppsala: A.-B. Lundequistka Bokhandeln; Leipzig: Otto Harrassowitz, 1939.

Eliade, Mircea. *The Myth of the Eternal Return.* Trans. Willard R. Trask. Bollingen Series 46. Princeton, N.J.: Princeton University Press, 1965.

Emmerson, Richard Kenneth. *Antichrist in the Middle Ages: A Study of Medieval Apocalypticism, Art and Literature.* Seattle: University of Washington Press, 1981.

Evans, G.R. *The Language and Logic of the Bible: The Earlier Middle Ages.* Cambridge: Cambridge University Press, 1984.

——. *The Thought of Gregory the Great.* Cambridge Studies in Medieval Life and Thought, 4th. ser., 2. Cambridge: Cambridge University Press, 1986.

Famulus Christi: Essays in Commemoration of the Thirteenth Centenary of the Birth of the Venerable Bede. Ed. Gerald Bonner. London: SPCK, 1976.

Festugière, A.-J. *La sainteté.* Paris: Presses universitaires de France, 1942.

——. "Lieux communs littéraires et thèmes de folklore dans l'Hagiographie primitive." *WS* 73 (1960): 123-152.

——. *Les moines d'Orient* 1: *Culture ou sainteté. Introduction au monachisme oriental.* Paris: Editions du Cerf, 1961.

(*La*) *filosofia della natura nel medioevo.* Atti del terzo congresso internazionale di filosofia medioevale. Passo della Mendola (Trento), 31 agosto-5 settembre 1964. Milano: Vita e pensiero, 1966.

Finucane, Ronald C. *Miracles and Pilgrims: Popular Beliefs in Medieval England.* London, Melbourne and Toronto: J.M. Dent and Sons Ltd., 1977.

Flusin, Bernard. "Miracle et hiérarchie." In *Hagiographie, cultures et sociétés*, pp. 299-316, with discussion, pp. 316-317.

——. *Miracle et histoire dans l'oeuvre de Cyrille de Scythopolis.* Paris: Etudes Augustiniennes, 1983.

Fontaine, Jacques. *Isidore de Séville et la culture classique dans l'Espagne wisigothique.* 3 vols. Paris: Etudes Augustiniennes, 1959-1983.

——. "Alle fonti della agiografia europea: storia e leggende nella vita di San Martino di Tours." *RSLR* 2 (1966): 187-206.

——. *Sulpice Sévère. Vie de Saint Martin.* SC 133-135. Paris: Editions du Cerf, 1967-1969.

——. "L'expérience spirituelle chez Grégoire le Grand. Réflexions sur une thèse récente." *RHSp.* 52 (1976): 141-154.

——. "Hagiographie et politique, de Sulpice Sévère à Venance Fortunat." *RHEF* 62 (1976): 113-140.

——. "Bible et hagiographie dans le royaume Franc mérovingien (600-750). Une soutenance remarquée à l'Université de Gand." *ABoll.* 97 (1979): 387-396.

——. "Le culte des saints et ses implications sociologiques. Réflexions sur un récent essai de Peter Brown." *ABoll.* 100 (1982): 17-41.

——. "Un fondateur de l'Europe: Grégoire le Grand (590-604)." *Helmantica* 34 (1983): 171-189.

Frazer, J.G. *The Golden Bough: A Study in Magic and Religion.* 3rd. ed., part 1: *The Magic Art and the Evolution of Kings.* 2 vols. London: Macmillan, 1911.

Frickel, Michael. *Deus totus ubique simul. Untersuchungen zur allgemeinen Gottgegenwart im Rahmen der Gotteslehre Gregors des Grossen.* Freiburger Theologische Studien 69. Freiburg: Verlag Herder, 1956.

Fridrichsen, Anton. *The Problem of Miracle in Primitive Christianity.* Trans. Roy A. Harrisville and John S. Hanson. Minneapolis: Augsburg Publishing House, 1972.

Fuhrmann, Horst. "Die Fälschungen im Mittelalter. Überlegungen zum mittelalterlichen Wahrheitsbegriff." *HZ* 197 (1963): 529-554; followed by "Diskussionsbeiträge" with contributions by Karl Bosl (555-567), Hans Patze (568-573), August Nitschke (574-579), a reply by Fuhrmann (580-601), and a final comment by Patze (601).

Gaiffier, Baudouin de. "Les héros des Dialogues de Grégoire le Grand inscrits au nombre des saints." *ABoll.* 83 (1965): 53-74.

——. *Études critiques d'hagiographie et d'iconologie.* Brussels: Société des Bollandistes, 1967.

——. "Mentalité de l'hagiographe médiéval d'après quelques travaux récents." *ABoll.* 86 (1968): 391-399.

——. "Hagiographie et historiographie. Quelques aspects du problème." In *La storiografia altomedioevale,* 1:139-166.

——. "Les 'doublets' en hagiographie latine." *ABoll.* 96 (1978): 261-269.

——. "Les thèmes hagiographiques. Est-il possible d'établir pour chacun d'eux une filiation?" *RHE* 77 (1982): 78-81.

Garfagnini, Gian Carlo. "La cosmologia altomedievale." In *La cultura in Italia fra tardo antico e alto medioevo,* 2:745-753.

Gastaldelli, Ferruccio. "Il meccanismo psicologico del peccato nei *Moralia in Job* di San Gregorio Magno." *Salesianum* 27 (1965): 563-605.

——. "Prospettive sul peccato in San Gregorio Magno." *Salesianum* 28 (1966): 65-94.

——. "Teologia e retorica in San Gregorio Magno. Il ritratto nei 'Moralia in Iob.'" *Salesianum* 29 (1967): 269-299.

Gatch, M.McC. "The Fourth Dialogue of Gregory the Great: Some Problems of Interpretation." *SPatr.* 10 (1967): 77-83.

Gautier Dalché, Patrick. "La représentation de l'espace dans les *Libri Miraculorum* de Grégoire de Tours." *MA* 88 (1982): 397-420.

Gillet, Robert. Introduction to *Grégoire le Grand, Morales sur Job, Livres 1 et 2.* sc 32. Paris: Editions du Cerf, 1952.

——. "Spiritualité et place du moine dans l'église selon saint Grégoire le Grand." In *Théologie de la vie monastique. Etudes sur la tradition patristique,* pp. 323-351. Paris: Aubier, 1961.

——. "Grégoire le Grand." In *DSp.* 6:872-910. 1967.

Ginzburg, Carlo. "Folklore, magia, religione." In *Storia d'Italia 1: I caratteri originali,* pp. 601-676. Torino: Einaudi, 1972.

Giordano, Oronzo. "Sociologia e patologia del miracolo in Gregorio di Tours." *Helikon* 18-19 (1978-1979): 161-209.

Goodich, Michael. *Vita perfecta: The Ideal of Sainthood in the Thirteenth Century.* Monographien zur Geschichte des Mittelalters 25. Stuttgart: Anton Hiersemann, 1982.

Gordini, Gian Domenico. "Aspetti e problemi degli studi agiografici." *SCat.* 109 (1981): 281-324.

Grange, Joseph. *Le miracle d'après saint Augustin.* Brignais: Imprimerie de l'Ecole professionnelle de Sacuny, 1912.

Gransden, Antonia. *Historical Writing in England* 1: *c. 550 to c. 1307.* Ithaca, N.Y.: Cornell University Press, 1974.

Grant, Patrick. "Redeeming the Time: The *Confessions* of St. Augustine." In *By Things Seen: Reference and Recognition in Medieval Thought,* ed. David L. Jeffrey, pp. 21-32. Ottawa: University of Ottawa Press, 1979.

Grant, Robert M. *Miracle and Natural Law in Graeco-Roman and Early Christian Thought.* Amsterdam: North Holland, 1952.

——. "Causation and the Ancient World View." *JBL* 83 (1964): 34-41.

Graus, Frantisek. *Volk, Herrscher und Heiliger im Reich der Merowinger. Studien zur Hagiographie der Merowingerzeit.* Praha: Nakladatelstvi Ceskoslovenské akademie ved, 1965.

Grégoire le Grand. Ed. Jacques Fontaine, Robert Gillet, Stan Pellistrandi. Chantilly, Centre culturel Les Fontaines, 15-19 septembre 1982. Colloques internationaux du Centre national de la Recherche Scientifique. Paris: C.N.R.S., 1986.

Grégoire, Réginald. "Il contributo dell'agiografia alla conoscenza della realtà rurale. Tipologia delle fonti agiografiche anteriori al XIII secolo." In *Medioevo rurale*, pp. 343-360.

——. "Il libro delle virtú e dei vizi." *Schede medievali* 5 (1983): 326-358.

Gregorio di Tours. 10-13 ottobre 1971. Convegni del Centro di studi sulla spiritualità medievale 12. Todi: Presso l'Accademia Tudertina, 1977.

Gregory, Tullio. "L'idea di natura nella filosofia medievale prima dell'ingresso della fisica di Aristotele—Il secolo XII." In *La filosofia della natura nel medioevo*, pp. 27-65.

——. "La nouvelle idée de nature et de savoir scientifique au XII siècle." In *The Cultural Context of Medieval Learning*, ed. John Emery Murdoch and Edith Dudley Sylla, pp. 193-212, with discussion, pp. 212-218. Dordrecht and Boston: D. Reidel, 1975.

Gribomont, Jean. "Panorama des influences orientales sur l'hagiographie latine." *Augustinianum* 24 (1984): 7-20.

Gross, Karl. "Der Tod des hl. Benedictus. Ein Beitrag zu Gregor d. Gr., Dial. 2, 37." *RBén.* 85 (1975): 164-176.

Grün, Anselm. *Der Umgang mit dem Bösen. Der Dämonenkampf im alten Mönchtum.* Münsterschwarzacher Kleinschriften 6. Münsterschwarzach: Vier-Türme-Verlag, 1980.

Guenée, Bernard. *Histoire et culture historique dans l'Occident médiéval.* Paris: Aubier Montaigne, 1980.

Günter, Heinrich. *Psychologie de la légende. Introduction à une hagiographie scientifique.* Trans. J. Goffinet. Paris: Payot, 1954.

Guillou, André. "L'école dans l'Italie Byzantine." In *La scuola nell'occidente latino dell'alto medioevo*, 1:291-311.

——. "L'évêque dans la société méditerranéenne des VIe-VIIe siècles. Un modèle." *BEC* 131 (1973): 5-19.

Gurevich, Aron IAkovlevich. "Au moyen âge: conscience individuelle et image de l'au-delà." *Annales E.S.C.* 37 (1982): 255-275.

——. *Categories of Medieval Culture.* Trans. G.L. Campbell. London: Routledge and Kegan Paul, 1985.

Guy, Jean-Claude. *Jean Cassien. Vie et doctrine spirituelle.* Collection Théologie, Pastorale et Spiritualité; Recherches et Synthèses 9. Paris: Lethielleux, 1961.

Hagendahl, Harald. *Augustine and the Latin Classics.* Studia Graeca et Latina Gothoburgensia 20. 2 vols. Göteborg: Acta Universitatis Gothoburgensis, 1967.

Hagiographie, cultures et sociétés, IVe-XIIe siècles. Actes du Colloque organisé à Nanterre et à Paris, 2-5 mai 1979. Paris: Etudes Augustiniennes, 1981.

Hale, Paolo. "L'imitazione di Cristo come ritorno in S. Gregorio Magno." *VMon.* 20 (1966): 30-42, 89-99.

Hallinger, Kassius. "Papst Gregor der Grosse und der hl. Benedikt." *SAns.* 42 (1957): 231-319.

Hardon, John A. "The Concept of Miracle from St. Augustine to Modern Apologetics." *TS* 15 (1954): 229-257.

Hay, Denys. *Annalists and Historians: Western Historiography from the Eighth to the Eighteenth Centuries.* London: Methuen, 1977.

Heiler, Friedrich. "Vom Naturwunder zum Geisteswunder. Der Wandel des primitiven Wunderglaubens in der hohen Religion." In *Festschrift Walter Baetke*, pp. 151-166. Weimar: Hermann Böhlaus Nachfolger, 1966.

Heinzelmann, Martin. "Neue Aspekte der biographischen und hagiographischen Literatur in der lateinischen Welt (1.-6. Jahrhundert)." *Francia* 1 (1973): 27-44.

——. "Sanctitas und 'Tugendadel'. Zu Konzeptionen von 'Heiligkeit' im 5. und 10. Jahrhundert." *Francia* 5 (1977): 741-752.

——. "Une source de base de la littérature hagiographique latine: le recueil de miracles." In *Hagiographie, cultures et sociétés*, pp. 235-257, with discussion, pp. 257-259.

Herrmann-Mascard, Nicole. *Les reliques des saints. Formation coutumière d'un droit.* Société d'histoire du droit, Collection d'histoire institutionnelle et sociale 6. Paris: Editions Klincksieck, 1975.

Hesse, Mary. "Miracles and the Laws of Nature." In *Miracles: Cambridge Studies in their Philosophy and History*, pp. 33-42.

Histoire des miracles. Actes de la sixième Rencontre d'Histoire Religieuse tenue à Fontevraud les 8 et 9 octobre 1982. Angers: Presses de l'Université, 1983.

Hofmann, Dietram. *Die geistige Auslegung der Schrift bei Gregor dem Grossen.* Münsterschwarzacher Studien 6. Münsterschwarzach: Vier-Türme-Verlag, 1968.

Holland, R.F. "The Miraculous." In *Religion and Understanding*, ed. D.Z. Phillips, pp. 155-170. Oxford: Basil Blackwell, 1967.

Holtz, Louis. "Le contexte grammatical du défi à la grammaire: Grégoire et Cassiodore." In *Grégoire le Grand*, pp. 531-539, with discussion, p. 540.

Howorth, Henry H. *Saint Gregory the Great.* London: John Murray, 1912.

Hunter Blair, Peter. "The Historical Writings of Bede." In *La storiografia altomedievale*, 1:197-221.

——. *The World of Bede.* London: Secker and Warburg, 1970.

Janik, Linda Gardiner. "Lorenzo Valla: The Primacy of Rhetoric and the De-Moralization of History." *HTh.* 12 (1973): 389-404.

Jones, Charles W. "Bede as Early Medieval Historian." *MHum.* 4 (1946): 26-36.
———. *Saints' Lives and Chronicles in Early England.* 1947. Reprint Hamden, Conn.: Archon Books, 1968.
Jourjon, Maurice. "Qui allait-il voir au désert? Simple question posée au moine sur son démon." *Lumière et vie* 78 (1966): 3-15.

Kardong, Terrence. "A New Look at Gregory's *Dialogues.*" *ABR* 36 (1985): 44-63.
Kee, Howard Clark. *Miracle in the Early Christian World: A Study in Sociohistorical Method.* New Haven and London: Yale University Press, 1983.
Keller, Ernst and Marie-Luise. *Miracles in Dispute: A Continuing Debate.* Trans. Margaret Kohl. London: SCM Press, 1969.
Kieckhefer, Richard. *Unquiet Souls. Fourteenth-Century Saints and their Religious Milieu.* Chicago and London: University of Chicago Press, 1984.
Kirschner, Robert. "The Vocation of Holiness in Late Antiquity." *VigC* 38 (1984): 105-124.
Koestler, Arthur. *The Roots of Coincidence.* London: Hutchinson, 1972.
Köhler, Ludwig. *Hebrew Man.* Trans. Peter R. Ackroyd. London: SCM Press, 1956.
Krusch, Bruno. "Kulturbilder aus dem Frankenreiche zur Zeit Gregors von Tours (†594). Ein Beitrag zur Geschichte des Aberglaubens." *ZBAW* (1934) 785-800.
Kurtz, Benjamin P. *From St. Antony to St. Guthlac: A Study in Biography.* University of California Publications in Modern Philology, 12.2, pp. 103-146. Berkeley: University of California Press, 1926.

Lacey, T.A. *Nature, Miracle and Sin: A Study of St. Augustine's Conception of the Natural Order.* New York: Longmans, Green, 1916.
Lambot, Cyrille. "La vie et les miracles de saint Benoît racontés par saint Grégoire-le-Grand." *RMon.* 143 (1956): 49-61; 144 (1956): 97-102; 145 (1956): 149-158.
Lamirande, Emilien. *Paulin de Milan et la 'Vita Ambrosii.' Aspects de la religion sous le Bas-Empire.* Recherches Théologie 30. Paris: Desclée; Montreal: Bellarmin, 1983.
Laporte, Jean. "Saint Benoît et les survivances du paganisme." In *Etudes Ligériennes d'histoire et d'archéologie médiévales.* Mémoires et exposés présentés à la Semaine d'études médiévales de Saint-Benoît-sur-Loire du 3 au 10 juillet 1969, ed. René Louis, pp. 233-246. Auxerre: Publications de la Société des fouilles archéologiques et des monuments historiques de l'Yonne, 1975.
Leccisotti, Tommaso. "Rileggendo il II Libro dei Dialoghi di Gregorio Magno." *Benedictina* 28 (1981): 223-228.
Leclercq, Jean. "L'Ecriture sainte dans l'hagiographie monastique du haut moyen âge." In *La Bibbia nell'alto medioevo,* pp. 103-128.
———. *The Spirituality of the Middle Ages,* part 1: *From St Gregory to St Bernard, From the Sixth to the Twelfth Century.* London: Burns and Oates, 1968.
———. "Pedagogie et formation spirituelle du VIe au IXe siècle." In *La scuola nell'occidente latino dell'alto medioevo,* 1:255-290.

——. *The Love of Learning and the Desire for God: A Study of Monastic Culture.* Trans. Catherine C. Misrahi. 2nd. corr. ed. New York: Fordham University Press, 1977.

Lecouteux, Claude. "Paganisme, christianisme et merveilleux." *Annales E.S.C.* 37 (1982): 700-716.

Le Goff, Jacques. "Culture cléricale et traditions folkloriques dans la civilisation mérovingienne." *Annales E.S.C.* 22 (1967): 780-791.

——. *La naissance du Purgatoire.* Paris: Editions Gallimard, 1981.

——. "'Vita' et 'pre-exemplum' dans le 2e livre des 'Dialogues' de Grégoire le Grand." In *Hagiographie, cultures et sociétés,* pp. 105-117, with discussion, pp. 117-120.

——. *See also* Bremond, Claude; and Patin, J. P. Valery.

Leloir, Louis. "Le diable chez les pères du désert et dans les écrits du moyen âge." In *Typus, Symbol, Allegorie,* pp. 218-237.

Leonardi, Claudio. "Il venerabile Beda e la cultura del secolo VIII." In *I problemi dell'occidente nel secolo VIII,* 6-12 aprile 1972, 2:603-658. Settimane di studio del Centro italiano di studi sull'alto medioevo 20. Spoleto, 1973.

——. "I commenti altomedievali ai classici pagani: da Severino Boezio a Remigio d'Auxerre." In *La cultura antica nell'occidente latino dal VII all'XI secolo,* 1:459-504.

——. "I modelli dell'agiografia latina dall'epoca antica al medioevo." In *Passaggio dal mondo antico al medio evo,* pp. 435-476.

——. "L'agiografia latina dal tardantico all'altomedioevo." In *La cultura in Italia fra tardo antico e alto medioevo,* 2:643-659.

Lewis, Clive Staples. *Miracles: A Preliminary Study.* New York: Macmillan, 1947.

——. *Undeceptions: Essays on Theology and Ethics.* Ed. Walter Hooper. London: Geoffrey Bles, 1971.

Lieblang, Franz. *Grundfragen der mystischen Theologie nach Gregors des Grossen Moralia und Ezechielhomilien.* Freiburger Theologische Studien 37. Freiburg im Breisgau: Herder, 1934.

Limone, Oronzo. "La vita di Gregorio Magno dell'Anonimo di Whitby." *SM* 3rd. ser. 19 (1978): 37-67.

——. "Agiografia latina nell'Italia meridionale." In *La cultura in Italia fra tardo antico e alto medioevo,* 2:755-769.

Linage Conde, Antonio. "La 'Regula Benedicti' y el 'Dialogo Segundo' de San Gregorio, obras literarias." In *Monastica 1: Scritti raccolti in memoria del XV centenario della nascita di S. Benedetto, 480-1980,* pp. 169-187. Miscellanea Cassinese 44. Montecassino, 1981.

Lindberg, David C. "Science and the Early Christian Church." *Isis* 74 (1983): 509-530.

Loomis, Charles Grant. "The Miracle Traditions of the Venerable Bede." *Speculum* 21 (1946): 404-418.

——. *White Magic: An Introduction to the Folklore of Christian Legend.* Cambridge, Mass.: Mediaeval Academy of America, 1948.

Loyen, André. "Les Miracles de saint Martin et les débuts de l'hagiographie en Occident." *BLE* 73 (1972): 147-157.

Lubac, Henri de. *Exégèse médiévale. Les quatre sens de l'Ecriture.* 2 parts in 4 vols. Paris: Aubier, 1959-1964.

MacCulloch, J.A. *Medieval Faith and Fable.* London: Harrap, 1932.

MacKay, Barry S. "Plutarch and the Miraculous." In *Miracles: Cambridge Studies in their Philosophy and History*, pp. 93-111.

MacMullen, Ramsay. "Constantine and the Miraculous." *GRBS* 9 (1968): 81-96.

MacRae, G. "Miracle in *The Antiquities* of Josephus." In *Miracles: Cambridge Studies in their Philosophy and History*, pp. 127-147.

Madden, Sister Mary Daniel. *The Pagan Divinities and their Worship as Depicted in the Works of Saint Augustine Exclusive of The City of God.* Washington: Catholic University of America, 1930.

Mähler, Maximilien. "Evocations bibliques et hagiographiques dans la Vie de Saint Benoît par Saint Grégoire." *RBén.* 83 (1973): 398-429.

Mandouze, André. "Saint Augustin et la religion romaine." *RAug.* 1 (1958): 187-223.

Manselli, Raoul. "L'escatologia di S. Gregorio Magno." *Ricerche di storia religiosa* 1 (1954): 72-83.

——. "Gregorio Magno e la Bibbia." In *La Bibbia nell'alto medioevo*, pp. 67-101.

——. *Gregorio Magno.* Torino: G. Giappichelli Editore, 1967.

——. "Gregorio Magno e due riti pagani dei Longobardi." In *Studi storici in onore di Ottorino Bertolini*, 1:435-440. 2 vols. Pisa: Pacini editore, 1972.

——. "Gregorio Magno nelle sue opere." In *Passaggio dal mondo antico al medio evo*, pp. 559-568.

——. "Resistenze dei culti antichi nella pratica religiosa dei laici nelle campagne." In *Cristianizzazione ed organizzazione ecclesiastica delle campagne nell'alto medioevo. Espansione e resistenze*, pp. 57-108. Settimane di studio del Centro italiano di studi sull'alto medioevo 28. Spoleto, 1982.

Margerie, Bertrand de. *Introduction à l'histoire de l'exégèse.* 3 vols. to date. Paris: Editions du Cerf, 1980-1983.

Marignan, A. *Etudes sur la civilisation française* 2: *Le culte des saints sous les Mérovingiens.* Paris: Librairie Emile Bouillon, 1899.

Markus, R.A. "Augustine: God and Nature." In *The Cambridge History of Later Greek and Early Medieval Philosophy*, ed. A.H. Armstrong, pp. 395-405. Cambridge: Cambridge University Press, 1967.

——. "Gregory the Great and a Papal Missionary Strategy." In *The Mission of the Church and the Propagation of the Faith*, ed. G.J. Cuming, pp. 29-38. Studies in Church History 6. Cambridge: Cambridge University Press, 1970.

——. "Ravenna and Rome, 554-604." *Byzantion* 51 (1981): 566-578.

——. "The Sacred and the Secular: From Augustine to Gregory the Great." *JTS* n.s. 36 (1985): 84-96.

Marrou, Henri-Irénée. *Saint Augustin et la fin de la culture antique.* 2 vols. with

"Retractatio." Bibliothèque des écoles françaises d'Athènes et de Rome, fasc. 145, 145bis. Paris: Boccard, 1938-1949.

Mayr-Harting, Henry. *The Coming of Christianity to England.* New York: Schocken Books, 1972.

Mazzarino, Santo. "L''èra Costantiniana' e la 'prospettiva storica' di Gregorio Magno." In *Passaggio dal mondo antico al medio evo,* pp. 9-28.

McCulloh, John M. "The Cult of Relics in the Letters and 'Dialogues' of Pope Gregory the Great: A Lexicographical Study." *Traditio* 32 (1976): 145-184.

——. "From Antiquity to the Middle Ages: Continuity and Change in Papal Relic Policy from the 6th to the 8th Century." In *Pietas,* pp. 313-324.

McNally, Robert E. "Gregory the Great (590-604) and his Declining World." *AHP* 16 (1978): 7-26.

Medioevo rurale. Sulle tracce della civiltà contadina. Ed. Vito Fumagalli and Gabriella Rossetti. Bologna: Società editrice il Mulino, 1980.

Mensching, Gustav. *Das Wunder im Glauben und Aberglauben der Völker.* Leiden: E.J. Brill, 1957.

Mercati, Angelo. "L'autore della Expositio in septem psalmos poenitentiales fra le opere di S. Gregorio Magno." *RBén.* 31 (1914-1919): 250-257.

Meyvaert, Paul. "Bede the Scholar." In *Famulus Christi,* pp. 40-69.

——. *Benedict, Gregory, Bede and Others.* London: Variorum Reprints, 1977.

Milburn, R.L.P. *Early Christian Interpretations of History.* London: Adam and Charles Black, 1954.

Miracles: Cambridge Studies in their Philosophy and History. Ed. C.F.D. Moule. London: Mowbray, 1965.

Momigliano, Arnaldo. *Essays in Ancient and Modern Historiography.* Oxford: Basil Blackwell, 1977.

Monaci Castagno, Adele. "Il vescovo, l'abate e l'eremita: tipologia della santità nel Liber Vitae Patrum di Gregorio di Tours." *Augustinianum* 24 (1984): 235-264.

Moody, E.A. *Studies in Medieval Philosophy, Science and Logic: Collected Papers 1933-1969.* Los Angeles: University of California Press, 1975.

Moorhead, John. "Thoughts on Some Early Medieval Miracles." In *Byzantine Papers: Proceedings of the First Australian Byzantine Studies Conference, Canberra, 17-19 May 1978,* ed. Elizabeth Jeffreys, Michael Jeffreys and Ann Moffatt, pp. 1-11. Byzantina Australiensia 1. Canberra: Humanities Research Centre, Australian National University, 1981.

Morghen, Raffaello. "Il culto dei santi nelle fonti agiografiche dell'alto medio evo." In his *Tradizione religiosa nella civiltà dell' occidente cristiano. Saggi di storia e di storiografia,* pp. 1-10. Studi Storici, Fasc. 112-114. Rome: Istituto storico italiano per il medio evo, 1979.

Morris, Colin. *The Discovery of the Individual, 1050-1200.* London: SPCK, 1972.

——. "Individualism in Twelfth-Century Religion: Some Further Reflections." *JEH* 31 (1980): 195-206.

Mourant, John A. "Augustine on Miracles." *Augustinian Studies* 4 (1973): 103-127.

Müller, Gregor. *Die Wahrhaftigkeitspflicht und die Problematik der Lüge.* Freiburger Theologische Studien 78. Freiburg: Herder, 1962.

Mundó, Anscari. "Sur la date de la visite de Totila à saint Benoît." *RBén.* 59 (1949): 203-206.

Murray, Alexander. *Reason and Society in the Middle Ages.* Oxford: Oxford University Press, 1978.

Musca, Giosuè. *Il Venerabile Beda, storico dell'Alto Medioevo.* Storia e civiltà 9. Bari: Dedalo Libri, 1973.

Nardi, Bruno. "Sguardo panoramico alla filosofia della natura nel medioevo." In *La filosofia della natura nel medioevo,* pp. 3-23.

Nie, Giselle de. "Roses in January: A Neglected Dimension in Gregory of Tours' *Historiae.*" *JMH* 5 (1979): 259-289.

———. "The Spring, the Seed and the Tree: Gregory of Tours on the Wonders of Nature." *JMH* 11 (1985): 89-135.

Nitschke, August. *See* Fuhrmann, Horst.

Ntedika, Joseph. *L'évocation de l'au-delà dans la prière pour les morts. Etude de patristique et de liturgie latines (IVe-VIIIe siècle).* Recherches africaines de théologie 2. Louvain: Editions Nauwelaerts; Paris: Béatrice-Nauwelaerts, 1971.

Oldoni, Massimo. "Gregorio di Tours e i 'Libri Historiarum'. Le fonti scritte." In *Gregorio di Tours,* pp. 251-324.

Orselli, Alba Maria. *L'idea e il culto del santo patrono cittadino nella letteratura latina cristiana.* Università degli studi di Bologna, Facoltà di lettere e filosofia, Studi e ricerche n.s. 12. Bologna: Zanichelli, 1965.

Oury, Guy-Marie. "Le miracle dans Grégoire de Tours." In *Histoire des miracles,* pp. 11-28.

Paronetto, Vera. "Gregorio Magno e la cultura classica." *Studium* 74 (1978): 665-680.

———. "A proposito di alcune recenti pubblicazioni su Gregorio Magno." *RSCI* 34 (1980): 174-187.

———. "I Longobardi nell'epistolario di Gregorio Magno." In *Atti del 6° congresso internazionale di studi sull'alto medioevo,* 2:559-570.

———. "Connotazione del 'Pastor' nell'opera di Gregorio Magno. Teoria e prassi." *Benedictina* 31 (1984): 325-343.

———. *Gregorio Magno. Un maestro alle origini cristiane d'Europa.* Nuova Universale Studium 46. Rome: Edizioni Studium, 1985.

Partner, Nancy F. *Serious Entertainments: The Writing of History in Twelfth-Century England.* Chicago and London: University of Chicago Press, 1977.

Passaggio dal mondo antico al medio evo. Da Teodosio a San Gregorio Magno. Roma, 25-28 maggio 1977. Atti dei convegni Lincei 45. Rome: Accademia nazionale dei Lincei, 1980.

Patin, J.P. Valery and Jacques Le Goff. "A propos de la typologie des miracles dans
le Liber de miraculis de Pierre le Vénérable." In *Pierre Abélard, Pierre le
Vénérable: Les courants philosophiques, littéraires et artistiques en occident au
milieu du XIIe siècle,* Abbaye de Cluny, 2 au 9 juillet 1972, pp. 181-187.
Colloques internationaux du Centre National de la Recherche Scientifique
546. Paris: C.N.R.S., 1975.

Patlagean, Evelyne. "Ancient Byzantine Hagiography and Social History." Trans.
Jane Hodgkin. In *Saints and their Cults: Studies in Religious Sociology,
Folklore and History,* ed. Stephen Wilson, pp. 101-121. Cambridge: Cam-
bridge University Press, 1983.

Patrucco, Marcella Forlin. *See* Desideri, Paolo.

Patze, Hans. *See* Fuhrmann, Horst.

Paul, Jacques. "Miracles et mentalité religieuse populaire à Marseille au début du
XIVe siècle." In *La religion populaire en Languedoc,* pp. 61-90.

Penco, Gregorio. "L'imitazione di Cristo nell'agiografia monastica." *CCist.* 28
(1966): 17-34.

——. "Significato e funzione dei prologhi nell'agiografia benedettina." *Aevum* 40
(1966): 468-476.

——. "Le figure bibliche del 'vir Dei' nell'agiografia monastica." *Benedictina* 15
(1968): 1-13.

——. "Il senso della natura nell'agiografia monastica occidentale." *SMon.* 11
(1969): 327-334.

——. "La dottrina dei sensi spirituali in S. Gregorio." *Benedictina* 17 (1970):
161-201.

——. "S. Gregorio e la teologia dell'immagine." *Benedictina* 18 (1971): 32-45.

——. "Sopravvivenze della demonologia antica nel monachesimo medievale."
SMon. 13 (1971): 31-36.

——. "Sulla struttura dialogica dei Dialoghi di S. Gregorio." *Benedictina* 33
(1986): 329-335.

Petersen, Joan M. "Did Gregory the Great Know Greek?" In *The Orthodox Churches
and the West,* ed. Derek Baker, pp. 121-134. Studies in Church History 13.
Oxford: Basil Blackwell, 1976.

——. "Dead or Alive? The Holy Man as Healer in East and West in the Late Sixth
Century." *JMH* 9 (1983): 91-98.

——. *The Dialogues of Gregory the Great in their Late Antique Cultural Background.*
Studies and Texts 69. Toronto: Pontifical Institute of Mediaeval Studies, 1984.

——. "The Garden of Felix: The Literary Connection between Gregory the Great
and Paulinus of Nola." *SMon.* 26 (1984): 215-230.

——. "The Influence of Origen upon Gregory the Great's Exegesis of the Song of
Songs." *SPatr.* 18 (1985): 343-347.

——. "Greek Influences upon Gregory the Great's Exegesis of Luke 15, 1-10 in
Homelia in Evang. II, 34." In *Grégoire le Grand,* pp. 521-528, with discussion,
p. 529.

——. "'Homo omnino Latinus?' The Theological and Cultural Background of Pope
Gregory the Great." *Speculum* 62 (1987): 529-551.

Petrucci, Armando. "Scrittura e libro nell'Italia altomedievale." *SM* 3rd. ser. 14 (1973): 961-1002.

Pietas. Festschrift für Bernhard Kötting. Ed. Ernst Dassmann and K. Suso Frank. Jahrbuch für Antike und Christentum, Ergänzungsband 8. Münster-en-Westfalen: Aschendorff, 1980.

Piétri, Luce. "Le pèlerinage Martinien de Tours à l'époque de l'évêque Grégoire." In *Gregorio di Tours*, pp. 93-139.

Poulin, Joseph-Claude. *L'idéal de sainteté dans l'Aquitaine carolingienne d'après les sources hagiographiques (750-950).* Travaux de laboratoire d'histoire religieuse de l'Université Laval 1. Québec: Les Presses de l'Université Laval, 1975.

Prinz, Friedrich. "Zur geistigen Kultur des Mönchtums im spätantiken Gallien und im Merowingerreich." *ZBLG* 26 (1963): 29-102.

——. *Frühes Mönchtum im Frankenreich. Kultur und Gesellschaft in Gallien, den Rheinlanden und Bayern am Beispiel der monastischen Entwicklung (4. bis 8. Jahrhundert).* München and Wien: R. Oldenbourg Verlag, 1965.

——. "Heiligenkult und Adelsherrschaft im Spiegel merowingischer Hagiographie." *HZ* 204 (1967): 529-544.

Puzicha, M. "*Vita iusti* (Dial. 2,2). Grundstrukturen altkirchlicher Hagiographie bei Gregor dem Grossen." In *Pietas*, pp. 284-312.

Radding, Charles M. *A World Made by Men: Cognition and Society, 400-1200.* Chapel Hill: University of North Carolina Press, 1985.

Ray, Roger D. "Medieval Historiography through the Twelfth Century: Problems and Progress of Research." *Viator* 5 (1974): 33-59.

——. "Bede, the Exegete, as Historian." In *Famulus Christi*, pp. 125-140.

——. "Bede's *vera lex historiae.*" *Speculum* 55 (1980): 1-21.

Reames, Sherry L. "Saint Martin of Tours in the *Legenda aurea* and Before." *Viator* 12 (1981): 131-164.

Recchia, Vincenzo. "La visione di S. Benedetto e la 'compositio' del secondo libro dei 'Dialoghi' di Gregorio Magno." *RBén.* 82 (1972): 140-155.

——. *Gregorio Magno e la società agricola.* Verba seniorum n.s. 8. Rome: Edizioni studium, 1978.

——. "San Benedetto e la politica religiosa dell'Occidente nella prima metà del secolo VI dai *Dialogi* di Gregorio Magno." *Romanobarbarica* 7 (1982-83): 201-252.

——. "La memoria di Agostino nella esegesi biblica di Gregorio Magno." *Augustinianum* 25 (1985): 405-434.

(La) religion populaire en Languedoc du XIIIe siècle à la moitié du XIVe siècle. Cahiers de Fanjeaux 11. Toulouse: Edouard Privat, Editeur, 1976.

Remus, Harold. "'Magic or Miracle?' Some Second-Century Instances." *The Second Century* 2 (1982): 127-156.

——. *Pagan-Christian Conflict over Miracle in the Second Century.* Patristic Monograph Series 10. Cambridge, Mass.: The Philadelphia Patristic Foundation, 1983.

Reynolds, Burnam W. "Familia Sancti Martini: Domus ecclesiae on Earth as it is in Heaven." *JMH* 11 (1985): 137-143.

Richards, Jeffrey. *Consul of God: The Life and Times of Gregory the Great.* London: Routledge and Kegan Paul, 1980.

Riché, Pierre. *Education and Culture in the Barbarian West: Sixth through Eighth Centuries.* Trans. John J. Contreni. Columbia, S.C.: University of South Carolina Press, 1976.

———. *Les écoles et l'enseignement dans l'Occident chrétien de la fin du Ve siècle au milieu du XIe siècle.* Paris: Aubier Montaigne, 1979.

———. "L'école dans le haut moyen âge." In *La cultura in Italia fra tardo antico e alto medioevo,* 2:561-574.

Rivière, Jean. "Rôle du démon au jugement particulier chez les Pères." *Revue des sciences religieuses* 4 (1924): 43-64.

Roldanus, Johannes. "Die Vita Antonii als Spiegel der Theologie des Athanasius und ihr Weiterwirken bis ins 5. Jahrhundert." *ThPh.* 58 (1983): 194-216.

Rollinson, Philip. *Classical Theories of Allegory and Christian Culture.* Duquesne Studies in Language and Literature 3. Pittsburgh: Duquesne University Press; Brighton: Harvester Press, 1981.

Rosenthal, Joel T. "Bede's Use of Miracles in 'The Ecclesiastical History.'" *Traditio* 31 (1975): 328-335.

Ross, J.P. "Some Notes on Miracle in the Old Testament." In *Miracles: Cambridge Studies in their Philosophy and History,* pp. 43-60.

Rouche, Michel. "Miracles, maladies et psychologie de la foi à l'époque carolingienne en France." In *Hagiographie, cultures et sociétés,* pp. 319-332, with discussion, pp. 333-335, and tables, pp. 336-337.

Rousseau, Olivier. "Saint Benoît et le prophète Elisée." *RMon.* 144 (1956): 103-114.

Rousseau, Philip. *Ascetics, Authority, and the Church in the Age of Jerome and Cassian.* Oxford: Oxford University Press, 1978.

Rousselle, Aline. "Du sanctuaire au thaumaturge: la guérison en Gaule au IVe siècle." *Annales E.S.C.* 31 (1976): 1085-1107.

———. "Paulin de Nole et Sulpice Sévère, hagiographes, et la culture populaire." In *Les saints et les stars. Le texte hagiographique dans la culture populaire,* ed. Jean-Claude Schmitt, pp. 27-40. Religions, Société, Politique 10. Paris: Beauchesne, 1983.

Rousset, Paul. "La croyance en la justice immanente à l'époque féodale." *MA* 54 (1948): 225-248.

———. "La conception de l'histoire à l'époque féodale." In *Mélanges d'histoire du moyen âge dédiés à la mémoire de Louis Halphen,* pp. 623-633. Paris: Presses Universitaires de France, 1951.

———. "Le sens du merveilleux à l'époque féodale." *MA* 62 (1956): 25-37.

Rusch, William G. *The Later Latin Fathers.* London: Duckworth, 1977.

Rush, Alfred C. "An Echo of Christian Antiquity in St. Gregory the Great: Death a Struggle with the Devil." *Traditio* 3 (1945): 369-378.

Russell, Jeffrey Burton. *Satan: The Early Christian Tradition*. Ithaca and London: Cornell University Press, 1981.

————. *Lucifer: The Devil in the Middle Ages*. Ithaca and London: Cornell University Press, 1984.

Sabourin, Léopold. "Les miracles de l'Ancien Testament." *BTB* 1 (1971): 235-270.

Savon, Hervé. "L'Antéchrist dans l'oeuvre de Grégoire le Grand." In *Grégoire le Grand*, pp. 389-404, with discussion, pp. 404-405.

Saxer, Victor. *Morts, martyrs, reliques en Afrique chrétienne aux premiers siècles. Les témoignages de Tertullian, Cyprien et Augustin à la lumière de l'archéologie africaine*. Théologie historique 55. Paris: Beauchesne, 1980.

————. "Die Ursprünge des Märtyrerkultes in Afrika." *RQCAKG* 79 (1984): 1-11.

————. "Zweck und Ursprung der hagiographischen Literatur in Nordafrika." *TTZ* 93 (1984): 65-74.

Schlick, J. "Composition et chronologie des *De virtutibus sancti Martini* de Grégoire de Tours." *SPatr.* 7 (1966): 278-286.

Schmitt, Jean-Claude. *See* Bremond, Claude.

Schneemelcher, Wilhelm. "Das Kreuz Christi und die Dämonen. Bemerkungen zur Vita Antonii des Athanasius." In *Pietas*, pp. 381-392.

Schoebe, Gerhard. "Was gilt im frühen Mittelalter als Geschichtliche Wirklichkeit? Ein Versuch zur 'Kirchengeschichte' des Baeda Venerabilis." In *Festschrift Hermann Aubin zum 80. Geburtstag*, ed. Otto Brunner *et al.*, 2:625-651. 2 vols. Wiesbaden: Franz Steiner Verlag GMBH, 1965.

Schreiner, Klaus. "'*Discrimen veri et falsi*.' Ansätze und Formen der Kritik in der Heiligen- und Reliquienverehrung des Mittelalters." *AKG* 48 (1966): 1-53.

————. "Zum Wahrheitsverständnis im Heiligen- und Reliquienwesen des Mittelalters." *Saeculum* 17 (1966): 131-169.

Scivoletto, Nino. "I limiti dell''ars grammatica' in Gregorio Magno." *GIF* 17 (1964): 210-238.

————. "Saeculum Gregorianum." *GIF* 18 (1965): 41-70.

(*La*) *scuola nell'occidente latino dell'alto medioevo*. 15-21 aprile 1971. Settimane di studio del Centro italiano di studi sull'alto medioevo 19. Spoleto, 1972.

Sepulcri, Alessandro. "Gregorio Magno e la scienza profana." *AAST* 39 (1904): 962-976.

Serenthà, Luigi. "Introduzione bibliografica allo studio di S. Gregorio Magno." *SCat.* 102 (1974): 283-301.

Sigal, Pierre-André. "Un aspect du culte des saints: le châtiment divin aux XIe et XIIe siècles d'après la littérature hagiographique du Midi de la France." In *La religion populaire en Languedoc*, pp. 39-59.

————. "Histoire et hagiographie: les Miracula aux XIe et XIIe siècles." *ABPO* 87 (1980): 237-257.

————. "Miracle in vita et miracle posthume aux XIe et XIIe siècles." In *Histoire des miracles*, pp. 41-49.

————. *L'homme et le miracle dans la France médiévale (XIe-XIIe siècle)*. Paris: Editions du Cerf, 1985.

Silvestre, Hubert. "Le problème des faux au Moyen Age (A propos d'un livre récent de M. Saxer)." *MA* 66 (1960): 351-370.

——. "Le 'plus grand miracle' de Jésus." *ABoll.* 100 (1982): 1-15.

Smalley, Beryl. *The Study of the Bible in the Middle Ages.* 2nd. ed. New York: Philosophical Library, 1952.

——. "L'exégèse biblique dans la littérature latine." In *La Bibbia nell'alto medioevo,* pp. 631-655.

——. *Historians in the Middle Ages.* London: Thames and Hudson, 1974.

Smith, Morton. *Jesus the Magician.* New York: Harper and Row, 1978.

Southern, R.W. *Saint Anselm and his Biographer: A Study of Monastic Life and Thought, 1059-c.1130.* Cambridge: Cambridge University Press, 1963.

——. "Aspects of the European Tradition of Historical Writing 1: The Classical Tradition from Einhard to Geoffrey of Monmouth." *TRHS* 5th. ser. 20 (1970): 173-196.

Speigl, J. "Die Rolle der Wunder im vorconstantinischen Christentum." *ZKTh.* 92 (1970): 287-312.

Speyer, Wolfgang. *Die literarische Fälschung im heidnischen und christlichen Altertum. Ein Versuch ihrer Deutung.* Handbuch der Altertumswissenschaft 1, 2. München: Beck, 1971.

Spörl, Johannes. "Gregor der Grosse und die Antike." In *Christliche Verwirklichung. Romano Guardini zum fünfzigsten Geburtstag,* ed. Karlheinz Schmidthüs, pp. 198-211. Rothenfels am Main: Burgverlag, 1935.

Stahl, William H. *Roman Science: Origins, Development and Influence to the Later Middle Ages.* Madison: University of Wisconsin Press, 1962.

Stancliffe, Clare E. "From Town to Country: The Christianisation of the Touraine, 370-600." In *The Church in Town and Countryside,* pp. 43-59.

——. *St. Martin and his Hagiographer: History and Miracle in Sulpicius Severus.* Oxford: Clarendon Press, 1983.

Steadman, John M. *Nature into Myth: Medieval and Renaissance Moral Symbols.* Duquesne Studies, Language and Literature Series 1. Pittsburgh: Duquesne University Press, 1979.

Steffens, Henry John. *See* Williams, L. Pearce.

Steidle, Basilius. "'Homo Dei Antonius'. Zum Bild des 'Mannes Gottes' im alten Mönchtum." In *Antonius Magnus Eremita,* pp. 148-200.

——. "Der 'schwarze kleine Knabe' in der alten Mönchserzählung. Beitrag zu St. Gregor, Dial. 2,4." *BenM* 34 (1958): 339-350.

——. "Die kosmische Vision des Gottesmannes Benedikt." *EuA* 47 (1971): 187-192, 298-315, 409-414.

Stephens, J.N. "Bede's Ecclesiastical History." *History* 62 (1977): 1-14.

(*La*) *storiografia altomedievale.* Settimane di studio del Centro italiano di studi sull'alto medioevo 17. Spoleto, 1970.

Strunk, Gerhard. *Kunst und Glaube in der lateinischen Heiligenlegende. Zu ihrem Selbstverständnis in den Prologen.* Medium Aevum: Philologische Studien 12. München: Wilhelm Fink Verlag, 1970.

Strunz, Franz. "Beda in der Geschichte der Naturbetrachtung und Naturforschung."
    ZDGG 1 (1935): 311-321.
Sumption, Jonathan. *Pilgrimage: An Image of Mediaeval Religion.* Totowa, N.J.:
    Rowman and Littlefield, 1975.
Swinburne, Richard. *The Concept of Miracle.* London: Macmillan, 1970.

Tateo, Francesco. "La struttura dei dialoghi di Gregorio Magno." *VetC* 2 (1965):
    101-127.
Thürlemann, Felix. *Der historische Diskurs bei Gregor von Tours. Topoi und
    Wirklichkeit.* Geist und Werk der Zeiten 39. Bern: Herbert Lang, 1974.
Torchio, Agostino Menico. "L'osservazione della natura nell'alto medioevo. Il
    contributo dei benedettini." *SCat.* 110 (1982): 254-271.
Tubach, Frederic C. "The Formation of the Miraculous as Narrative and Cultural
    Pattern: Remarks on the Religious Imagination of Gregory's *Dialogues.*"
    DVJS 54 (1980): 1-13.
Typus, Symbol, Allegorie bei den östlichen Vätern und ihren Parallelen im Mittelalter.
    Ed. Margot Schmidt and Carl Friedrich Geyer. Eichstätter Beiträge, Bd. 4,
    Abteilung Philosophie und Theologie. Regensburg: Verlag Friedrich Pustet,
    1982.

Van Dam, Raymond. *Leadership and Community in Late Antique Gaul.* The
    Transformation of the Classical Heritage 8. Berkeley, Los Angeles and
    London: University of California Press, 1985.
Van der Essen, L. *Etude critique et littéraire sur les 'Vitae' des saints mérovingiens
    de l'ancienne Belgique.* Louvain: Bureaux du Recueil; Paris: Albert Fonte-
    moing, 1907.
Van der Lof, L.J. "De san Agustín a san Gregorio de Tours. Sobre la intervención
    de los mártires." *Augustinus* 19 (1974): 35-43.
Van der Meer, F. *Augustine the Bishop: The Life and Work of a Father of the Church.*
    Trans. Brian Battershaw and G.R. Lamb. London and New York: Sheed and
    Ward, 1961.
Van Hove, Aloïs. *La doctrine du miracle chez Saint Thomas et son accord avec les
    principes de la recherche scientifique.* Universitas catholica Lovaniensis disser-
    tationes ad gradum magistri in facultate theologica consequendum conscrip-
    tae, series 2, 19. Wetteren: J. De Meester et Fils; Bruges: Charles Beyaert;
    Paris: J. Gabalda, 1927.
Van Uytfanghe, Marc. "La Bible dans les vies de saints mérovingiennes. Quelques
    pistes de recherche." *RHEF* 62 (1976): 103-111.
——. "La controverse biblique et patristique autour du miracle, et ses répercussions
    sur l'hagiographie dans l'Antiquité tardive et le haut Moyen Age latin." In
    Hagiographie, cultures et sociétés, pp. 205-231, with discussion, pp. 232-233.
——. "Modèles bibliques dans l'hagiographie." In *Le Moyen Age et la Bible,* ed.
    Pierre Riché and Guy Lobrichon, pp. 449-488. Bible de tous les temps 4.
    Paris: Beauchesne, 1984.

———. "L'empreinte biblique sur la plus ancienne hagiographie occidentale." In *Le monde latin antique et la Bible*, ed. Jacques Fontaine and Charles Pietri, pp. 565-611. Bible de tous les temps 2. Paris: Beauchesne, 1985.

———. "Scepticisme doctrinal au seuil du Moyen Age? Les objections du diacre Pierre dans les *Dialogues* de Grégoire le Grand." In *Grégoire le Grand*, pp. 315-324, with discussion, pp. 324-326.

Vauchez, André. *La sainteté en Occident aux derniers siècles du Moyen Age, d'après les procès de canonisation et les documents hagiographiques*. Bibliothèque des Ecoles françaises d'Athènes et de Rome 241. Rome: Ecole française, 1981.

Verbraken, Pierre-Patrick. "Le texte du commentaire sur les Rois attribué à saint Grégoire." *RBén.* 66 (1956): 39-62.

———. "Le commentaire de saint Grégoire sur le Premier Livre des Rois." *RBén.* 66 (1956): 159-217.

Vieillard-Troiekouroff, May. *Les monuments religieux de la Gaule d'après les oeuvres de Grégoire de Tours*. Paris: Librairie Honoré Champion, 1976.

Vinay, Gustavo. *San Gregorio di Tours*. Carmagnola, Turino: 'Barbaries,' Edizioni Medievali di G. Vinay, 1940.

———. *Alto medioevo latino. Conversazioni e no*. Napoli: Guida Editori, 1978.

Vitale-Brovarone, Alessandro. "La forma narrativa dei *Dialoghi* di Gregorio Magno: problemi storico-letterari." *AAST.M* 108 (1974): 95-173.

———. "Forma narrativa dei *Dialoghi* di Gregorio Magno: prospettive di struttura." *AAST.M* 109 (1975): 117-185.

———. "Latini e Germani nei *Dialoghi* di Gregorio Magno." In *Atti del 6° congresso internazionale di studi sull'alto medioevo*, 2:717-726.

Vogüé, Adalbert de. "Le procès des moines d'autrefois." *Christus* 12 (1965): 113-128.

———. *La règle de saint Benoît* 1: *Introduction, traduction et notes*. SC 181. Paris: Editions du Cerf, 1972.

———. "La rencontre de Benoît et de Scholastique. Essai d'interprétation." *RHSp.* 48 (1972): 257-273.

———. "Benoît, modèle de vie spirituelle d'après le Deuxième Livre des Dialogues de saint Grégoire." *CCist.* 38 (1976): 147-157.

———. "Grégoire le Grand, lecteur de Grégoire de Tours?" *ABoll.* 94 (1976): 225-233.

———. "La mention de la 'regula monachorum' à la fin de la 'Vie de Benoît' (Grégoire, Dial. II, 36). Sa fonction littéraire et spirituelle." *RBenS* 5 (1976): 289-298.

———. "Un cinquantenaire: l'édition des Dialogues de saint Grégoire par Umberto Moricca." *BISIAM* 86 (1976-77): 183-216.

———. "Un avatar du mythe de la caverne dans les Dialogues de Grégoire le Grand." In *Homenaje a Fray Justo Pérez de Urbel*, 2:19-24. Studia Silensia 3-4. Silos: Abadía, 1976-1977.

———. *Grégoire le Grand, Dialogues* 1: *Introduction, bibliographie et cartes*. SC 251. Paris: Editions du Cerf, 1978.

———. "Le pape qui persécuta saint Equitius. Essai d'identification." *ABoll.* 100 (1982): 319-325.

———. *Vie de Saint Benoît.* Vie monastique 14. Bégrolles-en-Mauges: Abbaye de Bellefontaine, 1982.

———. "De la crise aux résolutions: les *Dialogues* comme histoire d'une âme." In *Grégoire le Grand,* pp. 305-314, with discussion, p. 314.

Von den Steinen, Wolfram. "Heilige als Hagiographen." *HZ* 143 (1931): 229-256.

Vooght, D.P. de. "La notion philosophique du miracle chez Saint Augustin. Dans le 'De Trinitate' et le 'De Genesi ad litteram.'" *RTAM* 10 (1938): 317-343.

———. "Les miracles dans la vie de Saint Augustin." *RTAM* 11 (1939): 5-16.

———. "La théologie du miracle selon saint Augustin." *RTAM* 11 (1939): 197-222.

Voss, Bernd Reiner. "Berührungen von Hagiographie und Historiographie in der Spätantike." *Frühmittelalterliche Studien* 4 (1970): 53-69.

———. *Der Dialog in der frühchristlichen Literatur.* Studia et testimonia antiqua 9. München: Wilhelm Fink Verlag, 1970.

Vregille, Bernard de. "Ecriture sainte et vie spirituelle chez S. Grégoire le Grand." In *DSp.* 4:169-176. 1960.

Wallace-Hadrill, D.S. *The Greek Patristic View of Nature.* New York: Barnes and Noble; Manchester: Manchester University Press, 1968.

Walter, Emil H. "Hagiographisches in Gregors Frankengeschichte." *AKG* 48 (1966): 291-310.

Wansbrough, J.H. "St. Gregory's Intention in the Stories of St. Scholastica and St. Benedict." *RBén.* 75 (1965): 145-151.

Ward, Benedicta. "Miracles and History: A Reconsideration of the Miracle Stories used by Bede." In *Famulus Christi,* pp. 70-76.

———. *The Lives of the Desert Fathers: The Historia monachorum in Aegypto,* including a translation of the *Historia monachorum* by Norman Russell. Oxford: Mowbray; Kalamazoo: Cistercian Publications, 1981.

———. *Miracles and the Medieval Mind: Theory, Record and Event, 1000-1215.* Philadelphia: University of Pennsylvania Press, 1982.

———. "'Signs and Wonders': Miracles in the Desert Tradition." *SPatr.* 17 (1982): 539-542.

Wasselynck, René. "L'orientation eschatologique de la vie chrétienne d'après saint Grégoire le Grand." In *Assemblées du Seigneur* 2: *Temps de l'Avent,* pp. 66-80. Bruges, 1962.

———. "L'influence de l'exégèse de S. Grégoire le Grand sur les commentaires bibliques médiévaux (VIIe-XIIe s.)." *RTAM* 32 (1965): 157-204.

Weber, Leonhard. *Hauptfragen der Moraltheologie Gregors des Grossen. Ein Bild altchristlicher Lebensführung.* Paradosis: Beiträge zur Geschichte der altchristlichen Literatur und Theologie 1. Freiburg in der Schweiz: Paulusdruckerei, 1947.

Weidemann, Margarete. *Kulturgeschichte der Merowingerzeit nach den Werken Gregors von Tours.* Römisch-Germanisches Zentralmuseum, Forschungsinsti-

tut für Vor- und Frühgeschichte, Monographien Bd. 3. 2 vols. Bonn: Rudolf
Habelt GMBH, 1982.

Weinstein, Donald and Rudolph M. Bell. *Saints and Society: The Two Worlds of
Western Christendom, 1000-1700.* Chicago and London: University of Chicago Press, 1982.

Whitelock, Dorothy. "Bede and his Teachers and Friends." In *Famulus Christi,* pp.
19-39.

Wiles, Maurice F. "Miracles in the Early Church." In *Miracles: Cambridge Studies
in their Philosophy and History,* pp. 219-234.

Williams, L. Pearce and Henry John Steffens. *The History of Science in Western
Civilization* 1: *Antiquity and Middle Ages.* Washington: University Press of
America, 1977.

Wolpers, Theodor. *Die englische Heiligenlegende des Mittelalters. Eine Form-
geschichte des Legendenerzählens von der spätantiken lateinischen Tradition
bis zur Mitte des 16. Jahrhunderts.* Tübingen: Max Niemeyer Verlag, 1964.

Wood, I.N. "Early Merovingian Devotion in Town and Country." In *The Church in
Town and Countryside,* pp. 61-76.

Yerkes, David. "An Unnoticed Omission in the Modern Critical Editions of
Gregory's 'Dialogues.'" *RBén.* 87 (1977): 178-179.

——. "The Chapter Titles for Book 1 of Gregory's 'Dialogues.'" *RBén.* 89 (1979):
178-182.

Zangara, Vincenza. "L'*inventio* dei corpi dei martiri Gervasio e Protasio. Testimonianze di Agostino su un fenomeno di religiosità popolare." *Augustinianum*
21 (1981): 119-133.

Zoepf, Ludwig. *Das Heiligen-Leben im 10. Jahrhundert.* Beiträge zur Kulturgeschichte des Mittelalters und der Renaissance 1. 1908. Reprint Hildesheim:
Verlag Dr. H.A. Gerstenberg, 1973.

I regret that I have not been able to obtain a copy of Grégoire, Réginald. "Il volto
agiografico di S. Benedetto." In *Atti del Convegno di Bologna nel XV centenario della
nascita di S. Benedetto,* 15-17 sett. 1980, pp. 1-20. Ravennatensia 9. Cesena: Centro
di studi e ricerche sulla antica provincia ecclesiastica ravennate, Badia di Santa Maria
del Monte, 1981.

Index

abbots: among Gregory's informants 115; in the *Dialogues* 54-55
Adaloald 24n, 43
Adam 236n; and Eve 217n
Adelard of Bath 211
Adeodatus, former deacon of the church of Ravenna 199
adultery 142
Aemiliana, Gregory's aunt 93n, 107
Aeneas 74
Aesculapius 74
Africa 10-11, 14-15
Agapitus I, pope 1, 88
Agilulf, king of the Lombards 43-45
Agnellus, bishop of Terracina 42n
Agrigentum 216
Aigrain, R. 156n
Albinus, bishop of Rieti 261, 264
Amantius, priest 112n, 203
Ammonius, monk of St Andrew's 261, 269
Amoun of Nitria 130n
Anastasius, monk of Subpentoma 151
Anastasius, patriarch of Antioch 25, 30n, 197
Anatolius, false monk 74n
Ancona 10n, 102, 113n, 154, 228n, 237, 264
Andrew, bishop of Fondi 39, 54, 141, 144-145, 153
Andrew, Saint 22
Andrew, *scholasticus* 230
Andrew, *vir illustris* 25n
angels 75n, 137, 190, 228-229
Anglo-Saxon England 42, 196
Anglo-Saxons, conversion of 20-22, 37-38, 44, 64, 72

Angulus, baths of 99
Antichrist 30; medieval doctrine of 78n; miracles of 31, 78-81; precursors of 30n, 79-80; and Satan 81
Antony, monk of St Andrew's 112n, 270
Antony, Saint 130n, 235
Apocalypse of Paul 137n
Apocalypse of Peter 137n
Apocrypha 174
Apollinaris, martyr 199
Apollo, holy man 69
Apollo, temples of 39, 141, 144-145
apostles: commissioned by Christ 16, 18, 34, 35, 82; miracles of 18, 20, 34-37, 82, 209; preaching of 35; relics of 23. *See also* Andrew, Saint; Paul, Saint; Peter, Saint
Appian Way 141
Aptonius, *vir inlustris* 114n, 261, 265
Apulia 129n, 266
Arborius 223n
Arians and Arianism 43, 46, 81n, 254-255
Aristotle 226
asceticism, in the desert fathers 68-69
Asclipiodotus, patrician of Gaul 25n
astronomy 212n, 258
Athanasius, priest 261, 270
Athanasius, Saint 66; *Vita Antonii* 6, 46n, 101
Auerbach, E. 42n, 50, 177
Augustine, archbishop of Canterbury 22, 37, 72
Augustine, bishop of Hippo 2, 4, 66, 81n, 124, 188n, 190n, 191n, 197; attitude towards science 212-213;

attracted to the Manichaeans 11; baptism of 13n; conversion of 13, 158n; influence on Gregory 6, 8, 16, 28, 76, 134-138, 140, 187, 222, 225, 245n; witnesses miracles 13-14, 111
—, teachings on: allegorical fiction 165-166; the apologetic purpose of miracles 34-35, 37, 47n; the end of the world 27-28; the interpretation of Scripture 182, 195-196, 200n, 213n, 246, 252; lying 157-160, 170-171; miracles and nature 215-221, 225; the miracles of Antichrist 78n, 79n; the miracles of pagan gods 72-75; the miracles of Scripture 8, 34-35; modern miracles 8-15, 18, 37; the order in nature 227; the power of evil spirits 74n; the primacy of humility 69n; the science of his day 216-217, 227, 239; the seminal reasons 74n, 217-218, 220-221; spiritual miracles 9; the symbolic significance of nature 257; the various forms of vision 124n; the wonders of nature 8-9, 34
—, writings: *City of God* 10-11, 14, 215-217, 219-220; *Confessions* 13, 158n; *Contra Faustum* 220; *Contra mendacium* 158, 170; *De mendacio* 158; *De utilitate credendi* 8, 12, 219; *De vera religione* 8, 12; *Retractions* 12

Autharis, king of the Lombards 43
Avesgaudus, bishop of Le Mans 168

Babut, E.-C. 154, 175n
Bardy, G. 13n, 15n
Bartimaeus 33
Bartolommeo Facio 198
Basilius, magician 77
Batiffol, P. 47n
Bede the Venerable 51, 121, 162-163, 237, 242n, 255, 258; attitude toward *Dialogues* 92; Biblical character of his thought 243; conception of truth

164, 196; *Ecclesiastical History* 162-164; use of witnesses 196
Benedict of Nursia: attacked by Florentius 40; attacked by the monks of Vicovaro 128, 247-248; attitude toward secular learning 180-181, 185; aware of the dishonesty of Exhilaratus 131; charity of divinely rewarded 128; combats paganism 39; conversion of 119, 180-181; cosmic vision of 117-118, 125n; death of 120, 129-131; establishes Monte Cassino 39; expels demons 126, 234; Gregory's portrait of 99-100; meets Scholastica 118-119, 250-251, 253; meets Totila 118; miraculously repairs broken tray 103n; opens the eyes of Maurus 149n; produces water from rock 146, 149n, 250-252; rebukes wayward monk 127; restores a young monk to life 126, 248-249; retrieves iron blade from the lake 146, 149n; rule of 68n, 100, 253n; sees Germanus of Capua ascend to heaven 130n; sees Scholastica ascend to heaven 123, 130, 131n; significance of his name 249-251; spiritual insight of 104; temptation of 117-120; tested by Totila 129
Benedict, hermit 147, 148
Benevento, duchy of 43
Bertolini, O. 44-45
Bible. *See* Sacred Scripture
biography, ancient 163n, 165
birth, mysteries of 189n, 216-217, 240
bishops: in the *Dialogues* 54-55; among Gregory's informants 116; in medieval hagiography 97; in the writings of Gregory of Tours 55
Bloch, R. 210n
Boesch Gajano, S. 8, 26n, 30n, 40n, 44n, 45, 55, 75, 91, 92, 94n-95n, 101, 112n, 115, 116n, 152n, 204n, 215n, 231n-232n, 242n

Boethius 118; *Consolation of Philosophy* 185

Boglioni, P. 2, 45n, 58n, 75, 87, 179n, 212n, 213-215, 229

Bolton, W.F. 121-122

Boman, T. 168n

Boniface IV, pope 267

Boniface, bishop of Ferentis: curses a minstrel 94-95, 252-253; generosity of miraculously rewarded 88, 89-90, 128

Boniface, monk of St Andrew's 261, 267

Bonner, G. 61

Bosl, K. 161n

Brandea 23, 25

Brioude, church at 238n

Brown, C. 210

Brown, P. 16n, 243n-244n

Brunichild, queen of the Franks 22n, 42n, 61

Bynum, C.W. 97n

Byrhtferth 256-257

Caesarius, bishop of Arles 38n

Calama 10n

Calati, B. 55n

Campania 42, 141

Cana, miracle at 58, 107n, 154, 201n, 211, 225

canonization 68

Caphar Gamle 11

Carolingian Renaissance 183n

Cassiodorus 53

Castorius, monk 261, 264

Catry, P. 26n, 252

Centumcellae 109n, 133-134

Cerbonius, bishop of Populonia 254

Chadwick, O. 178n

chance 238-239

charity 75, 93, 107, 119, 172n, 181, 213; of Boniface of Ferentis 88, 89-90, 95; as the primary virtue 65n, 70; requires two persons 245; of

Sanctulus of Nursia 100; of Scholastica 253; in the thought of Augustine 70n; twin precepts of 195-196, 245

charms and Talismans 25

Chartres 139; school of 258

chastity 143

Chenu, M.-D. 258

Childebert II, king of the Franks 25n

Christ, Jesus 41n, 47n, 65, 70, 72, 76, 166, 209, 230, 244, 248; appears as a leper 19, 107; casts out demons 33; changes water into wine 58, 107n, 154, 201n, 211, 225; cleanses the temple 166; commissions the apostles 16, 18, 34, 35, 82; divine and human nature of 247; expels evil spirits 58, 105n, 147; feeds the five thousand 147, 225, 255; heals the blind 33, 58, 59-60, 106; heals the centurion's servant 105; heals the crippled woman 58, 105, 246; heals the deaf mute 58, 105n; heals the official's son 58, 105, 147, 200-201; imitation of 70; multiplies loaves and fishes 107n; passion of 247-248; prefigured by Jacob 160; produces miraculous drafts of fishes 58-59, 60, 106, 246; prophesizes his death and resurrection 59; raises the dead 58, 105, 107n, 149-150, 187; resurrection of 59, 60, 187, 189, 207; second coming of 27-29; sends out disciples by twos 244-245; shares meal with the disciples after the resurrection 60, 106n, 201, 246-247; virgin birth of 187; walks on water 58, 60

Ciccarese, M.P. 154

Cicero 118

Clark, F. 2n

Clement of Alexandria 158

Colgrave, B. 174n

Columbus, bishop of Numidia 25n

Consolino, F.E. 67n

Constable, G. 161n

Constantina, empress 22-25, 42

Constantine, abbot of Monte Cassino 114n, 261, 265

Constantinople 1, 20, 23n, 134, 135, 141, 151, 267; patriarchs of 30n

Constantius, priest 128

Constantius, sacristan 66n, 102-103, 153n, 228n

Copiosus, physician 112n, 113n-114n, 261, 271

Corsica 42

Courcelle, P. 117-118, 125n, 137n, 158n

Cox, P. 165n

Cracco, G. 8, 54n, 56n, 68n, 91n, 179-180, 181n

creation: days of 246; doctrine of 187-188, 189n, 228

credulity, about miracles 117, 176-177, 206, 210

Cremascoli, G. 93n, 94n

cupidity 184

Curma, curial official 134-137

Cusack, P.A. 118, 119, 125n, 249

Cuthbert, Saint 162, 242n, 255

Cyriacus, patriarch of Constantinople 30n

Dagens, C. 42n, 47, 47n, 49n, 55n, 57, 69, 83n, 84, 119, 178n, 180, 181, 182-183, 185

Daniel, prophet 146

Dante, *Paradiso* 257

Darida, Gothic commander 138, 140

Delaruelle, E. 46n, 222n

Delehaye, H. 67n, 96, 162, 222

Delforge, Th. 118n

Demm, E. 67n, 224n

demons 39, 82, 93, 137, 141-143, 144n, 145; illusions of 73-74; miracles of 73-75, 77; the pagan gods as 39, 73-74; possession by 77, 82, 98, 126, 127, 147, 176; role of, in temp-tation 233-237; subject to the apostles 65

desert fathers 81n, 129n, 160, 177n; ideal of sanctity 68-69; teaching on demons 233-235

Desiderius, bishop of Vienne 181, 182-183, 185

Deusdedit, *honestus senex* 134, 136, 261, 269

Dhanis, E. 95

Dialogues, of Gregory the Great: anti-heretical theme of 46; attitude of medieval authors toward 51; audience of 47-57, 85, 173, 252; authenticity of 2n; characterization of the saints in 97-104; clerical nature of 54-56, 85, 115; concealed meaning of 247-252; date of 2, 7, 20, 45; designed to be read 52; dialogue form of 173; doctrinal content of 4, 49, 89, 108-110, 190-191; fragmentary appearance of 55n; historical value of 2, 4, 117-122, 249-250; literary affiliations of 4, 117-120, 124-125, 137; literary culture represented in 179-181; narrative techniques of 96; portrait of the Goths and the Lombards in 45-46; purpose of 7, 42-47, 57; readers of 117, 173-174, 209-210; sophistication of 49-52; sources of 54, 113-117, 125, 128n, 129, 131-132, 133, 135-137, 140, 143-146, 148, 150-153, 174, 191-204; as spiritual autobiography 119n; stylistic character of 49-52; testify to paganism 38-40, 42-43; used as historical source 121

Diocletian, emperor 255

Dionysius Exiguus 118, 125n

Dionysos 39n

Dodds, E.R. 73n

Domnica 38

Donation of Constantine 198

Donatus, bishop of Arezzo 151
Donatus, grammarian 182
Dorn, E. 98
Doucet, M. 82, 119-120
Dudden, F.H. 176, 186, 192, 195, 203-204, 206
Dufner, G. 51, 121, 185
Dynamius, patrician of Gaul 24n, 25n

Eadmer, *Life of St Anselm* 97n
Easter Sunday 111
Eleutherius, abbot of St Mark's at Spoleto 132, 148n, 261, 266, 267, 269; exorcizes a demon 98, 202; overwhelmed by pride 98; raises a dead person 203; relieves Gregory's illness 111, 202
Eleutherius, saint and martyr 232n
Eliade, M. 168n
Elijah, prophet 146, 201n
Elisha, prophet 146, 149n, 150, 151n, 201n, 249
Elysium, fields of 137n
Emmerson, R.K. 78n
Empedocles 226
Empire, administration of 1, 42, 138-139
Ennodius of Pavia 169n
Epidaurus, serpent from 74
Epiphanius, deacon 174n
Equitius, abbot 56, 66, 78n, 89n, 90n, 102, 148; cures a nun 147; divinely vindicated 88; exorcizes the Devil 176; experiences a vision 86, 88; humility of 88, 90; not to be imitated 85-86
Ethelbert, king of the *Angli* 29
Eucharist. *See* mass
Eugendus, Saint 223n
Euhemerus 73
Eulogius, patriarch of Alexandria 22, 24n, 25, 30n
Eumorphius 122
Eusebius 154; *Life of Origen* 165n

Euthicius, cloak of 89n, 90n
Eutychius, bishop of Tyndaris 42n
Eutychius, patriarch of Constantinople 189
Eutychus, revived by St Paul 35-36, 64
evil spirits. *See* demons
Evodius, bishop of Uzalis 11
exempla 104
Exhilaratus, monk 131-132
exorcism, sacrament of 82

fall of man 213, 233, 246
false Christians 61-63
fasting 231-232; dangers of 69n
Felix III, pope 1
Felix of Nola 15n
Felix, bishop of Porto 133, 261, 269, 270, 271
Felix, prior of Fondi 261, 264
Ferentis 94
Festugière, A.-J. 68, 177n, 234
fiction, medieval ideas of 165, 174
Florentius, monk 99
Florentius, priest 40
Floridus, bishop of Città di Castello 112n, 203, 261, 266, 268
folklore 138n
Fondi 140, 141, 266; citizens of 143-146
Fontaine, J. 46n, 181, 258n
forgeries 160-161, 198
fornication 142-143
Fortunatus, abbot of Cicero's Bath 148, 261, 264, 265
Fortunatus, bishop of Todi 40, 77, 89, 94n, 192-193; exorcizes a demon 93; raises Marcellus from the dead 149-150, 152-153, 192-193
Fortunatus, nobleman of Ferentis 94
four elements, doctrine of the 226, 227n, 257
Fraser, J.G. 161, 254n
free will 236
Fridrichsen, A. 31

Frigdianus, bishop of Lucca 100-103
Fuhrmann, H. 161

Gahazi 146n
Gaiffier, B. de 121n
Galla, widow 232n
Garamantes, spring of the 216
Gaudentius, priest 128n, 262, 264, 265
Gaul 42, 54n
Gerald of Aurillac 56n
Germanus, bishop of Capua 99, 130n, 132-133
Gesta martyrum Romanorum 116n
Gillet, R. 55n
Ginzburg, C. 47n, 48n
God, existence of 186-187
Gordiana, Gregory's aunt 93n, 107-108
Goths 53, 134, 147, 148, 192, 249; as portrayed in the *Dialogues* 45-46
grammar 178, 181-183
Grant, R.M. 210n, 219n
Graus, F. 149n
Greece, ancient 206
Greek, language 6, 178, 233
Greeks, ancient 168n, 210n, 211
Gregory of Tours 6, 24n, 38n, 138n, 163n, 178, 238-239, 255-256; contrasted with Gregory the Great 89, 91, 111; emphasizes miracles 67n, 92n; on the end of the world 26; *Historia Francorum* 178n; ideal of sanctity 55; miraculously healed 111; reports scepticism 208; on the source of St Martin's power 222n; use of witnesses 196n; witnesses miracles 111, 208
Gregory Thaumaturgus 144n, 151
Gregory the Great: biblical character of his thought 118, 243, 259; biographical work of 96-101; cites witnesses 4, 92, 113-117, 152-153, 173-175, 191-194, 210; consistency of 8; conversion of 1, 119; credulity of 2, 176-177, 191; dealings with the

Lombards 43-45; earliest biography of 166-168; education of 1, 5, 178, 185, 191; emphasizes Christian practice 62-63, 82; episcopal *familia* of 53; Greek influence on 6, 178; influence of 1-2, 6; influenced by Augustine 6, 8, 16, 28, 76, 134-138, 140, 187, 222, 225, 245n; laments loss of the contemplative life 17; literary style of 51, 182; master of the contemplative life 63; miracles of 167; as a moral theologian 84, 87, 185, 232; relieved of his illness by Eleutherius 111, 202; reputation for moderation 61-62; sends *Dialogues* to Theodelinda 43, 44; verifies sources 201-204; witnesses miracles 111-112, 114n
—, teachings on: the communion of the saints 172n; demons 234-235; the devastation of the world 16-17, 28, 35; the efficacy of good examples 49, 86-87, 93; the end of the world 16, 26-31, 35; the existence of God 186-187; grammar 181-183; the ideal spiritual life 55; illness 230-232; the immortality of the soul 190-191, 206-207; the interpretation of Scripture 181-182, 195-196, 200-201, 244-246, 250, 252, 258; lying 4, 169-172, 175; the medical profession 231; miraculous visions 26, 29-30; rational enquiry 5, 177-178, 186-191; relics 22-26; the resurrection 186-191, 207, 226, 239-240; Satan 235-236; science 212-213; secular culture 4-5, 177-185, 191; spiritual vision 124; temptation and sin 232-237
—, writings. *See Dialogues; Homilies on Ezechiel; Homilies on the Gospels; In 1 Reg.; Moralia on Job; Pastoral Care; Register*
Gregory, monk 180

Gross, K. 119-120
Gurevich, A.J. 97n, 198n, 227n

hagiography, medieval: appeals to witnesses 173-174, 194; audience of 53, 85, 174; biblical character of 241, 243n; claims to truthfulness 155; conception of miracle 222-224, 228; conception of truth 160-169, 195; influenced by the *Dialogues* 2; literary invention in 155-157; medieval readers of 174; moral assessment of sources 197-198; punitive miracles in 95n; purpose of 10n, 46, 85; records disbelief 207-208; relationship of, to historiography 162-165; role of miracles in 3, 66-67, 96, 101-102; suppresses individuality of the saints 96-98, 165, 167
Hallinger, K. 121-123, 143
Hay, D. 243
heaven 82, 135, 136
Hebrews, ancient 168n, 170-171, 211, 223
Heinzelmann, M. 163n
hell 134, 135, 137; corporeal flames of 110; torments of 122-123
Helle, the abba 129n
heresy 42-43, 46, 81n, 106
heretics 175; miracles of 72, 75
Hermenegild, king of the Visigoths 70n
Hilary of Arles 66
Hippo 10, 11, 134
Historia monachorum 6, 233; emphasizes humility 69; role of miracles in 101
historians, ancient 74
historiography, ancient and medieval 162-165, 197-198, 243
history, medieval sense of 243
history, sacred, periods of 246
Hofmann, D. 200n
Holland, R.F. 238-239

Holy Saturday 202
Holy Spirit 54n, 72, 85, 107n
Homilies on Ezechiel 21, 187, 207; audience of 48n-49n
Homilies on the Gospels 7, 82, 93, 209, 226, 243, 244; audience of 48, 52; date of 16; miracle stories in 19, 107, 174n; presented orally 52; similarities with the *Dialogues* 49; stylistic character of 52
Honoratus, abbot of Fondi 56n, 85; sandal of 89n, 139, 146
Honoratus, abbot of Subiaco 114n, 129n, 148, 262, 265
Horace 117
hospitals 203
Hospito, duke of the Barbaricini 25n, 42n
Howorth, H.H. 177, 179n, 195
Hubert, Saint 174n
human nature 105-106, 246
humility 66n, 69, 72, 85, 139-140, 195, 212n; in Augustine's thought 70n; in Gregory's thought 69; nobility encouraged to practise 57n
—, of the saints: abbot Equitius 88, 90; Boniface of Ferentis 95; Libertinus of Fondi 139
hyperbole 156
hypocrites, miracles of 72, 76-77

idols 39, 42, 61-62, 73, 142
Illidius, bishop of Clermont 67n, 111n
illness 230-232
imitation: of Christ 70-71; of the saints 84-86
In 1 Reg. 58, 224
Incarnation, doctrine of 186
Innocentius, counsellor 14, 112n
Isaac of Spoleto 98, 131-132, 153
Isauria 174n
Isidore of Seville 66, 227, 258
Italy 1, 2, 7, 11, 44, 53, 84, 242

Jacob and Esau 159-160, 170

Januarius, bishop of Cagliari 42, 62

Jerome, Saint 157, 158, 208

Jerusalem 59

Jesse the Bethlehemite 171

Jews 39, 141, 143, 144, 153; unresponsive to Christ 34n; witnessed Christ's miracles 15. *See also* Hebrews, ancient

Job 79n, 229, 250

John Cassian 4, 6, 66, 80n, 224n; *Collations* 101, 141-146, 235; emphasizes purity of heart 69; *Institutes* 101-102; on lying 159-160; on the role of miracles 101-102; on temptation and sin 235

John Chrysostom 158

John I, pope 122

John III, pope 88n, 144

John the Baptist 24n, 39, 199

John the Hermit 68

John, archbishop of Ravenna 199

John, ex-consul 25n

John, monk of St Andrew's 112n, 113n, 270

John, patriarch of Constantinople 30n

John, Saint, the Evangelist, Gospel of 166

John, tribune 262, 266

John, vice-prefect of Rome 262, 266, 270

Jonas 71n

Jonas of Orleans 174n

Jones, C.W. 164, 195-197

Jordan, river 146, 149n, 201n

Judas 76

Judgment, Day of 19, 28-29, 65, 72, 76

Julian, bishop of Le Mans 168

Julian, *defensor* of the Roman church 193, 262, 265, 269

Justus, monk of St Andrew's 112n, 114n, 232, 271

Juvenal 117

Juvenal, bishop of Narni 232n

Lambot, C. 47n, 99n

Laporte, J. 39n, 40, 253n

Laurio, monk 113n, 151, 174n, 262, 264

law, medieval conception of 161

Lawrence, antipope 132, 179

Lawrence, *religiosus vir* 140, 262, 264

Lawrence, Saint, relics of 22, 24n

laying on of hands 82, 126, 203

laymen: as audience of the *Dialogues* 57; in the *Dialogues* 54-56; among Gregory's informants 116; and the medieval ideal of sanctity 56n

Lazarus 58, 105, 149-150, 187

Le Goff, J. 39, 104n, 120n

Leander, bishop of Seville 16, 181-182, 183

Leclercq, J. 161-162, 167

legend, the truth of 162

Leo I, pope 23, 24n

Leontius, ex-consul 25n, 76

Lerins 177n

Letaldus of Micy 168-169

Lewis, C.S. 225n

Libelli miraculorum 10, 209

Liberius, *vir nobilissimus* 262, 270

Libertinus of Fondi 56n, 66; restores a dead child to life 89n, 139-140, 146; robbed of his horse 138-139

lime, miraculous properties of 216-217

literacy, in sixth-century Italy 52-53

loadstone, miraculous properties of 216

logic 178

Lombards 1, 144n, 223n; administration of 53; conversion of 42-46; and literary culture 53; as portrayed in the *Dialogues* 45-46

Lorenzo Valla 198

Lubac, H. de 26n, 181-183, 185, 200n, 245n

Lucian 136n

Luke, Saint, the Evangelist 59, 113; Gospel of 166

lying, attitudes toward 4, 157-160, 168-172

Macarius of Alexandria 233
Macarius, abbot 126n
MacMullen, R. 210n
Macrobius 118
magic and magicians 40, 73, 74, 77, 253n
Mähler, M. 126n, 149n
Malchus, Saint 157
Malta 36
Manichaeism 11
manna 223
Manselli, R. 27n, 43n
Marcellinus, bishop of Ancona 237, 255
Marcellus, friend of bishop Fortunatus 149-150, 152-153, 192
Marinianus, bishop of Ravenna 48, 231-232
Mark, Saint, the Evangelist 112
Marmoutier 208
Marrou, H.-I. 227
Martin of Braga 38n
Martin the hermit 103, 238n, 250, 251-252
Martin, bishop of Tours 39, 74n, 118, 130n, 154; beaten by officers of the state 138-139; disbelief in his miracles 208; imitates Christ 241; as portrayed by Sulpicius Severus 99n
—, miracles of 24n, 46n, 81n, 102, 111, 223n, 138-140, 241; cures daughter of Arborius 223n; restores dead child to life 139-140
Martinianus, Saint 19
Martyrius, monk 19, 107
Mary and Martha, sisters of Lazarus 149-150
Mary, the Virgin 128, 187
mass 68, 130-131, 133; benefits of 109-110, 112n
Matthew, Saint, the Evangelist 72; Gospel of 166
Maurice, emperor 17, 22, 29, 45
Maurus, monk 127, 148, 149n; walks on water 146-147

Maximian, bishop of Syracuse 53, 113n, 151, 174n, 262, 264, 268, 269
Maximus, emperor 118
Maximus, father of bishop Probus of Rieti 232n
McCulloh, J.M. 23n
memoriae, of the saints 10
Menas, venerandus vir 113n
Merulus, monk of St Andrew's 112n, 270
midwives, the Hebrew 170-171
Milan 12, 28, 112n
minstrels 94-95
miracles: appeal of 48; belief prerequisite for 33; in the Bible 21, 34-37, 57-61, 200-201, 225; biblical archetypes for 47, 146-151, 209, 241-243, 251, 255; biblical doctrine of 33; consoling effect of 242-243; deepen faith 57-64; definition of 214-215, 218-219, 221-222; divine basis of 58, 168, 204-205, 221, 222-224; in the early church 8-12, 17-20, 35-36, 209, 210n; of evildoers 65, 72, 74-77, 81; grace of withdrawn 72; natural events conceived as 215-218, 224-226, 237-239; occasion for vainglory 72; of the pagan gods 72-75; relative scarcity of 30-32, 47, 80; of the reprobate 19; role of, in medieval hagiography 101-102; at the shrines of the saints 9-11, 14-15, 19, 24n, 37n, 38, 73, 89-90, 111n, 163n, 191, 238n; of the spiritual order 9, 18-19, 81-82; teach doctrinal lessons 4, 58-61, 105-107, 108-110; teach ecclesiastical discipline 58, 105, 107; teach moral lessons 4, 58, 87-89, 105, 107-108, 109-110, 135; and the work of conversion 17, 20, 22, 33-38, 46-47, 58-60
Miracula 163n
monasteries 89n, 126, 127, 130, 131, 138, 142, 146, 147, 148, 150-151,

163, 177n, 180, 208, 223n, 251; St Andrew's in Rome 1, 22, 53, 108, 111, 112n, 113n, 132, 148n, 151, 202, 269, 271; St Mark's in Spoleto 132, 148n, 202; St Peter's at Palestrina 89n

monks 22, 29n, 97, 115, 141-143, 233-234; of Equitius 85; of St Andrew's 111, 112n, 113n, 132, 269, 270, 271; of St Benedict 104, 126-127, 130, 242, 251, 268; of St Mark's in Spoleto 202-203; of St Martin 208; of St Peter's at Palestrina 267; of Spes 123, 130; of Vicovaro 128, 247-248

Monte Cassino 39, 119, 126

Moralia on Job 2, 7, 37, 49, 78, 86, 184, 187, 189, 207, 225, 233, 234, 236, 244, 245, 249, 250, 252; audience of 48; contrasted with *The Consolation of Philosophy* 185; date of 20

Moricca, U. 112n, 114n, 117, 121n, 152, 177, 211n, 194

Morris, C. 97n

Moses: and the burning bush 201n; denied entry to the promised land 72; divides the Red Sea 58, 187, 223-224; produces water from the rock 146, 187, 251

Mount Argentaro, anonymous holy man of 40n-41n

Mount Soracte, monastery of 151

Musca, G. 196n

Naaman 146n

Narcissus, bishop of Jerusalem 154

natural law 226-228

nature: as instrument of divine judgment 230; symbolic significance of 5, 214, 256-259; wonders of 8-9, 34. *See also* human nature

Nebuchadnezzar 147

Nepi 151

Nicaea, Council of 145

nobility: admonition of, in the *Dialogues* 57; among Gregory's informants 116; and the medieval ideal of sanctity 56n; as represented in the *Dialogues* 56; of Rome 53, 134

Nola, church of 265

Nonnosus, abbot 53, 150-151, 174n

nuns 86, 147, 176

Nursia 100, 148n, 180, 268

Odo of Cluny 56n

Origen 9, 87, 158, 165n

Orosius 196

paganism 142, 144n, 182-183, 185, 253n; survivals of 38-43, 57, 61-62

pagans: conversion of 20, 34, 36, 38, 39, 42, 46-47, 57, 144n; gods of 72-75, 144n; persecute the church 20, 34, 36; scepticism of 187n; superstitions of 210n; temples of 39, 73, 141, 142, 144, 144n, 145

Palestrina 89n, 146

Palladius 68-69, 101, 223n

panegyric 156

papal curia 88

papal estates 7n, 176-177, 204

Paphnutius 130n

parables 166; of Dives and Lazarus 107; of the fig tree 105; of the lost sheep 166; of the Prodigal Son 165n; of the sower 166n

Paronetto, V. 43n

Partner, N.F. 198

Paschasius, deacon 89n, 99, 132-133, 179-180

Pastoral Care 171, 231

Patze, H. 161n

Paul i, pope 24n

Paul the Deacon 44n, 121, 184n

Paul the Hermit 130n, 208

Paul the Simple 223n

Paul, Saint 64, 73, 158n, 167, 213, 217, 230; compared to St Peter 71; heals the father of Publius 36, 64; relics of 22, 24; revives Eutychus 35-36, 64

Paulinus of Milan 95n

Paulinus of Nola 11, 70n, 153n, 180, 194, 265

Paulus and Palladia 112n

peasantry, as represented in the *Dialogues* 56

Pelagius I, pope 144

Pelagius II, pope 1, 262, 266

Pelusium, monastery at 142

penance, sacrament of 105

Penates, images of the 74

Pentecost 107n, 201n

Peregrinus, monk 114n, 128n, 262, 265

Peter of Pisa 184n

Peter the Deacon, Gregory's interlocutor: acknowledges the primacy of virtue 66, 82n; astonished at miracles 30n; avid for wonder tales 65-66; doubts miracles 7, 209, 242; doubts the reality of the soul 123-124; function of, in the *Dialogues* 84n; identity of 7n

Peter, abbot of St Andrew's 262, 270

Peter, bishop of Corsica 42n, 61

Peter, brother of Gregory of Tours 112n

Peter, overseer of the church 137

Peter, Saint 158n, 199; compared to St Paul 71; cures the man lame from birth 223; relics of 22, 24-25; sepulchre of 24; walks on water 71, 147

Petersen, J.M. 6n, 88n, 89n, 94, 116n, 137n, 142, 143, 144n, 145, 148n-149n, 150n, 153n, 178n, 179n, 193

Pharaoh 74, 170

philosophy 185

physicians 231

Piamun, abbot 102n

Pityrion, monk 233, 234

Placidus, monk 146

Plato 158, 168n

Pliny the Elder, *Naturalis historia* 212

poets, ancient 182-183

Poitiers 208

Pompeianus, abbot 127

Poulin, J.-C. 56n, 67n-68n, 85n

preaching 38; of the Apostles 35, 63, 82; of Equitius 88; of St Martin 139; of Spes 130; use of the *Dialogues* in 57

predestination 80, 186

Pretiosus, prior of St Andrew's 112n, 113n, 262, 271

pride 66n, 69, 72, 75, 88, 186, 212, 236; the root of all sin 69, 233; the saints vulnerable to 98

Prinz, F. 177n

Probus, abbot of the monastery of Renatus in Rome 262, 268, 269, 270

Probus, bishop of Rieti 232n

Processus, Saint 19

Protasius and Gervasius, martyrs 12, 112n

Providence 74, 186, 213n

Pseudo-Augustine 71n

Publius, the father of, healed by St Paul 36, 64

Purgatory, doctrine of 132

Puzicha, M. 92n, 99n, 121

Quadragesimus, subdeacon 40n-41n, 262, 266

Quest of the Holy Grail 257

Quintilian 155n

Quirinus, bishop of Siscia 255-256

rationalism, error of 186

rationes seminales 74n, 217-218, 220-221

Ravenna 139, 199, 231

Ray, R.D. 163

reason, in defence of the faith 186-191

Reccared, king of the Visigoths 24n, 25n, 81n

Recchia, V. 27n, 118

Redempta, nun 107, 174n

Redemptus, bishop of Ferentis 30n, 262, 268

Reginald of Canterbury 157

Register, of Gregory the Great 44, 48, 151, 174, 230; testifies to pagan survivals 41-42

relics 22-26, 160, 208, 239

—, of the saints: Elijah 146n; Euthicius 89n, 90n; Honoratus 89n, 139, 146; John the Baptist 24n; Protasius and Gervasius 12, 112n; St Lawrence 22, 24n; St Paul 22, 24; St Peter 22, 24-25; St Sebastian 77; St Stephen 11, 14, 15

Renaissance 256

Reparatus, *spectabilis vir* 110, 134-136

repentance, in the thought of the desert fathers 69

resurrection, doctrine of 186-191, 191n, 207, 226, 239

resurrection-body 189-190; of Christ 201

rhetoric 51, 156, 163, 178

Richards, J. 41

Riché, P. 178n, 212n

Romans, credulity of the 210n

Rome 1, 7n, 20, 24, 43, 44, 45, 74, 77n, 100, 113n, 132, 136, 137n, 141, 148n, 151, 178n, 180, 193, 202, 231, 267, 269, 270, 271; prefect of 1

Romula, nun 19n, 174n, 231n; wondrous death of 107, 108

Rousseau, O. 149n

Rufinus 68-69, 178, 233; *Historia ecclesiastica* 144n

Rusticiana 22

Sabinus, bishop of Canossa 128-129, 254

Sacred Scripture: correct understanding of 63; factual reliability of 166; idea of miracle in 33-34, 65, 76n; in-

fluence on Gregory 118, 243, 259; interpretation of 181-182, 195-196, 200-201, 213n, 244-246, 250, 252, 258; symbols of 21; teaching on lying 159-160, 169-172

Samaritans 15

Samnium 113n, 138, 140, 267

Samuel, prophet 171-172

sanctity: medieval conception of 56n; popular conception of 67

Sanctulus, priest 181n, 263, 266, 268; Gregory's portrait of 100; miracles of 100, 147, 148n, 223n, 255

Sardinia 41-42

Satan 73, 142-143, 176; and Antichrist 81; appears as a dragon 19; attacks Benedict's monks 126-127, 248-249; attacks Martin the hermit 103; depictions of, in the *Dialogues* 234; role of, in temptation and sin 233-237; tempts monks of St Macarius 126n

Saul, king 171

Saxer, V. 10n, 13-14

scepticism: about Christ 33; about the immortality of the soul 190, 206-207; about miracles 7, 54, 117, 206, 207-211; about the resurrection 187, 207, 226

schism and schismatics 43, 44, 99, 106, 132, 179

Scholastica, St Benedict's sister 118-119, 124; death of 123, 129-130, 131n; produces a storm 40n, 251n, 253; significance of her name 249-251

schools 180-181, 183-184

Schreiner, K. 156, 160, 166

science: ancient and medieval 5, 212, 216, 226-228, 239, 258-259; modern 5, 226, 258-259

scientific revolution 226

Scivoletto, N. 183

Sebastian, Saint 77

self-knowledge 86

senate, of Rome 1
Seneca 118
Serchio, river 101
Servulus 181n
Severus, priest 103, 154
Sicily 1, 7n, 42, 113n, 122-123
Sigal, P.-A. 163n
sign of the cross 128-129, 141, 203, 248, 254
Silvestre, H. 74n, 160-161
Simplicius, abbot of Monte Cassino 114n, 263, 265
sin 222, 230-231; and temptation 232-237
Smalley, B. 243
Solinus, *Collectanea rerum memorabilium* 212
soul, immortality of the 89, 108, 190-191, 206-207
Spain 267
Speciosus, monk 180
Speciosus, priest 174n, 263, 268
Spes, abbot 123-124, 129-131
Spoleto 132, 202; holy woman of 147, 148n
Stahl, W.H. 212n
Stancliffe, C. 54n, 99n, 132n, 154, 174n-175n
Steidle, B. 118n
Stephen, abbot 263, 268
Stephen, *inlustris vir* 134-138, 140-141, 263, 270
Stephen, priest 267
Stephen, Saint 10, 11, 14, 15
Stephen, smith 134-135
Styx, the river 137n
Subiaco 40, 89
Subpentoma, monastery of 151
Sulpicius Severus 4, 6, 46n, 53n, 66, 71n, 74n, 81n, 130n, 132n, 138-140, 154, 155n, 173, 208, 238-239, 241; accused of lying 208; appeals to witnesses 174n-175n, 208; perceives himself as an historian 163n; on the role of miracles 102; on the source of St Martin's power 223n; truthfulness of 99n, 154, 155n, 174n-175n
—, *Dialogues* 102, 138, 175n, 208, 223n; audience of 53n
—, *Vita Martini* 102, 118, 125n, 154, 223n; audience of 46n, 53n, 54n; purpose of 46n
Symmachus, patrician 122
Symmachus, pope 132, 179
Syria 149n

Tarquinius 74
Tartarean Phelegethon, river of Hell 137n-138n
Tateo, F. 51
Tauriana 109n, 133
temptation: demonic source of 233-237; human source of 232-233
Terracina 144n, 180, 242
Tertullian 74n
Tharsilla, Gregory's aunt 19n, 93n, 107, 112n
Theoctistus, monk 126n
Theodelinda, queen of the Lombards 25n, 43, 44
Theodore, monk of St Andrew's 270
Theodore, physician 25n
Theodore, sacristan 146, 263, 267
Theodoric the Great, king of the Ostrogoths 122
Theodorus, monk of St Andrew's 19n
Thomas Aquinas 2, 165, 186, 224n; on the order in nature 227
"Three Chapters" schism 43, 44
Thürlemann, F. 163n, 196n
Tiber 74
Tiberias, Sea of 59, 60
Tiburtius, priest 134
Timothy, companion of St Paul 36, 64
Todi 93, 149, 150, 192, 193
tongues, speaking in 82
topoi 149n, 153n, 173, 194, 234

Totila, king of the Ostrogoths 118, 129, 254
Troas 35
Troy 74
truth, medieval conception of 4, 160-169
Tullium 134
Tuscany 77

Uranius, *Epistula de obitu Paulini* 265
Uzalis 10n

Valentinian, abbot of the Benedictine monastery at the Lateran 114n, 263, 265
Valentio, abbot of St Andrew's 263, 264, 267, 269
Valeria, pious priest of 89n
Van der Meer, F. 197n
Van Uytfanghe, M. 30n, 33, 76n, 209, 222n
Vegetius 196
Venantius, bishop of Luni 263, 266, 270
veneration, of the saints 85, 95, 253
vestal virgins 74
vices, hierarchy of 233
Vicovaro, monks of 128, 247-248
vigils 231, 232
Vinay, G. 43n, 119n-120n
Virgil, *Aeneid* 117, 137n
virtue, primacy of, with respect to miracles 65-72, 81-83, 84
virtues, hierarchy of 257
Visigothic Spain 183n

Visigoths, conversion of 70n, 81n
visions 86, 88, 108, 109, 112n, 117, 122-124, 125n, 129-131, 134-137, 146, 234; Gregorian doctrine of 124; on the increase 26, 29-30
Vita S. Pachomii 118, 119
Vitae patrum 4, 6, 69, 119, 141-145
Vitale-Brovarone, A. 50n, 51, 55n, 96, 209n, 247-249
Vogüé, A. de 30n, 43, 46, 47, 48, 51n, 54, 57, 68n, 89, 100n, 112n, 119, 119n, 120, 125-129, 131, 132n, 133, 135-136, 138, 140, 143-145, 148, 150, 152, 153n, 221n-222n, 244, 251, 253n, 265, 269
Volturno, river 138, 140
Voss, B.R. 163n

Walter Daniel, *Life of Aelred of Rievaulx* 97n
Walter, E.H. 163n
Wansbrough, J.H. 118, 121, 123-124, 249-252
Ward, B. 67n, 69, 97n, 101n, 196, 222n
Wearmouth-Jarrow, monasteries of 163
Weber, L. 8n
Whitby, anonymous monk of 67n, 81n, 121n, 166-168, 172
William of Conches 211, 258
William of Newburgh 198

Zimmerman, O.J. 50, 90
Zoepf, L. 97n